EQUIVOCAL CITY

Equivocal City

French and English Novels of Postwar Montreal

PATRICK COLEMAN

McGill-Queen's University Press
Montreal & Kingston • London • Chicago

ISBN 978-0-7735-5484-9 (cloth)
ISBN 978-0-7735-5485-6 (paper)
ISBN 978-0-7735-5569-3 (ePDF)
ISBN 978-0-7735-5570-9 (ePUB)

Legal deposit fourth quarter 2018
Bibliothèque nationale du Québec

Printed in Canada on acid-free paper that is 100% ancient forest free (100% post-consumer recycled), processed chlorine free

This book has been published with the help of a grant from the Canadian Federation for the Humanities and Social Sciences, through the Awards to Scholarly Publications Program, using funds provided by the Social Sciences and Humanities Research Council of Canada.

Funded by the Government of Canada | Financé par le gouvernement du Canada | Canada

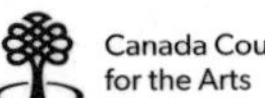

Canada Council for the Arts | Conseil des arts du Canada

We acknowledge the support of the Canada Council for the Arts, which last year invested $153 million to bring the arts to Canadians throughout the country.

Nous remercions le Conseil des arts du Canada de son soutien. L'an dernier, le Conseil a investi 153 millions de dollars pour mettre de l'art dans la vie des Canadiennes et des Canadiens de tout le pays.

Library and Archives Canada Cataloguing in Publication

Coleman, Patrick, author
Equivocal city: French and English novels of postwar Montreal/Patrick Coleman.

Includes bibliographical references and index.
Issued in print and electronic formats.
ISBN 978-0-7735-5484-9 (cloth). – ISBN 978-0-7735-5485-6 (paper). – ISBN 978-0-7735-5569-3 (ePDF). – ISBN 978-0-7735-5570-9 (ePUB)

1. Canadian fiction (English) – Québec (Province) – Montréal – History and criticism.
2. Canadian fiction (French) – Québec (Province) – Montréal – History and criticism.
3. Montréal (Québec) – In literature. I. Title.

PS8199.7.M66C65 2018 C813'.54093271427 C2018-903636-2
C2018-903637-0

This book was typeset by Marquis Interscript in 11/14 Garamond.

Contents

Acknowledgments

This book is the culmination of a personal as much as of an academic project, and its course has been shaped by a long history of fortunate experiences and encounters. Thanks to my parents' belief in the advantages of learning a second language as early as possible, my first education was in Montreal French elementary schools. This was in the pre-Quiet Revolution days, when, because of confessional as well as ingrained social divisions, that system attracted few anglophone students. Later, as an undergraduate at McGill, my interest in francophone Quebec literature was stimulated by a course with Jean Éthier-Blais, whose lectures combined passionate advocacy with wonderfully idiosyncratic displays of literary sensibility. His influence was counterbalanced by that of Marc Angenot, who became an important early mentor both in critical method and in ideological analysis. Beyond the university campus, I profited immensely from conversations at the Yellow Door, especially with the late Roger Balk and from summer jobs at *Our Generation* magazine under editor Dimitri Roussopoulos. I am grateful to Dimitri for encouraging me to write, and then for publishing, my first piece of criticism.

When I later made Canadian studies a field of academic research, I was lucky enough to participate in a number of projects that helped me find my way. Denis Hollier welcomed an entry on Quebec in the *New History of French Literature* he edited for the bicentennial of the French Revolution. A commission from Robert Lecker to write a short monograph on Gabrielle Roy's *The Tin Flute* (*Bonheur d'occasion*) for anglophone students provided not only an occasion for more sustained reflection on the work itself but also an education on how to convey complex ideas in accessible prose. I am also grateful to Robert and to Mary Williams for their warm hospitality over the many years since then. Thanks to Benoît Melançon, I had the privilege of speaking in a *Montréal imaginaire* colloquium during the celebration of Montreal's 350th anniversary. It was there, and in a lecture graciously arranged by André Brochu, that I first ventured a comparative analysis of French and English Montreal writing in and about the 1940s. Benoît, who is also a fellow *dix-huitiémiste*, has ever since been a conversation partner to whose insights and sense of humour I owe a great debt. In 1997 Pierre Nepveu and Lianne Moyes allowed me to take part in what I believe was the first conference on anglophone Quebec writing organized by a francophone institution, an event notable for the presence of both critics and creative writers. A conversation I had about my paper with Gilles Marcotte was particularly memorable, for he was as generous in his criticism in person as he was in his writing. The same was true of Micheline Cambron, at that time the director of the Université de Montréal's Centre d'Études Québécoises. In more recent years, Lianne has provided further opportunities to participate in discussions of Anglo-Quebec writing that have helped shape my views of the subject.

Over the course of my university career, the American Council for Québec Studies and the Association of Canadian Studies in the United States have provided (overlapping) intellectual communities in which to flourish. I have learned a lot from Paula Gilbert, Karen Gould, Mary Jean Green, Jane Moss, Karen McPherson, and Miléna Santoro, as well as, in earlier years, from Lorna Irvine, Bill Metcalfe, and Lee Thompson along with many others. Many of these friends have also been colleagues at *Québec Studies*, but Jane deserves special mention for her editorial leadership. I owe special intellectual as well as personal debts to Robert Schwartzwald, Sherry Simon, and Patricia Smart, three scholars whose work on topics related to the themes of this book I greatly admire, whose conversation has never failed to enliven my thinking, and whose encouragement has been a vital source of support.

Beyond the academic world, Linda Leith, enterprising editor, publisher extraordinaire, and, above all, valued friend welcomed me to the pages of *Matrix* magazine and helped me find my voice as an essayist. Her close editorial attention and the vitality of her own creative and critical work were a constant source of encouragement and inspiration. Later, as founder and long-time director of the Blue Metropolis literary festival, she gave me the opportunity to host a number of panels and readings and to experience the remarkable transformation of the multilingual Montreal literary scene she has helped to foster in the last two decades. Linda was the first to read what were very rough drafts of some early chapters of this book, and her firm confidence in the value of the project helped me so much to persevere with it. Thank you, Linda.

During the years I was writing this book, my department chair, Dominic Thomas, has been a constant source of encouragement, and work on the project has been assisted by several research grants from the UCLA Academic Senate. Ruth Jones, a former doctoral student now embarked on a promising career in creative non-fiction writing, read an early draft of the book and indicated ways to make it clearer. Friends and colleagues working in other fields, especially William Dyrness, Julie Hayes, and Nancey Murphy, helped expand my intellectual horizons. Thanks also to Adrian King-Edwards and Donna Jean-Louis for their hospitality during recent visits to Montreal. Finally, a word of appreciation for two book bloggers whom I have never met, Brian Busby of "The Dusty Bookcase" and Jean-Louis Lessard of "Laurentiana." Their archives of and on older Quebec and Canadian fiction have been of great help in my research.

At McGill-Queen's University Press, my editor, Jonathan Crago, knew when to be patient and when to prod, and I am grateful to him, as well as to Ryan Van Huijstee and Curtis Fahey, for shepherding the manuscript through the editorial process. Thanks also the anonymous reviewers for understanding what this book is about and for many helpful suggestions to improve it.

As always, I am deeply grateful to my family – Susan and Judy, John and Estelle Coleman, Veronica and Stephen Brownstein – for their love and support.

Note on Texts and Translations

For MacLennan's *Two Solitudes* and *The Watch That Ends the Night*, Graham's *Earth and High Heaven*, Loranger's *Mathieu*, Moore's *The Luck of Ginger Coffey*, Weintraub's *Why Rock the Boat?*, Bessette's *La Bagarre*, Gélinas's *Les Vivants, les morts et les autres*, and Ferron's *La Nuit*, I have used the text of the first (and in some cases, only) edition. For *The Apprenticeship of Duddy Kravitz* and *Beautiful Losers*, I have used more recent editions, which reproduce the original text. For *The Loved and the Lost*, I have used the 2010 edition published by Barry Callaghan's Exile Editions. It differs in some particulars from the first edition of 1951, though, as I indicate in the book, it is unclear if these are changes or misprints. For consistency's sake, it might have been better also to use the original texts of *Bonheur d'occasion* and *Alexandre Chenevert*, each of which has been revised more than once since their first publication. I have instead respected Roy's clearly expressed wish that the revised editions be taken as reflecting her intentions, and so I have worked with what Les Éditions du Boréal the *texte définitif*. Where it was relevant to my analysis, however, I have indicated where a substantial change to the original text has been made.

Quotations from French-language works appear in English translation, following the established practice at MQUP. I have used the published translations of Roy's *Bonheur d'occasion* by Alan Brown (under the title *The Tin Flute*, based on a revised state of the text) and of *Alexandre Chenevert* by Harry Binsse (*The Cashier*, based on the original text); and of Bessette's *La Bagarre* by Marc Lebel and Ronald Sutherland (*The Brawl*). I have not hesitated, however, to modify the English wording where I believe it to be mistaken or misleading, to highlight a particular nuance of meaning, or, in the case of Gabrielle Roy, to align the translation with the author's final version. In those passages of *La Nuit* that overlap with the text of *Les Confitures de coings*, I have adapted, though sometimes with significant changes, Ray Ellenwood's version of *Quince Jam*. Otherwise, I have provided my own translations, a practice that I have also followed for the quotations from Loranger and Gélinas as well for citations from critical works written in French.

EQUIVOCAL CITY

Introduction

This book offers a fresh approach to the Montreal novel by looking at French- and English-language fictions of the city in counterpoint with each other, not as speaking within separate literary traditions but as offering mutually illuminating examples of the kinds of story that could be written about the city at successive moments in its life. Just as important, I view them as instructive case studies of how writers articulated their understanding of that moment, and of the agency they could exercise in it, through their appropriation of the narrative forms available to them. The writers' relationship to their time, in other words, is reflected in, and revealed through, the interplay of temporalities in the tale and its telling. I see this book as a chapter in a new literary history of the city, another form of temporal narrative, and one concerned less with fashioning any specific collective identity, cultural or political, as such histories have often done, than with fostering an open-ended engagement with a past imagined as broadly shareable by all those who feel themselves addressed in some way by that past.

The segment of that history I sketch here is the period between the closing days of the Second World War, which saw the emergence of modern urban realism in the work of Gabrielle Roy, Hugh MacLennan, and Gwethalyn Graham, and the mid-1960s, when more experimental novels by Jacques Ferron and Leonard Cohen heralded the end of the political stasis and imaginative compartmentalization that the war had disturbed but not destroyed. Although obstacles of language and cultural habit often prevented novelists writing about Montreal in one language during this time from appreciating what their counterparts in the other language were doing, I am convinced it is now both possible and fruitful to locate their disparate achievements on the same timeline, provided we do not view that timeline as a simple linear sequence. Like the "common intellectual history" that Sean Mills argued – and showed – could be written about political movements in the multicultural Montreal of the 1960s,[1] the literary history I offer of the postwar novels recognizes that the artistic positions and projects it discusses most often developed independently of each other and focused on different issues. Yet it looks beyond these disparities to discern what Mills calls their shared "grammars," the evolving matrix of discursive possibilities and constraints within which these positions were articulated and transformed over time, in ways we can now see to be mutually illuminating.

The temporal concerns of my project distinguish it from other recent trans-linguistic studies of Montreal writing, which have tended (to speak very generally) to focus on the spatial dynamics of the urban imagination. For several decades now, francophone and anglophone scholars working with the tools of cultural and translation studies, or with the concepts developed by European francophone *sociocritiques*, have been redrawing the city's cultural map. Sherry Simon, for example, has in a series of pioneering works identified the real and imaginative spaces or "contact zones" where linguistic exchanges and cross-cultural encounters belie dualistic conceptions of the city's geography. Taking the notion of translation in its broadest sense, she has traced both the movement of texts from one language to another and the work of translation the texts themselves undertake in seeking to capture the city's diversity.[2] Simon Harel has followed the *parcours* (paths) and the *passages* of "migrant" figures as they negotiate their way through the host culture, as well as the ways in which contact with strangers has forced the culture's "native speakers" also to see it from the outside, with sometimes unsettling results. In addition, Harel has highlighted the role of *passeur* figures in Montreal fiction, translators of yet another kind, who broker the protagonists' access to alien cultural spaces.[3]

A broad cohort of scholars, formed or inspired by the massive *Montréal imaginaire* (Montreal of the mind) research project undertaken in preparation for the 1992 celebration of the 350th anniversary of the city's foundation, has investigated how the inescapable pressures and proximities of modern urban experience have undermined the defensive walls of cultural tradition, whether that of francophone Québécois long rooted in the province or of the city's more recently established "cultural communities."[4] Building also on more broadly focused critical enterprises such as Pierre Nepveu's influential "readings of places" and his conceptualization of artistic representation as an "ecology of the real,"[5] this group of scholars has revolutionized our understanding of the creative "traffic" not just between languages but between the various registers of the writer's mother tongue.[6]

Scholars from other disciplines and personal backgrounds have contributed to replace what Nepveu calls a "mosaic"[7] notion of diversity, whose elements are merely viewed side by side, with a dynamic form of linkaging that may lead us to revise the categories we use to discern them.[8] They have done so, however, largely by adopting more sophisticated conceptions of spatial connection. In work somewhat analogous to the sociological and anthropological explorations of the shifting geography of life on the ground, undertaken by scholars such as Annick Germain, Martha Radice, and Damaris Rose,[9] they have shed new light on local literary and cultural dynamics. Pierre-Michel Le Bel, for example, has studied the "metropolization" of the Montreal novel.[10] In English studies, the pioneering work of Barbara Godard[11] has been furthered by Lianne Moyes, Domenico Beneventi, and others.[12] Looking at Montreal from vantage points in a United Kingdom whose geopolitical imaginary has been increasingly contested in recent decades,[13] Rosemary Chapman and Ceri Morgan have offered new approaches to the representation of Montreal spaces, the former in a study of the key "sites" or meaning-saturated places in Quebec novels, the latter in a more self-reflective essay on how different city neighbourhoods have played crucial roles as enabling "mindscapes" for both the writers of contemporary Montreal novels and the critic becoming acquainted with the city through their work.[14] My understanding of the Montreal "seen" in its fiction is greatly indebted to all this research, and my account of how novelists of the postwar period articulated their perceptions would not have been possible without it.

As the last sentence suggests, however, the question of how Montreal has been imagined in the novel is inseparable for me from the issue of what kinds of *novel* those authors could envision and, more importantly, realize on the page. To give meaningful literary form to their perceptions, the writers had to put them into perspective, in both senses of that expression. First, they had to give their impressions artistic and not just psychological shape. They had to use the resources of the literary genres and modes that were available to them at the time, forms sufficiently familiar so that readers could appreciate what they were trying to do. But in this process of selection and organization, what did the authors have to overlook, sacrifice, or erase? Good writers also put their insights into perspective in another sense. They incorporate into the work some awareness of the partiality and incompleteness of even their best insights. To adapt the language of a widely cited political adage, good writers not only acknowledge what they know they don't know; they intuit and convey something of what they don't know they don't know.[15] Tracing a novel's representations of space – and using spatial categories to analyze the novels themselves – helps us locate fiction in relation to the city, but understanding how the novelists put these representations into literary perspective requires that we attend to the temporality of their formation.

Of course, the distinction between a spatial and a temporal approach is far from neat. When I speak of writers gaining an artistic perspective on their perceptions of the city and incorporating that perspective into the work – two of the criteria by which I judge their literary success – I cannot avoid spatial metaphors. Nor would such metaphors have proved so hermeneutically fruitful if the critics I have mentioned had not handled them with admirable sensitivity to historical context. Still, the difference in emphasis is significant. It can be seen, for example, in the development of a more historically oriented form of *sociocritique* in the work of Pierre Popovic and Michel Biron. Each followed up their early analysis of urban poetics in the *Montréal imaginaire* volume with full-length studies of literary genealogy and filiation I have found enduringly suggestive over the years.[16]

Perhaps the clearest illustration of this difference in emphasis may be found in the decision made by Gilles Marcotte, Quebec's greatest all-round literary critic, to divide his book of essays *Écrire à Montréal* (Writing in Montreal, 1997) into two parts.[17] Although many of the same authors and themes appear throughout the collection, the first group of texts, titled "Variations on a city" and composed largely of pieces that grew out of his work as co-director of the *Montréal imaginaire* project, concentrates on such issues as the presence (or rather the absence) of churches and other sacred spaces in Montreal fiction, and reflects more generally on what features of the cityscape nineteenth-century novels considered worthy of notice. The second set of essays, "Montreal Stories," gives more sustained attention to the relationship between history as it is represented in fictions of the city and the history one should now write about those fictions. The essays in this section include Marcotte's famous discussion of why Gabrielle Roy could not write a "high" realist novel in the Balzacian mode but was driven by the cultural circumstances in which she wrote, the culturally timid francophone Montreal of the war years, to feel her way toward what one might call a "minor" but more authentically local realism. This essay has been a critical touchstone for me ever since it first appeared in 1989. I first explored its implications in a detailed study of *Bonheur d'occasion* (*The Tin Flute*),[18] and the essay has remained in the back of my mind as I worked on this study.

The second part of *Écrire à Montréal* is also significant for including Marcotte's most extended and most critically self-conscious set of reflections on an English-language novel, and this essay has also accompanied me throughout this book. Composed of two sections written at different times, the essay records successive stages in Marcotte's effort to explain his admiration for Mordecai Richler's 1989 *Solomon Gursky Was Here* (which he declares to be the best Montreal novel ever written), despite the novel's cavalier treatment of the francophone city. Marcotte goes on to address the vexed question of whether Richler, and by implication other English-language writers, should be considered as belonging to the "same" literature as his (or their) francophone counterparts. Marcotte's readiness to entertain this possibility has encouraged me as I worked on my project, while his reservations about accepting that suggestion, grounded in the painful experience of finding his reality as a "Canadien français de Montréal" "excluded" from Richler's novel,[19] have reminded me that mistreatments and mutual misunderstandings cannot simply be overlooked or wished away. However, I take the city-wide and translinguistic convergence of the tributes to another anglophone Montreal writer, Leonard Cohen, after his death in 2016 as a sign that the obstacles to a fresh and more inclusive view of the city's literary past may now be less formidable than they once were.

My hope is that the obstacles to seeing novels of the still largely compartmentalized Montreal of the postwar period as moments within an inclusive literary history can be addressed by reflecting on three aspects of the temporal dimension of their art. The first, specific to the narrative fictions I study, is the way various features of the city's reality are "emplotted," to use Paul Ricoeur's term.[20] Emplotment turns a succession of events and experiences into a meaningful sequence. At the same time, the process of narrativization limits the authority and scope of the judgments on those events and experiences made by any speaker at any given moment of the story. What the work says never entirely coincides with what it says it is saying. By the same token, the temporal nature of narrative also undercuts any pretension on the interpreter's part to sum up the work's meaning in straightforwardly propositional terms, as if the temporality of reading it could be entirely transcended.

A second temporal dimension of the literary work is that of its genesis as a work of artistic imagination. Fulfilling the creative potential in its premise, recognizing the unexpected opportunities that emerge along the way, avoiding the challenges that can't be overcome in order to bring the work to completion, and, yes, finding a way to acknowledge what one doesn't or can't know even as one glimpses it – all these processes take place in what might be called the inner time of the writer's bringing the work into the world. Writers sometimes give us some insight into this aspect of their creation when they reflect on the result after the fact. Gabrielle Roy, for example, tells us how the character of Rose-Anna forced her way into the writing of *Bonheur d'occasion*, upsetting her initial idea of the novel.[21] Hugh MacLennan similarly recounts the way Athanase Tallard ended up dominating the first half of *Two Solitudes*, a story that was supposed to centre from the start on Athanase's son Paul.[22] Gérard Bessette realized only after his book was published that he had failed to say anything in *La Bagarre* (*The Brawl*) about the parents of his hero, giving the mistaken impression he was an orphan, though he could only speculate on his unconscious reasons for doing so.[23] Leonard Cohen came to agree with one of his critics, Dennis Lee, who thought the last part of *Beautiful Losers* did not give adequate expression to the vision it proclaimed.[24] These are all valuable clues, but in general one must reconstruct the inner temporality of the work based on the experience of reading – and re-reading – the text itself. The critic cannot prove but only hope to persuade, by offering a plausible account that makes sense of the novel as we have it.

Both these temporalities are in turn conditioned by the historical context in which they unfold. The range of narrative emplotments depends on the variety of genres and styles available at a given place and time as well as on the kinds of agency one can plausibly imagine being enacted in that context. As Marcotte showed in his essay on Gabrielle Roy, we cannot assume that when a Montreal writer set out to write a realist urban novel, she could find enabling models in the works of her great predecessors in the European literary tradition, even of her own language. On the other hand, writers may discover unsuspected potentialities in their marginal or belated situation. The avant-gardes of European modernism found ways to turn "backward" or "primitive" forms to innovative use; in quieter ways, writers in less confident cultural contexts may reconfigure "provincial" forms of consciousness from the inside.[25] To appreciate what was at stake in these choices, however, we need to keep in mind that in a city whose two main linguistic communities were still inhibited (though, of course, in very different fashion) by colonial cultural mentalities, finding an appropriate form of literary emplotment is not just a literary issue. It is a quest that cannot be entirely distinguished from the efforts of writers to "emplot" themselves as agents in the history of a literature they could not take for granted as being theirs.

On the other hand, the shaping power of historical context cannot be taken entirely as given, as a reality established prior to, and known independently of, the work of interpretation. Reflected *in* art, the particular mixture of enabling potentialities and inhibiting conditions that make up that context is fully revealed – and by that very fact transformed – only *by* art. Only in the effort to overcome those inhibitions and to realize those potentialities can the conditions under which a work of art is undertaken be properly identified and their influence accurately assessed. The object of that hybrid discipline called literary history might thus be defined as the ongoing tension between the reflective and the revelatory dynamics of writing over time, taking "over" in both its extensive and its transcendent sense. Its guiding principles are nicely articulated by Declan Kiberd in his *Invention of Ireland*: "to see works of art as products of their age; to view them not in splendid isolation but in relation to one another; and, above all, to celebrate that phase in their existence when they transcend the field of force out of which they came" (4). In speaking of transcendence as a "phase," Kiberd acknowledges that the transcendent element in the work is not outside history altogether but is itself a moment in the temporality of consciousness, one in which an enlarged conception of history is opened up.

A literary history of this kind might be undertaken from a variety of starting points. Hans-Robert Jauss and his school, for example, have used the history of reception as a hermeneutical key to the understanding of the inner dynamic of particular works.[26] This approach may be less useful where literary cultures are thinner and less well established, and even inappropriate in situations such as that of a bilingual city where speaking of *a* literary tradition is a step too far. For these reasons, I prefer to base my interpretations on the temporalities in and of the work as I am able to discern them. The understanding of the broader "moment" of their composition that I bring to this enterprise, though I hope well informed, is of an avowedly provisional, ad hoc nature. My aim is not to demonstrate how fiction reflects what we think we already know about the contrasting, parallel, and sometimes complicit "social imaginaries"[27] of the divided city in which they were written. Rather, it is to explore what the novels reveal about those imaginaries that changes how we perceive them.

By framing my study in these terms, I hope to minimize some of the problems that have traditionally bedevilled the writing of literary history, not least in Quebec and English Canada. As David Perkins has shown in his skeptical study of the genre, and as E.D. Blodgett has illustrated in his analysis of the various histories of Canadian and Quebec literature written over the years, a literary history generally assumes or projects the existence of an agent or collective subject whose birth and growth to maturity provides the unifying thread of its narrative.[28] This agent is most often the nation. In their classic, quasi-Hegelian form, literary histories identify the first adumbrations of a distinct national spirit, trace the travails of that spirit as it takes on a succession of forms, and celebrate the achievement (or imminent prospect) of some kind of political-cultural synthesis in which this spirit will (or should) find its full expression.

In Canada, not just the possibility but the legitimacy of writing such a history about the literature written in its two official languages (plus a variety of unofficial ones), and emerging from its different nations (with Indigenous peoples belatedly added to what used to be called the country's two "founding" nations), has long been contested.[29] In the 1960s and 1970s, francophone writers rejected attempts to read their work as contributing to the "bilingual-bicultural" pan-Canadian consciousness celebrated at the centennial of Confederation. They expressed impatience also with critics who drew on the discipline of comparative literature to study parallels and contrasts between what was being written in French and English, on the grounds that the basis for the comparison, if often articulated in terms of shared climatic and other geographical conditions as in Margaret Atwood's *Survival* (1972), was still assumed to be one of common or commonly understood nationality.[30] Though these early comparatists, many from English Quebec, were well intentioned and sought to respect the distinctiveness of the two literary traditions, the critics were right in pointing to the abstraction and dubious symmetry of comparisons based on broad similarities in theme or mythic substructure.

The francophone Quebec intellectuals of the day were largely convinced that the political nation building undertaken in the wake of Quebec's Quiet Revolution should go hand in hand with the development of Quebec-centred cultural institutions and critical discourses, and would do so in more organic, and monolingual, fashion.[31] Meanwhile, the rapid ethnic, regional, and gender diversification of English-language Canadian literature, or, perhaps better, the belated critical hospitality to that diversity, made it increasingly difficult to devise literary-historical narratives postulated on the projection of a unitary national subject. In addition, English-language literary institutions were in these decades definitively centralized in Toronto, turning that city into the main object of aspiration and resentment for English Canadian writers. In combination, these developments stripped Montreal critics of any lingering illusion that their city's writing in French and English would be the central two-ply thread around which the storyline of a pan-Canadian national literary history would be wound.

Two decades later, however, many francophone critics, including some who had laid the foundations for a distinctively Québécois literary history, felt increasingly ill at ease with the narrowness of what some had come to call the Quebec "national text."[32] This narrative had little room for writers from other countries who had settled in Montreal and who, even when they wrote in French, as they increasingly began to do, and participated in francophone institutions, drew on other wells of memory and dealt with the after-effects of other histories. Nor did the national text easily accommodate gender and sexual identifications at odds with the masculinist normativity of the Québécois identity it exalted.[33] Discomfort with the national text generated a new wave of work, sometimes undertaken from an explicitly "post-national" viewpoint, to honour the variety of the city's literary voices. While still primarily focused on writers expressing themselves in French, this scholarship was notable for retrieving the contributions made by Yiddish modernists, writing in what for a time was Montreal's third most important language, to the literary "invention" of the city in the early twentieth century.[34] In the 1990s this scholarship extended its reach to include the city's English-language literature. Though there remained (and still remains) some wariness about considering the latter as culturally as well as civically Québécois in any meaningful sense,[35] critics were increasingly willing to recognize the "otherness" of this literature at least as constituting one element of the inescapable "otherness" of all experience in the modern city, an otherness with which the Québécois consciousness would have to come to terms, even if it need not internalize it in all its particulars. Nepveu and Marcotte put it this way in their introduction to *Montréal imaginaire*. The questions debated in Quebec's "theatre of ideas," they declared, may take more starkly simplified form when expressed on Montreal's urban stage (as they did in the nationalism of the 1960s and 1970s), but they also become more complicated because that stage is not simply a mirror of a "national space," or what other theorists have sometimes called a "territory": a land to be conquered, mastered, and delimited by boundary markers, the objective correlative of a national identity in formation.[36] The city also and increasingly constitutes a node in a diverse global network of meanings and relationships.[37] It is a decentred, shifting set of paths to be traversed rather than a site of permanent settlement.

As linguistic and political tensions eased over the following decade, thanks in part to general acceptance of the primacy of French in education and the public square, critics began to integrate these flexible notions of cultural space into revisionary conceptions of literary history, extending the ideas sketched in Marcotte's *Écrire à Montréal*. For the authors of the 2007 *Histoire de la littérature québécoise* (History of Quebec Literature), recognizing the internal "de-centring of Quebec literature" of the post-1980 period meant including in the final part of their account chapters on *la nouvelle francophonie canadienne* (i.e., francophone cultures outside Quebec), as well as on *littérature anglo-québécoise* and its translations into French. It also entailed some reconsideration of the way earlier decades should be understood. The section of the same book devoted to the mid-century "invention" of a "Québécois" as distinct from the earlier "French Canadian" literature includes a chapter on the English-language poets of the wartime *Preview* group, though with the primary aim of highlighting F.R. Scott's work as a translator and literary mediator of French-language poetry.

A reconfiguration of Montreal's contemporary English-language literature as "Anglo-Québécois" writing had already been undertaken by other writers and scholars, including some from anglophone backgrounds.[38] Whether or not they would all accept the label as a definition of identity and not just as a way of framing one of the contexts in which they work, most anglophone Montreal writers today actively engage with the francophone city, having accepted their position as minority voices within it. The stress placed on their dual attachments to Quebec and English Canada in the referendum years has been transformed in the first decades of the new millennium into an energizing resolve to put their "de-centred" experience to creative use. The result has been a remarkable revival of the anglophone literary community.[39]

These are all welcome developments. Works in English are being translated into French in numbers that begin to approximate those of translation in the other direction. Novels and poems in both languages are beginning to be read alongside each other, often in the light of feminist, queer, or other transversal or intersectional concerns. There are striking instances of more intimate forms of intertextuality, a notable example being the explicit referencing of Réjean Ducharme's *L'Avalée des avalés* (*The Swallower Swallowed*) in Heather O'Neill's *Lullabies for Little Criminals*. Yet it is still rare for books in one language to affect significantly the genesis and formation of works in the other. There is also still little comparative critical work being done on the inner dynamics of that formation, and on what these dynamics might reveal about the history they reflect, or on their mutually enabling potential.[40] If, as I think likely, this situation will change, the reason, as Dominique Garand suggests, will be a shift in preoccupation away from the assertion of identity claims toward the negotiation of more flexible, more ad hoc forms of mutual answerability.[41] Daniel Weinstock makes a similar distinction in his reflections on what he calls "(post)nation building" in the multicultural state. "Arguments cast in terms of recognition and respect for the identities of citizens," he writes, "admit less easily of compromise and accommodation than those articulated in terms of citizens' values, interests, and preferences."[42] So, too, a basis for a common literary history may be found by focusing on the ways these values and interests are expressed, and on what Dominique Garand call the "historicity of the practices"[43] in which writers have engaged over time.

To be sure, the story I tell still has its telos: success in putting the recognition of Montreal's cultural complexity and linguistic diversity into novelistic perspective. But I do not conceive such success to be something that writers can attain once and for all. Those who pursue it will find their reach always and necessarily exceeding their grasp, if only because their work has to be delimited by an individualizing form. Indeed, the closer one approximates this goal the more it becomes clear that the route one has taken is only one approach among others and that in seizing one opportunity others have been left unrealized. As Joyce has Stephen say in *Ulysses*, that most capaciously pluralistic of novels, an authentic understanding of historical realities, including those of art, must always be chastened by a sense of "the infinite possibilities they have ousted" (30). The criteria for success, too, elude any final formulation. To use Kiberd's language, they transcend the works they judge only in one "phase" of their use before turning once more into another discourse itself subject to judgment. Still, one can speak of degrees of success and argue meaningfully about their achievement. Just how meaningfully will be a question for others to judge in their turn.

The fourteen works I examine here include most of the significant Montreal novels published in the two decades after the Second World War. By "Montreal novels" I mean fictions that, in addition to having the city as their primary setting, make some of its distinctive social or cultural features dramatically significant in the emplotment of its characters' actions. In many respects, the Montreal these books show us, though a city still within living memory, seems to belong to a long-ago era, so much so that, with the exception of *Bonheur d'occasion*, these novels tend now to be read more as documents than as works of art. Yet, to my mind, the greatest "documentary" value of these novels lies precisely in their "literariness": what in them tests and not just transcribes ideas, what dramatizes action rather than simply depicting it. And what ultimately reveals most to us about the mentality of the city they reflect is the mind at work in them.

To better understand the tension between what the novels say and what they do, I reconstruct as best I can the inner process through which they took the shape they did. In doing so, I take as reference points other texts from the same period, both French and English. As I see it, reading these Montreal novels in relation to each other is not only justified "externally" by the fact of their stories being set in the same city; it is also warranted by the operation of common or complementary forces in the internal dynamic I just mentioned. In struggling to gain an aesthetic perspective on Montreal, its writers had to deal, in one way or another, not just with the city's deep linguistic split – a division can always be turned into a dialectic – but with the pervasive mental compartmentalization by means of which the conflictual potential of that division was long contained. Ironically, these writers' literary responses to the city were complicated, sometimes self-consciously, as we will see, by a sense that what held the city together was precisely a consensus of non-agreement. I see the stubborn persistence of this paradoxical, perhaps even oxymoronic, sociability as inhibiting artistic expression, but also as provoking it, in forms distinctive to writers in both languages, even if they felt its effects in different ways. How were writers to speak about an urban reality defined by its non-articulation? How could they even be sure of having taken its measure? I am convinced that, however appropriate it may be to read the city's French and English fiction as forming two distinct linguistic traditions, putting these works in conversation with each other is essential to a better appreciation of the artistic challenges they faced as well as to a fuller understanding of the Montreal they portray.

Some of the fictions I study are more self-conscious about their composition than others, but differences in self-consciousness do not necessarily coincide with degrees of artistic interest. MacLennan's *Two Solitudes* (1945) and Gérard Bessette's *La Bagarre* (1958), for example, have each become canonical in large part because of their programmatic statements about their literary mission. Yet some of the most suggestive things these books reveal about the fictional possibilities actually available to them are to be found in details of the story whose significance the narrative consciousness seems to overlook. Conversely, Gabrielle Roy's *Alexandre*

Chenevert (*The Cashier*, 1954) is a novel that at first seems "unliterary" in the sense Roy gave to that term when she spoke about *Bonheur d'occasion*.[44] It is a book whose narrator does not adopt the distanced and impersonal stance Roy thought of as aesthetic but instead makes the moral commitment to hew as closely as possible to what her hero, a man of limited awareness, might plausibly perceive. Yet it dramatizes with unexpected sharpness the challenges of giving fictional representation to the agitated yet still petrified Montreal of the postwar years. Indeed all the novels I examine say something other than what they claim to say. This is not just because, like all works of art, they work through the indirection of metaphor and symbol, but because the cultural constraints and inhibitions with which they struggle give that indirection locally inflected twists.

Of the fourteen novels I have selected for detailed analysis, eight are English and six are French. This ratio no doubt reflects my personal predilections as an anglophone Montrealer of the baby-boomer generation whose early education was in a French public school of the pre-Quiet Revolution years but whose sensibility was shaped more by the English city of that era. Yet this ratio does, I believe, reflect the literary reality of the period I survey, for, even into the early 1960s, French-language novels set in Montreal and engaging concretely with the city were not as numerous as we might think. Some other works might have been added to my list, and I refer briefly to a few of them along the way,[45] but making more room for them would not, I think, significantly change the shape of my story. In a sequel devoted to the following decades, of course, the ratio of French to English works would have to be reversed, and dramatically so, though the accelerated rate of novelistic production in French would also necessitate the introduction of other kinds of selection criteria. But that is work for another day.

My starting point is conventional enough. That *Bonheur d'occasion* and *Two Solitudes* inaugurated the modern era of the Montreal novel has become a critical commonplace, though it is no less valid for that. I devote a chapter to each of these fundamental works, approaching them from new angles. In chapter 1, I show how MacLennan's use of the marriage plot for a national allegory is complicated by his ambivalent fascination with more promiscuous and unsanctioned forms of sexuality associated with city life. If the novel written within the story by MacLennan's idealized hero turns out to be lifeless (and it is significant that Paul needs his less inhibited partner Heather to tell him so), it is not only because the story is not "Canadian" enough. It is also because the character's work does not incorporate his creator's half-acknowledged intuitions about the unruly energies that drive the "double beat" of the city that is Canada's "heart" (4).

In somewhat similar fashion, my discussion of *Bonheur d'occasion* in chapter 3 shows how the "tenderness" that Roy sought to embody both in the maternal character of Rose-Anna and in her narrative perspective does not serve only to temper or transcend the harsh reality of conflict as it seems intended to do. It is, rather unexpectedly, also a source of tension in itself, both in the life of the characters and in the shaping of their story. Tenderness is not the opposite of the more assertive dispositions and desires exacerbated by the "temptations" associated with urban life and named as the source of the characters' unease. The purity of a sublimating or self-renouncing tenderness is itself a temptation one must sometimes resist in order to thrive – and to write a novel that is true to its urban setting.[46] In a later reflection on her novel, Roy claimed it was tenderness that gave it the "unliterary" quality I mentioned earlier, distinguishing her approach from the confrontational attitude she saw as characteristic of modern art. In fact, *Bonheur d'occasion*'s dramatization of the constraining effects of tenderness has its own kind of ruthlessness, a quality that saves her novel from sentimentality.

The distinctiveness of Roy's and MacLennan's achievements emerges more clearly when we locate them more firmly in the broader literary imaginary of the 1940s. Between the chapters on these novels, therefore, I include as chapter 2 a close comparative study of two lesser-known and less-appreciated novels, Gwethalyn Graham's *Earth and High Heaven* (1944) and Françoise Loranger's *Mathieu* (1949). The former was published the year before *Two Solitudes*, the other four years after *Bonheur d'occasion*.[47] Both authors focus on the barriers faced by talented outsiders who could potentially play leading roles in the city's social and cultural life. What prevents them from doing so is neither language nor poverty but another factor that complicates the sometimes schematic dualisms found in MacLennan and Roy's works. In Graham, it is anti-Semitism; in Loranger, the self-exclusionary power of envy and self-hatred. Interestingly, both themes are dramatized through the story of a male protagonist. In each novel, the heroine, though a career woman in her own right, serves primarily as an object of affection and as a mediator for the hero's social integration. I see this pattern as revealing something similar about the authors' literary status. By virtue of their privileged backgrounds, Graham and Loranger were themselves insiders in ways MacLennan and Roy were not, but as women they made themselves outsiders by becoming writers, and their narratives dramatize both the consequences of that fact and the sense of mission it fostered. I show how the remarkably similar family constellations in the two stories serve to dramatize personal predicaments suggestive of dysfunctions in the larger community to which the female protagonist belongs. The qualified hopefulness with which each story ends offers a thought-provoking contrast to the more wilfully asserted vision of the future offered by the novels of their more famous contemporaries.

The second part of the book divides the most important Montreal novels of the 1950s into three groups on the basis of the literary problematic I see as common to each group. Chapter 4 is devoted to stories about acts of witnessing framed by a conception of literature as itself having the mission of testifying to the moral and social weaknesses of the city. I look at three novels whose protagonists are fated to be spectators rather than actors, even in their own lives. I find it surprising that MacLennan and Roy's second Montreal novels, *The Watch That Ends the Night* (1958) and *Alexandre Chenevert* (*The Cashier*, 1954), have not been given the same comparative attention as *Two Solitudes* and *Bonheur d'occasion*. In both of the later books, an emotionally personalized narrative voice follows the life of a character whose imaginative vitality is linked to affliction by an ultimately fatal illness. The implied connection between the narrator's witness to weakness and the author's understanding of the Montreal in which the story is set only crystallizes, however, when we read Roy's and MacLennan's novels alongside Morley Callaghan's more allegorical *The Loved and the Lost* (1951). Because Callaghan never resided in the city, this novel, like Callaghan's other Montreal story, *The Many Colored Coat* (1960), is seldom included in lists of Montreal fiction. Yet Callaghan was a frequent visitor to Montreal in the early postwar years, and his portrait of the city is all the more illuminating for being the work of a writer very much aware of his outsider status.[48] Callaghan's attention to the specificity of the Montreal he portrays, a feature singled out for special praise by foreign critics such as Edmund Wilson and William Walsh, stands in sharp but often unremarked contrast to the vagueness of the Toronto he depicted in the 1930s moral fables that first brought him fame. The Montreal of *The Loved and the Lost* is governed by a set of clear but tacit racial, linguistic, and social understandings, and it is only because this implicit contract is threatened by the actions of the female protagonist, Peggy Sanderson, that the locals are driven to explain to her admirer and fellow Ontarian Jim McAlpine, the book's central character, what they do not yet dare say to each other's face. Callaghan dramatizes the enforcement of this tacit understanding in ways that highlight how differently MacLennan and Roy negotiate the tension between tacit and explicit civic consciousness in their 1950s novels. Speaking from within the city to which they bear witness, the latter writers oscillate between confident pronouncements on the city's character and insistent reminders of what they don't understand, but just as significant are those passages in which they only hint at things they are unable to spell out.

The two chapters that follow examine contrasting versions of the more assertive social criticism that emerged at the turn of the decade. In chapter 5, I look at the satirical novels published in quick succession by three English-speaking writers who in those days were also comrades in literary arms. Brian Moore's *The Luck of Ginger Coffey* (1960) and William Weintraub's *Why Rock the Boat?* (1961) illustrate the confident "knowingness" about Montreal's ways this generation of anglophone writers liked to display at that time, but the brittleness of their narratives suggests that the authority with which they speak of the city is more fragile than it appears. Mordecai Richler's *The Apprenticeship of Duddy Kravitz* (1959) shares both these features, but reading Richler's novel alongside his friends' less searching efforts allows us to see how the satirical portrait of Duddy is sharpened by a greater self-consciousness about the blinkered vision that made satirical confidence possible. The novel has long been celebrated for the exuberance of its comedy and wicked wit, but that exuberance is kept under tighter control than appears at first. The comic imagination is itself subject to narrative scrutiny, and it is this second level of irony that gives Richler's satire its deeper resonance.

In chapter 6, I look at two francophone novels published on the eve of the Quiet Revolution, Gérard Bessette's *La Bagarre* (1958) and Pierre Gélinas's *Les Vivants, les morts et les autres* (The living, the dead, and the others, 1959). When their heroes speak ruefully of a confidence they do not possess and can only envy in others inhabiting cultural worlds remote from their own, they seem to speak for their creators, as did many of these characters' predecessors in the anxiety-ridden psychological fictions francophone novelists were still writing in those years. A new ability to put this anguish into a concretely specified social perspective, however, allows Bessette and Gélinas to prepare the way for a more authentic and integrated form of local realism, one more ambitious in its scope and varied in its style than the realism of *Bonheur d'occasion*. In their work, irony becomes a means of discovery and not just of detachment, and self-deprecation a signal of openness to the other rather than a strategy of avoidance. Each novel includes satirical devices not unlike those found in the work of their anglophone contemporaries, but these are put to a more interrogative and thereby constructive use.

La Bagarre has long been considered a milestone in local literary history because of its "meta" dimension. In showing how and why Jules Lebeuf fails to write the great Montreal novel, Bessette does not lapse into lament. Nor does he resort to mechanisms of manic compensation, as Hubert Aquin will do in *Prochain épisode* (*Next Episode*) a few years later. Rather, Bessette suggests that the only way forward is, in Beckett's words, to "fail better." A complementary instance of better failure is found in Gélinas's awkwardly earnest, almost documentary, account of leftist politics, union militancy, and burgeoning nationalist consciousness in the early 1950s. In *Les Vivants, les morts et les autres*, Gélinas's insider knowledge as a member of the multi-ethnic Communist Party of postwar Montreal is conveyed in a manner very different from that of the anglophone satirists of the day. His disenchanted knowingness is shot through with longing for a truth always just beyond reach. In Gélinas's portraits of the striking workers at Dominion Textile and Dupuis Frères and the hockey fans who rioted at the Montreal Forum in support of Maurice Richard, ruefulness never dims the intensity of the narrator's fellow-feeling for his characters. In the decades following its publication, politically progressive critics uncomfortable with Gélinas's revelations about the deceptive (and self-deceptive) strategies employed by Communist Party leaders relegated the novel to the literary margins, but it has more recently come to be prized because of the wideness of its sympathies in depicting characters of a variety of social, ethnic, and linguistic backgrounds, and for its attempt to achieve a rounded view of the network of ideological forces in which they are caught. In his own way, Gélinas offers the "panoramic" view of the city Bessette's hero could only dream of attaining.

One of the ironies of Montreal literary history is that the successful reassertion of francophone cultural as well as political self-confidence in the 1960s would not find expression in more panoramic fictions of the kind projected by Bessette and exemplified by Gélinas. French-language novelists would instead intensify their focus on the psychological anxieties and other inner constrictions that were becoming more visible, and more amenable to representation, through the very process of their overcoming. The result was a series of wonderfully intense novels from writers such as Marie-Claire Blais, Hubert Aquin, and others. However, few of these works dealt in any detail with the Montreal that was rapidly beginning to modernize in those years. Such city-focused fictions as did appear, like Jacques Renaud's *Le Cassé* (*Broke City*),were monodies rather than multi-vocal works.[49] Otherwise, Montreal tends to be relegated to a marginal role in the narrative, even in such works as Jacques Godbout's *Salut Galarneau!* (*Hail, Galarneau!*, 1967). Perhaps the city's diversity could not be addressed until new modes of writing were first tried out for their own sake. In any case, it would not be until the late 1970s that the francophone urban novel took more expansive form in such works as Michel Tremblay's *Chroniques du Plateau Mont-Royal* (*Chronicles of the Plateau Mont Royal*, 1978–97). English-language Montreal novels, on the other hand, became rarer at the turn of the 1970s. As the political power and the cultural authority of the city's anglophone community rapidly eroded, it became difficult to discern what role the English-language writer was now to play. Interestingly, the first wave of renewal in the 1980s would be found in the less controversial domain of genre fiction, including the detective story, rather than in the "serious" realist novel.[50]

I therefore devote my final chapter to two works located at the tipping point when the balance of forces in the city's literary history was about to shift in dramatic fashion. The generic parameters within which these two fictions were written also contrast with those of the more conventional works examined in the preceding chapters. These novels are Jacques Ferron's *La Nuit* (The Night, 1965) and Leonard Cohen's *Beautiful Losers* (1966). At the centre of each book are two men, one anglophone, one francophone, a pair of long-standing "frenemies" whose relationship is at a point of crisis. Ferron's mildly fantastic novella combines a forward-looking nationalist fervour with a lingering, ambivalent affection for the old and odd intimacy-in-separation of the francophone and anglophone cultures with which he grew up. Cohen's apocalyptic fiction projects a new form of that intimacy into a messianic future in which it cannot quite believe, partly because of its melancholy attachment to a guilty past.

What makes these works interesting for us now is the unrealized historical potential they still carry within them, preserved, though to some extent also masked, by the sophistication of their literary technique. When Ferron produced a new and more militant version of *La Nuit* in the wake of the 1970 October Crisis and sought to exorcise the earlier text's ambivalence (notably by adding to it a polemical appendix just as long as the original text), the book, under the new title *Les Confitures de coings* (*Quince Jam*, 1972),[51] exerted significant influence on the *parti pris* generation of writers. Like *La Nuit*, *Les Confitures de coings* appeared under the *parti pris* imprint, and it fit more comfortably among the other polemical works in the catalog than did the first, more playful version of the novel. Yet the original *La Nuit* has never quite been forgotten, and it contains elements that give it enduring interest in its own right.

Conversely, *Beautiful Losers* made an immediate splash. It seemed to herald the appearance of a vigorous new cohort of anglophone Montreal writers ready and willing to take on the challenges thrown down by their francophone contemporaries. This expectation, however, was not fulfilled, at least in the decades that immediately followed. Cohen's novel has never been out of print in the fifty years since its first publication, but it found few emulators. Indeed, in retrospect it can be seen as marking the end of an era. If MacLennan's *Return of the Sphinx* (1967), which, like *Beautiful Losers*, mobilizes the resources of Greek myth, can be read as a kind of reply to its predecessor, it is an anachronistic answer, a throwback to a bygone era, not a message from the future Cohen imagined. Historically speaking, and independently of other forms of recognition, *Beautiful Losers*, like *La Nuit*, is a work without posterity. But perhaps these novels are simply waiting to be grandfathered into a new genealogy of Montreal fiction more attentive to the multiple and a-synchronic temporalities of the city's history. If that is conceivable, and this book wagers that it is, then these novels, like the others discussed here, may still have a great past ahead of them.

PART ONE

Solitude and the City in the 1940s

Montreal fiction is conventionally said to enter the modern era in 1945 with the publication of Hugh MacLennan's *Two Solitudes* and Gabrielle Roy's *Bonheur d'occasion*. These novels have been celebrated for two complementary reasons, and I believe it important to keep them both in view in any reassessment of their significance. First, these books addressed the city's ethnic and economic divisions in franker and fuller terms than had earlier novels whose action was set in the city, or at least than novels available to the two writers had done. If Roy and MacLennan had any predecessors, there had been none worth citing, let alone engaging in critical dialogue. Second, they incorporated into their narratives some critical awareness about the challenges of giving their insights literary form. Far from crippling the authors' creativity, as might easily have happened in this complex yet compartmentalized and culturally constricted city, this awareness energized their imagination, and the works that emerged from their efforts enlarged in turn their readers' horizons.

There were, of course, writers who came before them. The late nineteenth century, for example, had seen several French *Mystères de Montréal* and an English-language *Mysteries of Montreal*, but these weak derivatives of popular European melodrama would have had little to offer in the way of inspiration or challenge to writers of the mid-twentieth century even if they had not already faded from view.[1] The same can be said of the timid and often reactionary responses to the lures and letdowns of the Roaring Twenties and the Depression found in French-language fictions (English ones are hard to find) published in the interwar period.[2] Not that the new novels were entirely detached from local literary traditions. In *Two Solitudes*, the chapters about the Tallard family's life in the village of Saint-Marc owed much to Ringuet's *Trente arpents* (*Thirty Acres*, 1938), while in *Bonheur d'occasion* the Lacasse family's disastrous expedition to visit Rose-Anna's country relatives undercuts the idealism of the *retour à la terre* novels published over the preceding decades. For the writers of those novels, Montreal, and city life in general, was a threat not just to the moral virtue but the very identity of French Canadians. But the fact that these literary echoes are sounded only in Roy's and MacLennan's episodic depictions of rural life makes the absence of similar echoes in their representations of the city all the more significant. After 1945, however, even novelists who found the social vision of *Bonheur d'occasion* or *Two Solitudes* wanting in complexity, or who rejected the narrative aesthetic of these works, could react productively to them. The next generation could write their novels in part because Roy and MacLennan had written theirs.

When we speak of *Two Solitudes* and *Bonheur d'occasion* as works of urban realism, either to praise them for their pioneering vision or, in more recent years, to criticize the limitations of that vision (especially in the case of MacLennan), we need to remember that "realism" is as much a matter of the work's stance as of its statements. We prize the classic novels of nineteenth-century European realism partly for their willingness to discuss those "low" and local realities previously ignored by writers of "high" ambition, but also for turning that material to new imaginative account without unduly subordinating the stubborn particularities of circumstance to the universalizing demands of theory and form. What "unduly" means will vary from one cultural situation to another, and later readers may differ from earlier ones in their judgments of the same book. A Dickens or a Balzac novel, for example, may come to seem excessively melodramatic, the arc of a Hardy or Zola story too strongly bent to fit a reductively deterministic philosophy. Yet such critiques will not affect appreciation for the book as long we feel the writers have struggled against such tendencies and have incorporated some of that struggle into the dynamic of their work. The great realist novels, in other words, are also "realistic" about what I would call the conditioned, even conditional, nature of their enterprise. My discussion of Montreal fiction of the 1940s and 1950s will endeavour to keep both dimensions of realism constantly in view.

The tendency to single out *Bonheur d'occasion* and *Two Solitudes* as the emblematic novels of the period, however, has limited our understanding of the ways the city was, or could be, reflected and reconfigured in the French- and English-language fiction of the period. Since its origins in the Romantic period, literary history has largely been conceived as a story about the development of a nation's collective identity and artistic self-consciousness, and so these two novels have played key roles in critical narratives about the "coming of age" of Canadian and/or Quebec literature. If instead we look at these texts in the light of contemporary post-national explorations of urban diversity, we will discover a number of formal as well as thematic features earlier literary historians have overlooked. These features are well worth retrieving for what they tell us about what the authors were trying to accomplish as writers working in the Montreal of the 1940s, and worth pondering as we reflect on the state of the city today.

In pursuing this investigation, it will be helpful to move beyond dualistic comparisons that, in addition to being too closely associated with competing or abstractly complementary national narratives, too often obscure the peculiarities of their local literary contexts. Useful vectors for triangulating, so to speak, the cultural location of *Bonheur d'occasion* and *Two Solitudes* can be drawn by mapping these classics in relation to two other works of the same period. Gwethalyn Graham's *Earth and High Heaven* (1944), a far bigger best-seller in its day than *Two Solitudes*, is now little read; yet, in its romance plot, its social critique of the Anglo Montreal establishment, and its glimpses of the francophone world, this novel offers a suggestive contrast to MacLennan's book. Françoise Loranger's *Mathieu* (1949) has never been a best-seller, though it has come to enjoy a certain *succès d'estime*. Its focus on educated and culturally ambitious characters shows how moral preoccupations as well as artistic scruples similar to Roy's found expression in a story about a milieu very different from that of *Bonheur d'occasion*, too often taken as the paradigmatic picture of francophone Montreal. Expanding the comparison in this way will help us better appreciate the conditions and limits of literary realism in Montreal just before and after the Second World War.

More importantly, though, a broader comparative framework will help us track the authors' response to a dilemma that, with the partial exception of MacLennan, they do not articulate explicitly but that

I believe informs the shaping of all four novels at one level or another. On the one hand, appropriating the emancipatory potential of the realistic vision of the nineteenth-century European novel seemed to be a necessary step in building a literary culture whose development had been stymied by what one might call a semi-colonial mixture of impotent admiration for and defensive resentment of the city's European source cultures. The inhibitions and compensatory idealisms (differing in their French and English versions but much the same in overall effect) that structured the city's imagination of itself were clearly targets for the kind of critique articulated in the classics of European realism. Yet these writers also sensed that realism of this sort might itself be an anachronistic and therefore inadequate response to the mid-twentieth-century world to which the city also belonged, a world radically dislocated by a first and then a second world war, and by a catastrophic economic depression in between. This dislocation may have been registered and reflected more acutely in Montreal by poetic avant-gardes whose styles and sensitivities few local readers could comprehend, much less absorb, than by the city's novelists, who needed to think in terms of a broader reading public.[3] But, living as they did in Canada's commercial and industrial hub, a city connected by language and tradition to French- as well as English-speaking Europe, educated Montrealers of the 1940s could not avoid feeling echoing tremors of this dislocation, however much their imaginative force was muffled by the time-lags of a marginal, not to say backward, culture.

A modernist representation of the modern, in the mode of Proust, Joyce, or Woolf, was no doubt not a viable option for Montreal novelists who hoped, as my four writers did, to make writing their profession. For the avant-garde poets of the *Preview* group or a little later the painters and writers who signed Paul-Émile Borduas's manifesto, *Refus global* (*Total Refusal*), the absence of public acclaim, while financially and often psychologically discouraging (and sometimes tragically so, in the case of Claude Gauvreau), could be worn as a badge of artistic integrity. Not so for novelists who wanted to write for and to the city as well as about it. To do this, they had to speak from within the bounds of a cultural horizon whose limits they could not afford to ignore. Poets or pamphleteers could print and distribute small-scale works at their own expense, but novelists needed the mediation of commercial print. Unfortunately, local French-language publishers were financially fragile and vulnerable to clerical pressure, while the Paris publishing world was too hard to penetrate for a foreigner without the right connections. English writers who wanted a literary career could potentially gain access to the New York houses that dominated the North American scene. Indeed, they had no alternative, since the book industry was structured in such a way that no Toronto (let alone Montreal) publisher could effectively compete with American firms, even for the local market. Graham and MacLennan were lucky, in that wartime circumstances had stimulated greater American interest in Canada than had previously been the case, so that they did not have to disguise the setting of their novels as Morley Callaghan had done in the 1930s. Still, the need to "explain" Canada for the American market could easily limit the type of literary mode novelists could adopt if they hoped to compete in that market.

Yet it would be unfair to define the obstacles to novelistic modernism in exclusively economic terms, or to draw a potentially invidious contrast between poets and novelists. Perhaps the primary difficulty was that for the Montreal writer there did not yet exist a Montreal of the mind distinct from the French Canada (or Quebec) of the francophone imagination, or from the Canadian "Dominion" of the anglophone mentality, in the way that Joyce's Dublin, Woolf's London, Döblin's Berlin, or Bely's Petersburg stood apart from the nation in which they were located. Perhaps not coincidentally, while MacLennan, Graham, and Roy had spent some youthful time abroad,[4] their experience little resembled that of the expatriate modern artist. For writers of the next generation such as Mavis Gallant and Mordecai Richler, as earlier for the Toronto writer Morley Callaghan, European cities of temporary or permanent adoption provided crucial perspectives on the Canadian city they called home. European experience did play a key role in Gabrielle Roy's imaginative development, but her first stay in Europe occurred before she settled in Montreal, and the three years she spent there after the war were more important in inspiring her re-creation of the Manitoba world of her youth than in furthering her exploration of the city she had depicted in *Bonheur d'occasion* and to which she rather reluctantly returned in *Alexandre Chenevert*. MacLennan's European sojourn taught him only what he could not do, although he had to write "A Man Should Rejoice," his never-published Joycean first novel, to finally realize this after his return. Perhaps for this reason, MacLennan is the only writer of the four to incorporate the lesson into his Montreal novel. In *Two Solitudes*, Paul Tallard starts to write "Young Man of 1933," a novel explicitly focused on the contemporary crisis of values, but it is not about Montreal, and when he returns to the city from Europe he understands that such a book cannot speak authentically to the local situation.

Yet, although these writers could neither be satisfied with the realist model nor leave it behind, their inability to be "contemporary" either with their local public or with literary trends elsewhere does appear in their books in the form of a preoccupation that gives their belated realism a modernist twist. MacLennan's name for this feature was solitude. The "two solitudes" of his novel's title, taken from a quotation from Rainer Maria Rilke, have been widely misunderstood as referring to Canada's two main linguistic communities, and to the lack of communication between them. In Rilke's text, however, the phrase denotes a positive kind of separateness that enables rather than inhibits genuine love between persons. MacLennan made the phrase his epigraph precisely because the notion of two solitudes that "protect, and touch, and greet each other" in love expresses the need, not only to maintain healthy psychological boundaries, but also accept an essential aspect of the fundamental condition the partners share but which each must face alone.[5] The first misunderstanding of the author's intent thus conceals another one. Readers expecting a realist "novel of Canada," as MacLennan calls his book in his foreword, will naturally assume that "solitude" is a psychological or social condition of characters living in a particular time and place. Yet, as MacLennan makes clear, in a passage admittedly somewhat at odds with his effort to define and reconcile Canada's bedrock identities, there is also an "ultimate solitude" attendant on the realization that "all knowledge is like a painted curtain hung across the door of the mind to conceal from it a mystery that no one can face for long" (61).[6]

According to one of the characters, Captain Yardley, what lies behind the curtain is the paradox of a world wonderfully shaped yet devoid of morality or purpose, symbolized by the "self-centered, beautiful, dangerous and aimless" sharks he once saw swimming in constant motion in the water around his ship. We are told that Yardley "never let himself think" about this "ultimate solitude," though it seems clear that his glimpse of it has made him the tolerant and compassionate person he is.[7] Of course, if we take Yardley's attitude as a sign of his wisdom, then we, too, cannot contemplate this solitude too directly if we want to avoid a paralyzing "fear" (61) of the world. MacLennan himself never makes clear how Yardley's understanding of the ultimate solitude might inform the way other, less ultimate forms of solitude should be addressed. Nor does he do much to incorporate that understanding into the dynamic of his own novel. Still, it would seem that the reality of a "solitude" above and beyond the realm of ordinary experience must be acknowledged and appropriated in some way if our response to the world, whether as personal agent or as literary creator, is to be fully authentic. One could go further and claim with Maurice Blanchot that for the modern writer solitude has become a condition of possibility for literature itself, or more precisely, for what is literary in literature: that is to say, for what in literature transcends instrumental communication and opens the door to contemplation of the fundamental conditions of possibility – and impossibility – for such communication.[8]

We find something of this ambiguous, even inchoate, appreciation of solitude as both painful alienation and grounding insight in the other Montreal novels I will be discussing. The writers of *Bonheur d'occasion* and *Mathieu* draw their metaphysical vocabulary from Christianity (and in Graham's case from Judaism also), rather than from the Nietzschean language echoed by MacLennan, but it would be a mistake to make too much of this difference. The solitude that preoccupies these writers is best defined simply as the personal experience of an impersonal necessity. Depending on one's world view, such an experience may or may not be understood as pointing to an ultimate truth about nature, the cosmos, or the dialectics of history.[9] However variously and tentatively these writers may express it, what is common to them all is the intuition that a radical solitude of this kind is an experience linked to urban modernity. In the city, one can feel alone not just despite but because of the presence of other people, occupying yet not sharing a common space with the self. In this respect, the intuition of solitude in these Montreal novels may be less fully articulated than in the paradigmatic modern urban fictions of Joyce, Woolf, or Musil, but it is there. In all these European novels, solitude is a characteristic both of the characters' experience in the novels and of the authorial subjectivity out of which the fictions emerge. Unlike their European counterparts, however, the Montreal novelists who first sought to translate this experience into art also felt duty-bound to contribute to a more directly constructive project: that of fostering greater contact and communication among the city's communities and the individuals caught between them. As a result, they found themselves pursuing conflicting aims. Their persistence in bringing their works to completion reflects their conviction, or their gamble, that these aims cannot ultimately be at odds. Yet the thinness of local literary traditions and institutions made it difficult to imagine how the tension between these aims might be resolved, indeed even come to full articulation, at least in the here and now. In one way or another, all four writers could only gesture toward an abstract future where solitary imagination would go hand in hand with social solidarity. If the conclusions at which they arrive now seem disappointingly vague, the effort with which they seek to give literary expression to their basic commitment gives their novels enduring value.

1

Politics and Promiscuity in Hugh MacLennan's *Two Solitudes*

Hugh MacLennan's *Two Solitudes* is usually taken to be a novel about nationality, but while there is ample grounding in the narrative for reading it in these terms, other aspects of the text invite alternative lines of interpretation. The most interesting of these textual elements, I will argue, temper the strenuousness of the national allegory and account for the flaws in its consistency. The marriage of Paul and Heather, for example, is supposed to symbolize the union of "French" and "English" Canada, but today it is hard to take this relationship seriously as representing a true bridging of differences. The son of a mixed marriage, Paul is already half-English. Moreover, when he decides to write a novel, neither he nor Heather considers even for a moment whether he might write it in French. If, however, we situate the problematic realism of the novel's marital-national constructs within the novelist's modernist concern with what I call the promiscuity of urban life – not just its sexual unruliness but the potential of close spatial proximity to threaten social boundaries generally – then the awkward asymmetries in Paul's relationship to Heather and his conception of his career become aesthetically suggestive and not just symptomatic of an ideological impasse.

Near the end of *Two Solitudes*, Paul Tallard finally arrives at a clear understanding of his literary mission. He decides to jettison the novel he is writing about the crisis of the decadent modernity of Europe in favour of a story about the reasons why Canada is not yet modern. As MacLennan describes it, Paul's "Young Man of 1933" would have focused on the dilemmas of a hero confronting the economic conflicts, the ideological controversies, and the psychological confusion of the year Hitler came to power (301). This European novel was conceived by a Paul made uneasy by the presence of sexually adventurous, even predatory women when he visited the cities of the old continent. While we are not given much detail about the plot of Paul's new, "Canadian" novel, one clear difference between them is that his muse for the latter is a very different sort of woman. Heather Methuen is pretty, lively, and intelligent, to be sure, but she is no sexual threat. Paul loves her but is not in any way disturbed by her. Aesthetically and psychologically, therefore, Paul's decision appears to signal a defensive retreat from modernist realism to a moral allegory matching the political one.

In literature, however, realism is a relative term, and what looks initially like the more "realist" project of the two may in fact have been too distant from the writer's actual experience of his historical moment to be capable of realist execution. Whether or not "Young Man of 1933" succeeded in avoiding the temptations of allegorical abstraction, it would have been composed by a man who knew he was only a tourist in the Old World, one whose engagement with Europe was necessarily limited and one-sided. MacLennan's Paul can (he believes) "see" Europeans, but they cannot see him. As MacLennan says, Canada had not yet found a place in the international imagination. American writers such as Hemingway set their novels in a Europe for which the United States already represented a specific set of values and character types, just as Europe did for them, and so the encounters these expatriate writers depicted held the potential of mutual illumination. The Canadian writer, on the other hand, finds that his country means nothing abroad (330). Nor, given their compatriots' blinkered and defensive attachment to their mother countries, could Canadian novelists hope to mediate contemporary European developments for their public at home. Paul had clung to his project because he sought a topic worthy of his artistic ambition. He comes to realize what MacLennan himself had been forced to learn: literary realism does not draw its power solely from treating socially weighty themes, but from its willingness to portray people and things previously considered too familiar, too undignified (or too backward[1]) to warrant serious attention.

Two Solitudes is intended to be a realist work in this sense. Of course, MacLennan's book will have its idealistic side, since as an inaugural work of "Canadian" realism it must invent the model of Canada it wishes to embody. It is crucial to keep in mind, however, that Paul's work-in-progress differs in important ways from the novel MacLennan himself is writing. Most important, Paul's book is supposedly written by an author who, unlike MacLennan, already embodies the future ideal by virtue of his mixed identity. Yet, from what we are told, the vision developed in that novel is actually less complex than the one we are reading. Paul does not describe his novel in much detail, but even so it is significant that he never uses the word "solitude" either to describe some dimension of the personal or collective experience he is going to dramatize, or to name some aspect of the creative process itself. On the contrary, the success of his writing is closely linked to a marriage that happily blends erotic compatibility, legal sanction, and a happy reciprocity not just of individual but of collective minds, or to put it in MacLennan's old-fashioned language, of two "races."[2] Paul's book seems to presuppose the resolution of issues MacLennan's novel sees as not yet even addressed: not just the challenge of confronting the "ultimate," impersonal solitude, but the problem – related to the former through the experience of urban modernity – of integrating the disruptive force of sexuality into the social imaginary of both the English and the French communities.

According to MacLennan, an important reason for the inertia and defensive compartmentalization of these communities is the repressive power of (English) puritanism or (French) "Jansenism," and he is determined to show as frankly as he can the damage caused by sexual ignorance or repression. Healthy sexual relationships are as crucial to MacLennan's conception of personal and national maturity as is openness to political and cultural difference. It is, of course, possible that Paul's novel addresses these points, and perhaps MacLennan imagines it doing so, yet it is significant that Paul does not *say* this. Perhaps MacLennan felt it would be too provocative to make Paul speak as openly with Heather on this topic as the impersonal narrator does in addressing his anonymous readers. How could Heather respond without sullying her good-girl image? Both solitude and sex are absent from Paul's novel, at least as it exists within the pages of MacLennan's book. It is only the latter that attempts to address both.

This disparity should provoke more interpretive comment than it has among MacLennan's critics. Because the exemplariness of Paul and Heather's relationship has been defined in terms of national reconciliation, the textual work it does has also been assessed only in those terms. And from this point of view, the novel's limitations are obvious. Heather may be a unilingual English Canadian, but Paul is the thoroughly bilingual product of a mixed marriage, for he is the son of Athanase Tallard's anglophone second wife, Kathleen. The union of Heather and Paul bridges a divide that has already been crossed, but only in one direction.[3] Paul's status as a representative French Canadian is undermined perhaps even more by another factor, one that nowadays goes largely unremarked. While ancestry and language are still contentious issues in today's Quebec, religion is not, at least insofar as Christian affiliations are concerned. Until the middle of the twentieth century, however, the situation was very different. Catholics and Protestants went to different schools as well as to different churches, and mixed marriages were by no means a simple matter, among other reasons because Quebec did not recognize the validity of civil marriages (performed by a lay officer) until 1968.[4] Here again, MacLennan sidesteps the problem. Enraged by clerical resistance to his plans to modernize the town of Saint-Marc, and ostracized by a community that considers him a traitor for siding with English capitalists, Athanase becomes a Presbyterian. He converts his son along with him and sends him to a Protestant English boarding school. In other words, the Paul of the novel is no more fully Catholic than he is fully French. In order to marry Heather, he does not have to cross a religious divide or face an embarrassing legal problem. MacLennan avoids having to acknowledge this sleight-of-hand by letting the young couple marry outside Quebec, in a Nova Scotia civil ceremony. In contrast, there was no religious obstacle to Athanase's marrying the Irish Catholic Kathleen, and this fact should also make us wonder more than we do why neither Kathleen nor Montreal's anglophone Catholics generally are assigned any role in the novel's mediation of collective identities.

Before addressing this question, we need to ask another. Given these all-too-convenient plot devices, how could *Two Solitudes* have ever been thought of, even by English Canadian and American readers, as modelling a pan-Canadian consciousness that transcended differences without denying or erasing them? It is hard to understand how a writer so committed to working out his deepest intuitions about human relations would have taken what to us seem like convenient shortcuts, or how his first readers could have overlooked those shortcuts, unless doing so was the only way MacLennan could work through a problem he (and implicitly those readers as well) considered to be even more intractable than politics – the problem, indeed, evoked by the Rilke text from which MacLennan took his title. Paul's mixed origins may undermine the political import of his marriage to Heather, and beyond that of the novel of Canada he writes with her support, but it may be that in arranging things as he does MacLennan is setting the stage as best he can for dramatizing this other problem. The contours of the latter emerge if we read the novel less as triumphantly anticipating the fusion of political and literary energies in a new and assertive national culture than as ambivalently exploring the creative potential to be found in the promiscuity of modern urban life.

The opening pages of the book invite us to read *Two Solitudes* between the lines in this way. If the "sprawling half-continent" centred on the junction of the Ottawa and the St Lawrence rivers has a "heart," the narrator tells us, it is Montreal (4). The city's "pulse throbs out along the rivers and the railroads; slow, reluctant and rarely simple, a double beat, a self-moved reciprocation." The beat is a "double" one because it reflects the presence of "two old races and religions" that "live their separate legends" alongside each other. The image is nicely balanced between two kinds of connotation. On the one hand, the "double beat" of this heart is strong enough to infuse energy into arteries both natural and mechanical. In its "self-moved reciprocation," the heart appears to generate that energy within itself. On the other hand, this heartbeat is "reluctant," a word that in association with the term "double beat" suggests an arrhythmia that is potentially as debilitating as it is generously enabling.[5] The novel's Montreal is a strangely vulnerable engine of vitality.

Montreal's position as and at the heart of *Two Solitudes* is relativized in a number of ways. It is significant, for example, that the hero's creative consciousness is fully awakened in Athens, a cosmopolitan city of layered histories very different from the Montreal whose legends live separately, side by side. Athens is, of course, the cradle of democracy, and its ancient *agora* the symbol of political and philosophical dialogue. Yet Athens, too, is ailing. When Paul visits the city in the spring of 1939, democracy has disappeared from Greece as it has elsewhere in Europe. It is in Athens that a novel about the young man of 1933 begins to "press forward in his mind" (306). But Paul's creative responsiveness is not sparked by the political crisis alone. His literary awareness becomes articulate as he reflects on "the loneliness of all large cities" (305), and it is this experience of modern urban alienation – and not of "national" division, as is often assumed – that provides the occasion for MacLennan to insert the novel's title into his text. It is here that Paul is moved to picture himself and Heather as "two solitudes in the infinite waste of loneliness under the sun" (305). With the exception of the sun image, the language is not so very different from that used to describe the countryside from which rivers flow toward Montreal, for "nowhere has nature wasted herself" as she has in Canada, in the northern part of which "nothing lives" except a few isolated men and beasts (3, 4). Yet the teeming, Eliotic wasteland of Athens is very different from the uninhabited waste of the Canadian north.[6] Paul may be lonely in Athens, but he is not alone. More important, his perception of the city as a place where people of varying backgrounds and styles are to be found, mixing together in a constant negotiation of needs and desires, exacerbates his feeling of loneliness, but at the same time it provides his imagination with the crucial stimulation that depends on this aggravation of solitude. The passage about his novel "pressing forward" in Paul's mind is preceded by a vivid description of an Athens hotel bar where swaggering German tourists mingle with Greek locals and visitors from other countries. His gaze focuses on a sleek French woman engaged in sado-masochistic foreplay with a Nazi thug half her age, then on other women walking in the streets "with quiet knowledge, a sense of sex accompanying them like a subtle perfume" (305). For all his fastidiousness, Paul cannot but see his own desires mirrored in heightened form by the city around him, and it is this mirroring that enables him to identify his creative task. That identification is not definitive, as we will see, but without the impetus of his Athens experience his project would never have taken shape.

Unfortunately, MacLennan shares too much of his character's discomfort to do justice to his own artistic insight. Exchanging a glance with a woman at a bar, Paul "knew he could have her if he wished. Another time he might have let the routine take its course, but not now" (305). Nothing in the narrative suggests an awareness of the hollowness in Paul's pose of jaded sophistication. Paul has never shown any inclination to libertine conduct, and so his gesture of self-denial here would carry little weight if we did not suspect that for MacLennan the mere acknowledging of a vulgar sexual impulse is a sign of the city's impact on the hero's imagination. The novel assures us that its all-too-earnest and upstanding hero is a man of the world, but then goes on immediately to carefully distinguish artistic self-assertion from the troublingly aggressive and erotically unruly dimensions of desire. For all that, however, the message is clear: in a world scarred by the memory of one war and sensing the imminent outbreak of another, artistic innovation draws on an experience of solitude that does not in romantic fashion confirm the self in its identity. Rather, it sharpens the self's awareness of its implication in the depersonalized circulation of desire that characterizes the modern (Paul calls it "decadent") city. It is not the image of far-off Heather, after all, but that of the anonymous available woman of Athens who provides the catalyzing image for Paul's project.

In reflecting further on that project, Paul begins to see his protagonist's character as being shaped by his confrontation with the mass unemployment and mass political movements of that fateful year. Once again, however, he takes a step back. "Could any man write a novel about masses? The young man of 1933, together with all the individual characters Paul tried to create, grew pallid and unreal in his imagination beside the sense of the swarming masses heard three stories below in the shuffling feet of the crowd" (307). It is a puzzling objection, belied by MacLennan's own brief but vivid description of erotic degradation given in the scene we have just cited. What follows, however, helps us see what Paul is getting at. "A novel should concern people, not ideas, and yet people had become trivial" (307). If taken as inviting rather than foreclosing imaginative exploration, this personalized way of looking at the cultural moment might well provide the basis for a work in an ironic late-modernist mode, and it seems that such a perspective informs the novel Paul starts to draft.[7]

Significantly, however, we are never told anything more about the projected work except that Paul finishes it and then finds it wanting. In this respect, this novel is like the woman glimpsed in the bar: he could "have" it – it lies within his grasp – but it is not the right book for his "now," an historical moment that does not coincide with the time and place Paul had initially made his fiction's location. When he returns to Canada, Paul accepts Heather's judgment: "Many sections had extraordinary power and descriptions were new and vivid. But the balance was not right and the whole was curiously unsatisfying" (328). Persuaded by her also that the purpose of the novel should be to "celebrate life" (328) – an idea radically at odds with the artistic vision sketched in Athens – Paul burns his manuscript and begins to write a new novel set in Canada. What story this novel tells is never made clear either, but presumably the shift in focus allows Paul to achieve the "balance" he sought. How he achieved that balance we are not told, so we can only surmise it involved a recalibration of the relationship between fiction and reality. What had seemed in Europe to be a lucidly realistic and artistically enabling insight into the modern condition is revealed in the Canadian context to be a social abstraction and an imaginative dead end. As he begins to sketch a new novel set in Canada, Paul at last discovers "something the whole world has known for centuries. An artist has to take life as he finds it. Life by itself is formless wherever it is. Art must give it a form" (329–30).

The argument is only sketchily delineated, but a sympathetic reconstruction of what MacLennan is trying to say might go like this: "celebrating" life as it is found does not mean adopting a complacently positive attitude (though the author clearly feels drawn, or perhaps obliged, to move in that direction) but rather accepting and working with the reality of a place that is not already haloed by the prestige of existing cultural tradition. Even the tarnishing of that halo by the forces of decadent modernity only confirms the prestige of that tradition, symbolized by the enduring presence of the Acropolis above the streets of MacLennan's decadent Athens. The idealism of this celebratory impulse is not at odds with the novelist's realist intention, for without some enabling resource on which to draw the artist cannot give his material a form sufficiently pleasing to make that material interesting to other people. The critical edge of the project need not be blunted in the process, since the notion that "life is formless wherever it is" turns out be more than a platitude. As applied to Montreal, it implies that the city's long-standing "legends" are creative dead ends and so must be demystified in order to make room for new and culturally liberating narratives.

There is an unresolved tension, however, between Paul's determination to give form to a city that has not yet developed an integrated cultural personality and his initial intention of offering a creative response to the de-formation and depersonalization characteristic of the late-modern age. In choosing the new project over the original one, he cannot simply leave the latter behind, for the "Canadian" project is still a reaction to the "European" one, and not just a direct response to the local "material." The insights into the dilemmas of mass modernity MacLennan dramatized in his portrayal of Paul's travels cannot be forgotten. Nor should they be repudiated or repressed in the shift from an international to a local focus. Whatever he may say, Paul's creative energy is generated by the tension between these two perspectives. But how might this tension be "balanced" or mediated?

One road taken by modernist writers in a culture on the margins of modernity – early-twentieth-century Ireland, for instance – was to look behind the degraded current versions of the local "legends" to their older, more vital expressions. By appealing to past history, they did not seek to resist modernity but rather to redefine the terms of the conflict by historicizing modernity itself. In Canada, this strategy, and the vision of what one might call "leapfrog" development associated with it, was famously articulated by Marshall McLuhan, who prophesied that Canada would be able to move directly from the nineteenth-century provincialism in which its culture was still stuck, in his opinion by no means always for the worst, to the global village of the twenty-first century without suffering the travails of the twentieth. The "Red Tory" critique of technology and empire in George Grant offers another example of such a vision, one given passionate though rather inchoate expression in Scott Symons's Montreal novel *Place d'Armes*.[8] The philosophical anthropology of Fernand Dumont, like McLuhan and Grant a thinker who drew on a longer and broader Christian tradition than was typical of the clerical scolds of his day, offers a francophone version of the same basic perspective. Hostile to a reductively secular and materialistic modernity, yet understanding that what passes for conservatism in their culture is itself a product of that modernity, these intellectuals sought to redeem the future by retrieving the past. In retrospect, one may question whether they engaged the negative moment in this dialectic authentically enough to open the door to an alternative future, or whether by the 1960s that alternative was already foreclosed, a loss they could only lament.

In 1945, however, MacLennan might be forgiven for thinking that what might be called a progressive-conservative approach still represented a live imaginative option. Yet he is curiously reluctant to pursue it head-on. Instead of plunging directly after the prologue into the contemporary life of late 1930s Montreal, the long first half of *Two Solitudes* tells the story of Paul's father, a liberal-minded senator from an old Quebec family, and his efforts two decades earlier to get his home village of Saint-Marc to shake off its attachment to its traditional, church-dominated ways. With the wisdom of hindsight, MacLennan shows how Athanase was naive in thinking that economic development could bring the advantages of progress without the drawbacks associated with the establishment of a factory town. "Enlightened" as he was, Athanase was deluded in thinking that a provincial *notable* such as himself could outwit Montreal's capitalists and their unholy alliance with the francophone church.

Athanase's fate thus illustrates the truth of how even an individual endowed with all the advantages can, as Paul will later put it, "become trivial," even as MacLennan succeeds in making Athanase himself a distinct and memorable personality. He does this in part by situating his drama at a stage of economic development that, while still well within living memory, already belongs to a bygone age. Indeed, MacLennan's literary source for this episode, Ringuet's *Trente arpents* (*Thirty Acres*), had already dramatized this historical moment some years earlier. Yet in their mode of telling that story the two novels are very different. In Ringuet, past and present were linked by narrative as well as historical continuity. In *Two Solitudes*, by contrast, the events of the past are narrated with what Leith has called an "epic" sweep that contrasts with the twists and turns of Paul's education story. Perhaps even more important, at the moment of his decline, Ringuet's rural patriarch had become all he could ever be. By contrast, the liberal Athanase was a man of unfulfilled cultural promise, not just an historical dead end. However, the liveliness of the first parts of *Two Solitudes* comes at a price. Athanase's story does not shed much light on the more urgent questions of what the response to the "trivialization" of people should be or how one could find a way to enjoy the benefits of modernity without suffering its levelling effects. Novelists need not provide an answer to these questions, but they do need to confront them. It is curious that, in reflecting on his mission as an artist bridging past and future, Paul never once compares himself to his father or wonders whether Athanase's fate might prefigure his own.

This looseness in the articulation of past and future, especially in Paul's relationship to Athanase, may reflect something about the author's own position in relation to history. In the long first half of the novel, the anonymous narrator clearly speaks from an English point of view as he looks back with a mixture of nostalgia and superiority on a past whose distinctiveness of character (and thus its literary potential) he can claim as his inheritance because he is Canadian. At the same time, he need not assume any responsibility for the flaws and mistakes of the French past, or at least any direct responsibility for them. The past epitomized in the struggles of Athanase provides the narrator with a richness of historical memory, but one that does not burden him with an unchosen debt. From a Marxist or nationalist point of view, the author's response may thus be deemed inauthentic; it is certainly not that of what Gramsci called an "organic" intellectual, speaking from within the location being critiqued, rather than pretending to float above sectarian interests in a way that ultimately reinforces the existing hegemonic order. Yet, if we grant some validity to MacLennan's own sense of Montreal as the double-beating heart of a country where one's identity is defined in the first instance by the fossilized "legends" of two "races" living compartmentalized lives, MacLennan's mode of appropriating the past, if not the content he appropriates or sets aside, may be justified as the only one at that particular cultural moment from which a more open future could have been envisaged.

Looking at MacLennan's novelistic enterprise from this perspective, we can understand how he might not have been troubled by his decision to have French Canada represented by a man who is already half-English and who decides to write in that language. Another way of putting it, which may bring us closer to what MacLennan had in mind, is that Paul cannot be entirely determined by a "French" identity, since, except in the singular case of Athanase, MacLennan, in this respect like Ringuet before him, could only conceive of that identity in homogeneous terms, as all of a piece. Paul's half-brother Marius, the son of Athanase's first, French Canadian wife, Marie-Adèle, not only illustrates the point; he articulates it in polemical terms. Marius considers any mixing, whether racial, religious, or linguistic, to be a threat. The purity of his conviction makes him a dangerous man. Imagining Paul as the product of a mixed marriage may have been a way of allowing his marriage to Heather to avoid the real difficulties of bridging French and English mentalities, but it was also the only way McLennan thought he could provide his hero with some degree of internal complexity, given a French Canada that could not accommodate an Athanase. Whether the author's decision was historically justified depends on how much deep internal diversity in fact existed within French Canadian culture at the time, and perhaps more crucially, on how widely such diversity was acknowledged to exist by individuals or institutions with which MacLennan should legitimately have been expected to be familiar. In other words, to what extent was a creative (as opposed to a crippling) division within the French Canadian self imaginable at this moment? And imaginable by whom? Marius's failure to reach a position of power in his adopted city suggests that the character is not as representative of francophone Montrealers as he is of *bien-pensant* French Canadian discourse, but the gap between the two is no more than implicitly acknowledged.

However one answers this question, and I think there is some room for debate, one can at least see some literary reasons why MacLennan would want to make the protagonist of the main part of the novel someone rooted in a particular community of origin but de-centred enough not to be overwhelmed by an undifferentiated responsibility to it. Because of his mixed background, Paul finds himself rejected by the elite of both linguistic communities, and it is precisely this rejection – and the solitude it creates – that frees him from the burden of representing either community in any simple way. No doubt MacLennan's would-be novelist reflects something of the way his creator sees his own relationship to the world, a translation into temporal terms of a mediating imaginative position perhaps difficult to articulate in another vocabulary.

Because Paul is the novel's artist-hero, questions about the ethnic representativeness of MacLennan's characters have understandably focused on the male protagonist. Paul's fiancée, Heather, is generally taken at face value as the anglophone partner in the novel's symbolic marriage between the French and English "races." It is seldom noticed that her background is presented, somewhat puzzlingly, as ethnically mixed. As the granddaughter of Captain Yardley, she is one-quarter Nova Scotian (292) and so somehow not entirely determined by her Anglo Montreal heritage. Since Nova Scotia's European settlers came from the British Isles just as Heather's Montreal forebears did, this would seem to be a distinction without a difference, but not for Yardley or for his Nova Scotia-born creator. "Nova Scotia," Yardley muses, shortly before his death, "was as old as Quebec, but it seemed infinitely younger, without the Quebec sadness and the solemnity of the Catholic parishes … it seemed a separate country" (292). What the author seems to be implying is that, as a Nova Scotian, Heather comes from a background parallel rather than opposed to that of Quebec's French Canadians. Her "separate" roots run just as deep as theirs. Her identity is not entirely determined by one of the two "legends" that coexist in Quebec. No doubt MacLennan is investing Heather with something of his private mythology as a "Celt" from Glace Bay.[9] Whatever the case, the point to stress here is that Paul is not the only hybrid character in the book. Heather can become Paul's partner because she, too, experiences internal division, the pull of contrary tendencies.

In practice, however, what sharpens Heather's self-consciousness is not her genealogy but her gender. Although she admits to a culpable ignorance about French Canadians, as a woman she is not directly responsible for the oppressive actions of Montreal's anglophone elite. As an unmarried daughter financially beholden to her family, she cannot even exert any significant influence on those who bear that responsibility. Heather does what she can to assert her independence, notably by renting a studio apartment located, if not in a wholly French district of Montreal, at least in a mixed neighbourhood. There, she explores her vocation as an artist.[10] Heather also bridles at her mother's warning against marrying a man who is not the right social match. Yet, just as Paul never wonders whether he is recapitulating the idealistic career of his father, Heather never wonders if she might be repeating anything in the life of her mother, who married a man who was not of her class and never felt completely at ease in his world. Still less does she wonder if she might unconsciously be reproducing any of the attitudes of her Anglo family or community in the manner of her rebellion against it. In this respect, her imaginative relationship to her genealogy is as defensively limited as Paul's.

These disruptions, conscious and unconscious, of filiation and affiliation serve to individualize Heather and Paul and at the same time to insulate them from immediate, and therefore paralyzing, responsibility to or for the past. Their de-centred position, and the solitude that results from their awareness of it, becomes an enabling point of departure, and the reader understands that MacLennan would want to see that solitude preserved even in the consummation of their union. It is not just that each partner must be their own person if the marriage is to work. Nor is it simply a matter of casting off the inhibitions of tradition. What they need is to remain healthily distanced, as individuals and as a couple, from community claims on their loyalty. Only through the acceptation of separateness – and solitude – can they achieve, and thereby exemplify for their communities, that intimacy without fusion *Two Solitudes* names as its ideal.

The notion of intimacy without fusion is explored through MacLennan's treatment of what I have called promiscuity. Like its counterpart, solitude, in the novel it is by no means merely a negative phenomenon. The word itself never appears in the text, but if we take the notion of promiscuity in its broadest sense as encompassing not just sexual licence but any form of indiscriminate intimate contact or mingling – in crowded urban tenements, for example, denounced by social reformers as a threat to morals as well as to physical well-being – then it is a useful way of naming a phenomenon MacLennan views as a pervasive threat to social order. More provocatively, however, though with less fanfare, he also regards it as a healthy protest against an excessively puritanical and compartmentalized society. As a product of urban modernity that carries positive as well as negative potential, promiscuity is analogous to solitude, the apparent opposite with which it is in fact dialectically connected.

MacLennan's ambivalent attitude to promiscuous contact may be illustrated by comparing the description of 1930s Athens, where the prevalence of casual sexual relations illustrates the destructuring effect of machine-age modernity, with an earlier episode rarely mentioned by critics.[11] In 1919, just after the end of the First World War, Kathleen travels to Montreal to find a suitable city house for her family. Athanase's position in Saint-Marc has become untenable since he sided with Anglo industrialists against the local priest. Alone in her hotel, Kathleen allows herself to be picked up by an army officer reluctantly returning from the excitement of European cities to his home in Winnipeg. Far from condemning their tryst, MacLennan sympathizes with the impromptu couple's decision to seize an unexpected opportunity for sexual intimacy. The author's worry about the perniciously levelling influence of the modern age gives way to sympathy for a man condemned to live the rest of his years in the even more dispiriting flatness of the backward Canadian west. The easy frankness of this episode stands in marked contrast to the awkwardness of the scene in which Paul turns down Heather's sexual advances with an unconvincing speech about the ideal quality of their romance. The latter scene has been justly mocked,[12] yet if we think of the couple's relationship as already and inherently *socially* promiscuous, in that it fails to respect the boundary between the English and the French communities, then what appears to be a retreat into conventionality can be read as a strategic gesture designed to prevent MacLennan's first readers from avoiding the challenge that relationship represents by taking refuge in moral reproof. Similarly, readers today should beware of being content with ironic mockery, and even more of falling into the trap of looking at promiscuity solely in sexual terms. For, just as solitude needs to be understood as not just an element in a national allegory but also as a feature of the modern condition generally, the novel's treatment of promiscuity is also an attempt to address another aspect of that same condition.

This brings us to *Two Solitudes*' ambivalent portrayal of Montreal. Significantly, Paul's abortive sexual encounter with Heather occurs in a house in Montreal's still rural Lakeshore suburbs, while Kathleen's encounter with the officer, like that between the anonymous man and woman Paul observes in Athens, is a thoroughly urban moment. As a densely populated metropolis, Montreal inevitably provides occasions for promiscuous contact, and not just of a sexual nature. Promiscuity can involve religious and linguistic boundary-crossing as well. MacLennan generally portrays the city as neatly divided between French Catholics and English Protestants, but his novel includes a number of features that undermine these dualisms. What we are to make of them is not clear, and, as we shall see, the author himself doesn't seem to be entirely sure what to do with them.

As I mentioned earlier, aside from Paul's mother, Kathleen, there are no English-speaking Catholics, Irish or other, in the novel's Montreal.[13] Reference to other groups is equally rare, though sometimes symbolically significant. Heather has on her studio wall "a nude torso portrait of a Negro girl" done by a Czech painter, signalling the "modernity" of her artistic taste (257). There is passing mention of one Jew (199), the employer of Marius's fiancée, Émilie, but neither Mr Greenberg nor any person of colour actually appears in the book. Economic status is also neatly dualistic. With the exception of Athanase (who is not a city man) and one or two vaguely sketched political operators, the French are all poor, even Marius, whose law career is unsuccessful. Similarly, the English characters are all well-to-do. It is true that Heather's mariner grandfather, Captain Yardley, came up through the ranks, but he enjoys a comfortable income, and in any case he neither begins nor ends his life in Montreal. His wide experience of the world has enabled him to make friends easily with people of different backgrounds, but instead of using his money, and the limited but practical fluency in French he gained from his years in Athanase's Saint-Marc, to facilitate his integration into city life when he moves to Montreal, he is content to live comfortably as an outsider wherever he goes.

The same is even truer of Paul, though with an important and unexpected difference. Born to privilege but fallen into poverty after his father's death, educated at an English boarding school after his father becomes a Protestant, and then working his way through the Université de Montréal, Paul would seem to make a perfect hero for a novel about urban mobility. It is thus rather odd that we never see him interacting with other Montrealers, French or English, with the exception of Heather and, on one occasion, his half-brother, Marius. Unlike his mentor Yardley, Paul is never seen making new acquaintances or having significant conversation with anyone he does not already know from way back – something that is also true, as we shall have occasion to see, of Emmanuel in *Bonheur d'occasion*. Heather is no exception to this rule, for, as Yardley's niece, she has known Paul since childhood. Although Paul worked as a semi-professional hockey player to pay for his studies, he seems to have formed no friendships with his teammates. That he fails to find a job anywhere in the city after graduation is not entirely surprising, given the Depression context of the story, yet it is still curious that MacLennan's account of his efforts should be so sketchy. Not only does there seem to be no room for Paul in the divided city of *Two Solitudes*, the novel itself seems to be incapable of making room for that experience in the narrative.

The implication is that Paul is at a disadvantage because he is not a full member of either the English or the French communities and that, without support from either, his education and talent are not enough to secure a position. But none of this is shown. A fuller dramatization of Paul's interactions with the city around him would no doubt have required more familiarity with francophone Montreal than MacLennan possessed. Criticism of the author's ignorance on this score should, however, be tempered by consideration of the literary-historical context. The gap in MacLennan's narrative might have been bridged had he been able to build on some prior francophone novelistic representation of a versatile urban hero, as he done in the first parts of *Two Solitudes* using Ringuet's depiction of rural Quebec in *Trente arpents*. But there was no such work, certainly none that had attracted enough respectful attention in francophone circles to have prompted MacLennan to pay attention to it. Another striking but little-noticed feature of the Montreal of *Two Solitudes* is the absence of any reference to intellectual life of any sort in either language. In a novel set in another multicultural city, Paul might have found employment as a journalist. In *Two Solitudes*, Montreal's English newspapers are only briefly mentioned as mouthpieces for the Anglo establishment. The French press is not mentioned at all. That neither the press nor any other cultural institution ever appears on the imaginative horizon of an intellectually minded hero is a curious fact, one that surely says something about the imaginable city as much as the real one.[14]

The absence of cultural context and the thinness of Paul's interactions with the city may not, in other words, simply reflect historical reality. They tell us something about MacLennan's imagining of that reality. In portraying Paul's romantic and artistic struggles, MacLennan might at least have taken his hero to the waterfront. In other works, such as Roger Viau's *Au milieu la montagne* (In the middle, the mountain, 1951) or MacLennan's second Montreal novel, *The Watch That Ends the Night*, Montreal's port offers the characters a glimpse of broader sexual, social, and imaginative horizons, even when they cannot embark on an actual journey themselves. In *Two Solitudes*, the only character who looks out from the port is Huntly McQueen, and what he sees is his idea of British imperial order reflected back to him. In *Two Solitudes*, Paul must travel to Europe and experience its decadent modernity first-hand before he can even start to formulate his vision. A more circumstantial account of Paul's local interactions would have been instructive, and if it is not provided, the reason must be that these interactions generate none of the insights he needs to write his book, or furnish him with the vocabulary with which to write it. Nothing in the city, we infer, has the potential to surprise the characters or to enable them to see themselves and each other differently.

What kind of artistic perspective may be gained from a life lived only in Montreal can be seen in the novel's depiction of the wealthy men whose unfettered access to all the city has to offer does nothing to expand their mental horizons. MacLennan's depiction of Montreal's Anglo establishment is more concretely detailed than his account of Paul's struggles to find a job. It is also more confidently, more self-consciously, but also more narrowly "literary" in quality. By virtue of his position at the centre of urban power and as the target of MacLennan's attack, Huntly McQueen might theoretically have served as a means through which the narrative could describe the city from the inside while judging its mechanisms from without. Yet, while the narrator's ironic comments on McQueen and his world enliven the book, the mode of his narration is significant. By choosing to speak satirically, using the resources of broad-brush deflationary caricature, rather than the sober language of realism, the narrator suggests that he is less interested in analyzing the city's power structure than in the imaginatively easier task of mocking the narrow rigidity of the Anglo establishment outlook.

That Huntly McQueen, for example, should owe his success at least as much to his puritan upbringing in small-town Ontario as to his financial talent no doubt reflects something of the reality of the elite he represents. He is a man of pinched caution rather than bold risk, a man for whom the British Empire symbolizes order and restraint, not exploration and conquest. In making his deals, McQueen may upset traditional ways of life, as he does when he transforms the village of Saint-Marc into a factory town, but he does so in measured fashion, and ultimately with the blessing of the very Catholic Church that initially opposed him. His is not the capitalism of disruptive excess or transgressive desire; McQueen accumulates, but he does not spend. Yet the interesting implications of the curious symbiosis between his kind of capitalism and the equally distinct form of traditionalism that characterized Quebec life in this period are only sketchily explored. MacLennan's narrator is more fascinated by the bachelor McQueen's personal eccentricities, notably his exaggerated devotion to the memory of his dead mother. For those in the know, the allusion to the secret life of Prime Minister Mackenzie King adds spice to the story, but it does not offer any real key to understanding McQueen's success, or for that matter to that of his real-life model. The same is true of Heather's widowed mother, Janet Methuen, for whom McQueen feels a certain chaste affection, but what characterizes her best, and what he admires most, is the determination with which she upholds the social code of the Golden Square Mile family into which she had married. One could say that the defining feature of both characters is their opposition to promiscuity in any form.

All of this makes the novel's McQueens and Methuens excellent candidates for satirical treatment. By reducing complex psycho-social dynamisms to comically mechanical phenomena, MacLennan goes some way toward incorporating into his satire something of Paul's insight into the impersonality of machine-age modernity. Yet he does so in a paradoxically archaic fashion that trivializes the threat Paul saw in the European forms of that impersonality. For the Montreal capitalism of *Two Solitudes* is not really an impersonal system at all; it is constituted by the rivalry – and strategic collusion – of a few individuals. MacLennan's satire aligns with this in its old-fashioned focus on the exaggeration of personal eccentricities, and the simple identification of men such as Sir Rupert Irons with the industries for which they are named. The more troubling, quasi-expressionistic form of urban grotesque found in the Athens passage is not a mode of representation MacLennan thinks appropriate for the representation of power and desire in Montreal, which if corrupt is corrupt in reassuringly well-bounded ways.

The problem of literary mode is, of course, more complicated than this. On the one hand, by mixing the serious and the trivial, the high and the low, as in the description of the one book produced by a scion of the Square Mile, a compilation of after-dinner anecdotes entitled *Gentlemen, the King!*, satire can be promiscuous in its rhetoric, inventing incongruous juxtapositions such as the famous zeugma of Pope's "Rape of the Lock" about whether a girl will "stain her honour or her new brocade" (II, 107). Satire introduces a playful freedom into the narrative, breathing life into MacLennan's critique of McQueen's repressive puritanism. On the other hand, satire, especially of the kind employed here, restrained rather than anarchic in style, appeals to implicit and generally accepted standards of behaviour. In *Two Solitudes*, these standards are not all that different from the ones to which MacLennan's targets also appeal. The complacency with which the Methuens and their friends dismiss Americans as vulgar and view themselves as more solidly British than the British themselves may be mocked, but only because MacLennan holds a more complicated form of the same view. Kathleen's second, American husband, for example, is physically unrefined and devoid of intellectual distinction. Heather's more conventional sister, Daphne, marries an Englishman. The caddish and brutal Noel Fletcher might have come from a novel by Evelyn Waugh, except that the undercurrent of nihilistic anxiety that makes *A Handful of Dust* something more disturbing than most social satire is absent from MacLennan's moralistic depiction.[15] Noel is sexually demanding with his wife and quick to make a pass at Heather. Montreal's Anglo elite may be stuffy and conservative, but the very fact that they are behind the times has insulated them from some of modernity's unfortunate by-products. There is thus reason to hope that an original and authentic (English) Canadian identity may yet be shaped out of this material. Unfortunately, MacLennan's eagerness to discern this identity limits the creative potential of the mixing and incongruous – promiscuous, in other words – juxtapositions of his satire, which morphs too quickly into earnest advocacy for balance and moderation.

A similar ambivalence about the competing virtues of compartmentalization and promiscuity characterizes MacLennan's portrayal of Montreal's French Canadians, which is much less extensive, and more earnest in tone, than his satire of the city's Square Mile. Indeed, MacLennan does not venture into any francophone Montreal home except that of Paul's half-brother. True to stereotype, the Catholic Marius and his wife, Émilie, have more children than they can support, yet it is important that theirs is not a slovenly poverty. MacLennan's French Canadians may be narrow-minded in their attachment to religion and nation, but at least their way of life does not threaten to erode their moral character or, more crucially, their distinct cultural identity. Some of MacLennan's French Montrealers may be tempted to follow the kind of demagogic leader Marius aspires to be, but the more important point is that Marius does not succeed. The narrator of *Two Solitudes* prefers to believe that on an individual level French and English Canadians always find a way to get along (340). Given the patronizing way Athanase is treated by his English counterparts, and the absence of any significant personal engagement between French and English characters other than the romance between Paul and Heather, this claim is hard to credit. The contradiction is resolved only if we infer that, while regrettable in many respects, the city's social and religious compartmentalization has at least immunized the city against the worst psychological effects of the mass age. In so doing, it has preserved spaces in which healthy relationships

– personal, but perhaps political ones as well – might be nurtured, if the will to do so can be found.

The practical persuasiveness of this vision is debatable, but it would certainly have been more artistically convincing, as has been said, had Paul and Heather's union resulted from a negotiation of real otherness instead of being facilitated by the hero's half-English status. Yet I would suggest that it is just here, in the most egregiously compromised element of the story, that we may see evidence of MacLennan working against his own idealist impulses, or at least seeking to integrate into that idealism some of the unruly reality he otherwise seeks to downplay.

Despite the novel's clear distaste for its corrosive effects, there are in fact a number of moments when promiscuity of various kinds is given a more positive spin. Most of these are brief, and their implications are not explored. Perhaps the most startling of these is the report, near the end of the book, that Daphne's decadent husband, Noel, is not only "back in the R.A.F." but has his armaments factory working overtime; he had (just like Churchill) for years been warning Britain about the gathering storm (342). Noel may well be a willing accomplice in the triumph of the mass machine age, but it is he, and not the blinkered McQueen, who takes action to defend civilization against the worst products of modernity. How Noel's military commitment meshes with his overall selfishness, however, MacLennan doesn't say. Another instance of a character's readiness to adapt to changing times occurs earlier in the story. Before she married Marius, Émilie had shown an admirable willingness to cross social boundaries. In 1920, soon after her family had moved to Montreal from the country, and although she considered herself a good Catholic, she had no qualms about quitting a waitressing job she said "was no good for me" in favour of a better one in Greenberg's dress factory (199). Marius is shocked that she could work "for the Jews," but Émilie herself is quite comfortable with the mixed character of urban life. Nothing comes of this, however, for when we see her again toward the end of the book, she is merely the dutiful mother of Marius's many children.

Each of these passages introduces social and sexual complexities the novel ultimately declines to pursue, with one key exception. This is the curious biography of Paul's mother. Kathleen is the only significant character in the novel who is neither a French Catholic nor an English Protestant. She thus does not fit easily into MacLennan's dualistic image of Montreal. Kathleen is also the only major figure whose character has been marked by urban poverty and promiscuity. The street on which she grew up, and later the one where as an impoverished widow she raises her son Paul, are the only ones the novel describes in detail, and in each case, the key detail is the visible presence of prostitution.[16]

The promiscuity of prostitution undermines the overall pattern of segregation, ethnic and religious, in the first instance, but also psychological and moral, even if as an institution prostitution also serves to maintain social stability. Kathleen grew up in a mixed working-class neighbourhood that included Irish, Poles, and Jews along with the French and the English. The children, however, attended one of the three different school systems of the day: French Catholic, English Catholic, and English Protestant (which in practice served all non-Catholics, including Jews). Yet, when she later calls up her memory of that street, the first thing she mentions is something else. "An old whorehouse had stood on one corner of the Rue de l'Assomption and nobody worried about it" (107). MacLennan goes on to describe the comings and goings of the customers and how Kathleen learned from a neighbour boy that the madam "permitted no swearing or drinking in the house." Moral judgment is subordinated to sociological observation, and to an ironic appreciation for the orderliness of this disorderly house. The motif of prostitution reappears some chapters later, when the teenage Paul is looking out the window of the modest apartment where he lives with Kathleen after his father's death. The prostitutes walking below are presented as familiar figures rather than as unwanted outsiders. "At night the street was quiet enough. But three women, always the same three, wearing black fur-lined overshoes in winter and high heels in summer, patrolled the block regularly from eight to twelve" (220–1). A few lines later, MacLennan tells us that Paul decides to go out, since "it was Saturday, and a boy ought to make a special day out of a Saturday" (221). Of course, Paul is too young to think of a "special day" in terms of sex, but the juxtaposition of the two statements makes one wonder whether the narrative is gesturing toward an urban eroticism it cannot fully incorporate into the narrative.

There was a similar discrepancy between what is observed and what is acknowledged in the earlier passage as well, but, perhaps because it involves Kathleen and not Paul, the implications of that disjunction are developed more fully. After telling us how accustomed Kathleen and her neighbours were to having a brothel nearby, MacLennan begins the next paragraph by emphasizing the boundary that separated them from it. "But the whorehouse had little part in the life on the Rue de l'Assomption. It was not for the neighbors." What he means is that the working men of the street were too poor to enter its doors. Whether any of the street's young women were ever tempted to take a job there the narrator does not say, but Kathleen was sufficiently affected by her knowledge of what went on inside that she calls up memories of her old street just at the moment when, in 1919, she is searching for a Montreal house for her husband, Athanase, and ends up spending the night with Dennis Morey, the man on his way home to Winnipeg. We looked at this incident earlier, but we can now see it from a different angle.

MacLennan seeks to minimize the scandal of Kathleen's behaviour by stressing that she was not deliberately looking for sex; she only wanted "men who would look at her in a way suggesting that these things could be if she wished" (107). The phrasing is curiously parallel to the report of Paul's thoughts about the women he sees in the bars of Europe: he knows he is attractive enough to have one "if he wished" (305). Yet there is an important difference. Paul forsakes erotic in favor of imaginative initiative; for Kathleen, the two are the same. Back in Saint-Marc, she was portrayed as "lazy" (76), indifferent to politics, and disconnected from everything around her, including Paul (80). Here, she seeks connection and a sense of possibility, and MacLennan does not condemn her for doing so through her sexuality.

Even more surprising is MacLennan's account of Kathleen's other relationships with men. Her siblings left the Rue de l'Assomption as soon as they could, to seek a better life in the United States, but Kathleen stays in Montreal, finding a job as a hat-check girl in a hotel. Her position allows her to meet wealthy men whose advances, it is clearly implied, she did not resist. "She liked older men, especially the ones with no pretences, for they were more likely to be gentle, and they were always grateful to her for being what she was" (109–10). One of those older men turns out to be Athanase, whose first wife, the pious and puritanical Marie-Adèle, was already seriously ill at the time. Taking pity on his solitude, Kathleen becomes Athanase's mistress even before her rival dies. The irregularity of her relationship with her second married lover lasts even longer, since she and Henry Clayton, an American businessman, have to wait five years until he finally becomes a widower and they can marry without scandal. Kathleen accompanies Henry back to Pittsburgh, leaving Paul, now a young adult, to fend for himself. Indeed, she disappears from the novel altogether, except for the few letters she is said to send and for one curious reference to be considered in a moment.

Because it offended some *bien-pensant* Canadian reviewers, MacLennan's quietly provocative endorsement of Kathleen's sexual behaviour has been seen largely as a protest against the repressive power of puritanism. It is more than that. This is made clear in her encounter with Dennis Morey, the Canadian officer back from the war. Her encounter with Dennis is a meeting of two solitudes that calls for sympathy rather than judgment, a moment of promiscuity that, seen against the backdrop of the deeper solitude of the modern world made manifest in the war that has just ended, takes on positive value. We have seen how for Kathleen it is a moment of connection, not just with another person but with her urban past. For Dennis, it is a way to postpone his return to the solitude of a city that is the opposite of Montreal, in that far from being a "beating heart," his Winnipeg is devoid of any life-giving energy. Dennis's evocation of the Canadian west reminds us that, although the sweeping description at the beginning of the novel climaxed in the image of Montreal as the heart of the Canadian half-continent, the animating pulse of the city does not actually infuse the whole country with vitality. In fact, its beat is felt rather faintly out on the prairie, compared with the impersonal energy of the winds sweeping across the plains.

Thus, it is paradoxically in the portrayal of promiscuity that we see most clearly how the solitude of which MacLennan speaks is an historical and metaphysical condition as much as it is a psychological or sociological one. Solitude, these passages suggest, is not the absence of other people or an internal isolation that can be overcome by force of will; its effects can be mitigated only by the acknowledgment of vulnerability between people capable of being present to each other without defences. Because this is the case, Kathleen's erotic "promiscuity" does not, in fact, deny moral and social boundaries their necessary structuring role. Her promiscuity is not a matter of letting herself go. On the contrary, Kathleen's attitude and conduct throughout the book is in a way quite detached. This sense of distance is not to be equated with selfishness, although Kathleen certainly can be selfish. Rather, her behaviour is best understood in terms of the impersonality of the "ultimate solitude." This impersonality is most obvious in her encounter with the officer. Another man of his type would have served equally well, and the gift she gives him (and gets in return) is sex without passion and empathy without entanglement. A certain impersonality also characterizes her relationship with Athanase and, from what little we see of their interaction, her relationship with her second husband as well. The novel's treatment of Kathleen, therefore, goes some way toward incorporating the impersonality of the modern age into a distinctive creative vision, one in which "solitude," while painful, is a source of liberated initiative.

Not coincidentally, I think, Kathleen is the only character whose perspective on the city can be called comprehensive. The capitalist Huntly McQueen looks out from his St James Street office to the port and the British Empire across the sea, blind to the diversity of the city behind him. Before she meets Dennis in the hotel, Kathleen wanders through the streets of Montreal. As she does so, "her old sense of the city's wholeness returned to her; it gripped her feelings and imagination the way she remembered it from childhood" (106). This feeling of wholeness is grounded in her memories of the juxtaposition of order and promiscuity in her old neighbourhood, and her sexual encounter with Dennis is gratifying because it is an extension of this feeling of wholeness as well as an acknowledgment of mutual vulnerability. These two experiences, in fact, are two sides of the same coin.

In the end, though, MacLennan does pack Kathleen off to Pittsburgh. There seems to be no way, finally, to integrate her kind of agency into the city *Two Solitudes* wants to imagine. The conjunction of promiscuity and impersonality Kathleen represents is seductive, but apparently also too threatening to be incorporated further into the novel. Her sexual promiscuity has to be kept from contaminating the ideal of virtuous partnership symbolized by Paul's marriage to Heather. It is interesting to note that Heather never meets Kathleen; everything she learns about her future mother-in-law is mediated through Paul. The older woman is given no opportunity to educate the younger one. Nor does the adult Paul ever confront the mother who so often seemed indifferent to him. Heather's struggle to break free from her mother, the controlling yet needy Janet Methuen, is vividly dramatized in the last chapters of the book, but this kind of mother-daughter conflict is a familiar theme in romantic fiction.

Showing Paul coming to terms with the promiscuous Kathleen, a woman whose comforting yet detached presence seems to embody something of the essence of the modern city itself (a Montreal Molly Bloom, perhaps), would have been another matter altogether.

The book does include one moment when Paul might have confronted Kathleen, at least in his own mind. In Part Three of the novel, Heather asks Paul, whom she has not seen since they both were children and to whom she now feels romantically attracted, whether he has "known a lot of girls." Paul avoids the implied question about whether he is sexually experienced by replying that he has known only one *woman*, "though she never really grew up at all. She was so natural with all men she made it hard for me to be natural with any other woman." Heather's response to this provocative statement is the tentative "Do you know her still?" Paul tersely replies, "She's my mother," and the conversation stops there (288).

It would be tempting to pursue the Oedipal implications of this passage, so disappointingly curtailed and yet so critically disarming in the way it opens a doorway it refuses to enter. Paul's statement reduces Heather more effectively to silence than anything he tells her about the burden of being a French Canadian. What, indeed, could a well-brought-up young lady say in reply? How much of what Paul is hinting at could she even comprehend? More disappointing, however, is that the subject never comes up later on, after Paul and Heather are married. Nor does the narrator step in to provide any additional perspective, as he does in talking about the war and to herald, at the end of the book, the awakening in both the French and English "race-legends" of a new "felt knowledge" about their shared past and their common future (370). This optimism is rooted in the success of Paul and Heather's marriage, an achievement that implies that any obstacles to their sexual or psychological intimacy have been overcome. How exactly that happens the novel never explains. No doubt Heather's love, along with the sexual conjunction of her solitude with his, enables Paul to become "natural" with a woman who is not his mother. If this is true, then Heather is the key figure through which the novel projects the eventual resolution of the collective inhibitions and neuroses that have blocked a more intimate union between French and English Canadians. One wonders how conscious MacLennan was of once again making the woman, not the man – and not the writer – the mediator of this intimacy.

MacLennan will develop a more explicit and systematic Oedipal interpretation of Quebec nationalism in *The Return of the Sphinx*, a novel that unfortunately reduces political complexity to psychological allegory. This weakness is already present in *Two Solitudes*, but it is the merit of the earlier novel that its psychological explorations of solitude and promiscuity also serve to complicate the tidy dualism of its political message. I suggested earlier that the politically problematic decision to make Paul half-English could be read more sympathetically as the only way MacLennan thought he could give his "local" character some form of the internally divided self characteristic of the modern hero. Making him the *métissé* son of the socially and sexually promiscuous Kathleen could in the same way serve as a means of incorporating that promiscuity not only into the hero's character but by extension into the symbolic union of the two solitudes symbolized by his marriage to Heather, herself the granddaughter of a wanderer. Seen from this point of view, their union is potentially richer in its implications than a romance between two people of impeccable, and impeccably distinct, lineages.

Unfortunately, MacLennan as author is unable or unwilling to pursue his bolder intuitions. His determination to project a vision of a healthy and unitary national body prevents him from probing as deeply as he could have into the complexities of the city that serves uncomfortably as that country's double-beating heart. Yet he does not entirely deny the insights he is honest or vulnerable enough to let emerge along the way. One of these is that interaction with the impersonality of city life might well foster the emergence of a more capacious, less purpose-driven conception of personality than that associated with nation building as MacLennan conceives it. Another is the complementary realization that this wider conception of personality might in turn help foster new forms of political identity, in which unassimilated, uncategorized, and in-between elements are accommodated rather than denied.

In choosing the title *Two Solitudes*, McLennan recognized the need for a non-fusional form of connection, one in which individual selves become desiring subjects all the more fully and authentically in that they know themselves to be not just lonely people driven by personal neediness but separate beings shaped by the impersonal forces of modern (not to mention metaphysical) solitude. The last lines of the novel underscore the pervasiveness of this condition by declaring that, as the Second World

War began, Canada's achievement of maturity is evidenced by its (post-colonial?) awareness that it is "alone with history, with science, with the future" (370). In the end, *Two Solitudes* could glimpse but not quite fulfill the promise of its title. MacLennan judges his own book best in the words Heather uses about Paul's first attempt at a novel. "Many sections had extraordinary power and descriptions were new and vivid. But the balance was not right and the whole was curiously unsatisfying" (328). Perhaps the new novel on which the hero starts to work is not described because MacLennan realized he could not describe it. All he could do was create a space in which his readers could imagine what that imaginary novel had to say.

2

Gendered Mediations

Gwethalyn Graham's *Earth and High Heaven* and Françoise Loranger's *Mathieu*

Gwethalyn Graham's *Earth and High Heaven* (1944) and Françoise Loranger's *Mathieu* (1949) share a conception of the writer's calling that is very different from MacLennan's. Though only a few years younger than the author of *Two Solitudes*, these two writers do not seek, as MacLennan does, to model a triumphantly new literary consciousness through their novels. Their declared mission is the more modestly therapeutic one of diagnosing the hurt of social exclusion, including self-exclusion, and pointing the way to its healing. In their concern for the effects of deprivation, their projects bear some resemblance to that of Gabrielle Roy in *Bonheur d'occasion*. Yet, if we compare their novels to hers, we see that Loranger and Graham address the issue of the artist's mediating power in a more searching and specific way than Roy does. Unlike *Bonheur d'occasion*, *Mathieu* and *Earth and High Heaven* dramatize the difficulties faced by women writers seeking to appropriate that power in 1940s Montreal. Like Roy, Loranger and Graham justify their literary initiative by framing it as an act of compassion for others rather than of self-promotion. At the same time, they incorporate into their narratives a subtly penetrating reflection on their historical situation that contrasts as much with Roy's authorial self-effacement – or what we take to be such – as it does with MacLennan's explicit assertion of authority.

Because the working out of that reflection in these two novels takes interestingly similar and, as I will show, mutually illuminating paths, I propose to examine them together, and do so here, before discussing *Bonheur d'occasion*. Although in some ways, as I have suggested, these two works mark an advance in literary sophistication over Roy's first novel, in other respects it is *Bonheur d'occasion* that dramatizes more acutely the challenges Montreal novelists felt called upon to overcome in the following decade. Neither *Mathieu* nor *Earth and High Heaven* had any immediate posterity, and this is not only because Loranger and Graham published no further novels. In their focus on the gendered dimension of literary mediation, they were too much ahead of their time for their work to find an echo in the local culture. By the time they could be appreciated, moreover, their pioneering insights had been obscured by the somewhat awkward and didactic quality of their writing, as well as by the absence in the stories of those "representative" features the city's mainstream literary histories have been most concerned to map. A different perspective on their potential representativeness will emerge, however, when we see the surprising similarities in the configuration, not just of the two plots, but of the ways two writers who did not know each other incorporated into their narrative an awareness of the authorial agency available to them. It is through the unintended parallels between the books that we can locate their literary-historical moment.

In *Mathieu* as in *Earth and High Heaven*, the declared focus of the story is the integration into Montreal society, or more precisely into either the French or the English conception of city "society," of a male character whose talents have gone unrecognized because of his origins but also because of his doubts about himself. As in many such stories, the apparently unattainable, socially advantaged woman with whom he falls in love becomes a key mediating figure in his struggle. As the story unfolds, however, the question of how the "insider" heroine herself may flourish becomes just as urgent as her quest to assure the hero's integration. Through this female protagonist, the writer also explores her own mediating role in helping readers better understand and participate more fully in the city. The readers addressed by the text are of both sexes, since the weakness and vulnerability, as well as the social marginality, of the male protagonist are such as to provide ample opportunity for cross-gender identification. By the same token, both hero and heroine represent something of the author. Their roles are complementary but not gendered in a conventional manner, for the female protagonist is strong where the hero is weak. Most notably, Loranger's Danielle and Graham's Erica (each is given the feminine version of a male name) both enjoy a considerable degree of freedom and respect. They do more than assist the marginalized male protagonist with sympathetic understanding; they also push the community in which they move to re-examine its prejudices.

The heroine's role remains a problematic one nonetheless. Both novels attend closely to her thoughts and feelings but it is not her agency that drives the plot. When it seems that Erica will not be able to marry Marc in Graham's romance story, she wastes away until Marc gains the courage to claim her. In the more existentialist *Mathieu*, only the hero acquires the prestige that comes from looking death in the eye. On the meta-level of the narrative, however, it is the heroine, not the hero, who dramatizes the writer's struggle to achieve authorial status. The hero's discomfort with his liminal social status certainly mirrors in some ways the writer's dissatisfaction with the limited recognition she can expect, but it is the ambiguous narrative status of the female protagonist – is she heroine or helper? – that more fully articulates Loranger's and Graham's question about literary agency. In both novels, the prospect of hero and heroine uniting in marriage offers an imaginative resolution of both quest and question, but whether or not a wedding will actually be celebrated is at the end of the story still unclear. In this respect, these novels are not as optimistic as *Two Solitudes*; yet neither are they quite as disenchanted as *Bonheur d'occasion*, in which marriage offers Florentine the comfort and closure she seeks but does nothing to help resolve Emmanuel's anxiety about the prospects for social change.

In both *Earth and High Heaven* and *Mathieu*, the female protagonist works with language, though significantly only at a remove from the source of speech. As a journalist Erica Drake records, and as an actress Danielle Beaulieu performs, what other people have already put into words. Talented as they are, neither enjoys the scope for creative expression they deserve. Erica edits the women's page of the fictional Montreal *Post*. Even in the wartime gloom of 1942, the year in which the novel is set, this page continues to focus on society weddings, though it does offer hints about how cooks can cope with sugar rationing. *Mathieu* is set in the early postwar years, at a time when economic and cultural horizons should be expanding, but the only paid acting jobs Danielle can find are in commercial radio serials. Her more artistically rewarding work with the little experimental theatre troupe her brother directs is cut short when their performances of a Sartre play are cancelled under pressure from the Catholic Church. Both Erica and Danielle enjoy the security of bourgeois status and a considerable degree of independence from family as well as financial constraints, yet the social agency they can exercise is even more limited than that of the marginal man with whom each becomes involved.

Graham's Marc Reiser is a lawyer, but it is taken for granted that as a Jew he can work only for an all-Jewish firm. Another tacit but firmly enforced rule prevents him from renting an apartment in English Montreal's nicer buildings. As the story begins, Marc is also an army officer poised to go overseas, but even the more tolerant fellow officers with whom he trained do not welcome him into their homes. While *Earth and High Heaven* is a protest against prejudice, it never suggests that the attitudes it criticizes are likely to change any time soon, at least in Montreal. If Marc and Erica do marry – and at the end of the novel their wedding is still only anticipated – their union is not imagined as having any impact on the world around them. The obstacle standing in Marc and Erica's way is presented as being less amenable to negotiation than the one Paul and Heather face in *Two Solitudes*. The difference no doubt stems from Graham's conviction that anti-Semitism is a more stubborn and deep-rooted form of prejudice than the mutual stereotyping of French and English Canadians (both groups are shown to be equally hostile to Jews), but it probably also reflects the perspective of a woman writer who knows at first-hand how resistant social conventions can be, all the more so when they are taken for granted.[1] The contrast in perspectives is epitomized in the titles of the two novels. MacLennan's appropriates a melancholy-sounding but in reality tentatively optimistic statement by Rilke; while Graham borrows a phrase from "Be Still My Soul," a poem from Housman's *A Shropshire Lad* lamenting a love that can never be.[2] The poem is quoted at a moment near the end of the story when the lovers must confront the prospect of separation (275), and while the novel strives to conclude on a positive note, the despairing tone of the poem is still heard at the story's close.

Loranger's fervent belief in the possibility of breaking down the barriers separating individuals is also tempered by a pessimistic assessment of the prospects for change. With an acute and wide-ranging mind, a talent for writing, and a thirst for recognition, Mathieu Normand is poised to become the kind of public intellectual who in the following decade would lay the groundwork for Quebec's Quiet Revolution. In his notebooks,

Mathieu reflects on the psychological burdens of the French Canadian past, especially the debilitating hatred of the body in Quebec Catholic piety. His testimony on this issue, and perhaps even more on the liberating power of classical music, the only form of high art not subject to censorship or moral denigration in the Quebec of the day (217), echo and sometimes anticipate the essays that Jean Le Moyne was starting to write around the time the novel was published but that became famous only when they were gathered to striking effect in the landmark collection *Convergences* (1961). Through a family connection Mathieu is given a position as a drama critic at the Montreal *Matin*, a French-language paper no less conservative in its own way than Erica's *Post*. There, Mathieu can say more or less what he wants, but only because those who run the paper consider cultural reporting to be little more than a way to fill some space between the ads. Mathieu's freedom is that of a superfluous man.

As the descendant of an old Quebec Catholic family, Mathieu does not face the same social barriers as Marc, but the prospects for his full integration into Montreal life are just as bleak as his Jewish counterpart's. When he was a child, his profligate father ran away, and his mother took out her anger on the boy. After years of belittlement for being his father's son, but also for reminding his mother of a man she still misses, Mathieu seethes with resentment and self-hatred. Most crucially, Mathieu's hostile dependency on other people has prevented him from shaking off the killjoy religion of guilt in which he grew up. "Like every other child in the province, I had religion crammed into me. They stuffed me so full of it that now it comes out of every pore of my skin" (134). His inability to shake off this influence becomes an additional source of resentment as he gets to know Danielle, whose freedom from psychological or religious inhibition he can only envy. Convinced that Danielle could never find him attractive, Mathieu turns self-hatred into aggression, lashing out at her as he does at everyone and everything he admires but cannot enjoy. His perfidious review of the Sartre play staged by Bruno and Danielle invites its condemnation by church censors, and his critique is all the more devastating in that, unlike the uncomprehending Philistines around him, Mathieu understood and appreciated exactly what the actors were trying to do. Thanks to a last-minute qualm of conscience and the intervention of the influential patron who got him the job, his diatribe is pulled from the paper, and so Mathieu escapes any responsibility when the play's performances are indeed cancelled under church pressure. The incident shows us how Mathieu's despair might easily have driven him into the ranks of the reactionaries had not an unexpected convergence of circumstances opened up another future for him.

Mathieu ultimately arrives at a freer and more emotionally integrated outlook on life, but the prospect of his eventual union with Danielle is even less definite than Marc's with Erica. At the end of the book, Loranger's protagonists still prefer to think of themselves as friends rather than lovers; they are wary of acting on a mutual attraction that might be tainted by pity on one side and envy on the other. Nor does the novel indicate how Mathieu might flourish in a city still pervaded by cultural insecurity. Unlike MacLennan's Paul Tallard, who intends from the start to address the widest possible public, Loranger's Mathieu Normand confines his deepest thoughts to private *cahiers*. Only by accident do they come to be read by other characters, who might just as easily have remained forever unaware of Mathieu's torments and talents. While the notebooks are cited at length in the text, and thus offered to the reader along with the narrator's omniscient reporting of Mathieu's thoughts, nothing in Loranger's novel tells us how the character himself might bridge the gap between "private" and "public" expression. The same is true in *Earth and High Heaven*. Marc's status as a lawyer (and a military officer about to be commissioned) qualifies him for public roles Erica cannot play, but we never see him at work in his law office. Indeed, we never see him interacting with anyone in Montreal other than the people in Erica's circle. Whatever thoughts he has about the world around him he expresses only in conversations with Erica and in thoughts reported by the narrator. The kind of career he might pursue, assuming he survives the war, is no clearer than Mathieu's. The inference is that Graham, like Loranger, could not imagine the course of that career in any plausible detail.[3]

The relative situation of the male and female protagonists in these two novels is thus quite different from the one we find in MacLennan and Roy. In *Two Solitudes*, the author may have projected some of his own history into Heather's struggle to free herself from her family, but there is no question that Paul is the novel's central figure. Conversely, however much Emmanuel may speak for the writer of *Bonheur d'occasion*, Florentine remains the novel's pivotal character. By contrast, in *Earth and*

High Heaven and *Mathieu* concerns about the scope of individual creative agency are dramatized through a protagonist of the opposite sex as much as through one of the same sex as that of the author.

Yet the contrast is not simply one of gender roles; it also reflects a fundamental difference in the authors' fictional projects. Intent on showing how his writer-hero Paul will integrate French and English identities within his creative work, MacLennan did not worry too much about how Paul as an individual might be integrated, and his ambitions accommodated, within the ongoing life of the city. Roy was able to avoid the problem altogether by not making Jean Lévesque a central figure in the book, though, from what little she says about Jean's ascent, it is remarkably unproblematic. In *Earth and High Heaven* and in *Mathieu*, however, the accommodation of the hero's desires does not depend on the force of the hero's initiative or the attractiveness of his personal qualities alone, but on the heroine's embracing him as her partner. This decision is not taken for granted or inevitable, as in different ways it is in *Two Solitudes* and *Bonheur d'occasion*. The hesitations and deliberations of the "insider" heroine are not just personal in nature; they provide a measure of her society's capacity for renewal through the acceptance of an outsider. In this respect, Loranger and Graham offer variations on a key implication of the classic "marriage plot," and it is worth pausing for a moment to note how they differ on this point from Roy and MacLennan. Neither of latter views their protagonists' marriage as symbolizing the accommodation of difference within a closely knit community or the breakdown of the barrier between that community and another. For MacLennan, that community does not yet exist; it is the task of the marriage to help create it. In Roy, the marriage of Emmanuel and Florentine makes no difference to a community it doesn't even challenge.

In *Bonheur d'occasion*, the marriage of Florentine and Emmanuel does not represent a negotiation of differences, but rather a determination to collude in covering them up. Even though the bride and groom belong to what is essentially a single, homogeneous community, it is still remarkable how the disparities of outlook or expectation that do exist are neutralized by the silence of the characters and the structure of the story's conclusion, split between local disenchantment and a universalized idealism. The marriage portrayed in *Two Solitudes* is explicitly intended to symbolize the overcoming of communal differences, but that union is not as consequential, socially or aesthetically, as it purports to be. This is not just because of the well-known fact that Paul, as the son of a mixed marriage, already contains French and English identities within himself. Another reason, which seems to have escaped critical notice, is that marriage to Heather does not give Paul any status he does not already possess or agency he does not already enjoy. Her love gives him personal support, but through it Paul does not gain any additional social or economic advantage. As MacLennan portrays him, Paul is essentially self-sufficient. Even during the Depression, when he could not find a job worthy of his talents, he managed to scrape together enough money to write without contracting any debts, moral or financial. Likewise, whether Heather's family comes to accept Paul (or whether his half-brother, Marius, accepts Heather) doesn't matter. Heather is content to join Paul in a happy little world apart from everyone else.

Even more important, Paul's success as a writer does not depend on his access to, or participation in, any of the city's social or cultural networks – an issue of crucial importance for the heroes of *Mathieu* and *Earth and High Heaven*. Nor is the couple threatened with the ostracism that drives Graham's mixed marriage couple the Rosenbergs out of Montreal altogether and condemns them to a life of unhappy isolation in Toronto (248).[4] While Heather's snobbish mother, Janet, is prejudiced against Paul, she is herself an increasingly anachronistic and isolated figure. In any case, Paul and Heather are not presented as needing access to social networks. Like Canada, they bravely stand "alone with history" on the last page of the book.

Nor does Paul wonder whether his novel will find an audience. He may bemoan the absence of a local literary culture, but once he has hit his stride he never worries that his novel might not be accepted for publication or that it might be rejected or misunderstood by its readers. Heather's appreciation is taken as a sufficient guarantee of the positive reception of Paul's work. He never wonders how many people in the English community think enough like Heather to constitute a public for his book. Nor does he stop to consider who Heather's francophone counterparts might be, or what *they* might think. MacLennan seems to believe that Paul's novel, and by extension his own, will carry its own conviction.[5]

More modestly, neither Françoise Loranger nor Gwethalyn Graham claims to address, still less to speak for, any community beyond her own.

Their heroes are true outsider figures, in that they face obstacles of a kind neither Roy's nor MacLennan's protagonist has to confront. Both authors want their novels to represent the imaginative openness they wish their community to embrace, but they are at pains to make their vision a plausible one. Thus, they attend more closely and explicitly to the difficulties blocking the hero's integration. At the same time, the union they envision between hero and heroine – if it occurs – would be a more real achievement, in that it would embody (in contrast with MacLennan) already existing and (in contrast with Roy) authentic community values. The earnestness with which they pursue their project verges on the didactic, and yet both novels delineate in unexpectedly resonant ways what their reasonableness requires they refrain from imagining: the notion of a border-crossing intimate relationship whose dynamic would symbolize the possibilities and the problems of bringing the city's communities closer together. This uneasy combination of the expository and the exploratory finds expression in some peculiar features of characterization and plot which have gone unremarked in readings focused on the ideas the novels are supposed to convey. Just as unnoticed are the similarities in the way these features are configured – symptoms, I would argue, of an historical predicament peculiar to them both.

Both novels, for example, feature characters who move across the city's linguistic barrier, but in ways that do nothing to foreground the issue of trans-communal communication. Instead, these journeys provide implicit illustration of divisions no one thinks much about. Loranger's actor-director Bruno communicates effectively enough in English to win an invitation to perform in New York, but anglophone Montreal is entirely absent from *Mathieu*.[6] In *Earth and High Heaven*, Erica's brother Tony marries the francophone Madeleine de Savigny, but the reluctance with which their families accept their union serves only to show that for a Montreal Christian to marry a Jew, even if they are both English-speaking, is even more difficult than for an anglophone Protestant to marry a francophone Catholic. In itself, Tony and Madeleine's wedding (which pregnancy may have forced on them) cannot be considered a symbolic union of French and English Montreal. Madeleine's brother, the canny politician René, is in love with Erica, and their affectionately antagonistic conversations allow Graham to articulate some French Canadian views about anti-Semitism and the war, but these intellectual exchanges are primarily a foil designed to highlight the more intimate meeting of minds between Erica and Marc. Whether René would really be willing to jeopardize the soft-nationalist credentials that got him elected by marrying an anglophone Protestant is a question that never comes up, probably because it is assumed to be inconceivable. One suspects that René's gallantry is just a way for Graham to highlight Erica's attractiveness. In any case, apart from René, French Montrealers are as absent from Graham's novel as English ones are from Loranger's.

Both novels also limit their representation of the city to its bourgeois milieux. Neither story does more than vaguely mention working-class or immigrant neighbourhoods of any language group. Particularly striking is the fact that, although Erica and Marc spend much of their time walking or driving around town, they never visit a Jewish neighborhood or indeed interact with any Jews at all. The Montreal of A.M. Klein (who was active as a lawyer and editor as well as a poet at the time the novel was written) or the young Mordecai Richler is just as absent from the novel as the French Canadian city. The notion that Erica might be integrated into the city's Jewish community never arises, even as a controversial possibility. It is true that Marc's family lives far away, in a small northern Ontario town, but it is clear that the novel imagines the vector of social integration pointing in only one direction.

The social geography of *Mathieu* is no less remarkable for its narrowness. Danielle and Bruno share a flat above a Chinese laundry in what is presumably an economically mixed area (33), but the neighbourhood seems to hold no interest for these supposedly bohemian youth. Nor does the novel consider worthy of remark the fact that these francophone siblings grew up in Westmount, where their mother still lives with another, married daughter. Nothing is said about their relationship to Westmount's majority Anglo population, whose presence indeed goes entirely unmentioned. The urban landscapes depicted in *Mathieu* and *Earth and High Heaven* do overlap: the same downtown world of restaurants and nightclubs appears in both books, but even in those venues the city's linguistic communities are neither visible nor audible to each other.

It is striking that two novels championing the recognition of people marginalized by ignorance and social prejudice should present such a constricted view of the city in which they are set. For all their limitations, *Two Solitudes* and *Bonheur d'occasion* were broader in their geographic and demographic scope. One reason for the difference may lie in the circumstances in which the four books were written. *Two Solitudes* and *Bonheur d'occasion* were both published just as the Second World War was ending. *Earth and High Heaven* came out when victory in that war was not yet assured, and when French Canadian resistance to conscription was at its height. By the time *Mathieu* was published in 1949, the optimism associated with that victory had already faded. Indeed, the obstacles to social change may have appeared even more intractable than they were before, given Quebec premier Maurice Duplessis's resounding electoral victory in 1948. It is perhaps symptomatic that, although the war would still have been fresh in the memory of Loranger's characters, none of them mention it. Even when the well-to-do Nicole refers to a trip to Paris that must have occurred in 1939, she never identifies it as a prewar visit she now has the opportunity to repeat (25).[7]

Despite the concreteness and urgency of their calls for change, neither writer questions the essential immobility of the city in which they set their novel. On the contrary, they take it for granted.[8] Yet, if we look at protagonists' kinship context, we find that the configuration of family relationships tells us a lot about the authors' conception of Montreal's social imaginary and about the unexpectedly parallel ways Graham and Loranger seek to mediate the transformation of that imaginary through their fiction.

FAMILY CONSTELLATIONS AND URBAN ORBITS

A first feature common to the two books is the presence in the heroine's life of a father figure whose power is tempered by self-awareness and a considerable degree of intuition about other people. His vitality contrasts with the self-effacing, indeed remarkably ineffectual, presence of the maternal figures. In *Earth and High Heaven*, Charles Drake is a prominent businessman, a pillar of the Anglo establishment, but he is also a man with a taste for avant-garde classical music and a willingness to entertain, if not to endorse, advanced political ideas. He is also more closely attuned than his wife, Margaret, to his daughter Erica's moods. This father-daughter closeness becomes oppressive, however, when Charles pressures Erica into rejecting a suitor he considers undesirable. Only with the greatest difficulty will Erica resist this emotional blackmail, and in this crisis her mother, a prisoner to convention, is of little help.

The biological father of *Mathieu*'s Danielle Cinq-Mars is dead, but her uncle Étienne Beaulieu plays a paternal role analogous to that of Charles Drake. Like his counterpart, Étienne owns an important business, though he owes his success not to inherited privilege but to an ability to intuit his employees' unsuspected potential. He gives them jobs for which their training hasn't prepared them but in which they almost always flourish.[9] In this respect, Étienne plays a mediating role not unlike that of the novel's theatrical artists, who in their commercial radio work are described by Loranger as an "amphibious race" of cultural intermediaries providing the (missing) "link" between capitalists and the people (106). Indeed, Étienne has his company sponsor a radio serial that enables Danielle and her director brother Bruno to make ends meet while they pursue their dream of bringing cutting-edge French drama to the Montreal stage.

Like Margaret Drake, Danielle's mother, Marie, would like nothing better than to see her daughter settle into married domesticity, but she has little influence over Danielle and is largely content to busy herself with the family life of her other daughter. Étienne's equally conventional wife, Eugénie, Marie's sister, is similarly powerless to stop her daughter Nicole from pursuing a theatrical career. Less talented but no less driven than Danielle, Nicole wants to be an actress too. As a married woman whose husband, Albert Dupré, is entirely absorbed by his business and sexual affairs, Nicole enjoys independent agency of a more traditional sort. She ultimately finds her calling as a philanthropic hostess and impresario – as another kind of *trait d'union* between art and money.

There is one important difference between the two novels: unlike Charles Drake, Étienne Beaulieu encourages Danielle and Nicole to go their own way. One reason is that he is less possessive. Indeed, although intuitive about his family members and their needs, he is emotionally detached from them. He is more than willing to leave Nicole and her brother Bernard to their own devices. Like Erica's brother Tony, Bernard is weak-willed, but this hardly matters. Étienne is no more worried about his son-in-law's inadequacy than he is about his infidelities. But perhaps the main reason for the difference between Étienne and Charles, a reason that might explain the others, is that the French Canadian businessman is much less anxious about his economic future than his English counterpart, and so has no reason to put pressure on the younger generation.

Loranger's female protagonist may not need to rebel against her father figure, but the hero does. Graham's Marc feels no particular animosity toward Charles Drake since he neither needs nor wants his approval, but Mathieu is full of resentment toward Étienne. The latter in turn is fascinated by the tormented young man precisely because he does not know how to "place" him. His intuition fails to penetrate the psychological armor with which Mathieu defends himself against the world. Unlike Charles Drake, determined to keep Marc in the "place" to which his Jewishness should consign him, Étienne is not threatened by Mathieu, merely puzzled. Mathieu's mother, Lucienne Normand, a childhood friend of Étienne's wife, Eugénie, but much more assertive and controlling, was abandoned by her spendthrift husband, Jules, when Mathieu was still a child. Adept at playing the victim role, Lucienne sponges off the Beaulieus and demands total loyalty from her son even as she belittles him for lacking the charm of his profligate father. If Mathieu resents Étienne, it is for not divining how much he suffers, for not being the father figure he needs, the one man who could read his mind. Étienne's failure to "see" Mathieu may be less culpable than Charles's prejudice against Marc, but in the author's eyes it is no less indicative of society's failure to recognize and welcome the outsiders who might renew it. Luckily, the heroine is ready to do what the mother figure cannot, and what the father figure fails to do: take the initiative in mediating the hero's entry into the symbolic structure of the city.

Whether she can succeed, however, is a question to which the two novels offer only a tentatively positive answer. Although the prospect of Mathieu's marriage to Danielle is less definite than Marc's with Erica, Loranger is actually more optimistic than Graham. This is partly owing to the difference between the issues the books address. Fighting the anti-Semitism that excludes the hero from the community is a more daunting task than fostering the self-esteem of someone within that community whose marginality is to a large extent self-inflicted – though, as we shall see, Mathieu's handicap represents a collective disability, while Marc's alienation is, to an unexpected degree, self-induced. Another explanation, I would argue, may be found in the contrasting historical positions of Montreal's two language communities. The world of the Drakes is under threat. First, the Depression seriously damaged the market for the Caribbean sugar products on which the family business is based.[10] Now a second world war, which, unlike the first, has brought a multinational wave of refugees to Montreal, has led some in the English community (the French are portrayed as stubbornly isolationist) to question the city's tradition of ethnic and religious segregation. The Drake family legacy is also in jeopardy. Erica's brother Tony is already serving overseas, but the haste with which he enlisted has nothing to do with heroic commitment. Tony is a lost soul, unfit to take over his father's business and unprepared to shoulder his responsibilities to the baby born just before his departure. We later learn that he has been having affairs with women in England. The upshot is that Tony's social border-crossing sets no liberating precedent. It serves only to aggravate the difficulty of Erica's position, for her marriage to Marc is seen as accelerating the family's social decline. The anglophone Montreal of Graham's novel seems no more willing to loosen its rules than it was before the war. Given the circumstances, it is acceptable for Erica to take a job, even to occupy a managerial position at her paper (though only as editor of the women's page), but everyone still expects her to find a "suitable" husband, one who will shore up the established order, not reshape it.

Earth and High Heaven, in short, depicts a community whose vitality has been sapped but which continues to hold its members in a very tight grip. *Mathieu*, by contrast, deals with what seems like the endless deferral of the moment when the pent-up energy of the francophone community will find a creative outlet. As with Erica, Danielle's pursuit of a career is justified by her family's limited finances, though her reluctance to marry the wealthy but conventional Jacques would, if it were known, be greeted with as much incomprehension as Erica's relationship with Marc. Danielle's bother Bruno is a brilliant actor and director, more ambitious than Tony, yet socially just as inept, especially in comparison with his sister. Bruno allows his troupe to be hobbled by debt, and he fails to prevent their performances of Sartre's *Les Mouches* (*The Flies*) from being cancelled under church pressure.[11] Like Tony, Bruno flees the city rather than challenge its boundaries. When he is offered a theatre job in New York, he decides to abandon Montreal immediately, leaving Danielle to face the future alone, just as Tony had done with Erica.

In each case, the brother's departure disrupts the traditional pattern of filiation in ways that both help and hinder the heroine. The lack of competition from a male sibling, like the absence of a strong mother figure, gives Danielle and Erica wider scope for action in the public world of work. At the same time, lack of fraternal support deprives the heroine of a useful buffer against social and family pressure. For example, because Bruno shares her apartment, no one is scandalized at the unmarried Danielle's not living at home. She is thus free to come and go as she pleases, even stay out all night if she wants. Bruno's departure for New York could threaten that freedom. None of this, it should be noted, is actually said in the book, probably because Loranger didn't want to draw too much attention to her character's bohemian lifestyle. As in another free-thinking Quebec novel of the period, Charles Hamel's *La Solitude de la chair* (Solitude of the flesh), unconventional arrangements can be portrayed as long as no fuss is made about them.

One source of Erica's stress, by contrast, is the fact that she lives with her parents, constantly aware of and affected by their moods just as they always have their watchful eye on her. No doubt, lack of money, along with social convention, explains why she stays, but Graham may also have arranged things this way for dramatic purposes. Charles does not want Marc crossing the threshold of their home, and Marc himself does not want to go where he is not welcome. Perhaps significantly, we never see Tony's Catholic wife crossing the Drake threshold either. Similarly, Tony's absence means he is not there to mediate between his sister and their parents; nor can he host Marc at his own home as a first step toward integrating him into Gentile society. Bruno's exclusive preoccupation with his work has similar consequences. Mathieu is not actor material, and so Bruno has no interest in doing anything with or for him. Plus, he is a man, unlike the working-class Michelle, the Beaulieu's attractive former maid, to whom Bruno is happy to give the break she needs to launch her career. Like Tony's marriage to a francophone, however, Bruno's relationship with a lower-class woman is of no symbolic consequence.

Thus, the family structure in both novels is constructed in such a way as to make the heroine not just the principal but (at least initially) the sole mediator of the hero's quest for integration. That this arrangement is deliberate, and in its deliberation literarily suggestive, is confirmed by the similarities in the portrayal of Erica's sister Miriam and Danielle's sister-figure, her cousin Nicole. Both are worldly women, content to exploit the agency they enjoy rather than risk it for an uncertain reward. Yet their creators show remarkably little inclination to punish these compromised women for being less than heroic. On the contrary, their stories are told with as much sympathy as irony. Miriam Drake's marriage to a sexually inadequate Englishman (the polar opposite, therefore, of Daphne's husband Noel in *Two Solitudes*) has ended in divorce. Now, after her return to Montreal, she has been abandoned by the married American with whom she has been having an affair. Though she is reluctant to admit it, the rebellious Miriam finds herself needing the emotional security offered by a man from her own Montreal social circle. This man turns out to be the brother of Eric Gardiner, to whom Erica was formerly engaged but who died before they could be married. John Gardiner bears the traces of his repressive Anglo-Montreal upbringing and so must struggle to accept Miriam's checkered past, but fortunately he turns out to be a person not only of goodwill but of unexpectedly progressive political views.

The Catholic Nicole of *Mathieu* would never consider divorcing her boorish husband, Albert Dupré. She either does not know or does not care that Albert cheats on her with prostitutes, and she appears to be uninterested in finding an alternate sexual partner for herself. All Nicole wants is social recognition. When it becomes clear she has no talent, she discovers her true vocation as the philanthropist her money and taste enable her to be. Her skills as a social go-between, coupled with her initially irritating but finally admirable persistence in the face of rejection, make her one of the city's leading patrons of the arts, another "linking" species between the bourgeois and the bohemian. Like Miriam, in other words, Nicole finds a comfortable niche within the existing social order. The happy ending granted these two women of limited but genuine sensibility may reflect their creators' appreciation of the difficult conditions in which they, like Roy's Florentine, have to negotiate their desires.

Erica and Danielle are more ambitious in their aspirations to social agency, and better prepared to exercise it. When their stories begin, they differ from the Heather of *Two Solitudes* and the Florentine of *Bonheur d'occasion* in being independent-minded women in their late twenties, not young girls. Although unmarried, they are sexually experienced, a fact that carries with it no hint of guilt or shame. Perhaps surprisingly, given the conditions of the time, the French novel discusses its heroine's sex life more openly than does the English one. When Danielle confronts the classic novelistic temptation to choose a socially appropriate man over the problematic hero, she doesn't weigh the merits of the wealthy socialite Jacques Aubry only by engaging him in dinner conversation. She puts him to a more intimate test by spending the night with him in a rooming house in Montreal's lower downtown. The result is dispiriting, but the language used to describe their encounter only superficially resembles that of the conventional religious or moral discourses of the day. "This evening, she felt, did her no damage; it wasn't part of her life. She rejected and disavowed its every action, wanting only to hold on to what it had taught her. She understood, she knew now that if she had found it impossible to be herself it was because she had never stopped seeing herself according to Jacques's idea of her, the way you see without recognizing yourself in a distorting mirror" (181). Danielle's eagerness to put the incident behind her is not driven by remorse: erotic self-discovery is a moment of grace, not of sin.

Graham does not discuss Erica's first, and more positive, sexual experience with Marc so explicitly, no doubt because it is simply a natural next step in their relationship. Erica's previous engagement to another man seems to justify our assumption that she has had sex before (for if not, shouldn't her first experience with Marc be more of an event?), but there is something a little odd about this reference to the past. Erica's deceased fiancé, curiously named Eric, was the brother of John Gardiner, the man Miriam hesitates to marry because she suspects that despite his daringly socialistic talk this son of a good Montreal family is still a virgin waiting to marry an equally virginal woman, which Miriam is not and will not pretend to be. Whether Eric's outlook differed markedly from John's we are not told, and indeed one weakness of the novel is that Erica's relationship with a man whose name mirrored her own is left altogether too vague. In any case, Eric's death in an accident is less than tragic; on the contrary, it spurs Erica to seek wider professional and personal opportunities. Erica, one might say, takes Eric's place in the public world, just as she replaces Tony as the hope of the family.

Indeed, both novels show the heroine's desire as less conflicted than that of the books' male protagonists. Not only does Erica not depend on Marc for her sexual initiation, she is much less worried about the obstacles to their marriage than by Marc's inability to claim her in spite of them. Although *Earth and High Heaven* is known today primarily for its critique of the suffering imposed on Jews by Gentiles, the real issue for Erica (and, it would seem, for her creator) is Marc's lack of faith in himself. Graham's use of Housman is telling in this respect. She may not have known what kind of forbidden love the discreetly homosexual poet had in mind, but the pathos she found in the poem is not so much that of someone frustrated by prejudice than that of a man who cannot assert his desire. Likewise, in *Mathieu*, the eponymous hero, not Danielle, is the character hobbled by sexual as well as social inhibition. Having internalized his mother's image of him as physically unattractive and lacking in willpower, Mathieu can only envy the confident sensuality of Danielle's performances on stage. Unlike the heroes of other novels about social integration, Mathieu does not have to assert control over his passions; on the contrary, he must show he can own them.

In making a relationship between a hesitant, inhibited man and a confidently sexual woman, one who becomes an ideal object of desire precisely because she is free from the constraints of the conventional feminine ideal, the pivot of the plot, *Mathieu* and *Earth and High Heaven* recall some of the paradigmatic modernist novels: *Ulysses*, *A la recherche du temps perdu*, *The Magic Mountain*. There is, however, a key difference in the theme this plot is designed to illustrate. In those classic modernist works, the hero's erotic energy is directed toward aesthetic knowledge and the expansion of his mind more than it is toward the fuller social integration symbolized by marriage. Neither Proust's hero nor Mann's is looking to marry anyone, while the marriage of Joyce's Bloom is just as queer in its way as the erotic attachments of Hans and Marcel. To some extent, of course, Marc and Mathieu resemble their modernist forebears in being more reflective than active. In his conversations with Erica, Marc actually cites Mann (113) alongside the Canadian poet Wilfred Campbell (188), in contrast with Erica, who more conventionally quotes *Romeo and Juliet* (182). The notebooks of the more solitary Mathieu include poetic fragments as well as introspective meditations in a style reminiscent of the works of Julien Green and François Mauriac (French Catholic authors widely read in Quebec) and, closer to home, Saint-Denys Garneau.[12] Yet neither hero is yearning for spiritual or aesthetic transcendence as much as he is seeking social integration. Like Paul Tallard and Emmanuel Letourneau, though in different language, they look to a love anchored in community life as providing a way forward.

Still, the prospect of union with the heroine is not enough to spur Marc or Mathieu to immediate action. Each man must first deal with the deficiencies of his own psycho-social development. We have seen how family relationships (real and symbolic) in *Earth and High Heaven* and *Mathieu* enable and limit the heroine's agency in strikingly parallel ways. The same is true for the hero, although his problem stems precisely from the lack of a male parent figure similar to the one who plays so crucial a role in enabling (or forcing) the heroine to define her identity. Marc's responsible businessman father may be the moral opposite of Mathieu's profligate one, but the key point is that neither parent makes an appearance in the story until very late in the action. When the dying Jules does return to Montreal, Mathieu finds some emotional closure by being able to see him as he really is and not as his mother portrayed him. Marc comes to terms with his Jewish heritage when he visits his northern Ontario hometown and attends a synagogue service with his father. In neither case, however, is the father-son relationship a structuring force in the story, one that positively or negatively energizes the hero's growth to maturity. There are other older men of goodwill in the protagonist's Montreal, but for the most part they are confined to the sidelines. The head of Marc's law firm, Mr Aaronson, is no more than a benign background figure. Étienne Beaulieu plays a more active role in Mathieu's life, but until very late in the day there is no real communication between them.

Nor is the hero spurred to action by the presence of a social or erotic rival. Erica and Danielle are shown as attractive to and to some degree attracted by other men, but neither René nor Jacques is enough of a competitor to provoke Marc or Mathieu into taking action. In classic realist fictions of the city, the hero is usually obliged to vie for position with another man or to partner with him for their mutual benefit (the two scenarios, of course, are not mutually exclusive). In contrast, neither Marc nor Mathieu is ever portrayed in conversation with another Montreal man of his own age, of whatever background. Erica and Danielle have female foils to help them define their feelings, as well as a vague network of other urban acquaintances, but Marc and Mathieu stand alone.

This isolation of the hero is clearly deliberate, since it is maintained at the cost of some awkward narrative moves. If Étienne had known earlier who had written the notebooks he found in his car, he would have reached out to Mathieu sooner. Loranger's plot needs the discovery of the notebooks' author to be postponed as long as possible, though perhaps the difficulty of identifying their origin is meant to be thematically significant as well. The point may be that what Mathieu writes could have been said by almost any young educated francophone man of the period. Graham does not want anything to complicate Marc's relationship with Erica or her attack on the prejudice that excludes this eminently "presentable" man from Montreal WASP society, and so Marc is never portrayed in the company of other Montreal Jews. All these moves may also be motivated by the authors' desire to make the heroine's intervention more central to resolving the hero's difficulties than it would otherwise be. Yet neither her insight nor her social agency is by itself powerful enough to secure that result. Even as emancipated women, they do not possess the kind of authority needed to mediate the hero's emancipation. Both novels must therefore introduce a male figure endowed with just such authority.

What is curious, however, is that neither in *Mathieu* nor in *Earth and High Heaven* is this authority based on the male mediator's social prestige. On the contrary, this supporting character is just as marginal a figure in his way as the hero himself. He is free, at ease with himself, and available to assist others, yet he wields no actual power. All this suggests that we may see him as a male version of the heroine. At another level, one may also see in this figure a masculine incarnation of the influence the author imagines her book might exert on its readers. For, just as the novel's conception of the heroine's role reflected the limitations of the cultural situation in which Graham and Loranger wrote, the peculiar profile of their male mediators says something about the basis on which they offer transformative commentary on that situation. Perhaps the most striking fact about this male mediator is that, in contrast to the heroine, he is not based in Montreal. To find his way in the city, each hero must first leave it in order to get his help. Yet the male mediator does not inhabit another, bigger city, like the New York for which Bruno departs at the end of *Mathieu* or the London to which Tony has fled. On the contrary, and rather unexpectedly, he lives in the country. In *Earth and High Heaven*, the country is the Algoma region of northern Ontario; in *Mathieu*, the Quebec Laurentians. Yet the man the hero encounters in these hinterlands is no son of the soil voicing a traditional rural wisdom antithetical to city knowledge. Nor does he embody the "natural" erotic appetite the hero seems to lack and which he does not find modelled by a Montreal rival. Instead, the male mediator offers what today we would call a queer version of such features.

MEDIATING MONTREAL

In *Earth and High Heaven*, this mediating figure is Marc's older brother, David Reiser. When the Austrian Reisers came to Canada, they did not make their home among the mostly East European Jews of Montreal. They settled instead in a small town Graham calls Manchester, somewhere on the railway line north of the Great Lakes. A timber merchant in the old country, Marc's father now runs a mill, playing an integral role in the local resource economy. In contrast to Marc, David has stayed on in the area, working as a doctor for a nickel mine. Ironically, he interacts more with French Canadians than does his Montreal brother, since David also treats the francophone families of the bush country near the mine. He even enjoys a live-and-let-live friendship with the local priest, with whom he plays chess. The few Jews in Manchester do experience some anti-Semitic prejudice, but its effects are mild in comparison with what Marc encounters at a major Ontarian university and then in Montreal.

The contrast between the "country" David and the "urban" Marc is thus not what one might expect. By the 1940s, the Algoma hills had become one of the iconic spaces of Canadian modernist art, and whether or not Graham had the paintings of the Group of Seven in mind when she wrote, she makes David something of an aesthete. Before wartime currency restrictions put an end to his foreign travels, David would leave the bush twice a year to visit the theatres and fine restaurants of New York (79–80). Moving easily between Jew and Gentile, English and French, Broadway and the backwoods, David is a cosmopolitan figure unimpeded by social or cultural barriers. Only his face marks him out as different. He wears the windbreaker and baggy flannels of a local, but his "rather pronounced nose must have been a throwback to some fairly remote ancestor, for none of the recent Reisers or Mendels … were particularly Semitic in appearance" (270–1). Chief among those other Reisers, of course, is David's brother, Marc, and so this remark allows Graham to imply what it might be indelicate to say directly: her hero does not look Jewish. Marc's ability to pass does not make him any less alien to Montreal's Anglo elite, yet, despite his more obvious Jewishness, David feels fully at home in provincial Canada. The difference, however, is one of character more than of physical appearance: David more easily ignores social boundaries and so ventures where his brother dares not go. Passing through Montreal on the way back from New York and curious about Erica, David calls for her at her parents' home, something Marc had never dared to do. Satisfied that Erica is the right match for his brother, David then gives Marc the pep talk he needs to overcome his scruples about subjecting Erica to the social ostracism a mixed marriage would bring. He tells Marc to seize the only occasion for happiness he and Erica might have by marrying her before he has to leave to fight in a war from which he may never return.

This stirring speech makes us wonder why David himself is not married. Perhaps Graham simply wanted to avoid over-complicating her plot, but today's readers might be forgiven for thinking that David prefers to avoid heterosexual entanglements altogether, and that his New York trips have another, unstated purpose.[13] Whatever Graham may be implicitly or unconsciously suggesting in this regard – she mentions a "best friend" of David's being killed in Burma – she certainly presents him as a man unconcerned with social convention. David speaks, one might say, from a position of liminal mobility rather than of paralyzing alienation. He is thus able to open up an imaginative space in which his brother can envision new possibilities and find a reinvigorated sense of purpose.

David's speech is made all the more convincing for being delivered against the background of a landscape whose contours, as I suggested, had themselves been reimagined by Canada's modernist painters. If the natural world can be re-envisioned, why could the social world not be reimagined also? Yet Marc might not have been ready to hear what David says had not his moral imagination already been expanded by another crucial moment in his visit to his hometown. Graham enhances the drama of Marc's visit to Manchester by making the climactic day of his final home leave coincide with Yom Kippur, the most sombre date in the Jewish liturgical calendar. Marc's own religious convictions do not extend beyond a belief in "one God for everyone regardless of sect" (256), but he agrees to accompany his parents to the service in their makeshift synagogue. Manchester's small Jewish community can afford a rabbi only for the High Holy Days, and they have to bring him in from somewhere else. Like the rabbi, Marc too is a visitor, reconnecting with his community before he leaves again, in his case perhaps never to return.

The Jewish history recollected in the Yom Kippur service helps restore Marc's ability to "believe in himself" (248) by reminding him that his people have always embraced risk. Their trust that things will turn out well is a matter of faith, of course, but for Graham this faith does not necessarily entail belief in God, only confidence that the future is not closed. The words of the Yom Kippur service are probably cited at length (and in the English idiom of the King James Bible) in order to impress upon the reader the dignity of the Jewish religion, but in the economy of the novel they serve even more importantly as an emotional and literary counterweight to the sentiments expressed in the poem that gives the book its title. They rebut the charge that "earth and high heaven" are indifferent forces "fixt of old" and arrayed against the mortals who struggle against them in vain.[14] The poem's speaker regrets having awakened to awareness and asks "when shall I sleep again?"; the Yom Kippur texts transform remembrance of error and pain into praise of God's compassion and mercy. In turning despair into hopeful expectation, the ritual inspires in Marc a willingness to commit more wholeheartedly to Erica.

Graham's use of the Kol Nidre liturgy to facilitate Marc's marriage to a non-Jewish woman may well strike readers today as problematic. In response, one can only say that *Earth and High Heaven* is a work of its time in believing that religious particularities should be subsumed under a more generic, vaguely "Judeo-Christian" but effectively deistic – and thereby inclusive – spirituality. A question more relevant to my argument here is why the service Marc attends with such ultimately enabling results takes place in Manchester and not in Montreal. Neither Marc nor Erica attends any kind of religious service in that city. What prevents Marc's epiphany from occurring in Montreal? The obvious explanation is the same as for his lack of other contact with Jews there: Marc should not have any community ties or commitments that might complicate his integration into the city's Anglo elite. Yet in the Manchester episode Graham is able to integrate the Reiser family's Jewishness into a quintessentially "Canadian" setting. Could she not have found a way to do the same in the Montreal part of the book?

If we look at a key passage earlier in the novel, we find a reason why the answer is no. If Graham can be faulted for leaving out important aspects of the city, including its Jewish and francophone neighborhoods, in her description of the characters' Montreal, this passage highlights the felt presence of what they perceive to be not there, an absence more radical than anything missing from life in Manchester. In the course of their drives around and beyond Montreal, Erica introduces Marc to the geography of "her" Quebec:

> They drove past the monastery, then into a village by a steepled church … There was a shrine by the side of the road and a few people were grouped around it, old men and women and children and the village curé …
>
> This was Quebec, where you were born and brought up, and these are some of the things you would remember if you had to go away and live somewhere else – wayside shrines and fields of cornflowers, the view from the top of Mount Oka where you can look … out over the valleys of the Ottawa and the St. Lawrence … You would remember a village … a farmer driving a high-wheeled buggy down a dark country road at night …
>
> And you would remember Montreal, the incredible tropical green of this northern city in summer, the old gray squares, the Serpentine at Lafontaine Park with little overhanging casinos … the narrow gray streets of downtown Montreal like the streets of an old French provincial town … the steep terraced gardens of Westmount, and the endless narrow balconies of endless walled convents and monasteries, *where nobody ever walks* … "When they go on about preserving the French Canadian way of life, sometimes I think I know what they're talking about."
>
> "Yes," said Marc, adding after a pause, "Only their way of life is rather a luxury at the moment and somebody has to pay for it. I don't feel the way you do about Quebec. I feel that way about Ontario." (122–3, emphasis added)

While fully settled and humanized, the scene Erica surveys, and whose charm she tries to communicate to Marc, has no people in it. Yet it is not undomesticated wilderness; rather, it is as if the city were deserted, its inhabitants present only in their absence. If in the earlier parts of the novel the Jews of Montreal had remained almost entirely unseen, here the French, and in a sense, given the reference to Westmount, even the English are also missing from the picture. There is not even the equivalent of the old woman Gabrielle Roy's Emmanuel sees by the side of the tracks as he leaves the station on his way to war, the solitary symbolic figure onto whom he can project his desire for connection and in whom he can find a meaning for his mission. Erica's sympathy for "the French Canadian way of life" is predicated on what seems to be a total absence of contact. The Montreal with which she identifies is a city of the mind, not of actual mingling. It accommodates her desire insofar as it is a space that, while richly resonant with the vibration of other desires, Erica can inhabit in solitude, or alone with Marc. The city nurtures her capacity for self-expression, but perhaps it does so because it does not talk back. If this is the Montreal Erica mediates to Marc, we can see how gender is not the only factor limiting the kind of agency the heroine can model for the hero.

The one personal connection Erica does have with francophone Montreal is René. Her conversations with him do dramatize differences of outlook between the city's French and English, especially with regard to the war. Yet these talks have no transformative effect. Erica and René appreciate each other, but neither envisions an ultimate convergence of views. The Montreal they share, the downtown of restaurants, clubs, and backroom politicking, may be sophisticated and tolerant, but it would be futile, even dangerous, to think it capable of change. For Graham, the city is a brittle structure that could easily collapse if its defences were overrun by world events; meanwhile it manages conflict by keeping things exactly as they are. Erica reflects at one point that, if she were going to live her whole life in this Montreal, she would be content to marry a man from her own community. "You might be reasonably happy," she tells herself, "living with someone in Montreal and with that social and economic structure to absorb the inevitable stresses and strains, only to find that life on a desert island with that same person was quite unendurable" (247). On the surface, Erica is contrasting Montreal with a desert island far away, but one can also read her as making a statement about a potential polarity within the city. Should "the inevitable stresses and strains" be sufficiently aggravated by disturbances elsewhere, the city would itself become that desert island, devoid like it of any support structures at all – a nightmare version of the appealingly empty city Erica praised to Marc. What Erica now sees in Marc is a man with whom she could live on that deserted island as well as on this populated one. Except in her daydreams, however, Montreal as it exists cannot make room for them.

This pessimistic vision of the city colours the ostensibly happy end of the story. By the time Marc returns from Manchester, determined to marry Erica before leaving for Europe (286), Erica has already quit her newspaper job to enlist in the Canadian Women's Army Corps. This allows her desperate gesture of escape to take a more positive turn: Erica will join Marc in the wider, more turbulent world beyond the city limits. This open-ended conclusion is no doubt designed to strike a balance between romantic idealism and a realistic appreciation that anti-Semitism will not be eradicated overnight. Although not unexpected in a novel of this kind, this ending nonetheless comes as something of a surprise. At various points of the narrative, we have been told, rather ominously, that this or that event happened before the "end." At the beginning of chapter 5, for example, midway through the book, the narrator remarks that Charles Drake's "conduct from the Wednesday morning in mid-July … through to the end, sometime in September, represented three different and distinctive methods of attack" (141). The narrator goes on to add: "In the end, unlike his wife, he could not plead ignorance" (142). Later, "when [Erica] was trying to locate the exact moment when she had received the first warning, the moment which marked the beginning of the final stage in their relationship, she was to remember the way [Marc] had said, 'Or anyone else after you'" (189). The finality of this quotation is echoed by a sentence in chapter 13. The narrator's tour of Manchester ends at "the house in which [Marc's] parents were still living when he went home on his last leave in September, 1942" (253). The statement foreshadows a funeral more than it does a wedding.

Since the comments are made by a third-person narrator standing outside the story, they clearly signal that Erica and Marc's relationship is doomed. What then are we to make of the book's apparently more hopeful conclusion? Perhaps Graham changed her mind about the end of the story but failed to modify its earlier sections to make them consistent with her new thinking. I wonder, however, whether what seems like a defect of composition may not reflect an ambivalence the author was unable to fully acknowledge, let alone resolve. A further comparison with the end of *Bonheur d'occasion* may be pertinent here. In her 1947 reception speech to the Royal Society of Canada, Gabrielle Roy, whose optimism about a better world had faded rather quickly after the end of the war, said that she could not imagine Emmanuel surviving the battle and coming home.[15] The social disillusionment that would inevitably follow his return was too painful for her to contemplate. Graham may have already felt something similar as she was writing her book in 1943. She could not really imagine Marc and Erica living happily ever after, not even on a desert island. Their relationship is too deeply rooted in the Montreal where they met for that to be possible, yet the war had already gone on long enough for Graham to suspect that the postwar city would not be so affected by it as to change in any radical way.

Like David, the liminal outsider figure, the heroine of *Earth and High Heaven* enables the hero to envision new possibilities, and Graham's integration of these complementary mediating agencies into her narrative marks an important step toward a more complex and self-conscious form of emancipatory realist fiction. Yet imagining how these new possibilities might be actualized through the agency of such figures still lies beyond her capability. The last sentence of the book expresses an unwelcome awareness of this limitation: "The moment he caught sight of her, he began to run" (288). In assuming that Marc is running toward Erica and not in some other direction, we go beyond what the text says, and given the generally downbeat mood of these last chapters, we should perhaps ask whether Marc runs to embrace his fate or to flee it. Graham's failure to produce any further novels may be explained by the difficulties of her postwar personal life, including an unhappy marriage that took her away from Montreal to the even more rigidly segregated town of Charlottesville, Virginia. But the curiously self-cancelling ending of *Earth and High Heaven* suggests that the novel arrives at an internal, literary impasse revelatory of the cultural situation in which it was written.

The hero of *Mathieu* also finds the mentor and mediator he needs by leaving the city. Like Graham's Algoma hills, Loranger's Laurentians are saturated with symbolic significance, though of a metaphysical rather than aesthetic kind. Mathieu did not grow up there, but in a sense he is returning home, for in the Laurentians nature is "carved on a human scale" (262). With its summer camps and ski resorts, Val-Morin has none of Algoma's untamed grandeur, but it offers the feeling of a proper "fit" between self and world. Once he has internalized its lessons, Mathieu will, like Marc, be empowered to return to the city. Like Marc, too, Mathieu finds support from a liminal figure in whom seemingly contradictory interests and values harmoniously coexist. Émile Rochat is a Swiss fitness expert who runs a rustic hotel that is part fitness camp, part spa. He preaches an almost religious conception of physical and mental health. Though a foreigner, Rochat is more at home in his surroundings than the locals. An expert skier and swimmer, he thinks nothing of carrying an exhausted client on his shoulders over several miles of mountain trails. He is a francophone European, a man who has seen the world, but he is not a Frenchman, and still less a Parisian, and so the envy and resentment he provokes in Mathieu is not as paralyzing as the feeling of inadequacy experienced by many young French Canadian men of the period (in life or in fiction) in their encounters with the French.[16] This discomfort was often linked to sexual unease, the refinement of French manners being associated with effeminacy, and sometimes explicitly with homosexuality. This is emphatically not the case here. One might think that the unmarried Rochat's interest in shaping male bodies to make them not just healthier but more attractive would trouble someone as suspicious and susceptible to sexual panic as Mathieu. On the contrary, Loranger's hero has nothing but praise for the Swiss athlete's serene self-possession and his apparent immunity from the anxieties of desire – the very qualities exemplified by the David of *Earth and High Heaven*.

Under Rochat's tutelage, Mathieu is transformed from a fearful and skittish, deliberately off-putting misfit into a confident he-man. He discards the dark glasses behind which he hid from the hostile gaze of others and which concealed his own resentful gaze. He stands up straighter and his sour expression relaxes into a smile.[17] As he becomes more at ease in his body, he begins to assert himself sexually. Instead of scorning the advances of a bored bourgeois housewife, he seizes the opportunity they present. Mathieu's affair with Annette will only be a stepping-stone to further self-discovery, but, like Danielle's fling with Jacques, it is free from guilt.

Loranger makes clear her conviction that morality is not a matter of rules. Or rather, the only rule is to be yourself, to find and fulfill your true nature. The ultimate goal of this quest is the "joy" Mathieu suddenly discovers when he hears the music of Bach (217). Joy is more than a feeling of pleasure; it is an experience of fullness, in which anxiety is allayed and alienation overcome. The word is frequently found in Quebec writings of the period, most notably to designate a state of spiritual plenitude whose emblematic expression educated French Canadians would have found in Blaise Pascal's "Mémorial," which records the "Joy, joy, joy, tears of joy" that followed an overwhelming experience of God's nearness.[18]

The word's connotations, however, extended far beyond the religious sphere. In Saint-Denys Garneau, for example, "joy" refers more broadly to that state of psychological wholeness to which he aspired but which he could not enjoy. Ironically, what prevented him from doing so, according to his friend Jean Le Moyne, was precisely the joyless Catholicism in which their generation was raised.[19] When Garneau wrote in the most famous of his poems, "Accompaniment [*Accompagnement*]," that "I walk beside a joy / Beside a joy that is not mine / A joy of mine which I cannot share,"[20] he described a situation that almost from the first was read as diagnosing cultural just as much as personal dissociation.[21]

Le Moyne articulated his critique from the perspective of a progressive but still orthodox Catholicism. Loranger's attitude is more elusive. Mathieu's remark about having been "crammed with religion" (134) is a bitter one, though in fact no more virulent than what Le Moyne would write in his 1951 essay about the crippling effects of French Canadian Jansenism. Yet Loranger's insistence on being entirely what you are without regard for social convention (at least in the sexual sphere) gives her work something of a Nietzschean flavour. Not that her vision is devoid of moral stringency. We have seen how Danielle's commitment to authenticity made her turn her back on an easy future with Jacques in order to seek a more ennobling relationship. Similarly, Mathieu ends his affair with Annette once it has fulfilled its purpose. Like Danielle, he will seek a nobler kind of partnership. What Rochat's example shows, and what Mathieu comes to see after spending time with him, is what Danielle intuits for herself: that persons at one with themselves discover an internal imperative holding them to a higher standard.

They also become more attuned to what is genuine in the world around them. Like Danielle, Mathieu finds that he is better able to sympathize with Étienne and even with Nicole, whose quests, though worldly, are nonetheless authentic, each in its own way. As for those content with world as it is and their own place in it – Annette, Jacques, and Nicole's husband, Albert – Mathieu and Danielle will follow Étienne's practice of leaving such people to their own devices, bearing them no malice. Like *Earth and High Heaven*, *Mathieu* is sincere in its appropriation of religious language, but it uses that language to stake out a position somewhere on the border of the secular and the sacred. The novel seeks to mediate between these levels of reality, just as it does between the complementary values of self-containment and sexual connection, through its portrayal of the key liminal character. All of these mediations are designed to help the hero (and the reader) imagine how integration into the complex, multi-layered reality of urban life might be achieved without jeopardizing – indeed, while enhancing – one's personal integrity.

Despite this optimism, what the future holds for the central couple is no less uncertain in *Mathieu* than in *Earth and High Heaven*. The distance still separating Mathieu from Danielle, though theoretically more bridgeable, is in fact greater than the gap between Marc and Erica. The last pages of Loranger's novel show us Mathieu and Danielle communicating by letter, not face to face. In one sense, this represents progress: Mathieu's obsessive dialogue with himself in his notebooks gives way to a more relaxed two-way exchange. In these letters, the hero and heroine agree to think of themselves as friends living side by side and not seek an intimacy that might threaten their separateness. Each character has reason to be wary of fusional connection: Mathieu because of his mother's destructive identification with his father, Danielle because of her earlier professional and personal over-dependence on the charismatic but unreliable Bruno. The letters hint that Danielle and Mathieu may someday move closer to each other, but the two protagonists make it clear that their first priority is for each of them to develop their creative potential in parallel rather than partnership with the other. One might say that what the novel envisions is a positive form of the "accompaniment" of which Garneau wrote – or perhaps another version of that ideal of two solitudes touching and greeting whose formulation by that other poet, Rilke, had so inspired MacLennan.

The open-ended conclusion of *Mathieu* is thus more positive in tone than that of *Earth and High Heaven*. Still, one can ask why Loranger did not take her vision of intimacy in separateness any further than she does. I argued earlier that the sense of futility and despair belying the ostensibly optimistic ending of *Earth and High Heaven* reflected the author's inability to leverage the liminal characters' creative mediation for the benefit of the heroine and by extension for that of the novel's imaginative agency. I suggested that, in addition to the obvious difficulty of imagining an end to anti-Semitic prejudice, there was something curiously abstract about Erica's relationship with the city with which she – and her creator – so closely identifies. A similar difficulty arises in *Mathieu*, again in connection with a vision of Montreal.

When Étienne Beaulieu discovers that Mathieu is the author of the notebooks whose anguished meditations have stirred his sympathies as they have Danielle's, he stands ready to offer the young man all the resources of his wealth and social connections. Yet Étienne's final gift to Mathieu is not to find him a job in which he can show the world what he can do. Étienne had tried that already by getting Mathieu hired by *Le Matin*, with disenchanting results. It is the more modest gesture of offering Mathieu the keys to a little apartment he has been renting for his private use (343). In an earlier aside, the narrator had hinted that, although Étienne occasionally used this apartment for sexual rendezvous, what he really enjoyed was the opportunity to escape any kind of entanglement with other people. Theoretically, Mathieu will live in the apartment only until he finds his vocation (343), but the reader gets the sense that it is this same freedom from social demands that he, too, will enjoy most. Like Danielle, who intends to stay on alone in the apartment she had been sharing with her brother, Mathieu will enjoy that "room of one's own" which Virginia Woolf declared essential to artistic creativity (along with a sufficient income, of course, an issue *Mathieu* elides). Neither character will live in isolation, however. Danielle proposes that Mathieu take his meals with her. Her suggestion recalls a scene near the beginning of the novel when she had offered Mathieu a piece of fruit from her table (37). Mathieu had rejected what he took to be a patronizing commentary on his unhealthy appearance. Now, he can accept the favour as a sign of respectful mutuality and as the token of a new future. But what does that future look like?

Since *Mathieu* is a novel of apprenticeship whose hero expresses himself best through writing, we assume that, like MacLennan's Paul, Mathieu will use his independence to launch a literary career. Loranger is careful not to commit herself in that regard, and some earlier incidents in the book make her vagueness understandable. When he was writing theatre reviews, Mathieu could write what he wanted only because no one at *Le Matin* cared about culture. Even worse, he could expect his sophisticated appreciation of Bruno's staging of Sartre's existentialist play to be carefully read only by those worried about its morality. In the event, the play is banned, and though Mathieu bears no responsibility since he managed to get his review pulled from the paper, one wonders what would have happened to him had he given unqualified praise to a performance that incurred the ire of the church. Bruno can escape censorship by leaving for New York (where presumably he will work in English, though that issue is not addressed). That is not an option for Mathieu, rooted as he is in language and place. Nicole's successful campaign to support an amateur, and no doubt artistically less adventurous, theatre troupe after Bruno's departure is said to prove that Montreal is still "the city of miracles" (344), but the comment is tinged with irony. Certainly, the radiant future open to Mathieu – or to Danielle, for that matter – remains a matter of pious assertion rather than of confident prediction.

To appreciate how difficult it was for Loranger to go further in imagining Montreal as a space of creative interaction, we should look at a key scene early in Mathieu's spiritual awakening, one in which, like Graham's Erica, the hero attempts to grasp the essence of the city. It comes at that point in the story when Mathieu has just managed to avoid falling into complete abjection. He refused to take sexual advantage of Nicole when in the depths of her own loneliness she offered herself to him. However, his state of dereliction is still such that he decides to commit suicide after taking a last look at Montreal from the top of Mount Royal (209). Instead of taking the long but easy way up along the carriage road, he decides to get there quicker by scaling a slope too steep to be prudently attempted by someone in his debilitated condition. On the verge of a potentially fatal slide, however, he discovers in himself an unexpected determination not to let himself die. Summoning all his courage, he manages to reach the lookout at the top of the mountain. There, surrounded by a cloud of mist, he revels in his new-found love of life: "The city at his feet disappeared. In the depths of the fog, electrical signs as they came on lit up multicolored flares whose vapor trails as they rose seemed to move toward him. A feeling of power came over Mathieu. Forgoing any further self-analysis, he gave himself over to the lyricism of a new joy, which removed all traces of the fatigue he had felt, swept away old grudges, and cast out despair … 'I'm alive! … I might have died, but I'm alive! … I've won! All on my own! I've won! My life is mine!'" (212). Mathieu's refusal to analyze his experience is understandable. Under the pressure of an overbearing superego, he had analyzed himself almost to death. Now freed from morbid introspection, the hero turns his gaze outward to the scene around him. Yet, instead of emerging more sharply as a city to be embraced or conquered, Montreal disappears, leaving only traces of fireworks colouring the fog. The picture is a pretty one, and seeing the lights "rise" up toward him, as if in greeting, seems to validate Mathieu's feeling of joy. But this fullness of feeling is predicated on the absence of any concrete, external focus of desire. When in *Earth and High Heaven* Montreal appeared as an object of Erica's emotional contemplation, it did so as a landscape of unpeopled buildings and streets; here in *Mathieu* it takes the form of a blank screen onto which the hero can project his newly expanded self.

There is, of course, a fundamental difference in tone between the two texts. Where Graham was wistful, Loranger is energetic. Yet it is striking that, like *Earth and High Heaven*, *Mathieu* does not conclude with any clear indication of how the protagonists might actually engage with the city. Mathieu's mountain-top moment does not culminate in a renewed commitment to a struggle like that of Balzac's Rastignac, who at the end of *Le Père Goriot* (*Père Goriot*) shouts a challenging "It's between the two of us now!" to the Paris on which he gazes from the heights of the Père Lachaise cemetery.[22] Although Mathieu's "My life is mine!" sounds a similarly triumphant note, its focus is entirely inward. What social impact it might have is not explored.

Loranger's message of "joy" is thus limited in scope, just as Mathieu's perception of Montreal in the concreteness of its life and the diversity of its population is blocked by a fog about which he does not complain. More than Balzac, we are reminded of Gabrielle Roy. When Emmanuel looks down on the city from the Westmount lookout at a crucial moment in *Bonheur d'occasion*, he is invigorated by the belief that the war will unite the city's different populations in a common commitment to the self-sacrifice in which he has found personal meaning. His idealism, too, can be sustained only by keeping the terms of the sharing vague. In contrast with both Roy and Graham, however, Loranger depicts in her heroine Danielle a character at once intelligent, practical, and emotionally poised. She is presented as more fully ready than the hero to have an actual career. Yet that career is not sketched either. More important, the novel bears the hero's name, not hers. This split is important from a gender point of view, of course, but from the perspective of the author's writing self it is clear that Mathieu and Danielle are both projections of Loranger's reflections on what kind of mediating role she can play, given the cultural conditions of her time. As a novelist, Loranger could dramatize Mathieu's overcoming of his spiritual alienation, but she could not, it seems, make Danielle's better social integration the basis for a next-level story of problematic engagement with the city. After *Mathieu*, Françoise Loranger lived a rich professional life as a radio, television, and theatrical dramatist much like the one the novel allows us to imagine for Danielle – although what today's reader can extrapolate from the text probably goes much further than what Loranger's original audience could project with any confidence. In any case, the fact that Loranger published no novels after *Mathieu* suggests that even years later she doubted such a life could be given plausible, socially meaningful form in novelistic narrative.

Although the immediate impact of their novels was very different – *Earth and High Heaven* was a best-seller, while *Mathieu* was little noticed – neither Graham nor Loranger exerted much influence on the writers who followed them. It may be that the time was not yet ripe for the complex kind of literary mediation the two sophisticated women writers sought to model, and that this mediation had first to take more elemental form in order to be historically fruitful. One of the ironies of Montreal literary history is that, for all its author's reluctance to consider it a "literary" work, *Bonheur d'occasion* has held greater appeal for writers looking for artistic intertexts than have the more self-consciously literary works of Graham and Loranger, even though, in contrast to Roy (but like MacLennan), these authors included deliberate allusions to texts that inspired or provoked them. *Bonheur d'occasion* is, of course, a carefully crafted book, but it feels no need to position itself in relation to other works of art (though it does allude to the popular culture of movie and recorded song). This may be one reason for its continued and still current status as *the* foundational work of Montreal fiction. Because the "difference" of *Bonheur d'occasion* is best appreciated in relation to the more explicitly "literary" novels roughly contemporary with it, I have postponed my discussion of it to the end of my study of the novels of the 1940s. Analyzing Roy's first novel will also prepare the way for better understanding the novels of the following decade, including Roy's and MacLennan's second Montreal fictions.

3

Temptation and Tenderness in Gabrielle Roy's *Bonheur d'occasion* (*The Tin Flute*)

Gabrielle Roy's *Bonheur d'occasion* illustrates an understanding of fiction's cultural mission rather different not just from we saw in its English-language contemporaries, *Earth and High Heaven* and *Two Solitudes*, but also from that of *Mathieu*, which, though published in 1949, shows no signs of being influenced by its francophone predecessor. Whatever their differences, the three novels we have examined so far tell stories about the integration of outsider figures and dramatize their literary aspirations through the various conclusions they give to the "success" plot. As she makes clear by her deliberate decision not to follow Jean Lévesque's career once he leaves Saint-Henri, Roy finds such a plot entirely alien to her sensibility and moral commitments. Yet her decision to focus on the circumscribed lives of the downtrodden rather than of those seeking access to the city's inner circles also stems from a more tentative and cautious understanding of what a realist novel about the city should seek to accomplish.

As I hope to show, this view will find more of an echo in some key novels of the 1950s, notably MacLennan's *The Watch That Ends the Night* and Roy's own *Alexandre Chenevert*, than will the more assertive claims made by the other three books, the one notable exception, ironically, being the francophone novel most explicitly inspired by Roy's work. Roger Viau's *Au milieu la montagne* (In the middle, the mountain, 1951), like *Bonheur d'occasion*, is a story of a young woman's desperate search to overcome material and emotional deprivation, but in the energy and scope of her ambitions, its heroine, Jacqueline Malo, is more like Erica and Danielle than Florentine. More important, in dramatizing these aspirations, Viau displays none of that curious ambivalence about the disruptive power of desire that gives Roy's narrative its distinctive pathos, and that distinguishes her work from that of her 1940s contemporaries.

In various ways, *Two Solitudes*, *Mathieu*, and *Earth and High Heaven* all focus on a man of problematic social identity seeking to flourish in a city conceived as blocking the hero's integration yet needing to embrace the energizing diversity he represents to ensure its collective renewal. This dialectic is absent from *Bonheur d'occasion*, in which people need each other as individuals but the city does not need them. The only collective project in which they are invited to participate, other than the war (provided they are healthy enough to serve), is the consumption of material goods they can't afford. The shortage of the skilled labour needed for war production does give the orphan Jean a chance to climb the social ladder, yet there is nothing problematic about his rise: the city's institutions don't need to adjust in order to accommodate him, nor does he struggle to adapt to his new situation. Jean looks forward without looking back. As a consequence, Jean does not require the help of a female character to mediate his entry into higher networks of sociability or to recall him to his roots. His self-sufficiency is never seriously challenged by either external or internal forces. He neither changes nor provokes change, except in the woman left to bear his child alone.

In sidelining Jean, Roy is rejecting a paradigmatic story structure of the realist novel, but is also by implication repudiating the conception of individual and social development, and the relationship between them, this structure is designed to dramatize. In the other novels we have looked at so far, personal fulfillment and social progress are seen as mutually reinforcing. To the extent the hero succeeds in his quest, society at large also benefits. This is because the outsider hero also represents the very community that excludes him. That is to say, his alienation is a projection of the city's own alienation from what it could and should be: a more open and inclusive society that offers appropriate recognition to all. It follows that the hero's success is not imagined as coming at the expense of anyone else's legitimate material or moral claims. These books are animated by the conviction that the city could accommodate everyone's desires if only it embraced an enlarged idea of itself. Whether the city is up to the task, of course, is another question, one to which Graham and Loranger are unable to give as positive an answer as they would like.

In *Bonheur d'occasion,* Emmanuel expresses idealistic sentiments of this kind, but his yearning for a better world is not driven by a desire to exercise greater agency or to secure greater recognition. Nor does he imagine a society that more fully accommodates the distinct contributions of diverse individuals. His notion of an ideal community seems rather to be one that alleviates the burden of solitude by providing an opportunity for everyone to sacrifice their personal desires for the common good. Somewhat paradoxically, the first step to overcoming social and economic barriers is to overlook them for the sake of a higher solidarity. His view may have some validity in wartime, when everyone faces the same external threat and people are bound willy-nilly to a common fate. But it is a vision of emotional communion that elides the stubborn realities of class division and psychological defensiveness portrayed in the book. Moreover, it is notable that unlike Paul Tallard, who finds in Heather someone who understands and shares his ideals, Emmanuel cannot communicate his dreams to a Florentine preoccupied with her own survival. Significant, too, is that unlike Mathieu, Emmanuel cannot use his insights to engage the city in new ways. Mathieu's mountain vision may be blurred by fog, but Emmanuel achieves clarity only as he leaves Montreal on a trip from which he may never return. Emmanuel's projection of universal hope is thus disconnected from any local project.

In the wistfulness of its ending, *Bonheur d'occasion* may seem to echo Graham's *Earth and High Heaven.* At the end of that book, Marc is also on the verge of departing for the war, and his future with Erica is just as problematic as Emmanuel's with Florentine, but the difference is just as important as the similarity. Graham was tormented by a specific social problem, that of anti-Semitism. Her characters disturb society by making concrete demands on it, and their solitude is at least in part a by-product of their struggle. Neither Emmanuel nor Florentine really wants to rock the social boat; what they seek is a safe haven in which to escape the fundamental solitude of the human condition. Whereas the marriage of Paul and Heather and the potential union of Marc and Erica reconfigure social conventions, the wedding of Emmanuel and Florentine only reinforces them. Their *bonheur d'occasion,* what they "settle" for, is not the disenchanted culmination of a quest that might have ended better, had circumstances been otherwise. In Roy's book, there is no "otherwise" potentially in view, as there clearly is in *Earth and High Heaven.* The pessimism of Graham's story is relativized by the more forward-looking thrust of a narrative based on the dialectic of mutual accommodation I described a moment ago. Despite her existential doubts, Graham shares with MacLennan and Loranger a certain optimism about her work as a novelist whose mission is to convey the possibility of another, better world in such a manner as to encourage readers to feel its absence, and then to inspire in those readers the wish to make that world real. By dramatizing its protagonists' conflictual engagement with a society that as yet only dimly realizes that its continued vitality depends on such engagement, realist fiction justifies its own artistic confrontation with the status quo.

Roy's conceives of her mission in rather different terms. In depicting the isolation and deprivation of the people of Saint-Henri, she seeks less to foster a zeal for activism in her readers than a greater degree of fellow feeling. With the exception of Emmanuel's father, pious purveyor of vestments to the clergy, she does not give us anyone to hate. Even if we put Jean in this category, he is not there to hate for very long, since he disappears in the second half of the book. This novel about the Depression poor is remarkable for the complete absence of bankers, factory owners, or rapacious landlords. There are no criminals and no police. The economic and ideological pressures on the characters are very real, but the agents who embody those pressures, again with the very minor exception of an army recruiter mentioned but not portrayed, remain offstage. On the other hand, there are no sympathetic authority figures either: no doctor (only a nurse who can't speak French), and no priest – although whether to classify the clergy as good or bad is a question Roy is careful not to raise, no doubt to avoid a direct confrontation with the church. That none of the characters seek pastoral counsel is a statement in itself. But what are we to make of the absence of other authority figures, and thus of the opportunity for readers to discriminate between good and bad ones?

The answer would seem to be, first, that Roy is less interested in encouraging such discriminations than in eliciting the reader's sympathy for the characters she does depict. Second, in a society as hidebound and self-censoring as Roy's Montreal seems to be, calling people to exercise, develop, and diversify the capacity for sympathy that lies latent within them can itself be considered an aggressive move on the part of the artist, an assault on a homogeneous, and homogeneously judgmental, dominant culture. Moreover, I think that Roy did not just worry about the judgments of others; the scruple she experienced was also an internal one, born of her personal investment in a non-conflictual vision of the world. *Bonheur d'occasion* made a great initial impact with its heartfelt account of people struggling to hold on to their dignity, in large part by not desiring what they cannot have. But the source of the novel's enduring resonance lies in its dramatization of a deep ambivalence about the desire involved in writing the book. Roy only reluctantly accepts that conflict cannot be transcended without first being brought out into the open. Her effort to minimize the gap between the two stages of this process, so that in contemplating the conflictual reality the writer portrays in the novel the reader is already transcending the painful inner conflict that contemplation provokes, can sometimes work against the author when she wants too quickly to heal the pain she causes. But these weaknesses are offset by the authenticity with which she struggles with the disruptive implications of her own literary desire. She must *want* to reimagine what she sees in order to turn reality into art, and she must *want* to make the reader see that reality through her art. The difficulty of owning that desire, especially in the Montreal of the 1940s (and beyond), is the novel's deeper theme.

In an earlier study, I showed how uneasy Roy felt about being untrue to the given reality of people she met when she transformed them into literary characters.[1] Building on that earlier work, I will focus here on the connections between Roy's uneasiness about owning her desire to reshape the world through the effect of her art and the way she portrays the characters' desires in the story. The ultimate aim will be to read *Bonheur d'occasion* as the novel that emerges from the way Roy works through that uneasiness in her narrative. For the Florentine, the Rose-Anna, even the Emmanuel of *Bonheur d'occasion*, assertive desire represents a challenge to society, as it does in the novels we have examined. More immediately, however, it is a challenge to the desiring individual. The people of Roy's Saint-Henri have been conditioned to believe that moral and social merit consists in not wanting too much, and they have learned that letting yourself feel any desire too strongly only aggravates the pain of deprivation. Roy can portray her characters' dilemma so vividly because she knows it from the inside. A striking feature of her early Montreal career as a journalist and fiction writer was the diffidence that shadowed her ambition. Although she was not shy about doing what she had to do to get published and be paid what she felt she was worth, she kept to a minimum her participation in the networks of literary and sexual sociability to which she had been introduced by her mentor and would-be lover Henri Girard. For Roy, solitude was balm as well as bane: it sharpened the painful sense of longing that inspired her creative work yet it gave her the space she needed to write. When the resulting tension became too acute, she began to walk the streets of Saint-Henri in what Camus might call a solitary solidarity with the inhabitants of that neglected neighbourhood.[2] This experience of discreet and discrete accompaniment lies at the heart of the novel that became *Bonheur d'occasion*.[3] What makes the final book so vivid is the way the situation the story depicts is intensified by the sensibility that frames it.

Roy's pessimism about the successful mediation of desire becomes clear if we step back from the details of the story she tells and look at the overall narrative pattern of her book. *Bonheur d'occasion* is less interested in exploring the ways socially marginal characters might be integrated into the dynamic of urban life than in dramatizing their wish to escape, or just not think about, the stifling deprivation of the district they inhabit. Nothing in their experience has encouraged them to think of society as accommodating any demands they might make on it, and with the exception of Jean, who seems to get a new job out of the blue, none of them tests that assumption. The one big risk Azarius takes is to "borrow" a truck from his boss so he can drive his family out to the country to visit Rose-Anna's relatives. The point of this episode, however, is to show the impossibility of returning to the past rather than the difficulty of reaching for the future. One might argue that poverty confines the characters to Saint-Henri, but most of them never think of wandering beyond its limits anyway. Even the inveterate daydreamer Florentine only pictures herself living somewhere else after she has married Emmanuel and can in fact make a move. The dime-store lunch counter where she works as a waitress may be located at an urban crossroads, but it is not a place where different worlds intersect, or from which new pathways diverge. As Emmanuel says, Saint-Henri is a "village in the big town" (283–4) rather than a fully "urban" neighbourhood. One sign of this restriction of perspective is that Emmanuel is the only character self-consciously aware of it. He is the one character sufficiently detached from his neighbourhood by virtue of his middle-class status and his period of army training to gain a perspective on Saint-Henri, yet still sufficiently attached to his neighbourhood to want to see it clearly.

The people of Saint-Henri suffer, of course, from all the worst features of the city slum: crowded houses and streets, lack of privacy and personal space. Yet a comparison of their condition with the Montreal poverty depicted in *Two Solitudes* reveals some important differences. What I have called the promiscuity of urban life in MacLennan's Montreal is almost entirely absent from Roy's Saint-Henri world. This is most obviously true in the realm of sexual behaviour. Jean's one sexual encounter with Florentine only reinforces his desire to be self-sufficient. More characteristic of Saint-Henri than any sexual promiscuity are the hasty marriages that protect the husband from the threat of conscription: far from being motivated by desire or even by a longing for emotional intimacy, these weddings are prompted by the men's wish to be left alone. The one exception to this pattern is Alphonse, but, as we will see, his visit to a prostitute is a by-product of his disgust for "temptation" rather than of amoral acceptance of its presence and constant proximity.

No doubt Roy, a single woman writing for a morally conservative francophone public, could not have written explicitly about sexual pleasure even had she wanted to do so. But other kinds of urban promiscuity are equally absent from the world of her story. The population of *Bonheur d'occasion* is a remarkably homogenous one, ethnically speaking. This feature of the book does not seem to have been considered worthy of remark but it is surely significant, especially if we compare the city of the novel to the much more diverse Montreal portrayed in Roy's journalism of the time, journalism now widely praised for its pioneering documentation of the multicultural immigrant city.[4] In its depiction of a uniformly French Canadian Saint-Henri, the novel may accurately project the mental map of its characters, but it is curious that the narrator makes no mention of other populations. The substantial Irish working class of southwest Montreal, for example, is nowhere to be found. When Emmanuel walks up the hill into Westmount at night, the town's Anglo inhabitants are mentioned, but they are not seen, still less encountered. The novel's cast of francophone characters is, of course, large enough to provide sufficient dramatic variety, but it is still striking that only two very minor figures represent what one could call a de-familiarizing otherness: Jenny, the nurse Rose-Anna meets in young Daniel's hospital ward, and the recruiting officer who rejects Alphonse's application to join the army. In both cases, the shock leads not to confrontation but to retreat. The only person who really forces Rose-Anna to see herself from a "foreign" point of view is her mother, but she lives in the country, not the city. Far from representing a potential other life, Madame Laplante only symbolizes an existence whose potential has long been exhausted.

Other forms of transgression and promiscuous connection common to novels about city slums are also absent from *Bonheur d'occasion*. There are no drunken excesses; indeed, what little sociable drinking occurs is limited to Sam Latour's snack bar, which serves only soft drinks. Although Azarius and Rose-Anna are so poor they cannot pay the rent, the Lacasse family is not otherwise in debt. Alphonse borrows money once from Emmanuel, but otherwise no one in the story lives on credit. The point is worth stressing. It may have been a fact about Depression Montreal that the poor had little access to any of the sources of credit, formal or informal, legal or illegal, available in other cities, but, if so, it is a fact the author never thinks of noting, and it is one so much taken for granted that none of the critics I've read have mentioned it either, even when they have sought to compare Roy's realism with that of novelists elsewhere. In Dickens, Dostoyevsky, or Zola, credit and debt are key factors in the dynamic of urban life. This is not only because of their economic importance, but because debt is an important source of dramatic tension. The figure of the creditor is often used to personalize oppression and provides an equally personalized focus for resentment and revolt. Its absence from the world of *Bonheur d'occasion* is thus of psychological and literary as well as economic significance.

Absent also from Roy's Saint-Henri are two networks of informal communication and control: rumour and gossip. For better as well as for worse, Roy's Saint-Henri families live very separate lives, free from prying eyes but also isolated from community contact. The only two moments when this rule is broken are Montreal's annual moving day, when the family moving out may have to share their flat with the people moving in; and the day a woman gives birth, when, along with the midwife, neighbouring women enter the house to help. The characters' movements within the city are not just empirically confined to a limited space; their scope is restricted by the way the setting is represented in the text.

Jean Lévesque is only a partial exception to this rule. He succeeds, of course, in leaving Saint-Henri. But, though he is "out for the big things," as he puts it in his farewell letter to Emmanuel (293),[5] he does not, it seems, move to a more centrally located part of the city. When Florentine glimpses him at the end of the story, the expensive clothes he is wearing make him look like a man about town, but we are told he works in Saint-Paul-l'Ermite (293), a village on the mainland northeast of Montreal (it is now part of Repentigny). This makes sense in that an explosives plant was in fact located there,[6] but, given that the plot did not require that the location of his new job be mentioned, Roy's decision to relegate Jean to the outskirts of Montreal as well as to the margins of her narrative suggests the depth of her reluctance to imagine his urban integration even in geographical terms.

As the story ends, Florentine is also about to leave Saint-Henri, and again farther away from the central city, though in the direction opposite to the one taken by Jean. She is considering renting a little house on Boulevard Lasalle (382) southwest of Saint-Henri, perhaps in Ville Lasalle (where Roy herself would live with her husband for a brief period in the early 1950s), though more likely in nearby Verdun. Again, the contrast with *Two Solitudes* is instructive. Because of her willingness to "settle" for a comfortable but blinkered security, Kathleen was exiled from that novel by an authorial fiat not unlike the gesture that banishes Jean from *Bonheur d'occasion*. Roy's novel, by contrast, redeems Florentine's refusal to concern herself with anything beyond her immediate situation by making it the source of a morally worthy act. When she glimpses Jean across the street after saying goodbye to Emmanuel at the station, Florentine decides not to show off her married status to the lover who had humiliated her. By extension, moving out of Saint-Henri but away from the downtown Montreal that had once dazzled her on a date with Jean can be read as a rejection of urban blandishments. Florentine's obsession with material security, with the safe bet, makes her less than heroic, but it also helps insulate her from entanglements implicitly viewed as degrading.

Nor does the novel's other protagonist mount much of an assault on the city gates. Emmanuel scales the prosperous heights of Westmount not to disturb the peace, but only to ponder in solitude the weighty issues of war and social inequality that haunt him. He speaks to no one. In this respect, his contemplation of the English city from his vantage point on Westmount lookout bears some resemblance to the scene in *Earth and High Heaven* that shows Erica reflecting on her relationship to French Quebec. Even at the moment the character imagines the "other's" existence most vividly and most sympathetically, direct contact with that other remains unimaginable, either by the character or by the narrator who dramatizes the character's situation. That is to say, the possibility or impossibility of such contact finds no articulate negotiation at either level. Thus, it is not surprising that we never learn how much English Emmanuel can actually speak: it doesn't matter. Just as important as the absence of dialogue between members of the city's communities, however, is the missing link in Emmanuel's internal meditation on the city's predicament. When he asks himself whether the city's rich are as ready as the poor to sacrifice themselves for the common good, he does not wonder about their willingness to share the city's wealth, only how prepared they are to go off to war, as he himself is about to do (337). Solidarity is envisaged in terms not of mutual engagement but rather of parallel action.

TEMPTATION

The destitute Alphonse's attack on the social system from which he is alienated is at once more articulate and more vehement than Emmanuel's, and closer to what one would expect to find in a work of social realism. Yet its scope, too, is limited. In a way this is understandable, since Alphonse's defiance is outweighed by his despair. He directs his outburst only at his old schoolmate, not at anyone in a position of power, even the army recruiter who rejects him because he is too undernourished even to serve as cannon fodder. Alphonse tells Emmanuel about how it feels to walk down Sainte-Catherine Street and see all the goods he cannot afford to buy. In *The Watch That Ends the Night*, MacLennan also has a scene about the unemployed walking aimlessly down Sainte-Catherine, but the account given by his spokesman, George Stewart, is significantly different from Alphonse's. Where the former focuses on the people the Depression has thrown out of work, Alphonse focuses on the objects on display. He may be part of a crowd, but he speaks almost as if there was no one else there.

> Did you ever go walking along St. Catherine Street, an' you didn't have a penny in your pocket, an' you look at all the stuff in the windows? Yes, eh? Well, so have I … The great things I've seen, just bummin' along St. Catherine, you couldn't make a list of it. Packards,

> Buicks, cars for speed, cars for fun, and all those big wax dolls [*catins*] with fancy dresses on, and some with not a stich. There's nothin' you can't see on that street. Furniture, bedrooms, more dolls [*catins*] in frills an' silk, and sports stores, golf clubs, tennis racquets, skis, fishin' poles. If anybody has time to have fun with all those things, it must be us, eh? (57)

There is something a little odd about Alphonse's "us" in the last sentence. Since it includes the lower-middle-class Emmanuel, whose father does a good business in church supplies, it must refer, not just to the deeply poor, but to everyone who isn't well enough off to live a life of leisure – that is, the vast majority of the population (for surely the percentage of people who at this period could afford a car was rather small). But there is no sense in which this vast group exists as anything more than an abstract entity. The awareness Alphonse speaks of is really that of isolated and destitute individuals who are not imagined as being in potential communication with each other. There is nothing here even of that unspoken commonality of crowd experience in which language barriers dissolve.[7] The real problem with Alphonse's critique, however, lies in other features of his language. Twice, for example, he refers to department-store mannequins as *catins*. In Canadian French, *catin* can refer to a child's "doll" as the translation has it (and thus the word's appearance in a linguistically restrained novel is less startling than it seems), but in this context its other meaning of "trollop" must surely be present. Whether Alphonse's use of such a moralistic term just before borrowing a dollar from Emmanuel so he can visit a local Saint-Henri prostitute is meant to be read ironically is not at all clear (62), since the judgment it registers is consistent with the passage's overall perspective on the city's enticements. Morally corrupt or not, Alphonse defines them all as *temptations*. "Yeah, temptations, that's what they've given us," he says, as he wraps up his indictment of the consumer city. "This whole cheap show of a life is fixed to tempt us. And that's how society gets a hold of us, the cheater, and gets us good" (58).

That Alphonse should be taunted by pictures of pleasures he cannot afford is readily understandable. Yet to call them "temptations" is misleading. The word suggests an impulse one might act on, but this is not the case here. Not for a moment does the penniless Alphonse even consider resorting to crime or subterfuge in order to obtain the things that tempt him. What is temptation without the fantasy of indulging it? Also absent is any mention of the physical cravings that MacLennan mentions when he speaks of men looking hungrily at chickens roasting in restaurant windows as they walked down Sainte-Catherine in the 1930s.[8] Conversely, we think of resisting "temptation" as something morally admirable, but refraining from purchasing the cars and clothes with which consumer society entices you but which you never actually imagine buying can hardly be called a moral act. The contradictions in the rhetoric of temptation disappear, however, if the temptation Alphonse is talking about is not the temptation to acquire and possess, but the temptation simply to *want* one of the many and varied objects on offer. For Roy, it seems, the most insidious temptation of all, and the one hardest to resist, is the exacerbation and diversification of desire itself.

We see the same idea illustrated from another point of view when at the end of his speech Alphonse speaks of the kind of "temptation" uppermost in most people's minds when they think of that term: sex. Here, Alphonse moves from speech to action. He asks Emmanuel for a dollar to pay a prostitute plying her trade in their own neighbourhood of Saint-Henri. Financially as well as geographically, this makes sense, but curiously Alphonse does not speak in this context of a "temptation" being offered and indulged. Nor does he draw any connection between this discreet, local transaction and the more flamboyant enticements of the downtown city.[9] The reason for not speaking of temptation here would seem to be that Alphonse is imagined as seeking not erotic gratification but merely release from desire.

The same is even truer of Florentine in her relationship with Jean. Of course, Roy could not speak too explicitly about a young woman's sexuality if she wanted her novel to find a publisher in 1940s Montreal, the only place where, unlike English-language writers, she could think of seeing her book in print. Even so, it is clear that Florentine's desire is more for security than for sex. Or, to put it in terms that align her with Alphonse, what she wants is not to be troubled by want. Jean's attraction to Florentine is also curiously un-erotic. He takes advantage of the vulnerable Florentine primarily to exorcise his own vulnerability. He embraces the deprivation she embodies the better to allay the pangs of deprivation.

Modern writers often complain about the overstimulation characteristic of big cities, but a heightened and varied experience of desire, however painful, is nonetheless considered to be necessary for broadening our perception and refining our sensibility. Roy knows that "yielding" to the "temptation" of desire is not just excusable as a last-ditch defence against the anguish of inner conflict. Acknowledging and embracing one's nature as a desiring being (as distinct from indiscriminate self-indulgence) has positive value; it is a necessary step in one's psychological, social, and even moral growth. In having Alphonse speak of desire as "temptation," Roy is being admirably faithful to the character's point of view. Yet the fact that her narrator does not put this language into perspective but rather leaves it as the only language in which desire is discussed sets her novel at odds in interesting ways with the outlook characteristic of the modern urban novel.

We find a striking instance of this incongruity in Emmanuel's reply to Alphonse. At the moment of their conversation, Emmanuel has recently returned from basic training at a military camp somewhere outside Montreal. Unlike his poorer friends, Emmanuel's decision to join the army was motivated not by the prospect of being well clothed and fed but rather by a humanistic ideal. Yet when he is called upon to explain himself Emmanuel also uses the language of temptation.

> "You forgot one thing," the young soldier said after a pause. "You forgot the biggest temptation."
>
> "Now you don't say!" murmured Alphonse. "Is that right?"
>
> "The temptation," Emmanuel went on, "of animals in a cage or dwarfs [*naines*] in a circus. The temptation to break the bars and get out into life. A temptation you've forgotten: the temptation to fight." (59)[10]

This is surely an odd way for Emmanuel to describe his decision to fight in a war that, as an important fraction of French Canadian opinion insisted, did not directly threaten his life or liberty. One can imagine anti-conscription nationalists speaking of Emmanuel being seduced by imperialist propaganda, but they would hardly describe their francophone compatriots as living in cages at home. Conversely, one can scarcely imagine an English Canadian recruiter encouraging poor francophone Montrealers to join the army as a means of escaping their prison. Emmanuel is clearly offering his very personal belief that, given the dispiriting circumstances in which the people of Saint-Henri are living, and the limited options they have, joining the fight abroad is the only way to overcome the abjection so vividly described by Alphonse. He makes the point more explicitly later in the same scene, when another school friend, Boisvert, pushes Emmanuel to clarify what he means. Emmanuel replies that joining the fight is "your only chance to be a man again" (59). But why should he think of the prospect of becoming a man again as another form of temptation?

The most obvious explanation is not that the object of desire is unworthy but that the chances of obtaining it are so small as to make the struggle futile. In a society defined by long-ingrained and long-internalized prejudice, the "little people," like the feminized circus dwarfs (*naines*), might never be acknowledged as the "men" they aspire to be.[11] Emmanuel is clearly not someone to be discouraged by unfavourable odds. The circus image, however, suggests another interpretation. Freed of their cages, the bears and other beasts would simply not know what to do with their freedom. Indeed, from the confining but secure perspective of the circus tent, or the "village" that is Saint-Henri, even the prospect of unfettered freedom may be too disturbing to contemplate. As with Alphonse, greater immersion in the life of the city may awaken desire without providing any help, moral or material, about how to handle it.

Since Emmanuel is coaxing his companions to take the leap and not warning them against its dangers, one wonders why he frames the decision to enlist as one of yielding to temptation. Perhaps he uses this rhetoric as the only one capable of stirring the debased imaginations of people who have never received any positive forms of encouragement. Yet the novel does not suggest that Emmanuel is deliberately adapting his language to his listeners. On the contrary, he seems to be the vehicle through whom the novelist speaks to her public – and, I think, also to herself. Implicit in *Bonheur d'occasion* is that the story's unfortunate characters are not the only ones conditioned to think desire is dangerous. With the exception of Jean, all the characters the novel cares about think the same way, and on every level. Desire is dangerous from the point of view of practical calculation, because one is unlikely to obtain what one wants. It is dangerous psychologically, because to desire is to become even more vulnerable than one already is and to jeopardize what little independence one enjoys. Finally, it is morally wrong, because to want something more or something other than what one needs to subsist is not just presumptuous but fundamentally illegitimate.

What is perhaps most distressing about this view is that its judgments hold true even if the object of desire is in itself a worthy one: what is at issue is the valence of one's subjective experience more than the value of the thing sought. Even Yvonne's decision to become a nun has for her a transgressive quality not unlike Emmanuel's decision to fight. It is worth asking if the writing and reading of novels is an exception to this rule. If Emmanuel is Roy's spokesman, then the author may be expressing some doubt about her own effort to mediate the liberation of confined imaginations, even as she embraces the "temptation" of becoming a full human being through the struggle to write the book.

Emmanuel's conversation with his friends about temptation ends in mutual incomprehension, but Roy approaches the issue from another direction in the episode of the tin flute. The emblematic status of this object, already apparent in the original text, was confirmed early on by the choice of title for the novel's English translation.[12] Surprised and touched by Rose-Anna's air of vulnerability when they meet in the Five and Ten store, Florentine is moved to give her mother two dollars over and above what she contributes to the household from her waitressing job (119). The full significance of her gesture for the development of the narrative becomes evident if we look at how it differs from Emmanuel's gift of a dollar to Alphonse. The obvious contrast between using the money to buy a toy instead of the services of a prostitute – already somewhat attenuated by the rhetoric of temptation to describe material consumption generally – is less germane here than the fact that Florentine is far more identified with Rose-Anna than Emmanuel with Alphonse, and so she has a personal stake in how her gift affects and enables the recipient. As I argued earlier, Alphonse wants the money to satisfy a need rather than to fulfill a desire, but it is just this latter possibility that Florentine wishes to create for her mother, and to see reflected back to her. Emmanuel "lends" Alphonse the money in response to the other's plea; Florentine offers it as a free gift, in the hope that both recipient and giver will be transformed by the gratuitous nature of the gesture.

Whereas Emmanuel neither can nor wants to see what Alphonse does with his dollar, Florentine is forced to watch as Rose-Anna, emboldened by the unexpected money, considers giving a gift in her turn, the little toy flute her sickly son Daniel has long craved, instead of holding back the money to meet one of the family's many pressing material needs. But when a salesperson approaches her, Rose-Anna quickly puts the flute back on the shelf, as if she didn't want to be seen coveting it. "Florentine realized that between Daniel's wish and the shiny flute there would always be her mother's good intention – an intention repressed" (121). Florentine's joy immediately turns to ashes. She is disappointed with her mother for failing to mirror – as, no doubt, she had in earlier years failed to model – that capacity to display a freedom of spirit that she has unexpectedly found in herself. In *Bonheur d'occasion*'s world of scarcity, giving in to temptation may be wrong, but to resist temptation altogether, or perhaps better, to view certain opportunities negatively *as* temptations may be to fall into a constricted fatalism more demoralizing than any sinful indulgence.

The scene is a powerful one, and it marks the moment when Florentine's sympathy for her mother begins to give way to the resentment that explodes when she learns that Rose-Anna is pregnant again. Unlike Emmanuel's exchange with his friends, Florentine's confrontation with her mother in the latter scene is more openly conflictual, and thus carries the potential for bringing about a further development of consciousness with implications not only for the characters but for the dynamic of the novel as a whole. Florentine's irritation with Rose-Anna arises in part from her own unwelcome pregnancy, but its aggressive edge is sharpened by Florentine's perception of her mother as someone not just unable but unwilling to escape the cage of necessity. The judgment may be unfair, but it has the potential to lead to a conversation between the women that would force them to clarify their situation and challenge them to take a position in relation to it. As Emmanuel would put it, by engaging in active conflict they have a chance to free themselves, at least in their minds, from the cages that confine them and isolate them from each other. Indeed, the particular pathos of the moment stems in part from our sense that Rose-Anna acts almost automatically, as if not daring to think. This impression is reinforced by the fact that the narrator does not give us Rose-Anna's thoughts – if she formulates any articulate thought at all. No doubt the narrator prefers to focus on the shame Rose-Anna feels about being seen to be tempted, which is just another dimension of the external pressure on her, rather than on imagining her inner anguish. In contrast, Florentine's intuitive perception of her mother's predicament marks a dramatic departure from her usual tendency to avoid seeing things too clearly so as to avoid having to think about them.

Another element of pathos in this scene is the absence of communication between the women. The disparity of their perspectives, coupled with their ongoing mutual dependence, leads us to anticipate a more consequential confrontation than the abortive exchange between Emmanuel and his friends. This expectation, however, goes unmet. Florentine will gradually become more adept at negotiating other issues through a combination of risk taking and prudent calculation, but she deals with her mother by retreating into silence, engaging her no more than is strictly necessary. This silence is of a piece with her strategy of saying nothing to Emmanuel about the real father of her baby. Florentine falls back into her old pattern of not thinking too much about the choices she makes. What is striking is that Rose-Anna does not challenge her to face up to what she's doing. One could respond by saying she doesn't have to, since the narrator provides the necessary critical perspective, exposing what some critics have called a "Quebec" tendency to sweep inconvenient truths under the rug. What is more significant, however, and passed over in silence by the critics, is that the narrator aligns herself with Florentine in not turning the challenge back on Rose-Anna. In one sense, this, too, is understandable: unlike Florentine, Rose-Anna can't afford to become too self-reflective if she is to get on with all she has to do. Still, the fact that the novel avoids adding the pain of self-division to Rose-Anna's other sufferings results from a deliberate artistic decision, not simply from a pre-existing reality the writer merely reflects. A brief look at the way some key scenes are structured will illustrate the point.

The only moment at which Rose-Anna is led to reflect on her choices comes when she sees a newspaper headline about war-torn Europe (230–2). She realizes there is some tension between her sympathy for suffering mothers abroad and her unwillingness to let her son Eugène go off to fight. If she does not allow her thoughts to carry her very far, she has good reason: she has just been to the hospital in which another son, Daniel, is dying of leukemia. The episode is typical of the way the novel movingly depicts Rose-Anna's suffering as a mother while sparing her the additional torment of the reflective individual. Rose-Anna may at times experience conflicting impulses, but with the exception of the moment when she has to weigh her wish to see her country relatives against the prudence of allowing Azarius to borrow the truck (an incident, as I pointed out before, focused on the past rather than the future), her desires do not rise to the level of temptations she herself acknowledges to be such. Her hesitation about buying the tin flute, as we have seen, is reported by Florentine, not conveyed directly through Rose-Anna's deliberations, and the conflict is framed as one between prudence and "good intentions," that is, between two aspects of one unimpeachably moral disposition, rather than between rectitude and recklessness.

The accelerated pace of events in the last chapters prevents us from noticing how carefully these are arranged to forestall potentially awkward confrontations. That Rose-Anna does not attend Florentine's wedding, for example, is made plausible by her very advanced pregnancy (though it is interesting that no one says this), but the result is that she avoids witnessing, and thus implicitly endorsing, a marriage based on her daughter's lies of omission. Indeed, over the course of the narrative, Emmanuel apparently never meets Rose-Anna at all. There is thus no moment at which they have to confront their opposing opinions about war and sacrifice.

The most important evidence, however, of the novelist's protective attitude toward Rose-Anna is Roy's decision not to have her visit Daniel in his final days. After her one trip to the hospital, Rose-Anna is not made to witness his further decline, his increasing indifference to his mother (and attachment to his nurse), or his death. Rose-Anna's confinement, then the need to attend to her new child, again make this understandable, and perhaps Roy wanted to spare the reader, too, but the narrative is framed in such a way, and endowed with such a generalized pathos, that we don't question what might otherwise be seen as a problematic moment in the plot.[13] Rose-Anna is said to realize she will feel the pain of Daniel's death more acutely later, when she gets back to her daily routine, but for the moment what she feels is that "as if a balance were re-established" (368). That is, by dying Daniel has successfully struck back against the "part de malheur" his mother bequeathed to him by bringing him into the world.[14] This reassuring thought dispels Rose-Anna's resentment at being reminded by Azarius of Daniel's death in the first place, just when she has given birth. What Azarius doesn't know, but Rose-Anna does know from having plumbed the depths of sorrow, is that "death and birth, in that place, have almost the same tragic meaning" (367).

Here Rose-Anna does appear to articulate a considered, reflective insight, but the declaration needs to be read with careful attention to its meaning and context. In Roy's sentence, birth and death are equally tragic when seen from the "depths of sorrow." But the context of Rose-Anna's other thoughts belies that truth. A few lines earlier, she viewed the birth of the child as the token of new and better future (367). That view will in turn be relativized by her discovery at the end of the chapter that Azarius has enlisted in the army to escape his unhappiness. This seems to suggest that pain is the ultimate and not just the immediate context in which death and birth are equally tragic events. From a literary standpoint, however, that view stands at odds with Roy's use of Rose-Anna's pregnancy and childbirth to justify her absence at the wedding and the funeral and thus her insulation from the moral challenges they might present. The difficulty of reconciling these contradictory perspectives is resolved by limiting Rose-Anna's reaction at the end of this penultimate chapter to a single scream (394), and then excluding Rose-Anna from the final chapter, so that this inarticulate scream becomes her last utterance in the book.

Dramatically effective as it is, this climactic moment leaves both the psychological and the literary dynamic generated by the exploration of temptation unresolved. In saying this, I am not denigrating Roy's achievement. On the contrary, I think her effort to control the shape of her narrative is an aesthetically authentic response to a broader cultural necessity. The avoidance of self-divisive reflection, I will suggest, could not itself be avoided. To appreciate the reasons why this had to happen, we need to look at another dynamic informing the novel's composition, one that gave necessity resonant creative form.

TENDERNESS

In a speech she gave in 1947, two years after the novel was published, Roy described a decisive turning-point in the composition of the book. Like many other "social" novels, *Bonheur d'occasion* started out as a story about the aspirations of its youthful protagonists – about their temptations, one might say. Then the character of Rose-Anna unexpectedly forced her way into the centre of the narrative. "She disrupted its construction," Roy tells us, so much so that "she came in the end to dominate it by means of a single and most unliterary virtue [*qualité*], that of tenderness."[15] The influence of "tenderness" on the shape of the story in fact goes well beyond Rose-Anna herself. The word *tendresse* appears at a number of key points in the account of other characters' lives, and just as the notion of temptation took on positive as well as negative connotations, the dynamic of tenderness is sometimes presented, as it is in Roy's speech, as more disturbing or constraining than comforting. The two notions, I want to suggest, are complementary; by tracing Roy's ambivalence about tenderness we can bridge the gap in the novel's exploration of temptation.

Roy's definition of tenderness as "unliterary" surely calls for comment. Perhaps she wanted to distinguish her work from the more hard-boiled or judgmental forms of social realism, but she could hardly have forgotten that Dickens, George Eliot, and Chekhov, to name only three writers Roy admired, are not considered any less literary for displaying a tender attitude toward their characters. Roy's insistence that her achievement was based on sympathetic emotion rather than on literary crafting may possibly express the diplomatic self-deprecation of a writer wary of making artistic claims her audience might find pretentious, either because of her sex or because of their own lack of cultural confidence. Roy might well have wanted to forestall criticism of her boldness by emphasizing the feminine, even maternal, quality of her vision. But we should be wary of reading Roy's statement solely in defensive terms. Like some other anti-literary pronouncements of the past, Roy's statement should be taken as a kind of artistic manifesto.

If we look at what Roy does with tenderness in *Bonheur d'occasion*, we see that she puts this ostensibly non-literary disposition to eminently literary purpose. If a defining characteristic of nineteenth-century realism is that it gives aesthetic dignity to people and things hitherto deemed too humble or too vulgar to be worthy of literary representation; and if modernism can be defined by its determination to make art not just of sub-literary material, as realism did with its depiction of the low, the crass, or the sordid, but of anti-literary things – the random, the impersonal, even the inert or stubbornly resistant to interpretation – then Roy's "unliterary" tenderness could be taken as expressing a modernist literary sensibility, though one reflective of the author's (and her culture's) position on the margins of the modern. Roy's struggle with the "unliterary" may not take as complex a form as it does in, say, Joyce's *Ulysses*, a novel where hyperbolically "literary" elements are constantly juxtaposed with the most un-literary words and things (and a novel whose treatment of Molly and Leopold Bloom also belies the notion that tenderness must be unliterary), but Rose-Anna's takeover of what seems to have been a fairly straightforward project about the search for love in the slums clearly challenged Roy to become more self-conscious about the nature and purpose of her novel.

The language Roy uses to describe the disruptive emergence of tenderness is strikingly at odds with the supposed softness of the emotion, as well as with what we might assume to be the relationship between life and art. One might expect that a first-time novelist working from personal witness would want to offset with compassion the harshness of the circumstances she describes, but Roy's compositional experience is practically the opposite of this. As embodied in Rose-Anna, tenderness is a boldly intrusive force, so much so that it "disrupted" the construction of the novel and ended up "dominating" the book. These words do not describe a retreat from a critical into a sentimental attitude; rather, they record how a weak or inadequately energetic literariness gave way to an external force assertively making room for itself within the realm of the literary. In Roy's account, tenderness assumes an impersonal and demanding cast, shaking the writing subject out of her artistic comfort zone and forcing her to mobilize all the resources of her imagination. It is "unliterary" because, instead of offering a reassuring solution to an artistic problem, it asks an uncomfortable question about art itself, a question the author cannot easily address and whose reach extends far beyond the issue of Rose-Anna's role in the book.

In the novel as we now have it, the problem of *tendresse* first becomes explicit in the narrative's depiction of Emmanuel. When we meet him near the beginning of the story, he is making the rounds of his old haunts in Saint-Henri after returning from training camp. His decision to enlist in the army soon after Canada's entry into the war has turned him into an outsider. His former friends greet him with hostility, and his sense of isolation becomes more acute when Alphonse, after borrowing some money, leaves him to visit the prostitute. Emmanuel is seized by a "need [*désir*] for tenderness" (63). The forcefulness of the verb *s'emparer* [seize, hold], which curiously echoes the *dominer* in Roy's 1947 statement, suggests that what Emmanuel desires is sexual intimacy. This is not, or at least not quite, the case. While Emmanuel can remember the names of the various young women he has met over the years, he cannot call up any bodily images. "No emotion" is stirred when he thinks of these "phantoms" (63). Certainly, he does not feel driven to look them up when he returns to Saint-Henri after his army training and meets with his male friends. This may be because Emmanuel has not yet fallen in love, but the deeper reason is that sexual intimacy is too narrowly focused a conception of the tenderness he seeks. "Friendship" might be a better word: "The farther he walked the more conscious he was of a need [*plus il se reconnaissait avide*] for friendship," and we note that the forceful term *avide* is introduced only when Emmanuel frames his quest in terms of this somewhat hazy ideal, and not in relation to sex or to any other concrete form of interaction.

Looking back on *Bonheur d'occasion* many years later, Roy confirmed that in the novel Emmanuel's quest echoed that of his creator. She recalled the "desire for tenderness and fraternal exchange" that drove her out of the rented room in which she lived and worked in solitude to walk the streets of Saint-Henri that became the setting for her novel.[16] This statement would seem to clash with her 1947 claim that an un-literary tenderness disrupted the writing of a novel begun on another basis. Yet, if we look closely, there is no contradiction. The initial action is of tenderness sought, the subsequent experience one of tenderness offered; the second moment can be understood as an unexpected but complementary response to the first. Yet, just as Emmanuel finds that the tenderness offered him is not quite the tenderness he seeks, so, too, the tenderness represented by the appearance of Rose-Anna is disruptively different from the tenderness the writer was looking for when she first set out. The gap between the offering and the asking defines the space in which the story takes shape, and in which it will mediate between the literary and the unliterary.

In this respect, the structuring role of tenderness is much like the aesthetically provocative mismatch between temptation as lure and temptation as a necessary spur to self-realization. The two notions are in a sense complementary, in that just as sometimes it is good to give in to temptation, tender impulses are sometimes better kept in check. When Rose-Anna has to share her flat for a night with the new family moving in, she cannot resent them because she knows they are as poor as she is, but she doesn't reach out to them in sympathy. "She was accustomed to shutting off too much concern for others, economizing tenderness and keeping watch on her own impulses of generosity" (274). Rose-Anna defends herself against the exhaustion of her emotional resources just as she did against the temptation to spend money on the tin flute, with the important difference that here she is not criticized for her restraint.[17]

Remarkably, with one exception I will discuss below, this is the only time the word *tendresse* is actually used in connection with the character who supposedly embodies that emotion in the book. Rose-Anna generally treats her family with tenderness, of course, but without the narrative drawing attention to her attitude by naming it.[18] The answer, perhaps, is that in those instances there was no need for explicit articulation. Only when the family of strangers invades the family circle does it become necessary to mention the limits of tenderness, for it is at such moments that Rose-Anna is also confronted with the "literary," in the sense of that imaginative apprehension of social forces, and especially of the promiscuity of urban life, one expects a character in a mainstream realist novel to confront. If Rose-Anna is not made to explore the implications of what she sees, it is because for Roy she conveys an alternative vision.

To understand the dynamic of tenderness as it is associated with Rose-Anna in more implicit ways in other scenes, we must first look at its explicit articulation in relation to Emmanuel, who, to the extent that she consents to use one, serves as Roy's literary spokesperson, and to Florentine, who as the novel's heroine is also the mediating (or non-mediating) link between Emmanuel and Rose-Anna. In Emmanuel, the tension between the unliterariness of *tendresse* and the literariness of more concrete forms of sexual desire plays out in ways the narrative can more comfortably articulate than it can through the less self-conscious Rose-Anna. In the passage mentioned a moment ago, the narrator speaks of Emmanuel craving a friendship "new and unforeseen, measuring up to his strange expectations. Was it really friendship he was looking for? Or a part of himself that he only half understood, and which would become clear in the light of friendship" (63). In another novel, Emmanuel's quest for "friendship" would be exposed as a masked form of sexual desire, not yet recognized as such by an idealistic, emotionally under-developed young man. But here I think it expresses the truth of the character (and no doubt, of his creator, as she walked the streets of Saint-Henri). Emmanuel's goal is indeed an abstract one, involving friendship rather than a specific friend, and certainly not the intimate connection of lovers

– even lovers linked by their solitude. What he needs is not to see himself *in* another person; rather, it is to find someone who would serve as a light *by means of which* he could appear to himself. That is, the other person would not be seen as an object of desire, but rather in broader terms as the context in which other things could be seen, most notably himself as a desiring subject.[19]

We can now understand why we are not told whether Emmanuel wants to receive tenderness or to give it. No doubt he wants both, but what he wants even more is an experience of feeling in which the distinction between giving and receiving – and any potential disproportion between the two – is minimized. Friendship, at least the kind of abstract friendship in view here, is more likely to meet this demand than sexual partnership. It can satisfy the "avidity" of one's need for connection without the other – and, more important, the self – being summoned either to give or to receive any specific expression or proof of tenderness and thus being subjected to an obligation to act. One cannot help recalling the fact that, while Roy's visits to Saint-Henri resulted in moments of intense identification and intuitive communication for which she was grateful, they did not lead to the forging of any ongoing relationships.

The limitations – artistic as well as psychological – of such a quest for tenderness are illustrated in the sentences that follow. Emmanuel, we are told, "felt so isolated and exasperated that he would gladly have spoken to strangers in the street" (63). Yet the fact that he doesn't find, or take, the opportunity to engage with anyone is not noted with any sadness or regret on the part of the narrator. It seems to be taken for granted, like the absence of networks of gossip or other informal communication in the world of the story. Like MacLennan's Paul Tallard, Roy's Emmanuel Létourneau is never portrayed as speaking to anyone he does not already know. The one exception is Florentine, with whose mother he is probably acquainted because she used to do sewing for his family, and even then he speaks to her only after Jean has prepared the way. Whether Emmanuel's relationship with Florentine offers a resolution to his yearning for the "unforeseen" is a question I will take up in a moment, but the sentence just cited highlights another curious aspect of Emmanuel's quest. He moves through the city streets in silence, addressing its inhabitants only in his thoughts. This lack of personal contact is, of course, to be attributed in part to the psychological isolation, pervasive in Saint-Henri, which has shaped Emmanuel's outlook almost as much as it has that of the more destitute characters. But it also reflects the artistic terms in which his quest is framed.

Once Emmanuel's yearning becomes focused on Florentine, it takes on a more erotic cast. While he never stops acting tenderly toward Florentine, he no longer thinks of "tenderness" as an enabling field of feeling, but rather as an impediment to sexual fulfillment. Leaving his home to look for the woman he will soon marry, Emmanuel feels as if he were escaping from prison, "a prison of tenderness."[20] He feels guilty about abandoning his affectionate family, but he must seek out the object of his desire. In other contexts, this painful decision to separate would be presented simply as a fact about growing up. In *Bonheur d'occasion*, however, it takes on more pathetic connotations. Emmanuel is not just claiming his independence as a desiring subject; he is turning his back on a feeling, or perhaps better, a fundamental emotional disposition that Roy wishes could serve as the undifferentiated basis for all one's relationships, indeed for one's relationship with the world as a whole. At the same time, she knows that such a wish is unrealistic. Relationships with family, friends, and partners make different kinds of demands on the self and elicit forms of affective response. These may in some cases appropriately be combined but the maturing self must learn, often painfully, to discriminate among them.[21] The same is true of the novelist. In a fable or a romance, with its intimations of a higher world, the opposition between these impulses can be portrayed as a provisional one, destined to be abolished; in realist fiction, this opposition is a fundamental truth that must acknowledged even when there is hope for reconciliation.

The novel's hesitation about differentiating tenderness from desire finds dramatic expression in the last scenes of the book. When Emmanuel marries Florentine, his tender devotion makes him indulge her spendthrift ways. It also prevents him from suspecting that the baby she tells him she is carrying might not be his. Yet he cannot help realizing that something is off. As he boards the train leaving Montreal at the end of the book, he thinks about Florentine's mood swings. The "coldness" and the "silence [*réticence*]" he mentions are traits he had observed before. What puzzles him is something new: Florentine's "sudden fits of tenderness" (378). Given the similarity of the language with that in Roy's later discussion of *Bonheur d'occasion*, these *accès* are unlikely to be bursts of a sexual passion to which Roy, like other novelists of the day, could allude to only indirectly. If that is what is implied, Emmanuel would surely be flattered and gratified rather than puzzled. Since he is already used to Florentine's appreciation for the material things he gives her, tenderness as return for a favour can't be what mystifies him either. What Emmanuel can't understand must be what he did not expect Florentine to display: precisely that tenderness divorced from any concrete desire that he has felt in himself. If so, then for a moment Florentine is just as "unliterary" as her mother. By an ironic twist, the puzzlement this generates offers a very literary illustration of the difficulty of understanding another person's motives even and especially when they appear to mirror one's own. What is most significant, however, is that neither Emmanuel nor the narrator clarifies the situation any further. Some things, it would seem, are better left unexplored.

Florentine's relationship with her mother is also given greater complexity by the tension between tenderness and desire, but, again, in such a way that its implications are not fully explored. At the end of the long evening when, suspecting she is pregnant, Florentine goes looking in vain for Jean, she masks her desperation by deciding to do what it takes to create at least the illusion of happiness. With this thought, she is seized by "tenderness [*attendrissement*]" (256) for her mother, who has devoted her life to doing the same thing for her family. The feeling dissipates when she arrives home to find her family evicted from their flat. As in the episode of the tin flute, the bitter disappointment that overcomes her stems primarily from discovering that the harshness of reality, and even more, the harshness of having to think about reality, cannot be avoided by falling back into the fuzziness of good feeling. The result is a feeling of hostility even greater than the resentment Florentine felt when faced with Rose-Anna's inability to indulge a saving temptation. Remarkably, this hostility is not Florentine's alone. It also arises in her mother when a few pages later Florentine's morning sickness makes her realize her daughter is pregnant. Florentine sees Rose-Anna looking at her, not just with a disappointment equal to her own, but "without pity, without friendship, without kindness; only with eyes filled with horror" (261; translation modified). The result is that "the two women stared at each other like enemies" (262).

The moment when tenderness is disrupted, first by an overwhelming experience of neediness, then by the spectacle of desire's consequences, is the one truly dramatic confrontation between Rose-Anna and Florentine, and the word Roy uses to describe what happens to the relationship between them is a surprisingly strong one. When Florentine had earlier despaired of avoiding the shame of pregnancy by finding Jean and getting him to protect her, she concluded that men and women are "enemies" (252). Now, this enmity extends to her relationship with her mother. A few pages later, it is said to characterize her relationship to herself. Looking in a mirror, "Florentine … stared long at this new image of herself as enemy [*en ennemie*]" (265). Like the face-off between Florentine and Rose-Anna, this moment of unwelcome but fateful clarity is eminently "literary," first by virtue of its dramatic vividness, and then because it echoes similar moments of discomforting self-examination in other novels. Precisely for this reason, however, it is for Roy a moment of "enmity" and not just distress: the ultimate source of enmity is the seeming incompatibility between seeing the world from a "literary" perspective, here that of a critical realism about desire, and a more "tender" one that keeps that perspective from becoming too distressingly clear.

The "enmity" of which Roy speaks is more than a simple feeling of rage or hate. Like its opposite, the tender "friendship" Emmanuel sought, it designates a field of vision within which people appear to each other and to themselves. The intensity of the emotion derives from its structuring effect: the hostile gaze clarifies the identity of the person seen (the other or even oneself) by locating her, indeed pinning her down, within a space of conflictual action. In this key respect, enmity marks an advance on the more inchoate and ultimately inconsequential resentment expressed by Emmanuel's friends. Even the verbally articulate Alphonse quickly falls back into passive resignation because his anger floats in a psychological void. Bemused as he is by the city's temptations, Alphonse is not the object of anyone's gaze; nor can he direct his attack on anyone in particular. Because it situates one subject in relation to another, enmity is a disposition with positive as well as negative potential.

Thus, far from being incompatible with desire, enmity can give it the assertiveness that otherwise might be inhibited by social conditioning or moral censorship. Earlier in the novel, Roy had shown how it was Jean's anger at being reminded by Florentine's avid vulnerability of his own discarded past that drove him to have sex with her. Jean then abandons Florentine for the same reason he seduced her: in seeing her he saw himself with an uncomfortable clarity. This ambivalence of enmity, which forges and destroys bonds through a dialectic of opposition and attraction, is familiar to us from many works of literature, and notably from the kind of realist fiction Roy rejects when she refuses to follow Jean's story any further. The hostility between Estella and Pip in *Great Expectations*, or between the humiliated hero and the haughty noblewomen of *Le Père Goriot*, are only two examples of the way enmity in one form or another drives the novelistic protagonist's pursuit of social success. At a more popular level, the "hostile meet" has long been a standard opening trope of Hollywood movies of the kind to which Jean invites Florentine at the beginning of their abortive romance – but which they don't see because he decides to stand her up (37).

Dynamic enmity of this kind was not yet, however, a major feature of Montreal fiction, French or English. Not until *The Apprenticeship of Duddy Kravitz* do we find a gleeful representation of hostility, and the scandal Richler provoked arose in part from the transgressive novelty of his decision to place that feeling at the centre of a story set in a city that preferred not to let its latent enmities come too close to the surface. Even in that book, as we shall see, the clarity brought about by enmity is limited, in the sense that it does not extend to the representation of sexual desire. Duddy acts aggressively so that people will "see" him, but there is no clear seeing in his relationship with his French Canadian girlfriend. Even when Yvette finally rejects him, we do not really see Duddy through her eyes. In *Bonheur d'occasion*, as soon as Jean Lévesque "sees" Florentine, he leaves the scene. The question to ask, then, is what emerges from Rose-Anna and Florentine's clarifying moments of enmity?

The answer, simply put, is very little. Rose-Anna's hostility turns first to a sense of shared shame (341), then to a despairing sense that Florentine has become a stranger whose feelings she cannot hope to understand – and therefore need not try. Rose-Anna's one attempt to engage her daughter in a conversation about the seriousness of marriage is cut short when Florentine accuses her of preaching, the same reproach Rose-Anna had directed at her own mother (344). As in the scene when the Lacasse family went to see their country relatives and Rose-Anna was forced to see how frail and ragged her children looked next to their cousins, the confrontation between Rose-Anna and Florentine clarifies their relationship to the past more than it illuminates future possibility. Thus, it is understandable that both women quickly retreat to the safety of their separate corners. Florentine makes no further acerbic remarks about Rose-Anna's giving birth to yet another child. Soon reassured by her success in making an economically advantageous marriage, Florentine's internal enmity toward herself is transformed into a more flattering self-image, enhanced by the thought of using some of her husband's money to help her mother after Azarius follows Emmanuel off to war. Any further experience of the "enmity" between men and women is precluded by her avoidance of Jean at the train station, and by her confidence that her lack of passion for Emmanuel will actually make life easier in the long run (381). Meanwhile, Rose-Anna refocuses her attention on her baby, with a "concentrated tenderness" (363) uncomplicated as yet by any differentiating individuality in this infant, who in the novel remains unnamed.

Perhaps in an attempt to offset its unwillingness to follow up on the confrontation between Florentine and her mother, Roy underscores the pathos of a second scene in which Rose-Anna is forced to experience a moment of painful clarity. In the novel's penultimate chapter, Rose-Anna is lying in her darkened bedroom when Azarius comes in and begins a convoluted story of regret and farewell she can't understand. She asks him to turn on the light and the sudden sight of him in army uniform, which explains everything, gives her a shock so great that her only reaction is a single scream (372).

It's a powerful moment, one whose impact is enhanced when we realize, after closing the book, that Rose-Anna's scream is her last recorded utterance. After all she has been through, we think, what more could she say? The distressing clarity of this scene is quite different from that of the confrontation between Rose-Anna and Florentine. That scene was also one in which language failed: unable to bring herself to say the word "pregnant" out loud, Rose-Anna lapses into silence. But the hostile silence of that scene carried the potential for further conversation. As I suggested earlier, the space of "enmity" was one in which the relationship between mother and daughter could develop into something deeper. Such is not the case here. Rose-Anna sees Azarius in the impersonal, disempowering clarity of a fate revealed, not the energizing "enmity" of interpersonal discovery. Nothing can come from this clarity or be made of it. Fate's decree is not up for debate; its impact can only be registered on a body rendered incapable of articulate response.

Or at least, this is how the novel presents the situation. The agonistic tension of contending desires dissolves into the fundamental pathos of the human condition. This tension is more usually the matrix of a realism that exposes the hidden causes of social conflict as a first step toward mediating a solution. The central dynamic of this critical realism is temptation, and its emblematic locus the city. The pathos of suffering is the source of an emotional realism about the effects of those causes insofar as they lie beyond one's control. The guiding principle of this realism is tenderness. Its emblematic moment is Rose-Anna's contemplation of her new baby, whose birth contextualizes Daniel's death and Azarius's departure as moments in the cosmic cycle of life.

Bonheur d'occasion itself remains poised uneasily between these two realisms. The ambivalence of Roy's stance, or, perhaps better, her reluctance to grasp the nettle of the conflict between them, may be one reason the Montreal writers who followed immediately in her footsteps did not find literary inspiration in her book, even when they appreciated her pioneering achievement. The one exception proves the rule. Roger Viau's *Au milieu la montagne*, as I remarked earlier, tells a story very similar in outline to Roy's, but despite its greater frankness it fails to resonate as deeply as *Bonheur d'occasion*. Viau did not realize that one cannot write a more knowing or worldly version of Roy's book and still achieve the unique and fragile equilibrium of her "unliterary" art. That equilibrium is closely linked to the possibility of plausibly imagining a Montreal neighbourhood as a "village" (283), something that the writers who followed her, determined to "catch up" with urban modernity in a postwar Montreal that was itself rapidly changing, neither could nor wanted to do. One immediately sees, for example, that *Bonheur d'occasion* offers no guideposts by which Françoise Loranger could orient her exploration of *Mathieu*'s city. I think it significant that the most eloquent literary tribute to *Bonheur d'occasion* should appear only many years later, in a novel that, thanks to the resources of Latin American "magic realism," recreates the village-in-the-city atmosphere in sophisticated postmodern form: Michel Tremblay's *La Grosse femme d'à côté est enceinte* (*The Fat Woman Next Door Is Pregnant*, 1978). In the 1950s, by contrast, even Roy's own *Alexandre Chenevert* will still strain to meet the challenge of urban realism. Not coincidentally, I think, Roy set the pivotal chapters of the later book in a rural setting far more hospitable to her protagonist than the countryside briefly evoked in *Bonheur d'occasion*. The outcome of the struggle to write what would be her second and last Montreal novel was the conviction that her vision could be authentically realized only by setting future stories in places less completely defined by the temptations of desire than the modern city. Of course, *Mathieu* had no immediate successors either; and it cannot be said that *Earth and High Heaven* or even *Two Solitudes* established an enabling literary paradigm with and against which subsequent writers could define their project. As we shall see, it is as if the novelists of the early 1950s, English or French, still had to self-start.

Yet I would argue that, in one aspect, *Bonheur d'occasion*'s wariness about a thoroughgoing social realism finds an echo in the novels we will examine in the next chapter, one whose reverberations in turn allow us to better sound the depths of Roy's work. This concern appears most explicitly in the passage just before the one in which Florentine and Rose-Anna face each other in enmity. Florentine has just arrived home seeking the reassurance of familiar surroundings, only to discover the flat crowded with the incoming tenants: her parents had not found a new home in time. Florentine's immediate reaction to this spectacle, which in another moment of clarity lays bare the extent of the family's distress, is to call it *inimaginable* (translated as "It can't be," 270). This kind of hyperbole is common in everyday speech, but Roy's word choice here seems to me significant. What is all too vividly real not only could not have been imagined by Florentine, in the sense that it is something she would never have wanted to envisage. It is a reality that resists the character's, and perhaps even the narrator's, imaginative effort to comprehend it here and now. In other words, what we have here is another anti-literary moment, though one very different from the unliterary tenderness associated with Rose-Anna's disruption of the author's initial project.

Florentine finds the spectacle of disorder unimaginable because up to this point she has always been able to assume that, however hostile the outside world may be, she will still find a stable space of tenderness at home not unlike the one from which Emmanuel tears himself away in order to seek out the woman he desires. Now, for the first time, Florentine faces the prospect that the tenderness she seeks is not to be had. "For the first time in her life, she saw Rose-Anna in a dusty dress and with disheveled hair. The dejection of this woman who had kept her courage through all their misfortunes seemed to her a sure sign of the family's breakdown [*effondrement*], and her own in particular" (260; translation modified). It is probably a similar experience of *effondrement*, or psychic breakdown, that makes Rose-Anna scream when she sees Azarius in uniform. The question this scene raises for Florentine, as later for Rose-Anna, is not how desire can be negotiated or temptation handled, but how the complete disintegration of the desiring subject can be averted. Florentine's world does not collapse because, as we have seen, she transforms her distress into revolt. I argued earlier that the resulting experience of enmity opened up a clarifying perspective on the future the novel did not develop, but this expectation may have been misplaced if, as the scene I have just described suggests, the primary function of aggressive self-assertion is to fend off an *effondrement* that becomes "imaginable" only in the desperate effort to distance oneself from it.[22]

By sustaining that effort over the long period of the novel's gestation, Roy was able to bring her book to completion and give it the deep inner resonance that mysteriously belies the novel's surface conventionality. At the same time, Roy ends up in a difficult position in relation to the constructive intention of her project. She wants to believe in a tenderness that transcends or defuses enmity, but can the "unliterary" tenderness she embraces, even if with some ambivalence, as I have tried to show, do more than ward off the threat of breakdown? Roy's determination to protect her characters from the anguish of inner conflict works against her intention to compose a novel that could effectively mediate the unwelcome reality of such conflicts. That worry in turn leads to further defensive gestures, to the point where even the idea of collapse cannot, within the world of the narrative, be contemplated too directly. In the end, Roy's reluctance to entertain a conflictual vision of the world, which limits the scope of her realism, stems not only from an idealistic yearning for an unliterary transcendence; its ultimate source is an anxiety about breakdown so pervasive as to require any exercise of the imagination, literary or unliterary, to be kept carefully in check.

If this problem were peculiar to the Gabrielle Roy of *Bonheur d'occasion*, I don't think her novel would have the enduring popularity it still enjoys in today's Montreal. What the more self-conscious Montreal novelists of the early 1950s – especially the self-consciousness of Roy and MacLennan about what they did or didn't do in their own earlier work – will make clear is that the anxiety about breakdown displayed in her novel was not just an individual and psychological problem. It was a defining characteristic of the carefully compartmentalized Montreal of her time, a disposition whose dynamic would become more visible in the postwar years, and whose memory still lingers in the city's collective consciousness. Roy's achievement was to have turned an inchoate intuitive experience of that anxiety into a work of art in which that experience found authentically unresolved expression.

PART TWO

Shaky Solidarities: The 1950s

Gabrielle Roy's second Montreal novel, *Alexandre Chenevert* (1954), disappointed the many readers who hoped for another *Bonheur d'occasion*.[1] The title character, an anxious and irascible bank teller, had none of the *élan* that in different forms drove Jean, Emmanuel, or Azarius, while Alexandre's long-suffering wife, Eugénie, was haloed by none of Rose-Anna's maternal aura. The couple's daughter has some of Florentine's grit, but Irène makes only a cameo appearance in a story largely focused on the hero's medical and metaphysical worries and then on his death from cancer. Though the narrator gathers all the minor characters around Alexandre's deathbed and assures us he will never be forgotten, there is no sense, as there was in the scene of Emmanuel's departure for the war, of a sacrifice being made for the sake of a better future. Whatever doubts coloured its hope for social transformation, *Bonheur d'occasion* certainly conveyed a sense of artistic confidence: a new cultural era was dawning, in which the Montreal novel could and would deal creatively with the realities of modern life and in so doing enable readers to imagine new urban possibilities. When they finish *Alexandre Chenevert*, by contrast, many readers find themselves sharing the author's palpable relief that the story has at last been brought to an end. That Alexandre should live on in the hearts of those who knew him may be more than a pious wish, but it is not a notion that offers much in the way of imaginative promise.

Roy was not the only writer to shift from an idealist to a more disenchanted view of artistic possibilities in the Montreal of the early 1950s. Quebec Premier Maurice Duplessis had consolidated his power with a resounding electoral victory in 1948, while in Montreal Camillien Houde, imprisoned early in the war for his anti-conscriptionist views, had been re-elected mayor in 1944 and would stay in office for ten years. The hope expressed in various ways by the novelists of the 1940s, that the end of the war would unleash new civic energies, now seemed naive, and it is remarkable how even in the later years of the new decade many writers, English as well as French, remained convinced that the existing order would long endure. We will be looking at some of the more important of their works later in this part of the book. To frame that discussion, it will be helpful in this introductory section to complement my comparison of *Alexandre Chenevert* with *Bonheur d'occasion* with a few remarks about the relationship of MacLennan's *The Watch That Ends the Night* (published in 1959 but begun several years earlier) to its predecessor which, though equally brief, will set the stage for the analysis to follow, and then to say a little about other fiction written in the intervening period.

Although *Bonheur d'occasion* has often been paired with *Two Solitudes* as symbolizing the emergence of Montreal realist fiction, the parallels between the two authors' second novels about the city have gone unremarked. Like *Alexandre Chenevert, The Watch That Ends the Night* describes a central character's long decline into terminal illness, again in contrast with the earlier novel's focus on new birth. In *Two Solitudes* the birth was that of a book, Paul's novel, not a baby as in *Bonheur d'occasion*, but the symbolic import of the event as a token of a new imaginative future was much the same. At the end of *The Watch*, Catherine Stewart lives on through her daughter Sally, just as Alexandre Chenevert is said to survive in the hearts of the people who gather around his deathbed, but, for MacLennan as for Roy, consolation comes more from memory than from hope.

This is not to deny that in fiction a character's death can have an energizing effect on the collective imagination, but for this to happen that death needs to be plausibly imagined as a sacrificial event, one in which the character is felt to represent the community as a whole in a plot resonating with tragic overtones. The hero's suicide in Anne Hébert's "Le Torrent" (1950) has this quality, as will later the death of Jean-le-Maigre in Marie-Claire Blais's *Une saison dans la vie d'Emmanuel* (*A Season in the Life of Emmanuel*, 1965). These stories, however, are allegorical fables rather than realistic fictions. André Giroux's sincere but schematic *Le Gouffre a toujours soif* (The bottomless pit, 1953), which anticipates some of the themes of *Alexandre Chenevert*, tries to find a balance between realism and allegory, but it fails to place its hero's terminal illness in a sufficiently specific and variegated social context for the attempt to succeed; its Quebec City is as schematic a landscape as the rural locales chosen by Hébert and the early Blais. In their second Montreal novels, Roy and MacLennan dramatize the tension between the two modes in a more reflective and challenging way. Their parallel and in some ways converging struggles to handle the tension between the circumstantial factors and symbolic forces determining their character's fate tells us something important about a city that for them was and yet was not the kind of community whose condition could be represented in the life of one person and whose commonalities could be disclosed by collective imaginative participation in his or her fate.

The difference between Roy's and MacLennan's second and first Montreal novels, however, goes beyond the obvious thematic contrasts between death and birth or between doubt and trust. In working through a deeper and more internal experience of negativity reflecting their experience both as individuals and as increasingly public figures,[2] both writers arrived at a new degree of literary self-consciousness. In their earlier novels, MacLennan and Roy had given literary dignity to local experience. But they had not yet fully faced the issue of how this process of ennoblement could – and should, given the temptation to idealize or schematize that experience – itself be put into perspective. They had not, in other words, tested the authenticity of their literary enterprise within the work itself. In *Two Solitudes*, for example, Paul talks about the difficulty of getting a handle on his material, but his struggle does little to dramatize MacLennan's own effort to transform his intuitions into a work of art. It is as if the author were simply carried along by the idealized projection of himself in the character he invented. Similarly, Roy's banishment of Jean from the world of *Bonheur d'occasion* meant that she could avoid confronting the artistic limits of the sympathy with which she treated the other characters of that world.[3]

Such elisions were understandable, given the precariousness of each author's budding career. Simply to give some degree of imaginative form to the world they wanted to depict was already to have overcome the considerable cultural inhibitions that hobbled their efforts. To have looked too closely at the partiality and conditioned character of their enterprise might have foreclosed the possibility of gaining even some degree of artistic perspective on their material. That these writers should now find themselves wondering about how to put their initial perspectives into perspective, so to speak, is evidence of their willingness to address the problem of artistic creation at a higher, more sophisticated level. How fully they met this new challenge may be debated, but the importance of their endeavour to imagine the city as a setting in which that challenge could be given literary articulation is, I think, unquestionable. The issue was this: Could Montreal be conceived of as a place enabling the writing subject to dramatize the process and not just the distant prospect of representing it? Could the city's distinctive way of mediating (or minimizing) relationships between and across linguistic and other divides provide resources the authors could use in reflecting on the mediating potential of their own artistic constructs? In *Bonheur d'occasion* and *Two Solitudes*, Roy and MacLennan had shown what they could do for the city. In *Alexandre Chenevert* and *The Watch That Ends the Night*, the question is what the city can do for them.

Other novels of the early 1950s can also be read as addressing problems of literary perspective on the issues they raise. A.M. Klein's *The Second Scroll* (1951), for example, displays through the radical heterogeneity of its component parts – memoirs, poems, "glosses" on other texts – an acute awareness of the difficulty, not just of telling the story of the elusive Uncle Melech, but of conveying through that story something of how the Holocaust and then the establishment of the state of Israel affected a Jew of the Montreal diaspora. Klein's immersion in a long tradition of linguistic doubleness (Yiddish alongside Hebrew), expanded by his appreciation for the complex co-existence of French and English in Montreal, prevented his protagonist from embracing that fusion of personal consciousness and public cause we find projected by MacLennan's Paul or Roy's Emmanuel. Despite the fervour of his Zionism, Klein could not abandon the diasporic identity whose legitimacy was now challenged by those who declared that the new state of Israel was a Jew's only real home. In *The Second Scroll*, it seems at first as though the Uncle Melech the hero yearns to meet will help mediate that conflict, yet in the end Melech eludes his nephew's grasp. He remains a legendary figure whose reality cannot be defined and whose mediating power cannot be counted on. The result was a kind of psycho-literary impasse that anticipates Klein's eventual collapse into total silence a few years later, *The Second Scroll* having failed to win its author the fame he hoped for.

On the francophone side, Robert Élie's *La Fin des songes* (*Farewell My Dreams*, 1951), with its juxtaposition of third-person narrative and first-person diary entries, recalls the form Loranger gave to *Mathieu*. The key difference is that Marcel, the diarist, has no sympathetic listeners to help him get outside himself, only a double, his brother-in-law Bernard. Élie's book includes some poignant passages about Marcel's ambivalent attachment to his hometown, but not seeing any prospect of resolving that ambivalence, or turning it to productive use, Marcel carries out the suicide Mathieu only contemplates. Worse, because he is haunted by his own ghosts, Bernard's determination to find in Marcel's self-destructive act a spur to greater social involvement is less than convincing, either on the level of the tale or on that of its telling. For all its generic heterogeneity, *La Fin des songes* is essentially a monody, just as the unattainability of the "fabled city" evoked in Klein's poem "Autobiographical," the first and most artistically eloquent gloss on the narrative of *The Second Scroll*, is implicit in the poet's eloquence fading into one "sobbed Oriental note" (65).

The English-language Montreal fictions of the early 1950s that found their city setting most congenial for reflection on its representation were novels far less ambitious than Klein's. They are hard-boiled detective stories such David Montrose's *The Body on Mount Royal* (1953) or Douglas Sanderson's *Blondes Are My Trouble* (1954). These writers traded on Montreal's postwar reputation across North America as a city of easy morals, where corruption came with an exotic French accent. As often in such works, the private-eye protagonist speaks about the difficulty of uncovering the city's secrets while displaying his mastery of its unwritten rules. While conventional in form and limited in scope, detective fiction was a congenial genre for offering a certain amount of meta-commentary about what could or could not be known about Montreal's urban life.

The situation will begin to change with the splash made by Mordecai Richler's rebellious *Son of a Smaller Hero* (1955), and with the more discreet appearance of those early stories in which Mavis Gallant offered a more oblique and stylistically innovative approach to writing about Montreal.[4] These authors belong to the generation after Klein's, and both found it necessary to write about home from the distance of Europe. Among the significant francophone fictions of the same period, the "existential" novels of André Langevin offer what can be seen as more sophisticated, or at least more intellectual, versions of the English-language hard-boiled novel, though relayed through the work of Sartre and Camus, both admirers of that genre. In Langevin's most successful book, *Poussière sur la ville* (*Dust over the City*, 1953), the fictional mining town of Macklin, with its characterless buildings dwarfed by the inhuman features of the surrounding wilderness and its sharply stratified population united only in the myopia of their perceptions, provides a plausible and effective context for a "modern" self-conscious exploration of the powers and limitations of literary representation. On the other hand, the stark, quasi-allegorical nature of the setting belies the gritty detail of its narrative surface. Despite its title, *Poussière sur la ville* is a single-dimension fable like Hébert's "Le Torrent" rather than a work of differentiated realism.

The few explicitly urban francophone fictions of the early years of the decade tended to give the realism of *Bonheur d'occasion* a more conventional, documentary turn, while at the same time projecting a rather artificial sophistication. Roger Viau's *Au milieu la montagne* and Charles Hamel's *Solitude de la chair* (Solitude of the flesh, both 1951) exemplify this split in different ways. The authors offer a number of intriguing sociological observations. For example, both novels refer to queer sexuality as an accepted fact of life, one that does not call for any special comment or judgment. Yet, on closer inspection, this worldliness is only notional; it is not informed by any real acknowledgment of the diversity of desires, or even of the consciousness-shaping effect of desire as such.[5] When in a landmark study André Belleau examined the way the city's literary life was represented in novels of this period (including Hamel's), he was struck by the contradiction between the substantial infrastructure of publishers and critics the Montreal of those fictions is said to have and the cultural underdevelopment of the real city at that time, a contradiction the novels refuse to acknowledge.[6] There is a similarly awkward disparity between the veneer of sexual and social sophistication of Viau and Hamel's narratives and their disconcerting vagueness about phenomena they do little more than name. In this respect, "literary" novels like theirs differ only superficially from the ostentatious frankness of anglophone detective stories. For, in works such as David Sanderson's *Hot Freeze* (1954), the private eye's seen-it-all attitude to deviant sexuality, far from reflecting a genuine worldly tolerance, is merely a form of prurience masking an underlying moralism as simplistic in its views as the earnest goodwill displayed in the more literary francophone fictions.

The spiritual anxieties of the existential francophone novels of the early 1950s and the anglophone crime novel's hard-nosed focus on the facts of life converge in more creative fashion in what is surely the most significant Montreal novel, English or French, of the early part of the decade: Morley Callaghan's *The Loved and the Lost* (1951). With neither prurience nor moralism, Callaghan tells a story of how a white woman thought to be sexually fascinated with black men is first ostracized then murdered. Nor is race the only theme addressed in a novel full of shrewd observations about the city. Callaghan's anglophone characters move about the city with ease, but theirs is only "the small part of [Montreal] that was not French" (5), and we are reminded in subtle ways of this limitation throughout the book. Callaghan's lean style has some of the efficiency and brittle sophistication of the anglophone detective writers, yet this explicitly Catholic author also explores the recesses of moral conscience in a manner that recalls his French-language contemporaries and co-religionists.[7]

The Loved and the Lost, unfortunately, has been largely neglected in accounts of Montreal fiction. For most Quebec critics, English as well as French, local residency or a Quebec identification seems to be a prerequisite for inclusion in their literary histories, and Callaghan was essentially a Toronto writer.[8] However, after years of remarkable productivity during which he had written in quick succession a number of books and short stories set in and around that city, Callaghan found himself on the eve of the Second World War afflicted by a writer's block that lasted almost ten years. When he recovered, he decided to set his first new adult novel not in Toronto but in Montreal.[9] This is surely a gesture worth pondering, and not only for its significance as a turning-point in Callaghan's career. It seems to me that Callaghan was energized by a perception of the city that was not his alone but that, because of his outsider status, he was the first to articulate in novelistic form. Perhaps even more important, given his earlier experience of writing about another city (including the practical necessity of ensuring that nothing in the Toronto setting would affect its immediate "readability" to an American audience), he was well positioned to put that articulation into literary perspective within the new book. Worthy of study for its own sake, Callaghan's handling of this twofold process also invites us to approach some of the key Montreal novels that followed it, including *The Watch That Ends the Night* and *Alexandre Chenevert*, with this "new" predecessor in mind. That is to say, if until now the appearance of *The Loved and the Lost* has not been treated as a "moment" in the history of the Montreal novel, it is a moment whose time may have come, now that this history is being rewritten from a more inclusive point of view. Callaghan's project, I will argue, can help us account for aspects of MacLennan's and Roy's vision that hitherto have been slighted or ignored, and to arrive at a better assessment of their achievements and limitations. These three novels will be the focus of chapter 4, centred on the dramatization of what I call "witnessing" as a means of providing a critical perspective on the city that is also a critical reflection on the literary enterprise itself. In chapers 5 and 6, I go on to show how the writers of the late 1950s found other ways to mediate between these two forms of critical perspective. In chapter 5, I examine the use of satirical norms and devices by a trio of anglophone writers: William Weintraub, Brian Moore, and Mordecai Richler. In chapter 6, I show how two francophone novelists reflected on the heuristic value of their work in relation to other interpretive discourses: philology for Gérard Bessette, political ideology for Pierre Gélinas.

4

Witnesses to Weakness

Compassion and Civic Consensus in Fictions of the 1950s

Morley Callaghan's decision to set his first postwar novel in Montreal marked an important change in his approach to writing about city life. The Toronto of his 1930s novels had largely been scrubbed of its identifying features, and the city itself was never named. By contrast, the Montreal setting of the new book is explicitly identified on *The Loved and the Lost*'s first page, and some of the distinctive features of that setting become crucial elements in the story. The drama of *Such Is My Beloved* (1934), for example, could have unfolded in almost any large North American city; the events of *The Loved and the Lost* could have occurred only in Montreal. Even more important for my purposes here, *The Loved and the Lost* anticipates *Alexandre Chenevert* and *The Watch That Ends the Night* in two important ways. First, the long-foreshadowed death of one of its central characters reflects, and in turn illuminates, the fragility of the city's life force. Second, like Roy and MacLennan after him, Callaghan seeks in *The Loved and the Lost* to gain a new perspective on his own creative work, a more reflective understanding of what he could and could not do in providing his public with an updated version of the urban morality tale that had made him famous.

Because the basic plot structure of *The Loved and the Lost* so closely resembles that found in *Such Is My Beloved*, one of the best of Callaghan's prewar books, I will look briefly at the equally important differences between the two novels to illustrate the nature of the change. I will then use *The Loved and The Lost* as a reference point from which to map in a preliminary way the uneasy relationship to the city in *Alexandre Chenevert* and *The Watch That Ends the Night*. For, in addition to their focus on a morally significant, potentially redemptive death, Roy and MacLennan's 1950s Montreal novels share two other key features, one thematic, one structural, with the Callaghan work that preceded them.[1]

The common theme is that of helplessness. The doomed protagonists cannot avoid their fate and the people close to them cannot avert it. The characters are also unable to overcome racial intolerance and sexual violence, as well as the more elusive evils of loneliness and anxiety, in the city at large. For Bouchard, the police detective in *The Loved and the Lost*, these things are just as much part of what he calls the "human condition" as death itself (268). One would expect Bouchard, who prides himself on his familiarity with modern writers such as André Gide (263), to distinguish between the constitutive features of this condition and the contingent products of historical circumstance, between those things that can be changed and those that can't, and to act in consequence. Yet neither he nor any of the other leading characters in Callaghan's novel feels called upon to make such distinctions, and still less to act on them, least insofar as the tenor of Montreal life is concerned. The same will be true in *Alexandre Chenevert* and *The Watch That Ends the Night*, although with complications we shall examine in due course.

Callaghan, to speak for the moment only of him, mocks the complacency of Montreal's Anglo elite, deplores class inequalities, and exposes the tacit segregation of the city's "races" (both in the old sense used in *Two Solitudes* and in the modern one that highlights colour differences), but it is not at all clear that he expects his critique to have any practical effect. Not only does Montreal seem to be a city impervious to change, it may be that nothing *should* be changed. Despite its faults, the city of the early postwar years (the story is set just after Jackie Robinson's successful 1946 season with the Royals baseball team) is a place where minority populations feel more comfortable than they would elsewhere, and so they don't want to see the boat rocked. The main black character in *The Loved and the Lost* says so explicitly. His sentiments are echoed by George Stewart in *The Watch That Ends the Night*, and even Roy's humble bank clerk Alexandre Chenevert, acutely aware of how much worse things are elsewhere in the world, would probably concur. Generous spirits, French or English, may well find Montreal too compartmentalized for their taste, socially, morally, or otherwise, but their dissatisfaction tends to modulate into a lament about the limitations inherent in the human condition as such.

The dramatization of helplessness in these novels is not, however, intended only to justify a reluctant acceptance of things as they are. It also serves to test the imaginative limits of the authors' literary enterprise. The question of what can be changed in society is inextricable from questions about art's power to model the possibility of change. In fiction, expressions of social pessimism may signal a failure of literary confidence, but in some of the best modern writing they are signs of aesthetic energy, of an energized willingness to face the worst and not let it overwhelm one's capacity to comprehend it. To what degree such energy is present here, and to what extent the authors' artistic energy succeeds in putting helplessness into an ultimately helpful perspective, are matters of debate. The second, structural feature these novels share suggests, at least, the writers' determination to face these issues.

This feature is a narrative device: the actions of one protagonist are mediated to us largely through a second, observing consciousness. In Callaghan and MacLennan, this consciousness is embodied in another protagonist within the story; in Roy, its presence is dramatized through the voice of a narrator who, though ostensibly external to the story world, is so identified with the feel of that world as to become an emotional participant in it. The technique itself is hardly new – one need only think of *The Great Gatsby*, written by Callaghan's Paris acquaintance F. Scott Fitzgerald – but these Montreal works give a distinctive twist to the relationship between the two characters or voices.

Unlike Jean and Emmanuel in *Bonheur d'occasion*, or Paul and his half-brother Marius in *Two Solitudes*, or any number of other fictional pairings, the twinned characters in the novels of the early 1950s do not represent alternative understandings of the same social circumstances. Nor do they pursue complementary quests, like those of Erica and Marc in *Earth and High Heaven*, or Mathieu and Danielle in *Mathieu*, converging on the same goal from different directions. While they are given contrasting temperaments – one being more socially assertive, the other more retiring and reflective – the difference between these figures is one of degree rather than kind. One protagonist provides a perspective on the other, but not from a radically different position. Nor is the distinction one between involvement and detachment. That is to say, the "observing" character is not just a spectator, while in certain key respects the "observed" character is as much an observer as a fully engaged actor. The doubling of the characters explores the tension between action and reflection, but it does so, in the first instance, by giving two versions of that tension rather than by undertaking directly to resolve it. Neither consciousness is detached enough from the scene of action to discern its limitations clearly, yet neither is so wholly absorbed as to be blind to those limitations. Having one protagonist's struggle echo the other's enables the author to portray the relationship between reflection and action from different points of view. It also carries the risk of collapsing dialectic into duplication, and of ending up with characters who mirror rather than cast new light on each other. Before looking at the individual novels in detail, it will be helpful to map the relative positions of the protagonists across the three books and to say something more about the analogy I have drawn between them.

The Loved and the Lost is told in the third person by an external narrator, but the narration hews closely to the perceptions of Jim McAlpine, a young Toronto history professor. He has come to Montreal at the invitation of Joseph Carver, an influential newspaper publisher looking for an opinion columnist. Jim appears initially to be a familiar kind of novelistic hero, a man torn between his ambition to scale the social heights (he is not called McAlpine for nothing) and his instinctive identification with all those who, like himself, know what it is to have their livelihood, indeed their whole sense of worth, depend on what other people think of them. As befits the hero of such a tale, he immediately attracts the attention of Carver's daughter Catherine, and if Jim hesitates to act on his own attraction, she respects him for his scruples about using her as a stepping-stone to success.

Yet it quickly becomes clear that Jim has other reasons to procrastinate. While Carver keeps him on a string to test his nerve (and his subservience, too), Jim is introduced to a woman who works in the same advertising firm as his friend Chuck Foley. Like Jim, Peggy Sanderson has come to Montreal from a modest Ontario background. She has already found a job in the media and she, too, becomes a focus of desire in her new situation. The difference is that she shows little interest in getting ahead, professionally or personally. She spends most of her free time in Montreal's black neighbourhood, befriending its people and hanging out in its nightclubs. So intense is this pretty young white woman's interest in this world, and so clear is her indifference to Chuck Foley and his crowd, that she is assumed by them to be sexually enthralled by black men. The swirl of desire, resentment, and racism around Peggy becomes the real focus of the story.

Despite himself, Jim becomes obsessed with Peggy, but though he wants her to prefer him to any other man, black or white, he hesitates just as much to commit himself to her as to Catherine. In pursuing a notorious woman like Peggy, he runs a more serious risk of losing his reputation for integrity than he would by marrying the boss's daughter. Moreover, Jim wonders what Peggy's motivations are. Over the course of the novel, what Jim thinks of Peggy becomes just as pressing an issue as what those further up the social ladder think of him. In both cases, however, what precipitates the crisis is not that Jim acts without thinking but that, as Callaghan put it in a later interview, he thought when he should have acted.[2] Jim cannot take Peggy's goodness on trust, and it is this failure of faith, more than anything he actually does, including his slighting of Catherine, that condemns him irrevocably in the Carvers' eyes. Yet Peggy herself is also more a spectator than an actor. Beyond hanging out in clubs and bars, she doesn't seem to do much of anything except provoke reactions in other people by the mere fact of her presence. We never see her engaging with black people in anything more than passing fashion. Other characters criticize her for not thinking enough about how her actions appear to others, but her rashness consists precisely in the deliberateness with which she focuses on serving as a witness to the actions of others. Like Jim, she gets into trouble primarily because of what she doesn't do. It becomes clear that, more than her suspected promiscuity, her air of impervious self-possession is what makes other people mad. Like Jim, Peggy fails to clarify by her actions what she really thinks. Both are punished for it, Peggy more than Jim, since as a woman her lack of transparency, or better, openness to inspection and judgment by others, is a violation of social codes as well as of moral norms.

The Watch That Ends the Night is told in the first person by George Stewart, the son of an impoverished branch of an old Montreal family who in middle age has attained modest success as a radio commentator and a part-time university teacher of history. His profile is thus much like that of Callaghan's Jim: a partial outsider whose claim to status is based on a talent for communication. The novel's active protagonist is Jerome Martell, another outsider, an orphan from a Maritime lumber camp, whom the young George got to know in the 1930s after Jerome's reputation as a surgeon earned him a position at a Montreal hospital. Like Peggy, the Jerome of the Depression years had reached out to the poor, but instead of remaining in the city he left to fight fascism in Spain. At the moment the story begins (the winter of 1951), Jerome, who had gone missing sometime before the Second World War and had been declared dead, has unexpectedly returned to Montreal. George and Jerome are linked through their love for the same woman, the daughter of a Montreal family more prominent than George's. Like Callaghan's character from that same class, she is called Catherine, but she is less fortunate in that she suffers from a congenitally weak heart. When George was young, he had neither the money nor the nerve to defy family opposition to his marrying Catherine, and later he watched from the sidelines as Jerome claimed Catherine for himself and ignored the experts who said she should never try to have a child. George's jealousy did not prevent him, however, from admiring Jerome's vitality and his social commitment, or his success in giving Catherine a new lease on life. When it seemed that Jerome was dead, George became Catherine's second husband, serving as her caretaker as her heart gradually does begin to give out. Jerome's dramatic return after surviving torture by both Nazis and Communists now threatens both his personal happiness and his political complacency.

The threat does not materialize. Jerome makes no attempt to reclaim the wife he abandoned. Nor can his medical talent save her from death. He can only join George in watching helplessly as Catherine slowly dies. Less dramatically charged but no less significant is Jerome's decision not to confront Montreal's Anglo-Scottish medical establishment, even though he finds it just as hidebound after the war as it was before. Given the traumas he has endured, his diffidence is understandable, but Jerome's subsequent departure for the Canadian west reminds us that even in his prime he had focused his activism on the world beyond Montreal, and that he had never taken his defiance of the city's power structure very far. He had mocked the absurdity of Montreal's Anglo elite much as MacLennan's narrator had done in *Two Solitudes*, but other than founding a free clinic he had taken little concrete action. Ironically, the mild-mannered George is now more politically engaged than Jerome, though significantly as a commentator rather than an actor. It is also interesting that his field is foreign affairs, not local matters: in this respect George unwittingly mirrors Jerome.

We find a similar displacement of intellectual energy away from the local urban context in the presentation of *Alexandre Chenevert*'s title character. The story begins in 1947, with Alexandre avidly following world politics: admiring Gandhi, worrying about the rights and wrongs of the conflict in Palestine, and wondering if the Russians are good or bad. Alexandre's daily life, however, is one of anxious absorption with his job as a bank teller, so much so that except for the billboards he sees during his commute –another example of the key role played by the media in all three books – Alexandre hardly engages with the city around him. Despite his expansive humanist sympathies, he cannot help exploding in resentment when anyone near him demands his attention. This could easily have made him a figure of fun, but provoking laughter is not really Roy's intention (nor is it her literary forte). Instead of having his actions, or inactions, witnessed by another character, with a few episodic exceptions Roy makes Alexandre the observer of himself. His own anxious self-consciousness pre-empts the role that might have been assigned to a second protagonist. In the imaginative worlds of MacLennan and Callaghan's novels, the distinction between observer and observed, between spectator and actor, may be narrowed, but Roy's world seems to collapse it entirely.

A closer look at the narrative of *Alexandre Chenevert*, however, shows that it does include a second, observing consciousness: that of the narrator. Alexandre's story is told by an external third-person speaker, but one who emotionally is as close to Alexandre as George, the first-person narrator of *The Watch That Ends the Night*, is to Jerome. It is through the relationship between this personalized narrator and a hero whose anxieties mirror, or are mirrored by (it is sometimes hard to tell), those of the narrator that Roy will seek to put her fictional enterprise into perspective. The narrator of *Bonheur d'occasion* was, of course, sympathetically close to the characters, but in that novel the narrator's involvement in the story world was counterbalanced by the determination of that organizing consciousness to give coherent shape to the various lines of the plot. In other words, the consciousness that identified with the characters also firmly – and quite visibly, through the careful sequencing of the chapters – controlled the arc of their stories in order to give the narrative its overall artistic cohesion. While the intention is nominally the same in *Alexandre Chenevert*, the laboriousness of the novel's construction suggests an author uncomfortable with her task – perhaps because, as the writer of

Bonheur d'occasion, she cannot pretend it is not a "literary" one.[3] The narrator still represents the writer,[4] but not in the masterful and sometimes necessarily ruthless handling of narrative economy. Rather, what links them is the constant struggle with a story in whose awkward unfolding she is caught up. Alexandre's death does put a decisive end to a story we feel could easily have dragged on longer (and apparently in earlier drafts did so), but that event cuts the string rather than unties the knot.

The novel's frequent recourse to the rhetorical question is symptomatic in this regard. In contrast to other ways of reporting the character's thoughts, such questions simply echo the character's perplexities (cf. 43, 44, 49, etc.). An early example is especially suggestive: "Truly, without the war, what would Alexandre have known of the great, groaning world, resplendent and more thinly populated than most people said?" (5). The question does not tell us something we haven't already guessed about the hero's outlook. It merely underscores the narrator's identification with the character's point of view, even as it unwittingly highlights the fact that what Alexandre knows of the world derives from the imagination that conceived him.

The important differences between Roy's two-protagonist narrative and that of the other books should not, of course, be ignored, just as we should not overlook the differences of class between Roy's French Montreal characters and Callaghan's and MacLennan's English ones. Still, I think it worthwhile to begin with what the three novels have in common. The similarities in the way they articulate the perennial artistic tension between engagement and detachment reflect something about the broader historical context they share, and to which they speak. This becomes clear as we see the commonalities in the ways they give that tension self-conscious literary form through their adoption of the double-protagonist structure. In these narratives, one character or consciousness serves as witness, not so much to the actions of another, but to that other's own witnessing.

The kind of witnessing I am talking about here goes beyond mere spectatorship. It is a self-involving form of observation, a presence to and for another. That is to say, it is a form of moral engagement. Witnessing of this sort is surely one of the things literature is called to illustrate, but it may say something about the possibilities for literary witness in the Montreal of the early 1950s that in the three novels we are considering the observed protagonist is just as much confined to a witnessing role in the civic drama as the ostensible observer. The sense of responsibility that drives Peggy, Jerome, and Alexandre to wish for a better world and to seek signs of promise in the city around them far exceeds the scope of the actions they undertake to fulfill that promise. The doubling of the witness allows this discrepancy to be registered and addressed. This happens first, at least in a limited way, within the story world; then, more comprehensively, through the ways the narrative dramatizes the difficulty of mediating between reflection and action in its portrayal of that world.

The artistic potential of the procedure is considerable, but finding the right degree of distance between the two witnesses or their modes of witnessing is a delicate matter. If the gap is too great, the novel risks becoming too abstract and moralistic in its judgments. If it is too narrow, if one witness simply mirrors the situation of the other, then the doubling may fail to open the new perspectives the novel seeks. Perhaps the reason these early 1950s Montreal novels have not generally been seen to be culturally transformative to the same degree as the authors' earlier works is that, despite their literary sophistication, they did not avoid the second of these traps. Yet, even if the novels fell short of their authors' ambitions, their projects are worthy of attention in that they fall short within the realm of the literary rather than in the sense of falling short of being literary at all.

THE LOVED AND THE LOST

The outline of Peggy's story in *The Loved and the Lost* so closely tracks that of Stephen Dowling in *Such Is My Beloved* (1934), perhaps the best of Callaghan's prewar, Toronto novels, that a brief comparison will show what changes of emphasis the shift of setting to Montreal brought in its train. Dowling is a Catholic priest who becomes involved with two prostitutes in an unnamed North American city hit by the Depression. He spends so much time with Ronnie and Midge, trying to find them respectable jobs but mostly offering them sympathetic company, that everyone in the church suspects his zeal is really sexual attraction. So do Ronnie and Midge, and even when they come to recognize his good intentions, they resent him for scaring away their customers and bringing them unwanted attention by the police. Misunderstood and rejected,

Dowling loses his sanity and is consigned to a mental institution. There, he finds solace in composing a commentary on the *Song of Songs*, the most erotically charged book of the Bible.

While with this parting gesture Callaghan mocks the church's long history of insisting that the eroticism of the *Song of Songs* was only allegorical, *Such Is My Beloved* is a bit too allegorical itself to be a satisfactory novel. The problem, though, is less Callaghan's treatment of sexuality as such than his depiction of the setting in which the characters' desires are played out. He avoids giving any of Toronto's topographical features its proper name, and he provides only minimal detail about the characters' personal backgrounds. This vagueness has long been deplored by Canadian critics, especially in the early years of Canadian literary nationalism.[5] In the author's defence, one could argue that to appreciate what is at stake in the story we don't really need more contextual details than we are given. That two working-class women of the 1930s should have turned to prostitution does not require "local" explanation; nor does a priest's decision to minister to them as redeemable sinners. However dubious his motivation, Dowling has clear Christian justification for his outreach. Similarly, forcing the prostitutes to leave town may not be something a judge can legally do in every jurisdiction, but it falls within the range of what we think judges might do in some places. And so, while more psycho-social detail about the local culture might be desirable, it is not needed for Callaghan's Canadian, American, or even European readers to be satisfied with the plot's basic plausibility. The only exception to Callaghan's bare-bones treatment of his setting, interestingly, is the apparently gratuitous detail he provides about one of the two prostitutes. All we learn about Ronnie is that she comes from Detroit, but Midge is more specifically identified as the child of a francophone Montreal family, and we are given her real and full name: Catherine Bourassa. We are thus invited to wonder more about her background than we do about the other characters, who are nothing more than they appear to be.

What was exceptional in *Such Is My Beloved* becomes the rule in *The Loved and the Lost*. Like Dowling, Peggy Sanderson befriends members of an outcast social group with an intensity that disturbs her colleagues and her employers. She, too, is a loner, driven by social conscience but also by erotic fascination. The black men she meets respond warily, questioning her motives and complaining of the trouble her sympathy brings them.

Like Dowling, Peggy becomes disillusioned and fatalistic, but her transgressive behaviour is punished more severely: instead of being driven mad, she is murdered. The greater hostility she encounters may partly be explained by the fact that, unlike Father Dowling, Peggy has no social warrant for hanging around a black neighbourhood. As Wagstaffe, a black nightclub owner points out, she is not a missionary, a social worker, or a political militant. Wagstaffe has seen all these types of women. He has also learned to recognize the kind of bourgeois white girl who simply likes to go slumming. But Peggy baffles him (104). What does she want? Nothing, it seems, except to be present to and with black people, without discrimination. It is other people's inability to understand why anyone would want to do this, and thus to "place" Peggy using their usual moral categories, that makes them angry and eventually condemns Peggy to a fate more violent than Dowling's. On one level, therefore, Peggy's murder by an unknown assailant (most likely a sexually enraged white man, but the novel leaves the question unanswered) is less improbable than Dowling's mental breakdown. On another, the violence of the dénouement disrupts the ordered world of the story in a way Dowling's peaceful exit does not. For all these reasons, we expect the author to contextualize the events of this narrative to a much greater degree than he did in the earlier one. Alluding to allegorical archetypes is not enough, and it is no doubt in implicit acknowledgment of this problem that, unlike *Such Is My Beloved* (and other early Callaghan novels such as *They Shall Inherit the Earth* or *More Joy in Heaven*), *The Loved and the Lost* is given a title that sounds like a phrase from Scripture but is not actually biblical.[6]

Callaghan does provide some context for understanding Peggy's behaviour, but curiously he does so only in an early episode about her life before she arrived in Montreal, not in the chapters set in that city. Peggy's father, a Methodist minister worried about what his white congregation might think, forced her to break off her childhood friendship with the one black family in their small Ontario town. Peggy's involvement with the black community as an adult stems, it is suggested, from a mixture of gratitude to that family and guilt for abandoning them, but also from the erotic after-effect of seeing the teenage son of that family emerge nude one day from a swim in the lake. The lasting impact of these early experiences is hard to measure, however, since the narrator does not say anything about Peggy's private thoughts after she arrives in Montreal. Nor are we shown in any detail just how she interacts with individual members of the black community. She has a brief friendly conversation with a black woman, for example (62), but what they say to each other is not reported, and one suspects that the only purpose of the episode is to show that Peggy is not interested only in black men. What she actually wants remains unclear. That people (and not just white men) jump to unwarranted conclusions about what she must be after is surely meant to caution us against doing the same. Yet the fact that she returns repeatedly to the club yet never talks about the music suggests she *is* looking for something else, though, since we don't see Peggy doing more than sitting and listening, it is difficult for the reader to imagine what that is. Peggy refuses to explain or justify herself to Jim, on the grounds that any man who claims to care for her should take her integrity on trust. What he believes *about* her is irrelevant; what matters is whether he believes *in* her. We can understand why Callaghan should want readers to confront the prurient aspect of their curiosity, as well as their own lack of trust in the tale even when we think the teller fails us. Still, the author's decision to withhold any information, not just about what Peggy does but also what she herself is thinking, in a narrative told from an external third-person viewpoint seems to be artistically self-defeating.

Such, at least, was the judgment of many of the novel's early critics.[7] Perhaps the pithiest formulation of this view appears in one of the letters Hugh MacLennan wrote in 1957 to the future novelist Marian Engel, who was writing a master's thesis on the Canadian novel under his direction. According to MacLennan, "Morley has failed to understand the true moral situation posed by his book. Whether or not he knew that the girl who was Peggy's model was a psycho-neurotic, I don't know, nor does it matter. The NOVEL ITSELF DOES NOT KNOW THIS VERY IMPORTANT FACT. If she is a psycho-neurotic, then the moral emphasis is wrong. If she is not, then she is not credible."[8] For MacLennan, as for other Canadian commentators of the day, Peggy's behaviour is explicable only in terms of a desire distorted either by mental instability or by the author's substituting a fantasy construct for a realistic female character. The contrast with the reaction to *Earth and High Heaven* and *Mathieu* is striking. Like her forebears, Peggy Sanderson is a mature and independent woman (although, of course, in this 1951 novel everyone refers to her as a "girl"). Yet the plausibility of her behaviour is scrutinized to a degree that Erica Drake's or Danielle Beaulieu's has never been, even though these well-brought-up young ladies were having guilt-free sex in a story set in 1940s Montreal. The demand for more precise information about Peggy was surely prompted by racial anxiety more than by scruples about realism and morality.

Still, MacLennan raises an important issue about the essential under-determination of the narrative. In asking us to take the integrity and coherence of Peggy's character on trust, the novel is really asking us to trust that the universe in which she dwells has a meaning beyond what we are given the means to perceive, at least with earthly eyes. Some of the Catholic novelists with whom Callaghan has been linked[9] might speak of the mysterious unknowability of souls and encourage us to abandon ordinary explanatory categories in seeking answers to our questions. Graham Greene's *The End of the Affair*, published the same year as *The Loved and the Lost*, a novel that also features a heroine whose motives the hero (not coincidentally, a successful worldly novelist) cannot grasp, offers a good example of this attitude. Whether this kind of religious outlook is compatible with that of realist fictional narrative (as opposed, say, to romance) is a point on which critics disagree.[10] Certainly, if *The Loved and the Lost* were clearly written in Greenian mode, MacLennan would have understood the intention, even if he would not have found the result congenial. His perplexity reflects his assumption that Callaghan was attempting something different, and that the deliberate under-determination of novelistic knowledge must therefore have another rationale. But he cannot see what it might be.

MacLennan is right in claiming that Callaghan's novel does not "know" a key fact, but what he misses is that lack of knowledge is precisely the predicament of the novel's second protagonist. Unlike Greene's Maurice Bendix, Callaghan's Jim McAlpine is not just Peggy's hapless lover but a character engaged on a quest of his own. Indeed, it is Jim's story that provides the context for Peggy's, and it is through Jim that Callaghan dramatizes the problematic intersection of social perception and aesthetic cognition in the "world" projected by the novel. Because Jim does not learn from Peggy what he should think of her, and cannot divine it on his own, he must turn for clues to the people and places her presence affects. That is, to know what to think of Peggy, Jim needs to know what to think of Montreal. It may be that to really understand

Peggy, or at least to understand what and why he cannot understand, Jim needs to glimpse a higher reality, but in the first instance he has to become acquainted with what Charles Taylor would call the "social imaginary" of the city, which, though earth-bound, is also hidden from casual view.[11] The actions of individuals take their meaning, though not necessarily their ultimate moral valence, from the framing ethos of the stage on which they take place.[12]

This, of course, is a lesson taught by many modern novels, but in *The Loved and the Lost* the mode of instruction takes a peculiar form. Peggy's intention, to the limited extent that she articulates it, is simply to *be* in Montreal. Most of what she does consists simply of showing up, of being present in and to the scene she witnesses. Her one general statement about the city, which is belied by subsequent events but which she never recants, is limited to a sunny appreciation of the ways things are. "I think I've been happier here than I've ever been," she tells Jim early in the story. "It's an old city and yet it's new; and it's a seaport, and the different races get used to each other" (35). The same embrace of a perceived state of harmony characterizes her attitude at the shoe-polish factory somewhere in the city's industrial southwest, where she finds a menial job after being fired from Foley's advertising agency downtown. She tells Jim that she fits in well with her fellow workers (89–90), and there is no reason to think otherwise. Jim may worry that "Peggy the Crimper" isn't the right companion for a media intellectual on the make, but Peggy is no rabble-rouser out to make trouble. Aside from going alone to a black nightclub, we never see her do anything more socially transgressive than venturing out in public without a hat.

It has been argued that, in portraying Peggy, Callaghan was obliged to pull his punches, inhibited by moral or practical concerns from portraying Peggy as the sexually and socially liberated woman she "really" is.[13] To put the point in MacLennan's terms, the novel does not know what to think of Peggy because censorship makes her unthinkable. This argument identifies a real problem in the narrative, but it fails to locate it properly. In his short stories, Callaghan proved quite capable of dramatizing the lives of sexually non-conforming characters when he wanted to do so. The problem is that, while a transgressively mobile Peggy might have been thinkable in the Parisian setting of "Now That April's Here," or in the more generic North American locale of "The Autumn Penitent," she is not thinkable *in Montreal*.[14] Or rather, her freedom in that city is thinkable, but only in the form of an unfettered witnessing to the peculiar character of the place. For what Peggy's presence reveals by its very lack of determination is postwar Montreal's characteristic refusal to draw an explicit boundary line between what you can or cannot do, even if there are, as we shall see, implicit lines you cross at your peril. What is more, the city's famously tolerant atmosphere results from a consensus that is itself the product of tacit rather than explicit agreement. The fuzziness of Peggy's motives draws our attention to the fuzziness of the collective will. Callaghan may want to use Peggy to convey an insight into the fallen "human condition" (268), but her role is also to help Jim come to terms with the distinctive imaginary of the city in which her character moves.

Like Peggy, Jim McAlpine comes to Montreal from a small-town Ontario family of modest means, but whereas she was forced to shun the poor black family that befriended her, Jim suffered the shunning: his wealthy white neighbours looked down on him. Now, as his name suggests, he is out to climb the mountain of success. Unlike Paul Tallard or Marc Reiser, he suffers from no ethnic handicap; on the contrary, he is an excellent candidate for integration into Montreal's Anglo elite. He has a distinguished record as a naval officer in the Second World War, a doctorate in history good enough to secure an academic position at the University of Toronto, and the promise of international recognition. Carver invites him to Montreal on the strength of an article Jim has just published in the *Atlantic Monthly* on "The Independent Man." Like Graham's Charles Drake, Carver likes to pride himself on his broadness of mind, and Jim would seem to be just the kind of columnist to enhance the prestige of his *Montreal Sun*. Like Drake, Carver also has an intelligent and good-looking daughter, and Callaghan's Catherine resembles Graham's Erica in being a woman matured by experience (she is divorced) rather than a young ingénue. She and Jim seem destined to enjoy a happy future in a renewed but still comfortably familiar Montreal.

Jim's weakness, though, is that he has failed to learn the lesson of *Luke Baldwin's Vow* (1948), the young adult novella Callaghan published just before *The Loved and the Lost*. To be independent, Luke discovered, you must first have "some money on hand" so you can "protect all that was truly valuable from the practical people in the world."[15] To show Carver just how self-confident and independent he is, Jim has given up his university job and taken an expensive room at the Ritz. His boldness impresses the older man even as it enables the canny publisher to test the financial and moral limits of that independence by delaying his decision to hire him. Until he gets the job, Jim can do nothing but wait and walk around town. This is not as much a problem as it seems, however, because the job Jim seeks is one in which "action" takes the form of commenting on what other people do. It is tempting to read Jim's move from the university to the media rather than to business or government service as a sign that in the postwar world this is where one finds the widest scope for exercising real power,[16] but the truth is that Jim is more interested in the prestige of being a columnist than in what his writing might accomplish. Though Carver's paper is said to have national influence (28), none of the Montreal characters, including Carver himself, ever refer to anything published in it. All we learn about Jim's first column is how pleased he is to see his work in print. He is less fascinated by the media's power over the public than by its potential to reflect a flattering self-image.

Jim is not alone in thinking of cultural institutions primarily as the means through which to prove his agency to himself. This seems to be the general tendency of everyone in the (almost exclusively English) Montreal portrayed in the novel. Jim's old friend Chuck Foley is in advertising. Peggy's nominal boyfriend, Henry Jackson, whom she seems to have met while working with Foley, is a commercial artist (19). Wagstaffe's nightclub is supported by a white musical taste-maker named Rodgers, who delights in his image of urbane sophistication. Wagstaffe's club has a white counterpart in the bar owned by Wolgast and his partner Doyle. They pride themselves on the selectivity of the people they admit to the so-called "Earbenders Club," named for the regular customers who, though they may be judges or other worthies in real life, find their greatest gratification in getting other drinkers to listen to their stories.[17] The few francophone characters with whom these English-speakers interact are of the same ilk. Wolgast's sole French customer, Claude Gagnon, is a newspaper cartoonist (52), and even the police detective Bouchard wants Jim to see him as a sophisticated literary man familiar with the works of André Gide (263).

French or English, white or black, all these characters are united in defining their relationship to the city in ways that will shore up their self-image. What Callaghan's characters appreciate about Montreal, in contrast with other places they have known, is the city's tacit social agreement to minimize overt humiliation. Individuals and ethnic groups may not enjoy equal freedom – on the contrary, everyone acknowledges that (like everywhere else) blacks and whites, French and English, not to mention religious minorities, don't have the same scope of action – but there is one thing on which everyone can count and which is highly prized: whatever positive self-image people have managed to construct for themselves will not be openly denigrated by others as long as they don't rock the boat too hard. Provided this implicit consensus is maintained, every Montrealer can be one of Jim's "independent men," at least in his own mind. The one exception, an overweight reporter at the *Sun* forced to endure the mockery of his superiors, is brought briefly to Jim's notice only to prove the rule and to remind the newcomer that respecting the prohibition against openly insulting others is in his own interest as well.

That this social consensus involves a willed blindness to important aspects of the city's empirical reality is made clear at the very beginning of the novel, when the narrator says of Catherine that Montreal "was her town, at least the small part of it that was not French" (5). Catherine's privilege is real, but it consists as much of the freedom to ignore francophone Montreal as of the power to exercise the agency her wealth affords her. The foundations of this freedom needn't be looked at too closely, since to the extent that the city's majority francophone population comes into the novel's view, which is very little, it is portrayed as being content with the status quo. The French, too, prefer to live among themselves rather than engage with other communities in potentially conflictual ways. Early in the story, Jim and Catherine attend a cocktail party at which a society hostess welcomes French and English guests with easy cordiality. No one but Jim seems to notice the moment when "the French Canadians gradually retreated to the drawing room, where they could relax with one another, and the English-speaking Canadians moved toward the dining room and possession of the cakes and sandwiches" (127–8).[18] Jim, who is said to know Montreal and to speak French easily, and who at the party is concerned to display his independence from Carver, doesn't even think of disrupting this arrangement. On the contrary, he instinctively knows that to draw attention to it would provoke a reality check everyone would rather avoid.

After this incident, no further mention is made of the linguistic divide. With only rare exceptions, the events of the story all take place in a Montreal that can be called "English" in the sense that for practical purposes the characters don't have to take francophone opinion into account (16). This Montreal promises to become Jim's city as much as Catherine's, but as he becomes involved with Peggy, the novel discreetly but deliberately narrows his English metropolis even further to the downtown rectangle bounded by Pine and Saint-Antoine, Atwater and Bleury. Near the beginning of the story, we see Jim visiting the St James Street financial district and the *Sun* building nearby, but only at end of the story, when he is interrogated about Peggy's murder, will he again venture beyond the little world centred on Sainte-Catherine Street West. In our fascination with the novel's social and racial heterogeneity, we may overlook the smallness of the space in which Jim moves: Peggy's Crescent Street basement apartment is located almost around the corner from the Ritz, while Wagstaffe's club is within easy walking distance of both (at least, when it isn't snowing). In Montreal, however, geographical proximity – and a certain degree of that urban promiscuity MacLennan hinted at – does not preclude imaginative compartmentalization, far from it, and so Jim assumes he can keep his relationship with Peggy a secret. He takes it for granted that Catherine won't look for him except in the places she would expect to see him and into which she is accustomed to go. What Jim forgets, though, is that while compartmentalization is the basis of the city's overall ethos, "in Montreal a great many of the English were acquainted" (35), precisely because their world is so small. News of his interest in Peggy soon reaches two men who would normally keep quiet about it but who feel compelled to seek Jim out. They fear that Peggy's behaviour will force them to suffer the humiliation they have so far avoided and to inflict it in return. They believe Jim will understand their reaction because he too is at risk. Novels of social initiation often include a mentor figure whose status allows them to school the protagonist in the ways of the world while maintaining an ironic perspective on the moral limitations of that world. The Étienne Beaulieu of Loranger's *Mathieu* is one example. *The Loved and the Lost* assigns the duty of spelling out the city's rules to two characters who differ from Beaulieu and other similar mentor figures in that they are men anxious about losing the precarious status they enjoy should that consensus collapse.

In the first of two long speeches that dominate the middle chapters of the novel, the black club-owner Elton Wagstaffe tells Jim that "things weren't so bad in Montreal, and the Brooklyn ball team made no mistake when they first broke in their colored ball players with the Montreal team. It was important that they picked on Montreal. It's a town where there are a lot of minorities, but the French like the Negro ball players and give them a hand, and if a colored boy kept his head, and kept his eyes closed a little and didn't want to go to too many places he didn't get into any trouble. The eyes didn't have to be closed too tight and the Negro ball players swinging around the circuit with the team were glad to get back to Montreal" (105). Readers will recall that, before Jackie Robinson broke the colour bar in major league baseball, he was sent to Montreal in 1946 to test the waters by playing a season with the Royals of the International League. As a close friend of the prominent Montreal sports reporter Dink Carroll, Callaghan would have known all the details of the story, no doubt including the unexpected ease with which Robinson and his wife were able to rent a house in a francophone area of the city.[19]

The phrasing of Wagstaffe's account, however, is interestingly ambiguous. The "but" that immediately follows the mention of minorities could be read as distinguishing those minorities from the French majority, but the flow of the sentence seems to suggest that the French "like the Negro ball players" because they, too, know what it is to be a minority, psychologically at least, in their own city. Whatever its demographic and economic reality, the city seems to be a place where no group enjoys majority status and the imaginative dominance that goes with it. The Montreal of the text is composed of a set of minorities, or of people who consider themselves members of a vulnerable minority and whose sensibility to humiliation is minimized by a system of ad hoc arrangements. The success of these arrangements is measured primarily by the absence of "trouble" (41). Ironically, Wagstaffe's apprehension of "trouble" has nothing to do with black people violating the unspoken rule that excludes them from the city's "good hotels" and "select bars" (41), but with a white woman's presence in a club he controls. He fears that, however noble Peggy's intentions, she is a threat to his livelihood and, even more, to his pride, because of the kind of scandalous incident her witnessing presence is bound to provoke. Yet he will not ban Peggy from the club, precisely because he does not want to insult her either (111). He counts on Jim to persuade her to stay away, and if he can't, to distance himself from her. If Jim defends Peggy he will be tainted by association.

Wolgast is blunter than Wagstaffe when he tells Jim how Peggy brought one of her black acquaintances into his bar. He needs Jim to understand why he cannot allow her to do it again. As Jim "unhappily" acknowledges, Wolgast is right in predicting that, if blacks start coming to his bar on a regular basis, it will lose its "fine class of customer" (182). But this is not what bothers Wolgast most. He suspects that Peggy picked his bar to make her point because she knows he is Jewish (181). She may assume that his own experience of prejudice would make him an ally, but just the opposite is true. Like Wagstaffe, Wolgast is grateful for the relative tolerance of Montreal, which has allowed him to "get something of my own – on the legit" (180) despite his past practice of fixing boxing matches. Montreal is "a grand town," he says, a place where people don't look down at him, and he is determined not to be "belittled" by anyone, including a woman who thinks his own experience of prejudice should make him willing to put his livelihood on the line (182).

To drive home his point, Wolgast tells Jim a long story about the humiliations his family suffered in prewar Poland. Wolgast's peasant father was once ordered to sell a white horse he had come to love but which belonged to the landowner. His deathbed injunction to his son was to get a white horse of his own that no one could take away (179; an echo of the advice given in *Luke Baldwin's Vow*). Wolgast's white horse is the bar he and his partner Doyle run just as they please, and he is not about to let anyone else decide who he will or will not admit (he also refuses entry to white people he doesn't think fit the ethos of the bar). He stresses that he won't attack Peggy's friend. "The jig won't be belittling me," Wolgast says, because the black man won't be assuming he can get in. But Wolgast is ready to smash Peggy's face with a bottle for presuming he will do what she would not ask of a Gentile (182). Wolgast is confident Jim will agree with his position. Like Wagstaffe, Wolgast knows about Jim's precarious social position, and like his black counterpart he warns Jim about the humiliation he will face if he doesn't "keep his head" about Peggy: in other words, if he lets his fascination with the mystery of Peggy's character – is she otherworldly or perverse? – go too far.

Today's readers may find it curious that a novel that refers to the friendly welcome received by Jackie Robinson should not question

Wagstaffe's and Wolgast's conviction that the city's remaining racial barriers cannot be torn down. But we need to recall that, in the social imaginary of the novel, the idea of "race" is complicated by its historical use to designate national lineages. Montreal's official flag, as adopted in 1939 (only a decade before the publication of *The Loved and the Lost*, not way back in the nineteenth century), honours four peoples considered distinct enough for each to merit one of its quadrants: French, English, Scottish, and Irish, united but also kept separate by the flag's central cross.[20] The social boundaries that affect blacks and Jews thus overlay an older imaginary of ethnic and linguistic divides that still defines, not just the everyday life of the city, but the very foundations of its existence. For this reason, these boundaries cannot be subjected to explicit scrutiny without putting the city's cohesiveness at risk. So, at least, Callaghan's (anglophone) Montrealers believe. The best that can be done – and for the novel's characters, Montreal does it well – is to keep things fuzzy enough so that everyone can keep their pride as long as they don't press their claims too much. Clarity can be a bad thing.[21]

The disturbing effect of the story Callaghan tells can therefore be defined more precisely. The tacit urban consensus emerges as an object of thought only in order to discourage further thinking. For the Montrealers of the novel, being forced to think about the terms of that consensus is itself a form of humiliation, as "belittling" in its way as any actual insult, since it brings into the open inequities and compromises they would rather not face. This insight is given dramatic expression in the only episode of the book where we see the city's diverse population gathered together as one: a hockey game. Standing up in his seat in the Forum, Jim surveys the crowd: "They came from all the districts around the mountain; they came from wealthy Westmount and solid respectable Outremont and from the Jewish shops along St. Catherine, and of course a few Negroes from St. Antoine would be in the cheap seats. There they were, citizens of the second-biggest French-speaking city in the world, their faces rising row on row, French faces, American faces, Canadian faces, Jewish faces, all yelling in a grand chorus; they had found a way of sitting together, yelling together, living together, too" (187).[22] This happy consensus, however, soon turns sour. *The Loved and the Lost* anticipates a number of novels that later in the decade will also use a hockey game to dramatize a moment of collective humiliation. Callaghan's game is fictional, but Pierre Gélinas's *Les Vivants, les morts et les autres* (1959), echoing Eugène Cloutier's *Les Inutiles* (The useless ones, 1956), will dramatize a real event: the 1955 suspension, widely regarded as unfair, of Maurice Richard from the league playoffs. In different ways, these later novels show how the riot that followed transformed the long-standing but still largely inchoate political resentment of Montreal's francophone population into a more focused national consciousness. Perhaps for this reason, neither of these books says anything about black people being present in the Forum crowd or mentions the absence of the truly poor, as Callaghan's does.

The fictional game of *The Loved and the Lost*, set in the late 1940s, centres on a penalty that isn't imposed. A New York Rangers player instigates a fight, and though his culpability is obvious to the crowd, the referees somehow don't see it. What the fans protest is not punishment but impunity. But what really angers the spectators – all of them, whatever their background – is the way the scofflaw skates around the ice as if he bore no responsibility at all for the fracas. Catherine Carver, who is watching the game with Jim, is just as indignant as the French Canadian priest sitting next to them, and her reaction expresses what everyone feels. "'Look at the fake innocence,' Catherine cried" (191).[23] But why is she so vehement? Some of Catherine's anger arises from her irritation with Jim. She is aware of a recent cooling of his ardour, and this makes her suspect that his relationship with Peggy is not as innocent as he claims. Like the hockey player, Jim is pretending nothing is wrong and assuming he can get away with violating the rules of the game. Catherine's pride prevents her from challenging Jim directly, so she takes out her anger on the player. But her outburst is presented as also expressing the collective judgment of the crowd.

In recent years, it has become commonplace to claim that, whatever else may divide the citizens of Montreal, they are united in supporting their hockey team. Monique Proulx's 2015 novel *Ce qu'il reste de moi* (What remains of me, 2015), for example, puts this commonplace at the heart of her optimistic vision of Montreal's civic harmony.[24] The Montrealers of *The Loved and the Lost*, by contrast, may have learned to sit, yell, and live together, but their unanimity really consists of a set of parallel but separate susceptibilities to hurt. In contrast to later books about the 1955 Forum riot, Callaghan's novel does not see that hurt as generating a new and more dynamic collective consciousness, but on the contrary as exposing the fragility of the combination of denial and tacit agreement on which the city's peace depends. The uncomfortable truth the Montreal crowd sees reflected in the New York player is that at bottom the "innocence" they enjoy at the hockey game is just as false as that of the player they are quick to condemn.

For Jim, the crowd's reaction to the hockey player is a premonition of what will happen to Peggy. Yet, despite having glimpsed the disciplining impulse beneath the tranquil surface of the civic imaginary, Jim fails to defend Peggy from its violence. His fear of being humiliated by his association with Peggy proves to be stronger than his faith in her goodness. This faith is already under strain. A "doubt … had entered his mind" about Peggy's virtue because of the offhand manner with which she speaks about other men (233). He wonders whether her willingness finally to have sex with him is evidence of promiscuity and not proof that he is the one man she loves. Piqued at the idea he may not be as special as he thinks, but wrapping his offended pride in a mantle of virtue, he turns down her offer and leaves her apartment. Peggy is murdered that same night.

We never learn the killer's identity – most likely it is one of the jealous white men who saw Peggy at the club, though we cannot be sure – but this doesn't matter. The crime is a collective one. Jim is initially a suspect because he had visited Peggy late that night in her room, and, because he feels guilty for betraying her, he is willing to take the blame. Detective Bouchard, a confessor-figure out of Dostoyevsky, soon realizes that Jim is not the culprit, but he does not let him entirely off the hook; rather, he declares that "the human condition" is ultimately responsible for Peggy's death (268). Yet, while it may be true that jealousy and wounded pride are universal motives, the hockey-game episode makes it clear that Peggy's challenging of Montreal's social consensus was going to end in violence. Jim is tormented by guilt not only because he failed a woman he had come to love. He also failed to appreciate the implications of what Wagstaffe, Wolgast, and the hockey fans had revealed to him about a city he had boasted of knowing. Not only does Jim not defend himself when attacked by a Catherine herself humiliated by public evidence of his involvement with another woman; he welcomes his social ostracism and the loss of his newspaper job.

Jim, it seems, intends to take on the scapegoat role Peggy had unwittingly played, anticipating and accepting his expulsion from the city that earlier welcomed him. He will also deliberately shoulder the moral burden of the "belittlement" that of all things is what the city most dreads. Although he can do no more than Peggy could to bring about change, Jim can turn his witnessing presence in Montreal from that of someone observing the city's contradictions into that of a man carrying them in his suffering body. Jim, it would seem, becomes one of the testimonial hero-victims found in the novels of Callaghan's Catholic contemporaries, Graham Greene or Georges Bernanos.

The final pages of the novel, however, complicate this interpretation, for they suggest that Jim's self-abasement is only another form of grandiosity. The new Jim, eager for redemption, is as confident in the autonomous power of his mind as the old Jim who wrote about "the independent man" for the *Atlantic Monthly*. George Woodcock pointed out long ago that Jim's inability to trust Peggy recalls the story of Orpheus' failure to rescue his beloved Eurydice from the underworld.[25] If the parallel were exact, Jim, like Orpheus, would go on to turn grief into poetry, loss into lyric, and this is the direction in which he starts to go. After leaving the police station, he seeks out a beautiful little French church somewhere east of the English downtown he had visited on a walk with Peggy when their relationship had just begun. The implication is that he leaves the scene of his ambitions and delusions to seek refuge in a place where he can put what he has loved and lost into a more transcendent perspective.

The story ends, however, with Jim unable to locate the church: not only has Jim suffered loss, he is himself lost, and the reader is left to interpret the meaning of this conclusion unaided by the narrator. Jim's "lostness" may be another symbol of the "human condition," but Callaghan was insistent that his book was a novel, not a moral fable. Taking him at his word, and looking more closely at how Jim is depicted, we see that, unlike, say, the pilgrim of Dante's *Divine Comedy*, whose redemption also begins with an experience of disorientation, Jim has not left his old, controlling self behind. Instead of accepting loss, and the guilt that goes with it, he seeks out the church as part of an inchoate but egotistical "plan" to "hold on to Peggy forever"; his hope is that "in some way he would keep her with him" (272). The tone here is clearly critical, since the words echo those Callaghan used earlier to convey Jim's desire to control Peggy when she was alive. Jim's final mission is more defensive than truly redemptive.

But what about the authenticity of the novel's poetic project? The sympathetic but critical portrayal of Jim's conversion in the concluding pages of the novel can also be read as the author's reflection on his own work. Jim's failure to find the church he once glimpsed is linked to a suspicion about aesthetic perspectives that appears at various points throughout the narrative. When Jim had first proposed to Peggy that they look for the church, it was for artistic rather than spiritual reasons: he had heard the building had "very good lines" (36). They gaze at the outside of the building but do not go inside. Similarly, when Jim had sketched Catherine as he watched her being interviewed on the air about her charity work, and when he drew Peggy in her factory smock, he presented his drawings as tributes to the model who inspired them. However, the titles he gives his portraits ("Madame Radio," "Peggy the Crimper") show his artistic gaze to be a patronizing one, just as there is something complacent in the way he thinks about his newspaper column. It is therefore ironically apt that Jim's reputation is ruined by Catherine's discovery that the portrait of Peggy found in the dead woman's apartment is just like the one in her own room. Catherine might have been able to forgive Jim for loving another woman, but being twinned with Peggy as objects of undifferentiated aesthetic scrutiny is a humiliation she cannot abide.

Jim himself seems to acknowledge the perversity of putting aesthetic above or even alongside moral considerations in his interview with detective Bouchard. To gain Jim's confidence, and no doubt also to show off his cultural sophistication, Bouchard mentions Gide, a writer considered dangerously daring in the Catholic Quebec of the day. His remark about Gide's "fine style" provokes Jim to an angry response: "Oh, my God, we all have a fine style! Where am I?" (263). Bouchard's remark recalls the *bons mots* Jim himself had earlier used to impress Carver. He is exasperated mostly with himself, though he cannot help expressing his exasperation in egotistical form.

However, the question "where am I?" is more than rhetorical. There is a real problem of place in the story. A police station in which confessor-policemen quote Gide: it seems too thematically apt to be real. In praising Gide's style, we should note, Bouchard flatters Jim by assuming that his suspect has read that writer in the original French. Indeed, Jim prides himself on being fluent in that language, and what's more, on being able to "read" French Canadian people. We have already seen how Jim immediately grasped the dynamic of French and English interactions at the party he attended with Catherine. In another early scene, Jim is shown taking pride in guessing what a French Canadian priest and his sister must be like simply from watching how they step out of a taxi and enter a hotel. Now, even in his self-abasement, Jim feels he has taken Bouchard's measure. His exclamation "where am I?" may be one of disorientation, representing the first stage of his aesthetic and moral self-questioning, but it also reveals that, socially speaking, he remains convinced that he knows where he is and what he has a right to expect. He dismisses Bouchard as a fool without bothering to consider where the detective is coming from or what he is getting at.

Confident in its own social knowledge, the novel has up to this point been closely identified with the observing, and observant, protagonist through whom that knowledge has been mediated. Whether or not it knows "what to think" of Peggy, morally or aesthetically, it knows what to think of Montreal. I have argued that questions about Peggy are secondary to questions about the urban context in which she moves, and that these are effectively articulated through the witnessing experience of the novel's second protagonist. But, in assessing the novel's achievement, we need to ask whether Callaghan puts the authenticity of the second protagonist's social knowledge into adequately critical perspective.

The answer will depend on how plausible it is to read Jim's "where am I?" as a genuine question about his social location. Jim's failure to find the church he seeks may reflect his moral disorientation, or the bankruptcy of the detached aesthetic perception that had led him there before. But all these allegorical explanations should not obscure the fact that Jim simply does not know his way around that part of town as well as he thinks. That is to say, Jim's moral and aesthetic failing is rooted, at least in significant part, in inadequate acquaintance with the city. Jim may think he knows French and the French, but he does not know French Montreal, or, perhaps better, he does not know Montreal as the French know it. When he embarks on his final quest, he orients himself only in reference to anglophone landmarks such as Phillips Square and St Patrick's Basilica (273). His failure to find the little French church may well be a consequence of his inability to locate it in relation to other kinds of places or urban itineraries. Jim cannot really take on the representative scapegoat role he would like to play because his vision of the city and of his relation to it is not comprehensive enough. To put the city's moral and aesthetic perplexities fully into perspective, to answer the question "where am I?," would require mapping it from a French as well as from an English point of view. But, while the novel suggests this may be the case, it is unclear if it knows "what to think" about that suggestion. Nor does it do much to incorporate ignorance on this point into what is otherwise a very "knowing" narrative. More than the mixed messages MacLennan accused Callaghan of giving about Peggy's moral character, what will trouble readers today is the gap between the author's confident analysis of Montreal's civic consensus and the clues he leaves us about the foundation on which it rests.

THE WATCH THAT ENDS THE NIGHT

If Jim McAlpine's reaction to Montreal's governing "rules" is that of an unhappy and isolated liberal, a would-be "independent man," George Stewart, the narrator of *The Watch That Ends the Night*, describes these rules with the tolerant indulgence of an organic intellectual of Red Tory bent. George comes from a long-established Montreal family, and, although he grew up in straightened circumstances and chafes at the limitations of the tacit consensus that governs the city, he takes pride in what he considers to be a great historical achievement. "Montreal," he tells us, "is the subtlest and most intricate city in North America. With her history she could not have been otherwise and survived, for here the French, the Scotch and the English, over two centuries, have been divided on issues which ruin nations and civilizations, yet have contrived to live in outward harmony. This is no accident. They understand certain rules in their bones" (255). George does not spell out what the rules are, but, as the story makes clear, they function much like those articulated more explicitly in *The Loved and the Lost*: they maintain social peace through the peaceful because tacit compartmentalization of urban life. As MacLennan put it in one of the essays he wrote while he was working on the novel, Montreal "has learned to live harmoniously by the simple expedient of recognizing that its social problems are insoluble … Finding itself burdened with internal barriers, Montreal has avoided trouble by building the barriers higher still."[26] To make those barriers a topic for discussion is to put the whole system in jeopardy. "You know how we are in Montreal," Catherine says to George at one point, "the way we keep our opinions to ourselves if we think people will disagree with them" (151). The inclusiveness of this "we" is itself a question *The Watch That Ends the Night* feels no need to raise.

These disenchanted pronouncements are a far cry from the utopian projections of *Two Solitudes*, which envisioned its protagonists and the peoples they represent united through intimate, boundary-respecting but nonetheless boundary-crossing communication, and through the art that arises from solitudes "touching" each other. Yet, as we have already seen, the depiction of Montreal in *Two Solitudes* turned out to be more complex and disenchanted than the novel's programmatic statements would lead us to expect. In *The Watch That Ends the Night*, these urban complexities take centre stage, and the personal relationships dramatized in the novel are more backward than forward looking. The story begins at a moment in "the first winter of the Korean War" (3), that is, in the early months of 1951. The middle-aged George learns that his friend Jerome, who had left Montreal fourteen years earlier to fight for the Spanish Republic and whom everyone assumed had perished in the world war that followed, is alive and has returned to Montreal. Over the intervening years, George has risen from genteel poverty to a solid social position as a Canadian Broadcasting Corporation (CBC) commentator on foreign affairs and part-time McGill professor of history, thus enjoying both the media career Jim McAlpine had craved and the secure academic position Jim had forsaken in his quest for celebrity. George has also taken his friend's place as husband to Catherine and father to Sally. Jerome's unexpected and upsetting return prompts George to revisit the days when he was a fellow-traveller among the left-wing, sexually adventurous youth of 1930s anglophone Montreal. It was a time when he discovered how the city could at once stimulate and stifle the energy of its citizens. The contradictory nature of Montreal's influence is much like that of the strong-willed yet physically fragile Catherine, who makes George feel strong and helpless all at once. As the observing protagonist, George is as helplessly fascinated with Catherine as he is with Montreal, but he is also driven to reflect on how the marriage and the city that fulfilled his desires failed to satisfy Jerome. In making George his narrator, MacLennan subjects his own artistic trajectory to scrutiny. Frustrated by what proved to be *Two Solitudes*'s limited political impact, yet acknowledging his affinity with the more careful and socially integrated narrator of the new book, MacLennan takes a more nuanced view of his literary mission.

So it is that in *The Watch That Ends the Night* the generic tension between the broad historical saga and the more inward story of personal and artistic growth, unacknowledged in *Two Solitudes*, is now integrated into the narrative structure. Or at least, such is the author's intention, for the difficulty of holding the polarities together is dramatized by making the narrator one of the book's two main protagonists. The novel begins tentatively: "There are some stories into which the reader should be led gently, and I think this may be one of them" (3). It soon becomes clear, however, that the "reader" who most needs to be gently led is George himself, as he begins to revisit an often-painful past. George gradually grows in narrative confidence, and he later tells the story of Jerome's childhood escape from a New Brunswick lumber camp with an epic sweep reminiscent of the first parts of *Two Solitudes*. At the same time, we are made to realize that the mythic quality given Jerome's tale is rooted in George's perception of Jerome as larger than life, a figure he also needs to keep at an imaginative distance. If Jerome exists on a different plane from George, then one can no more judge the two men by the same criteria than one can narrate their story in the same mode. Still less can one conclude that George's story is less significant than Jerome's.

George recalls Paul Tallard in suffering from paternal weakness and financial hardship in his youth, a crucial difference being that George's story is told in a manner that draws attention to the teller. George dwells on the slowness of his psychological emancipation with a blend of rueful humour and sly self-justification reminiscent of Dickens's *Great Expectations*. The forbidding figure of his aunt Agnes bears some resemblance to Miss Havisham, at least to the extent that we wonder whether there might not be something as deficient in the young George's view of Catherine as there is in Pip's attitude to Estelle.

These nuances of point of view give *The Watch That Ends the Night* a complexity of perspective greater than that found in *Two Solitudes*. In other respects, however, MacLennan's second Montreal novel, like the first, veers uneasily between earnest realism and satirical whimsy in its depiction of society. On one side, we have powerful scenes such as the documentary-like description of the masses of unemployed men walking up and down Sainte-Catherine Street, killing time as they look into shops and restaurants they can't afford. This passage has rightly become an iconic literary image of Depression Montreal. On the other, we have the comic satire of George's weekday life teaching in a private boarding school, a rickety, anachronistic outpost of British colonialism in the Quebec countryside. The headmaster whose eccentricities George is forced to indulge is even more a caricature than the Huntly McQueen of *Two Solitudes*. And, while no doubt George adopts a comically satirical tone in order put some mental distance between himself and the forces that hinder his participation in the life of the city to which he escapes on the weekends, the device is itself imaginatively constricting, just as there are times when Aunt Agnes sounds too much like P.G. Wodehouse's Aunt Agatha to be taken seriously as a symbol of authority.

George's satirical perspective on his past is equally problematic, though in a more suggestive way, in the chapters devoted to his Communist or fellow-travelling friends of the 1930s and early 1940s. Some of these figures are of a type that invites satirical treatment. Arthur Lazenby, for example, anxiously avoids being implicated in any militant action that might jeopardize his future career. We are not surprised to find him later serving as a deputy minister in postwar Ottawa, a well-oiled cog in the gears of Canada's federal bureaucracy. The naivety about communism displayed by other acquaintances is also a legitimate target for George's derision. But in each of these cases there is more attitude than action. None of these characters is described engaging in any actual political work other than attending rallies for the Republicans fighting in the Spanish Civil War. Otherwise, these characters, envied by George because they live in Montreal and have jobs that allow them considerable freedom, are witnesses rather than participants in civic affairs. They spend most of their time parading their avant-garde sensibilities and sexual sophistication within their own circle. George neither reproaches nor excuses them for failure to get involved in the kind of local projects (union organizing, for example) later dramatized by Pierre Gélinas in his depiction of Montreal Communists. The issue simply doesn't come up. MacLennan's satire focuses on "character quirks," referring us to implicit and agreed-upon norms of right behaviour as opposed to inviting debates about those norms. This satire allows the narrator, and the novel, to expose the foibles and delusions of George's friends without making us wonder what that they might or should have done. Nor does George compare his friends to other, more authentic activist characters. None of George's friends comes from the ranks of the Sainte-Catherine Street masses, just as none is a francophone or a non-anglophone immigrant, but these facts go unmentioned. To notice them would also be to raise questions about the scope of the novel's city that the satire serves to foreclose.

More troublingly, we find a similar avoidance of imaginatively serious and specific engagement with the urban scene in the depiction of Jerome, the one character George respects, whose actions he takes seriously, and to whose flawed heroism he gives respectful witness. Jerome's brilliance as a surgeon has brought him to Montreal and to a prestigious position at the Beamis Memorial Hospital, whose board includes Sir Rupert Irons (a minor character carried over from *Two Solitudes*) and other members of the Anglo-Scottish elite. Jerome likes to see himself as an independent outsider, toughened by service in the Great War and ready to take bold action in the public sphere just as he has done in his private life. Having married Catherine some years after George had been forced to give her up because his family declared the semi-invalid girl an unsuitable match, Jerome dismisses her other doctors and persuades her to have a child with him despite the risk to her heart.

Sally's birth augurs well for the success of Jerome's other enterprises. In another bold gesture, he and Catherine take up residence in what George calls "the most interesting part of Montreal … the no man's land between the English and French blocs, almost unknown to them, which contains people with interests all over the world" (155). Further clues in the narrative allow readers familiar with the city to locate the Martells' apartment on Lorne Crescent, a small street just east of McGill University. Identifying their social location, however, is another matter. Jerome, George tells us, "seemed to know everyone in Montreal whose brain was alive, and most of them came from Europe or other parts of Canada. The old dynasty still ruled the city, as oblivious as mandarins to new faces and new ideas, but they were there: after a long, long time they were there at last and they were turning Montreal, in spite of itself, into a real world city" (223). Who these people are, however, and what they are like, we never learn. They remain "unknown," even though a few chapters later George insists they were playing a much more significant role in the city than any of the friends whose lives he describes in detail.

There is something of a puzzle here. If these "new faces" were really turning Montreal into a "world city," how could the English and French "blocs" remain so ignorant of their existence? Even George's left-wing friends seem to know nothing about them. The transformative effect of these immigrants remains beyond the ken even of the narrator looking back on the period when this transformation supposedly began. Perhaps, though, the contradiction is not as great as it seems. Because these people's interests are "all over the world," it may be that they are making Montreal a "real world city," not by changing anything in the city's internal dynamic, but rather by making it a place more attentive to what is happening elsewhere than it was before. In this respect, there may be an implicit connection between the "new faces" and the Anglo Montrealers of George's circle. One would think that greater awareness of world conflicts would lead to more acute perception of local contradictions, but this does seem not to be the case. On the contrary, this disjunction between the importance and the visibility of the "new faces" only underscores the pervasive compartmentalization which defines the novel's Montreal. It is taken for granted that whatever political consciousness is fostered in this diverse and divided city can only be projected outwards.[27]

This is certainly the case for the older George. He has found his niche as a CBC commentator, but his field is foreign affairs, not local politics. But it is even more strikingly true of the novel's more active protagonist, the Jerome of the 1930s. His chief political concern is the conflict between Fascists and Republicans in Spain. This was, of course, an issue of critical importance for progressive 1930s intellectuals, but it is striking that it is the only political cause *The Watch That Ends the Night* analyzes in any detail. The Spanish Civil War engages Jerome more intensely than anything going on in Montreal, in Quebec, or in Canada at large.[28] Indeed, other than a brief reference to his efforts to establish a free clinic for the poor, we learn nothing about Jerome's public life except that he attends meetings about the situation in Spain.

There is nothing satirical, however, in the novel's portrayal of Jerome. His single-minded, somewhat naive pursuit of international justice is exploited by Communist ideologues and by Norah Blackwell, the nurse who latches on to him and accompanies him to Spain, but the authenticity of his commitment is never questioned. Lazenby later describes him to George as "a divine fool" (297). This epithet puts him in the same category as the Peggy of *The Loved and the Lost*, though the differences between the way the two characters are seen by other people, and portrayed by the narrator, are equally important. Callaghan may consider Peggy to be a divine fool, but the characters in his novel do not, and that is her tragedy. Jerome's motives are understood and admired by everyone, even those who disapprove of his actions. No doubt gender plays an important role here. When questioned about her husband's obliviousness to the effect his actions have on other people, Catherine tolerantly replies that "he's just Jerome" (139). Jim would never be tolerant enough to say the same about Peggy. For men, Peggy is a puzzle they need to solve so they can possess or control her. Jerome can be allowed to depart with his enigma unresolved.

This is not to say that Jerome is not scapegoated, as Peggy was, by Montreal's governing consensus. Although he leaves voluntarily and eventually returns alive, there is a sense in which the city had to expel him in order to maintain its internal equilibrium. When Jerome goes public with his political commitments and appears on stage at a rally for the Spanish Republicans, an event that disintegrates into a fight between (largely French Canadian) conservatives and (largely English-speaking) leftists, he can no longer be ignored by the city's governing "blocs." Jerome is subjected to vicious attack in the press. According to George, the newspapers (both French and English, he implies, though only the latter are actually in view) don't care about the workingmen or immigrants who attend such rallies. What they do doesn't really matter, since, although they presumably include some of those who are supposedly making Montreal a world city, their actions do not threaten its political order, or its social imaginary. They are "outsiders" (255) who can be safely ignored by a Montreal confident of keeping them in their place. But Jerome is different. "By virtue of his position at the Beamis Memorial," we are told, "Jerome had been at least half-way inside the Montreal Thing whether he wanted to be or not." As a consequence, he finds himself subject to its discipline. "Had he been a born Montrealer," George continues, "he would have realized what he had done, but he was not a born Montrealer, and I was sure that even now he did not" (256).

Unlike Callaghan's Jim, who for all his familiarity with the city remains an outsider in certain key respects, MacLennan's George is one of those old-stock Montrealers who understand the city "in their bones" (255). Thus, he is neither surprised nor emotionally shaken by the brutality with which the Montreal media unite in condemning Jerome when he openly challenges the city's complacent consensus. George notes with cynical detachment that the reporter who goes after Jerome most vehemently is himself a "crypto-communist" hoping to deepen Jerome's alienation from the civic establishment and drive him into the arms of the Party (256). This reporter, Irving Dublin, is given a name suggesting he may well be one of those "new faces" living in the interstices between the French and the English and whose "interests all over the world" are making Montreal more international. If so, the convergence of Dublin's agenda with that of the "Montreal Thing" offers ironic confirmation of the power of that "Thing" to co-opt or contain dissent.

In any case, it soon becomes clear Montreal has no room for someone like Jerome. Far from enabling him to be an agent of social mediation, his liminal position on the border between inside and outside proves to be untenable. When he returns to Montreal after the war, this is still the case. George's one trip abroad coordinating a tour of Russia in 1937 gave him a glimpse of totalitarianism he turns to good account when he begins his career as a radio commentator on the eve of the Second World War. By contrast, Jerome's traumatic experience as a prisoner of the Germans and then the Soviets only reinforces his disdain for the petty divisions of Montreal's anglophone medical establishment, torn between a patrician Englishman who is the hospital's chief physician and the parvenu "Ulster boy" (165) who chairs its board. A career in Montreal no longer interests Jerome. In any case, his hands are now too mangled by torture to resume work as a surgeon. Jerome will survive – he speaks of a job out west where he won't have to operate – but in postwar Montreal he is no longer an actor, only a spectator, and like George can only watch as a recurrence of Catherine's illness precipitates her death.

The last section of the novel focuses on the quality of the two men's witness. Satire and social irony are left behind as George's narration takes on a more solemn, elegiac quality. After Jerome's departure for Spain, George had become Catherine's caretaker and later, after Jerome was declared dead, her second husband. Seemingly fated to love Catherine only from afar, George finally won the prize he sought. Yet, although he has taken Jerome's place, George can do no more than witness Catherine's decline along with his old friend. Questions of worldly agency, however, become moot as Catherine confronts the elemental struggle between life and death. *The Watch That Ends the Night* is admirably unflinching in its portrayal of Catherine's suffering. At the end, Jerome can do nothing but be there (362), but his attentive presence redeems his earlier failure to be truly present at all. Similarly, the intensity with which George identifies with Catherine in her struggle goes a long way toward offsetting his bourgeois complacency. It gives his role of sympathetic witness a gravitas it had previously lacked. The relationship between the two male protagonists is ultimately mediated more through the woman they love and lose than through any public attachments.

I would argue, however, that in shifting its focus from the public to the private sphere the novel has not abandoned its attempt to gain a literary perspective on its civic ambitions. On the contrary, in the concluding chapters MacLennan shows a new willingness to acknowledge the limitations of the vision projected in *Two Solitudes*. What is more, he displays a readiness to incorporate into that vision something of the wilfulness of the artistic imagination, which, in his determination to make *Two Solitudes* a constructive, socially useful work, he couldn't allow himself to acknowledge. George's tribute to Catherine's "spirit," for example, goes beyond conventional pieties in reflecting on the ruthlessness of her will to live. If the human spirit she embodies "is the sole force which equals the merciless fate binding a human being to his mortality," it is because that spirit "creates, destroys, and recreates" (341). As George's allusion to Goethe's *Faust* a few pages earlier makes clear (321), the middle term is the key one. The spirit George admires in Catherine includes her willingness, even while married to Jerome, to feed on George's devotion in almost vampirical fashion. Only now, and in this context, can George express his long-suppressed resentment of the woman he loved. Although he does not say so in so many words, George's subsequent reflections about religion and music make it clear that the dissonant note of protest, even aggressive self-assertion, must be incorporated into any authentic harmony (341–2).

These cosmic considerations, like the references to the Bible, Bach, and Beethoven, to "Everyman" and the "Unknowable," that multiply at the end of the book (343–4), seem to lead us away from concrete urban issues, but two key metaphors in the last part of the novel bring us back to earth. In "the first year after the war," George confides, his preoccupation with Catherine's health had changed his relationship with the city. "My orbit in Montreal," he writes, "had narrowed to the city's heart" (307). Geographically speaking, this means the (English) downtown "between Sherbrooke and St. Catherine," and on one level George is saying he no longer wandered too far from his home on the edge of that district (the Stewarts' apartment seems to be that of the author, located on Summerhill just off Côte-des-Neiges above Sherbrooke). George's use of this image also implies that he is seeking some reassurance about the viability of Catherine's heart through contact with the vitality of the city's figurative organ. Catherine's name, after all, is that of Montreal's main thoroughfare, and so person and place are connected. The connection is a distinctive one, somewhat at variance with other such allegorical relationships. *The Watch That Ends the Night* is not a book in which a character dies because of the city's heartlessness or as a symbol of it. At the end of the novel, the city's "heart" is prized because, behind the cynical solidity of its rules, there is something about Montreal that is as fragile as it is vital, and it is to this deeper reality that George, in shrinking the circle of his orbit to that "heart," finds himself drawn.

In the opening pages of *Two Solitudes*, MacLennan's external narrator had said that, if the "sprawling half-continent" that is Canada "has a heart," Montreal was it. The city's "pulse throbs out along the rivers and railroads; slow, reluctant, and rarely simple, a double beat, a self-moved reciprocation" (4). There may, of course, already have been a negative undertone in the image of the "double beat," which ostensibly relates to the "two old races and religions" of the city's French and English settlers but which surely also refers, deliberately or not, to the flawed heart of MacLennan's first wife, Dorothy Duncan. By the time *The Watch That Ends the Night* was completed, Duncan had died, and it was widely known that MacLennan drew on personal experience in dramatizing George's relationship with Catherine. It seems likely, therefore, that the author was aware that his reference to the "heart" of Montreal in the last pages of the book might be read as a gloss on his use of the image in the earlier novel. George's admission of vulnerability here, in the first instance a personal vulnerability but implicitly a collective one as well, hints that despite the confidence with which it speaks of Montreal's rules, *The Watch That End the Night* is more aware than it first seems to be of the precarious contingency of its pronouncements.

The Watch That Ends the Night further complicates its vision of the city with the reprise of a second and more curious body metaphor. We saw earlier how, in contrast with strangers, immigrants, and even exceptional individuals like Jerome, born-and-bred Montrealers like George, who have inhabited the city for more than "two generations," understand how to behave. They help maintain the city's social and "racial" equilibrium because they know the city "in their bones" (255). The declaration takes on different connotations, however, in a conversation between Catherine and George a few pages later. Shortly before Jerome leaves for Spain, George visits Catherine in a Laurentian cottage where she is trying to distract herself from her emotional and physical troubles by learning to paint. As they look out on the springtime landscape, George, citing Ecclesiastes 1:4, "murmur[s] the line about one generation passing away, another coming and the earth remaining" (263). Catherine replies: "I don't know about all these big things. Only about the little human specks passing through what I'm looking at now. I never knew before that the earth has bones" (263).

The perspective encapsulated in this metaphor is presented as the vision of a genuine because vulnerable artist, not that of a mystic or, as seems to be the case in the earlier citation, of a complacent political conservative. The world Catherine perceives may have a hidden enduring structure, but the defining features of that structure, far from being immune to time or change, become apparent only with the erosions of time, like a face individualized by age. Knowledge of the earth's bones may not lead one to challenge the existing social order, but it does open a perspective from which the imaginative grip of that order can be loosened by appreciation of a deeper temporality that puts the urgency of other issues into perspective. In this respect, MacLennan's "organic" images of heart and bone are more subversive than his satire, whose ironies mock convention in what in the end is a rather superficial way. Unlike the comic satirists who followed him and whose work we will examine in the next chapter, MacLennan could not muster much enthusiasm about the emancipatory potential of generational renewal – his portrait of Sally's relationship with her clean-cut boyfriend is distressingly bland – and so his satire is not buoyant enough to be really transformative. Unfortunately, the deeper vision hinted at in the metaphor of heart and bone is also blurred by the fuzzily pious rhetoric to which the author reverts at the end of the book. One wishes that MacLennan had instead done more to integrate the novel's more adventurous personal insights into his portrayal of the Montreal with which he so lovingly quarrelled.

ALEXANDRE CHENEVERT

The Loved and the Lost and *The Watch That Ends the Night* expose the limitations of the civic consensus, but in dramatizing the drastic consequences befalling those who question the city's "rules," bourgeois anglophone writers of the early 1950s ran the risk of reinforcing their power even as they sought through their characters' sacrificial witnessing to lay the groundwork for reform. As well intentioned as they might be, these relatively privileged writers could hold this contradiction at arm's length – as perhaps they needed to do in order to display it in their work. What is more difficult to understand is why a francophone writer as conscious as Gabrielle Roy was of the constrictions of the civic consensus should also confine herself in her second Montreal novel to lamenting its immutability. *Bonheur d'occasion* may have pulled some of its critical punches and counted too naively on wartime solidarity and sacrifice to energize social reform at home, but it was driven by a powerful sense of indignation at injustice. The language used in *Alexandre Chenevert* to attack economic inequities and linguistic alienation is more precise in its articulation than that of *Bonheur d'occasion*, yet readers who expected a parallel development in the sharpness of the novel's social critique were disappointed. Roy's second Montreal novel remains one of sympathetic witness rather than conflictual engagement.

Some of the initial disappointment with *Alexandre Chenevert* no doubt stemmed from a misunderstanding about the fundamental orientation of Roy's creative personality, which she herself had only begun to clarify as she composed her first memoir-fiction, *La Petite poule d'eau* (*Where Nests the Water Hen*, 1951). If *Alexandre Chenevert* took much longer to write than Roy had planned, part of the reason was a growing unease with the realist form adopted so successfully in *Bonheur d'occasion*, and with the obligation she felt to meet her public's demand for a second work in that mode. The novel she produced out of that unease is a somewhat disconcerting one. Appreciation for the book as a work of art, though widespread, has from the first been less than universal. Praise for the author's sensibility sometimes substitutes for searching critical appraisal. I suggest that we can account for this interpretive embarrassment by reading *Alexandre Chenevert* in terms of the problematic of self-conscious witnessing developed in the English-language novels that preceded and followed it.

A surprising feature of *Alexandre Chenevert* is that, while it refers in more explicit and concrete terms than *Bonheur d'occasion* did to contentious local issues, these issues play little role in shaping the characters' lives. A notable example is linguistic inequity. In *Bonheur d'occasion*, the dominant position of the English language was not directly critiqued, but it was dramatized in the speech of the francophone characters. Examples include Jean's casual use of English phrases to express his ambitions and Alphonse's speech about life on Montreal's garbage dump. The critical edge of Rose-Anna's abortive exchange with the unilingual English nurse Jenny may have been blunted by the scene being set in Daniel's hospital room, where pathos trumped politics, but the emotional impact of the incident was nonetheless considerable. In *Alexandre Chenevert* the subordination of French to English in Montreal becomes a topic for explicit comment. The narrator notes of a streetcar conductor that "he was instinctively more polite when he spoke English" (175), this "instinct" being a name for internalized social conditioning. When the bank manager Émery Fontaine imagines asking his English superiors to adopt a more sympathetic attitude to Alexandre, he thinks as well as speaks in English. "'What about the old employees?" wondered Monsieur Fontaine, thinking in English, as he often loved to do" (62). Fontaine's use of English is what today we would call "aspirational," a means of projecting himself mentally into the social position he would like to occupy.[29]

Provocative as these moments are, however, they prove to be surprisingly inconsequential in the unfolding of the story. The characters remain oblivious to, and their actions are unaffected by, what the narrator observes about their behaviour. The one instance of language juxtaposition that significantly inflects the arc of the book's plot does so in a paradoxical way. The text draws our attention not once but twice to a sign outside the (French Catholic) hospital where Alexandre will eventually die. The sign reads: "SILENCE/HÔPITAL/HOSPITAL ZONE" (71, translation modified).[30] The irony that French takes precedence over English only in this "zone" of disease and death is pointed enough. Yet even more significant is that the two languages converge in the word "silence," that is, in a negation rather than a negotiation of speech. The SILENCE of the hospital sign enjoins us to suppress speech for the sake of the sick. In his final days Alexandre will be more concerned with making peace with the life he has lived than in engaging with a future that would differ from the past, as Emmanuel at least tries to do at the end of *Bonheur d'occasion*.

Similarly, Alexandre avidly consumes newspaper and radio news about peoples around the world and obsesses about the international conflicts that in early 1947 dominated the headlines: religious violence in an India about to become independent, Cold War tensions, fighting between Jews and Arabs in Palestine. Yet the hero's one extended interaction with someone not a *pure-laine* French Canadian never addresses questions of ethnic diversity or political difference. Looking for a way to earn extra money to reimburse his bank for an accounting error he supposedly made, Alexandre somehow learns that a fabric wholesaler named Markhous, a Hungarian Jewish immigrant on the Boulevard Saint-Laurent, needs a temporary bookkeeper (76). Alexandre expresses no curiosity about Markhous's background or identity.[31] All we are told of their conversations is that they talk about the burden of income taxes, a topic on which they easily agree (78). The omission is all the more curious in that Alexandre has been shown to be torn in his own mind between his sympathy for the Zionist migrants to Palestine and the anti-Jewish prejudices with which he has grown up. Given Alexandre's diffidence – he hardly ever speaks to anyone outside his family and co-workers, not even his neighbours – it would also have been interesting to know how he came to meet Markhous, and what their first impressions were of each other. The whole encounter, in fact, calls for an explanation Roy does not supply.[32] Once the scene is over, Markhous disappears from Alexandre's imaginative horizon, along with the glimpse of difference he represents. While the tentativeness of the characters in relation to each other may reflect a socially plausible habit of caution and, in Alexandre's case, a deep-rooted inhibition, the scope of the scene is clearly limited by authorial decision.

In comparison with *Bonheur d'occasion*, the narrator's imaginative horizon has narrowed in other ways as well. Markhous is accorded no more than a perfunctory expression of the sympathy the earlier novel extended even to its minor characters, or of the concern to name feelings the characters themselves would have been unable to put into words. In *Alexandre Chenevert*, the narrator's emotional as well as observational range is not much broader than that of the protagonist whose perspective she voices. No doubt, the intention was to make up in depth for what is sacrificed in breadth. Roy's adoption of a point of view so closely identified with her title character signals her determination to convey Alexandre's predicament even more fully and intimately than she did that of Florentine, Emmanuel, or Rose-Anna, who shared the stage in the earlier story. Indeed, so close is the identification with her single protagonist that Roy's narrator becomes less an external presence than a second consciousness within the story, a double of the character's own mind problematically positioned on the border between the story and its narration, between teller and tale.

This instability of viewpoint is apparent from the very beginning of the book. In a passage about Alexandre's notions of national character, we are told that Alexandre doesn't think much of the English. "You only had to watch their actions here in Canada to discover their taste for domination. Of course for Alexandre the English were the hereditary enemy, nominated by history, the schools, the environment – the enemy he could scarcely do without, for were he to lose him, what would become of his grievances?" (16). In the second sentence the narrator captures the deadening effect of traditional French Canadian discourse in the same way that she notes the linguistic automatisms of the streetcar conductor's colonized speech. Alexandre also mirrors this discourse in identifying the "English" in Canada as British, whereas when he goes on to speak about the distinctive qualities of the "French" national character only the inhabitants of France are in view. French Canadians owe nothing to their European heritage: the land of naughty books and free thinking is a foreign country with which they have nothing to do. Alexandre's ideas about Jewish financial power and American materialism are equally conventional. Each nation is associated with a stereotypical fault.

What about the French Canadians themselves? At first, Alexandre seems to be even more unsparing in his critique of his "compatriotes" than of other nations. "Their faults at once sprang to view: envy, the habit of feeling sorry for rather asserting themselves, hate rather than love; yet very arrogant when they proved to be the stronger" (10). The language of this list contrasts so strongly with what has gone before – it is hard to imagine Alexandre has picked it up from the press – that we are entitled to attribute it to the narrator at least as much as to the character, the former inflecting the latter's consciousness through the use of free indirect style. Yet, just as we start to take in the force of this criticism, its impact is softened by the words that follow: "in short, the faults of men in general …" French Canadians, in other words, are guilty of no distinctive fault. The narrative thus avoids assigning any specific moral responsibility to Alexandre's people, just as he accepts none himself. Even the insight into humanity's faults is not really Alexandre's, in the sense that he is given responsibility for articulating and then dismissing the thought. In that case, we could read his prudent retreat into a dismissive "in short" as a comic gesture of avoidance. But the sentiments expressed seem to be as much the narrator's as the hero's, and the indeterminate position of that narrator precludes any attribution of them to an individualized agent.

Another and to my mind crucial instance of how the authorial shaping of the narrative serves more to mirror than to mediate Alexandre's point of view is found near the end of the novel. The obtuse, well-fed hospital chaplain is compared unfavourably with a former curate in Alexandre's parish, "a man who had been ill all his life" but who had preached a message of solidarity, supported trade unions, and "concerned himself specially with community service projects" (210, translation modified). The critical point here is clear. Yet one wonders why this priest was never mentioned before. His name never comes up in Alexandre's ruminations about the state of the world. No doubt, the author had to be careful about going too far in criticizing the church and so withheld her comments until the narrative arrived in the "hospital zone," where expressions of resentment and rebellion could be excused by the imminence of death. Whatever the case, the curate's sermons clearly had no more impact on Alexandre's behaviour than they had on his thoughts. His focus on Gandhi allows him to indulge a comically narcissistic identification with the Indian leader's heroic asceticism without having to wonder – as he would have had to do if he compared himself with the priest – about what emulating his model would actually mean.

Alexandre may be obsessed with poverty and suffering, but he never does anything about either other than to make an occasional and grudging donation to charity. While petit-bourgeois anxiety about hanging on to his hard-won position may deter him from joining a political party or pressure group, he never considers even ordinary, non-political actions such as volunteering in a local soup kitchen or distributing old clothes. The question of what Alexandre might do in his spare time, other than read more newspapers, is never asked. We may assume that poor health limits his activities, but the question doesn't come up. Nothing is said either about how Alexandre's wife, Eugénie, spends her days, even though, with no job, no child at home, and apparently no relatives or friends, she has few demands on her time. That the self-obsessed Alexandre never wonders what Eugénie does during the day is plausible enough, but the narrator's lack of interest is striking. Indeed, the novel is so successful in making us take this lack of curiosity for granted that no critic I know of has made it an issue. It may well be that the couple's lack of social involvement was the norm for lower-middle-class people of their time and place. In the French Montreal of the 1950s, Catholic nuns, priests, and brothers were numerous enough to run the francophone city's charities on their own, and the laity perhaps happy – or habituated – to leave them to it. Nevertheless, the absence of any narrative comment is another way *Alexandre Chenevert* differs from *Bonheur d'occasion*. There, too, the Lacasses' lack of connection with other families was taken for granted, but given the shame associated with their poverty, a theme the book does develop, this estrangement was more readily understandable.

Despite the constant reference in *Alexandre Chenevert* to datable events – the assassination of Gandhi and the Berlin airlift among others – and despite the greater variety of its characters' class origins, the novel's post-war Montreal is in some respects more stifling than the isolationist Saint-Henri of Roy's earlier book. The geography of *Alexandre Chenevert* is centred on a bank branch located at the French end of the city's downtown, probably at the corner of Ontario and Alexandre-de-Sève, not far from the Hôpital Notre Dame.[33] Such an institution is a place where Alexandre could plausibly become acquainted with people of varying status and temperament. However, while branch manager Fontaine's wealth may put him in a higher economic bracket than Madame Mathieu, the old widow who comes each month to deposit her meagre pension check, and while the complacent good humour of another bank teller, Godias, makes Alexandre more conscious of his dyspeptic disposition, all these characters share the same basic imaginary. Not only does *Alexandre Chenevert* avoid staging any encounters between potentially clashing cultural viewpoints other than Alexandre's brief experience with Markhous, but the novel minimizes the impact on the story of the differences that do exist within its homogeneous group of francophone Montrealers. The Saint-Henri portrayed in *Bonheur d'occasion* may have been exclusively French Canadian too, a neighbourhood its inhabitants rarely leave and which no outsiders (other than the narrator) ever visit, but its Depression poverty made its isolation readily understandable. More important, it included several characters of sharply contrasting outlooks on life. *Alexandre Chenevert*, by contrast, is never distracted for very long from its focus on the hero, the other characters serving only to add a little shading to the portrait.

One could argue that the narrowness of the novel's social horizon is simply an inevitable consequence of an artistically legitimate decision to portray the city from its hero's limited point of view. But it is a decision that itself invites interpretation, especially given what we know about the long and difficult genesis of the book, not to mention Roy's unexpected determination to focus her story on a depressive and querulous man rather than on a woman's hopes and dreams.[34] This is not to say that Alexandre does not mirror some of the author's own anxieties; far from it. But paradoxical as it may seem, Roy may have found this distancing gesture to be necessary in order to gain a perspective on the city and on her literary mission more searching and self-critical than that of *Bonheur d'occasion*.[35]

If *Alexandre Chenevert*'s French Canadians are distinguished from other peoples in that their only flaws are the ones they share with humanity in general, life in the novel's Montreal is also distinctive in the way it merely mirrors universal human concerns. The city's peculiar character shows itself in its preoccupation with the problem of illness. As he commutes to and from work, Alexandre sees billboards encouraging contributions to help build new (French) Catholic and (English) Jewish hospitals (70).[36] The general effect of these billboards is similar to that of the bilingual hospital sign discussed above, and to that of the ads displayed in the streetcars Alexandre uses to get around town. Some of these ads are conventional come-ons, urging him to buy a new shirt to ensure business success (60). These messages recall the "temptations" Alphonse criticized in *Bonheur d'occasion*. But Alexandre's attention is captured most by public-service messages encouraging him to be checked for cancer (193), and these messages do more than mirror Alexandre's hypochondria. The parallel fundraising campaigns for new hospitals are the only forms of collective action mentioned in the novel. The other characters mention no other civic cause, and the narrator never alludes to any local public issue. It is in their concern for health, or rather, with the threat of illness, not their enthusiasm for political action or, still less, any promiscuous expression of desire, that Montreal's divided communities, and the individuals isolated within them, display their underlying commonality.

There are intriguing even if distant echoes here of Camus's *La Peste* (*The Plague*, 1947), published just at the moment Roy began her stay in France.[37] In both novels, a city's political tensions, hitherto kept in check only by a tacit social consensus, are entirely eclipsed by a shared preoccupation with disease. It is also interesting to compare the outlook of the novels' main protagonists in relation to their city. Dr Rieux captures the mood of Camus's Oran by balancing emotional solidarity with philosophical detachment. His witness is of a more active and persevering kind than that of Alexandre, torn between grudging compassion for other people's ailments and guilty irritation with their impinging proximity. In this respect, Alexandre also represents the city in which he lives. While Camus's hedonistic Mediterranean city is struck by a sudden epidemic of plague that shocks Rieux into action, Roy's wintry Montreal suffers from the pervasive fatigue of chronic low-level ailments that sap whatever energy Alexandre is able to muster.

The difference in the nature of the disease finds interesting reflection in the ways people use language to talk – or not talk – about the threat they face. The force of denial is such that the French Oranais of *La Peste* refuse at first to name the plague whose symptoms are all too apparent. The francophone Montrealers of *Alexandre Chenevert* face a less catastrophic situation, but their inhibition is even greater: they cannot name their illness, since the self-pity, timidity, and resentful defensive pride that are its symptoms make it impossible for them to give it a name at all. In *Alexandre Chenevert*, a "real" crisis, one that clarifies the community's situation, is an event that can occur only somewhere else, not in Montreal. The relation of the novel's characters to their environment and to each other thus takes less extreme and varied forms than it does in Camus.

Indeed, it is much the same in every case. The tension between compassion and irritation in Alexandre's attitude toward others is much like that experienced by other characters in their relationship to him. Whether they have known him for a long time, like his wife, Eugénie, his friend Godias Doucet, or his boss, Émery Fontaine, or whether they have just made his acquaintance, like the doctor who treats him and the hospital chaplain who hears his confession, they all experience the same "slow burn" exasperation when they talk to him that Alexandre also feels when he listens to them. They also experience the same discomfort, if not guilt, about not being able to move past that feeling.

La Peste ends with a revelation that is somewhat analogous to the one that concludes *Alexandre Chenevert* but again differs from it in illuminating ways. Dr Rieux reveals that the narrator who up this point had referred to himself in the third person is none other than himself, not just a witness but a participant in the story. The tension between the insider and outsider perspectives the novel offered on its Oran is thus at once underscored by highlighting their narrative expression and resolved by this dramatic dénouement. At the end of *Alexandre Chenevert*, Alexandre realizes that far from being fundamentally different from other people, in fact he is just like them. The character's realization, however, does not have the same provocative effect on the way the preceding narrative is to be understood. Roy's narrator does highlight the tension between inside and outside perspectives by loosening her adherence to the hero's point of view in order to present a critique of religious dogma much more pointed than anything her protagonist would have expressed. Yet, in the rest of the book, the narrator rarely distinguishes this point of view from that of the hero, even if the two perspectives clearly differ in their degree of articulation. Roy's intention was no doubt to offer the most authentic testimony possible to her character's struggle, but one might ask whether that narrator is sufficiently distanced from the hero to give adequate testimony. Where Rieux's impartial self-presentation is in striking and creative tension with his intimate involvement in what he describes, Roy's narrator seems in relation to Alexandre only to oscillate between the same feelings of compassion and resentment that define the hero's relationships with the other characters.

Roy's portrayal of Dr Hudon, like Dr Rieux a physician who serves as the author's spokesman, though only in one episode of the novel, unwittingly dramatizes the difficulty. When the hypochondriac Alexandre finally agrees to be examined by a physician, Hudon is unable to diagnose his illness. On a symbolic level at least, the reason is that the doctor is too much like his patient. "For of course he himself lived a crazy life; meals gobbled in haste at irregular hours, his sleep often interrupted" (123). The "of course" of this sentence is odd: why should the idea that family doctors lead crazy lives be taken for granted, unless the narrator's world and that of the characters were one and the same? In a sense, of course, it was. Roy's husband was a physician, and her remark may be her way of acknowledging that she was not the only one in the marriage to suffer job stress. The literary effect, however, of characterizing the doctor in this way is to prevent the episode from giving us the perspective on the character it was clearly designed to provide. Even as he contemplates Alexandre with compassion, Hudon worries about the limited time he can spend with his patients of modest means and still earn a living. In other words, he is compassionate, but irritated. When Alexandre starts to complain about insurance companies, "the doctor at once agreed with him" (104), abandoning his initial effort of detachment in order to identify with his patient. This agreement over money recalls that of Alexandre and Markhous over income taxes: real contact between the two men begins with solidarity in grievance; it also ends there. Alexandre is not different enough from Hudon to stimulate the latter to any creative thinking – a fact that irritates the doctor as much as does his patient's failure to seek follow-up care. When some time later Hudon discovers Alexandre's prostate cancer, it is too late to do anything.

It is not only as a patient that Alexandre is ill served by a doctor who resembles him too much to see him clearly. He is also disadvantaged in his role as the embodiment of the city's ailing condition. Like Jim McAlpine and George Stewart, Dr Hudon is a means by which the author seeks some perspective on the collective life of the city as it reveals itself in that character's witnessing of another person's sacrificial witness. Unlike the secondary witness figures in *The Loved and the Lost* and *The Watch That Ends the Night*, however, Hudon too closely mirrors the protagonist's point of view to mediate it to us with any kind of illuminating perspective.

Roy may well have been aware of this. Perhaps she thought that, if she could not cast new light on Montreal and its ills because of the difficulty of dramatizing in the world of the story the differentiating kind of relationship Callaghan and MacLennan were able to imagine, she could provide such a perspective by other means: first by narrowing the imaginative horizon of the story world, then by devising an alternative form of observing consciousness to mediate the intensification of perception that results from that gesture. Thus, unlike the Lacasses in *Bonheur d'occasion*, for whom the traditional life of the countryside retains a certain hold on their minds, Alexandre is a Montreal native, or at least enough of one not to compare urban life with another mode of experience. Nor does he expose the problematic foundations Montreal's social imaginary by transgressing its rules, as Callaghan's Peggy and MacLennan's Jerome do. Like these other protagonists, Alexandre reveals the city more by the intensity of his witness than in the extent of his action, by what he is rather than what he does. Unlike these "outsider" figures, however, his being embodies a central feature of that imaginary, its paralyzing mixture of compassion and irritation, so completely that it reflects it back uncomfortably to the people whose gaze he attracts.

Just as Roy dramatizes the collective condition of *Alexandre Chenevert*'s Montreal through the intensity of the protagonist's mirroring rather than by the effect of his disruptive presence, she puts the hero's testimony into perspective by means of a second figure who also mirrors the hero, but from outside the story world. Given the peculiarly homogenous nature of that world, it would in fact be difficult to imagine a character capable of "seeing" Alexandre from a point of view substantially different from his own. In *Bonheur d'occasion*, Roy had provided such a character in Jean. He "sees" Florentine in ways no one else can or wants to do. Although Jean's view of Florentine is subjected to negative narrative judgment, it continues to inform the reader's view of her in significant, indeed indispensable, ways. No character in *Alexandre Chenevert* "sees" its hero with eyes as shrewd as Jean's. As a consequence, the only way to insert a witnessing consciousness into the story, as I suggested earlier, is to personalize its narration, to make the narrator herself a quasi-protagonist of its action. One way in which this happens is the narrator's frequent resort to rhetorical questions. These give personalized voice to the character's anxieties and in turn invite readers to join both character and narrator in acknowledging, if perhaps reluctantly, the reality of a situation they all share. Reflective awareness is to be achieved through participatory intimacy rather than distanced yet sympathetic witness, since the novel's Montreal makes no room for such witness.

Of course, in adopting this strategy, the author risks collapsing the critical distance she also wishes to create, as happens in Dr Hudon's perspective on his patient. Roy's apprehension of this danger I think explains her most radical narrative move: she kills off her hero. What's more, in contrast to Dr Hudon, the narrator anticipates Alexandre's death early on. Almost from the start we are given hints that Alexandre's ailments will turn into terminal illness. This is because, in a world seemingly devoid of any other incentive, only imminent death will prompt Alexandre to look at himself from the outside. Just as important, Roy seems to need the prospect of Alexandre's impending fate in order to round out her portrait of the character and his relationship to his environment. In *Bonheur d'occasion*, the death of little Daniel provided the necessary background shadow against which the idealistic temptations of the book's final scenes could be illuminated, but the death of this secondary character occurred offstage. In *Alexandre Chenevert*, an author famous for her generosity toward her creations kills off the hero, and we are not spared the details of his dying. Such a radical decision can only have been taken under considerable artistic pressure. In a later conversation with Ben Shek, Roy declared that she was not yet done with Alexandre.[38] It is hard to imagine Roy writing a second book about her character; more likely, she is referring to her unresolved feelings about having "sacrificed" Alexandre for the sake of her art.

How deliberate that sacrifice was is unclear, however. Nothing much is made of the delay in diagnosing Alexandre's disease, which is judged in the end to result less from a failure of care than from fate's decree. There is none of the rage, resentment, and self-questioning with which MacLennan's George watches Catherine die, or of the more ambiguous mixture of self-accusation and redemptive compensation in Jim's mourning of Peggy. Roy's other characters, including Alexandre's wife, react to his decline with nothing more complicated than ordinary sadness and regret. The sole but significant exception is the chaplain, whose name, Marchand, symbolizes the crassness of his spirituality. Here, as I mentioned earlier, the narrator goes beyond a sympathetic mirroring of her hero's limited point of view. She attacks the narrow dogmatism of a church intent on silencing awkward questions and instilling obedience, and unwilling to accommodate doubt and protest. The sudden adoption of a critical external viewpoint here is made plausible by the move to a hospital setting, but, as with the belated reference to the left-wing priest Alexandre used to hear preach, we realize with regret that critical comments such as these had not been expressed before, to the detriment of the book. They would have situated Alexandre's life within a more concrete and differentiated context of clashing perspectives.[39] When Dr Hudon first examined Alexandre, he asked his patient whether he had religious faith and got only a perfunctory yes for an answer (111). In that scene, Alexandre's refusal to discuss the matter, like his reluctance to talk about his sex life with Eugénie (102), was presented as characteristic of a Montreal francophone of his time and place. At the same time, this local realism about habits of mind that were taken for granted allowed the narrator herself to postpone any critical discussion of these sensitive topics until the end of the book, when its consequences for the characters are limited and its potential for complicating the depiction of their world in the manner of what Gilles Marcotte, citing Georg Lukacs, called "high realism" is minimized.[40] What is said in the hospital zone, it seems, stays in the hospital zone.

On the other hand, this final episode of the novel does make a crucial point about the social imaginary of Alexandre and his city. If Father Marchand begins to take a humbler view of his role as chaplain after talking to Alexandre, and if other characters are drawn to visit the dying man, it is not just because the spectacle of the protagonist's suffering is so pathetic, or because their irritation simply fades away in the face of his imminent demise. As he approaches death, Alexandre himself becomes less irritated with the world and thereby less irritating to other people. His compassion for another patient in his room is no longer spoiled by the urge to lecture him about the world's ills. Alexandre's dispirited and dispiriting reflection of the anxieties and contradictions of the city around him is replaced by another, more enabling form of mirroring, one that exercises a positive influence on his visitors. In fact, they come to form an unexpectedly diverse and newly energized, if no doubt only temporary, community around his bed. The hospital setting may serve to "contain" the narrator's attack on distortions of religious belief, but it provides a context for mutual communication free from resentment and complacency, one that reflects back to its participants an ennobling rather than belittling image of themselves.

One wonders, though, why the novel cannot imagine such communication – and communion – occurring in the city at large. Part of the answer may be found in the other episode that most explicitly displays the author's artistic shaping of Alexandre's story: the hero's trip to the country that constitutes the second of the novel's three parts. Willing for once to take someone else's advice, and while he still feels relatively healthy, Alexandre follows Dr Hudon's suggestion that he take a vacation in the Laurentian countryside. There, in a little lakeside cabin, he communes with nature and enjoys the simple hospitality of the Le Gardeurs, a family of farmers who own the property. Alexandre' idyll is spoiled, however, when he decides to translate his experience into socially useful words. He tries to write a letter to the editor of a newspaper which long ago had published his ideas about the world situation. Unable to muster his thoughts, the normally voluble Alexandre fails to compose even a first sentence (162).[41] In his distress, he decides to return home early, carrying in his pocket the one thing he was able to write during his vacation: a letter to his wife saying he loved her. But, just as Alexandre could not have expressed such a sentiment when immersed in his Montreal life, Eugénie will read that letter only after her husband has died and left that life for good.

This sad episode also says something important about Roy's communication with her readers in this, her second and last Montreal novel. It has long been noted that Alexandre's vacation destination lies somewhere just beyond the village of Rawdon where Gabrielle Roy found peaceful refuge, first during the composition of *Bonheur d'occasion* and again during the time she struggled to bring *Alexandre Chenevert* out of what she called the "limbo" of amorphous drafts.[42] Not enough is made, I think, of the symbolic implications of this connection between life and art. The hospitable surroundings of her Rawdon retreat had helped Roy write a first book that readers loved, but with which she did not want to be identified as she began to feel more and more uncomfortable writing in the mode of social realism. That Alexandre cannot write in the very place Roy had found congenial underscores the difference between author and character. Yet, in showing us that character trying ineffectually to give inchoate inward feeling social articulation, Roy is also dramatizing her own discomfort, when she returned to that place, about producing the kind of social panorama her readers expected.

The Lac Vert episode itself does not give us any clues about the reasons for this discomfort, but we can get some idea from the episode that immediately precedes it. This is the one moment in the story that shows us Alexandre relating to his urban environment in a positive way. He is in a good mood after his second medical consultation. Dr Hudon's remark that he was "too thin-skinned for this world" and "made to suffer" (115) has flattered his self-image as a Gandhi-like martyr. He wanders over to the Carré Saint-Louis. Bathed in sunlight and comfortably warm, empty but in an inviting rather than (as in *Earth and High Heaven*) a desolate way, the square is one of the very few positive city spaces shown in the book. It is certainly the only one Alexandre ever stops to enjoy. "'This is a little corner of Montreal I've always rather liked,' Alexandre ingenously [*naïvement*] confided to himself" (117–18, translation modified). Roy's choice of adverb suggests that for once Alexandre speaks without obsessing about what he should think and without worrying about how to put his feeling into words. At ease in his surroundings, he becomes more attentive to them, in a way that anticipates the heightened perceptions of the Lac Vert countryside but also foreshadows his sympathetic observation of the patients who later share his hospital room. All is well until Alexandre sees something that reawakens his moral scruples. "In the interests of honesty, he tried to tell himself that he had no more right to pamper himelf than had, for instance, that poor policeman glued to the asphalt in the sun's full glare, and signalling so continuously with his arms that the mere sight of it began to fatigue Monsieur Chenevert" (118).

Alexandre gives himself permission to turn away from a distressing spectacle and focus on his own happiness, but just at this point the narrator intervenes, using the character's thoughts to convey what seems to be a message of her own: "Then, as, when you get down to it, he had been perfectly free to do all his life, he looked at something else. Perhaps it was bad to keep telling people that they had the right to be happy. Such a relaxation of barriers might one day produce a strange confusion – no more policemen on street corners, no more miners, no more spinners and weavers at their unhealthy trades" (118).

The first step toward happiness, this passage suggests, is to turn away from other people's problems. It is a plausible claim to make in the case of man so obsessed with misery that he can never be happy or make anyone else happy either. The sentence that follows is more problematic: if everyone had a right to be happy would anyone still be willing to work as a policeman or a miner? The inference is far from self-evident. The spinners and weavers of Pierre Gélinas's *Les Vivants les morts et les autres*, as we will see, want to be happy, but they don't leave their jobs; they fight for better wages and working conditions. Roy's way of framing the question suggests that it is she who has fallen into "a strange confusion" by assuming that happiness is to be equated with escape from the realities of social existence. Or, to put it another way, that to engage with these realities means you can't be happy. Absent here is any sense that such engagement might foster both creative imagination and practical change. It may indeed be necessary to "look away" at times in order to relieve the pressure of obligation and give oneself room to breathe. It hardly follows that one cannot look back again without being suffocated.

We can, of course, understand why Roy's anxious Alexandre, dominated as he is by his social superego (and hostage to a rather grandiose image of himself as bearing the weight of the world), might come to this conclusion. We can also understand why he should feel so relieved when he hears nature speaking to him at Lac Vert in "the consoling language of indifference" (134), lifting from his shoulders the burden of responsibility, indeed of response altogether, that weighed him down in the city. Yet, in this passage, as earlier in the scene in the Carré Saint-Louis, Roy does not distinguish the narrator's perspective from that of her protagonist. She speaks of the world, and of her work, in terms as polarized as Alexandre's. The writer, she seems to be saying, can submit to the undoubtedly moral but rather dreary obligation of identifying with her character's limited consciousness, and end up mirroring in her writing the mixture of compassion and irritation that defines his relationships with other people, or she can claim her right to creative happiness and abandon the "unhealthy trade" of "mining" his life to make a novel. We see now why Roy, in order to resolve this dilemma, had to take Alexandre out of the world of work, first to a countryside vacation spot, then to a hospital, the one place where you can legitimately leave to other people the "insalubrious" tasks that keep society going and focus on your own well-being.

Conversely, neither the characters who come to Alexandre's bedside nor the narrator herself feel driven to "look somewhere else" in order to avoid being entangled in the hero's predicament. On the contrary, as I have suggested, they find consolation in contemplating the dying Alexandre, whose fate, they may well be relieved to hear, they can do nothing to change. Their only responsibility is to find in his mortality a salutary reminder of their own and of the precious fragility of human life. In turning her back on the urban novel in favour of the fictionalized memoirs of the lost world of *Rue Deschambault* (*Street of Riches*, 1955), Gabrielle Roy would make this responsibility the basis for an artistic mission more congenial to her personality than that of social realist.

The honesty of Roy's struggle to put her urban writing into perspective through the story of the title character gives *Alexandre Chenevert* enduring value as a novel of Montreal, over and above its importance as a document about a way of life and as the expression of a distinctive literary sensibility. What keeps her struggle from culminating in a fully satisfactory work of art, however, is that even though her novel offers an intuitively acute conception of the city's collective imaginary in depicting – and enacting – its controlling syndrome of compassion and irritation, with the exception of brief references to linguistic hierarchies it does not present that imaginary as a contingent phenomenon shaped by specific historical forces. Roy's protagonist and the narrator who accompanies him may in the end view the city's ills from a transcendent point of view, but they do not put them into a perspective from which the prospect of a cure can be glimpsed.

Of course, Callaghan and MacLennan had offered other reasons not to look too far beneath the surface of Montreal life. Flawed as it is, that surface is as pleasant to skate across as it is dangerous to probe. As we turn to novels of the later 1950s, we will see both francophone and anglophone writers sapping the foundations of the urban consensus whose solidity Callaghan, MacLennan, and Roy still took for granted. In Richler, Moore, and Weintraub, the pleasurable enjoyment of social stasis by those who feel superior to it becomes the target of a satire more thoroughgoing, and therefore more deeply ambivalent, than any found in earlier English writers. The anxious and ineffectual earnestness of Roy's Alexandre is recast by Bessette and Gélinas as the more subversive inadequacy of wilfully immature characters. With the partial exception of *Les*

Vivants, les morts et les autres, none of these subsequent novels appeals to transcendent realities of nature or spirit. The limitations and contradictions of the city's life, they suggest, need to be experienced in aggravated form before their transformation can be imagined.

5

A Precarious Maturity

Anglophone Satire at the End of the 1950s

Between 1959 and 1961, Mordecai Richler, Brian Moore, and William Weintraub, three English-language writers who were also friends, published satirical novels about Montreal life. In these stories, the (male) hero's ambitions are frustrated as much by the comic naivety of his outlook as by society's culpable resistance to renewal. MacLennan's two Montreal novels had included satirical portraits, but these depicted the city's fossilized elites, not the hero struggling against them. Athanase's naivety in *Two Solitudes* was tragic rather than comic, and while Alexandre Chenevert's grandiosity does have something comical about it, it is not really a laughing matter. Of course, these three satirical novels criticize social rigidity as well. Curiously, that critique is strongest in Richler's *The Apprenticeship of Duddy Kravitz*, the first of the three to be published and the one whose story, which begins in 1947, is set farthest in the past. Although the two other books appeared after the death of Maurice Duplessis, amidst the first stirrings of the Quiet Revolution, and are set, at least ostensibly, in a more recent period – the action of *The Luck of Ginger Coffey* takes place in 1956, while that of *Why Rock the Boat?* unfolds in an indeterminate present – they are predicated on the resilience, not the imminent doom, of the established order. Moore and Weintraub anticipate no radical change, and if anything they are less angered by the stultified city than Richler was.

One reason is that the experiences dramatized by Weintraub and Moore relate to crises in their personal lives they felt they had resolved. Ginger Coffey's Montreal is largely the one the unknown author encountered on his arrival in 1948; by 1956, the publication of *Judith Hearne* had brought him critical success. Similarly, the journalistic experiences of Weintraub's hero, Harry Barnes, hark back to the author's apprentice years at the Montreal *Gazette*, which he left in 1950. By 1961, Weintraub was enjoying a productive career as a journalist and as a scriptwriter for the National Film Board. But the very fact that these authors could portray their earlier experience of Montreal without any indication of temporal distance suggests they assumed the immediate future, too, would not be all that different from the present.[1] Even Richler's *Duddy Kravitz*, whose youthful wounds were still fresh and whose satire of his hero's Saint-Urbain Street world cuts more deeply, does not detect any stirrings of structural change. The increasing prosperity of the postwar years, it seems, is doing nothing to diminish the city's linguistic divisions and imaginative compartmentalization. Although the satires of Weintraub, Moore, and Richler vary in range and tone, they are alike in directing their critique, not so much at the inability of Montrealers to modify the tacit civic consensus that according to MacLennan and Callaghan defined the historical particularity of their city, as at the stubbornness and stupidity that prevents their fellow citizens – the English speakers among them chiefly in view – from living up to standards of moral enlightenment applicable in every time and place.

On the surface, at least, this appeal to universal standards makes comic satire a genre less context-dependent than the realist novel, with its focus on historical contingency. That flexible common sense should prevail over prejudice; that money should neither be squandered nor hoarded; that the elders of society should not prevent their children from choosing their life partners for themselves: few of the premises on which comic satire is usually based is likely to provoke much disagreement, in theory if not always in practice. While deliciously concrete in their selection of telling local detail, these satires – even, as we shall see, the more circumstantially discursive *Duddy Kravitz* – distance themselves from the messiness of real-life decisions, the better to highlight general absurdities of judgment. They succeed not by dramatizing conflicts between equally cherished but opposing values but rather by exposing the mechanical consistency of people's behaviour and the unthinking way they cling to their ideas as if they were all of a piece.

Of course, satirical fictions are inevitably shaped by the culture in which they appear. Vanity may always be foolish, but what counts as vanity, and what distinguishes vanity from appropriate self-esteem, may vary according to local customs and codes. By and large, however, the satirical depiction of such local variations, while inviting discussion of how moral principles are best applied, does not undermine the universality of the principles themselves. Still, the decision to write in this literary mode in preference to others available to the author may well be conditioned by the cultural context in which that decision was made. That these anglophone Montreal writers of the late 1950s should choose to write a comic satire suggests a considerable degree of confidence that the city has reached a point where, although still hidebound, it is sufficiently sophisticated to "get" what they say. Most important, they assume that satirizing the city is a culturally acceptable, even welcome, exercise. These novels are free of the anxiety that informed the more earnest fictions of MacLennan and Callaghan, whose obsession with the cultural precariousness of the city found expression in their realist "problem" novels. No doubt, the achievements of those elders gave the younger ones some of the confidence they needed to write. Another basis for that confidence was the privileged status still enjoyed by an anglophone minority whose ranks were being renewed and diversified by waves of new postwar immigrants (such as Moore himself) and the increasing social integration of the local Jewish community from which Richler and Weintraub came. In some ways, it was more plausible than it had been in earlier decades for anglophone writers to see themselves as speaking for modernity as such, as being cosmopolitan rather than "race"-bound in their outlook.

On the other hand, this universalism could be given convincing expression only by limiting its scope. The modern, disabused "knowingness" the novels project requires that they eliminate from their field of vision anything about which they cannot speak knowledgeably. In discussing *The Loved and the Lost*, I argued that MacLennan's criticism of the novel for "not knowing" what it thought of Peggy was misplaced. The limitation of the novel's knowledge was integral to the dramatization of what it could mean to "know" Montreal. Such a question does not arise in the stories told in *The Luck of Ginger Coffey* or *Why Rock the Boat?*. Adhering to the conventions of comic satire, the authors do not need to raise it either. To do so would be to spoil the fun. If the more complex *Duddy Kravitz* hints at the issue, it too, as we shall see, discourages the reader from following up that hint very far.

One could make a plausible case that this restriction of scope also betrays an indirect or unconscious awareness of the increasingly problematic authority with which anglophone Montreal writers could speak of "their" city. The detective novels that played such a prominent role in the anglophone Montreal fiction of the 1950s and early 1960s could also be enlisted to support such an argument.[2] Like comic satirists, writers of detective novels with sufficient command of insider information about practical matters within the purview of the genre can claim literary authority without raising questions about what they don't know and why they don't know it. Since the mysteries of the "noir" city can by definition never fully be elucidated, the failure to address (let alone remedy) certain specific forms of social ignorance can be taken in stride.

However, we should beware of assuming that generic conventions define a work's artistic potential in any straightforward way. In practice, some conventions may end up clashing with others. Comic satire often attacks moral corruption or social backwardness through indulgent depictions of childish pranks, ruthless caricature, or vulgar humour. While not necessarily irreconcilable, these elements of satire never mesh entirely, and so a space is created in which new possibilities can be explored.

Indeed, at certain times and places, writers may even find satire, despite its conventions, a more congenial genre for such exploration than what Henry James called the "loose and baggy" genre of the realist novel. The English Montreal of Moore, Weintraub, and Richler at the end of the 1950s, I suggest, was one such place and time. From a political point of view, or from the perspective of a teleological view of historical development, the turn to comic satire might seem to signal a retreat from the challenges of attempting a comprehensively "realist" representation of a city whose governing ethos was becoming increasingly brittle. From a psychological point of view, on the other hand, to choose this genre might be seen as a repudiation of the "maturity" found in *The Watch That Ends the Night*, or earlier in *The Loved and the Lost*, a maturity that had come to seem more willed than real, shaped by a semi-colonial superego rather than secured through the agency of a fully integrated because concretely grounded cultural self.[3]

This force of this counter-argument will be felt if we compare the beginning of Richler's *Duddy Kravitz* with that of his first Montreal novel, the more conventionally "realist" *Son of a Smaller Hero* (1955).

After briefly introducing its protagonist, Noah Adler, the earlier novel opens with a panoramic survey of the urban space occupied by the Montreal Jews in the summer of 1952. The omniscient narrator begins by declaring: "The ghetto of Montreal has no real walls and no true dimensions. The walls are the habit of atavism and the dimensions are an illusion" (10). The sociological language of this opening statement – if not its thesis – echoes that of the B'nai Brith report on the decline of anti-Semitism in Canada to which the narrator refers a little later. Richler goes on to describe the different classes of Jews to be seen on the main streets of three different neighbourhoods: the poor of St Lawrence Boulevard, the well-to-do of Queen Mary Road, and the people of Park Avenue, gradually moving from poverty to plenty. Each description includes details about the stores, cars, and other material features that characterize each area of the city. The writing is lively and the tone wonderfully confident – indeed, at times too confident. When the narrator declares that "each street had its own technique of walking, a technique so finely developed that you could always tell a man off his own street" (12), the phrase "so finely developed" applies less to the people in the story, whose behaviour merely indexes their class position, than to the narrator, who seems to be congratulating himself on the fineness of his observations.

Or rather, the phrase conveys the self-satisfaction of an author standing outside and apart from his work. For it is by no means clear from the story the novel tells how anyone within its world, even Noah, could arrive at a position from which such insights could be gained. It is not a question the narrative feels compelled to address. Nor does the novel present these insights as generalizations to be tested in the story. *Son of a Smaller Hero* is often said to be too directly autobiographical to be successful, but the real problem is that Richler strives so hard for literary gravitas that he fails to bridge the gap between the experience the story relates and the authority with which the story is told. But one could also say that, unlike the writers discussed in the last chapter, Richler was simply not as interested in the problem of how to put his artistic perceptions into perspective as his predecessors were. If he could not convincingly assert narrative authority by mere force of will, which would seem to be the lesson he drew from *Son of a Smaller Hero*, than the alternative is to abandon the ideal of a mature, reflective authority in favour of the peremptory and irreverent authority of satire.

Thus, in *Duddy Kravitz*, the reader is introduced to Jewish street life through a comic episode, the "March of the Fletcher's Cadets." The boisterous students of Fletcher's Field High School are not subjected to solemn sociological analysis as they parade through their neighbourhood under the baton of one of their teachers, W.E. James. James likes to draw his students' attention to his initials: "that's 'Jew' spelt backwards, as he told each new gym class" (36). Just as this statement ironizes claims to clever "knowingness," the description of the kids' "way of walking," their schoolboy gestures and jokes, trivializes the skill of "telling people off their street." What is there to learn about these boys that isn't already obvious? Serious authorial commentary gives way to gleeful citation of the insults the marchers and the onlookers hurl at each other. Though less ambitious in scope and lighter in tone than the beginning of *Son of a Smaller Hero*, the opening scene of *Duddy Kravitz* is more vivid, more alive, and thus aesthetically more fully realized. The narrative also probes more deeply into the situation it depicts, using comedy to suggest realities it would be too heavy-handed to spell out. Near the end of the episode, one of the kids tells his father: "Mr. James says that in the first world war sometimes they'd march for thirty miles without stop through rain and mud that was knee-deep." The father replies: "Is that what I pay school fees for?" (40). There is nothing original about parental exasperation with pompous teachers and out-of-date and irrelevant lessons, but Richler sets that exasperation in a particular historical context. His scene takes place just after the Second World War, whose horrors eclipsed anything seen in the first, especially for the Jews. The father's flippant reply makes us realize that neither the characters in the scene nor the narrator describing the parade mentions the Holocaust. Any direct allusion to that event would, of course, spoil the joke. On another level, this silence provides an effective illustration of what the earlier novel had called the "invisible walls" of imaginative self-limitation that for Richler characterized Jewish Montreal (and other Montreals, too, according to the other writers we have examined). Complicit in that limitation, while quietly drawing attention to it, Richler's narrator adopts an interestingly ambiguous attitude toward the authority with which his narrator speaks.

Although *The Apprenticeship of Duddy Kravitz* was published several years later than *Son of a Smaller Hero* and carries a title that suggests a progression from childhood to young adulthood, Richler's second hero is younger than his first by about the same number of years that his creator is older than the man who wrote the earlier book. Noah Adler is twenty when his tale begins in 1952, three years before *Son of a Smaller Hero*'s publication date of 1955. *Duddy Kravitz* came out in 1959, but the story starts in 1947, when the central character, whose family background is essentially the same as Noah's, is still a teenager in high school. The greater distance between the time of writing and the time of the story allows Richler to attain a greater objectivity in the portrayal of his protagonist. But in doing so through satirical excess instead of through measured realism he does so without over-asserting his claim to knowledge. As a consequence, when Richler introduces the chapter that follows the comic account of the cadets' parade with a more serious observation – "Where Duddy Kravitz sprung from the boys grew up dirty and sad, spiky also, like grass beside the railroad tracks" (41) – this lapidary declaration carries a force all the greater because of the contrast with the exuberant comic scene that first showed us that "where."

There is much more to *Duddy Kravitz*, of course, than a strategic retreat (if that is the right word) from strenuous realism to sprightly satire, from earnest "maturity" to an "immaturity" whose irresponsibility is acknowledged but whose vulgar vitality the narrative is not ashamed to make its own. The radical heedlessness of Duddy's character gives Richler permission to be ruthless with the rules of decorum, while the impact of the hero's actions on other people is sobering enough to make the reader think hard about the aesthetic and moral appropriateness of the author's enterprise. As a result, Duddy Kravitz turns out to be a more effectively self-conscious work of art than *Son of a Smaller Hero*. This does not mean that Richler's novel transcends the cultural moment in which it was written. To understand the relation between text and context, however, it will be useful to postpone further discussion of Richler's novel until we have examined the comic satires written by his friends. Although published after *Duddy Kravitz*, their novels offer simpler forms of the satiric strategy Richler will exploit to more memorable effect.

WHY ROCK THE BOAT?

William Weintraub's *Why Rock the Boat?* offers a comic send-up of life at the *Daily Witness*, a paper said to be typical of Montreal's timid, self-censoring press.[4] The paper's coverage of civic life is limited to summarizing the after-dinner speeches given by local bigwigs and listing the mourners at the funerals of prominent citizens. Reporting on world affairs means interviewing visiting dignitaries in their hotel rooms,[5] making sure to get these dignitaries to attack communism and praise free enterprise. For the journalists, a desirable assignment isn't one that deals with a controversial topic. They know that any story likely to "rock the boat" by attacking entrenched interests will be spiked by the paper's dictatorial editor. What counts is whether they can wring a free meal or some other little perk out of their assignments, to supplement their meagre salaries. The story's central question – will cub reporter Harry Barnes, freshly arrived in Montreal from the Eastern Townships, fulfill his dream of becoming a "real" journalist, or will the need to make a living force him to compromise his principles? – seems to be answered even before it is asked.

The novel's premise is a familiar one, and the bittersweet ending comes as no surprise. What makes the story successful is the skilful pacing with which one comic complication follows another in breathless but carefully controlled succession. Weintraub also sprinkles his narrative with little "knowing" details that give the satire a particular local twist. The collusion between organized crime and a corrupt police force, for example, is dramatized not by the cover-up of some gruesome crime but by a comic misunderstanding about a "victimless" offence. A fake "raid" on illegal gambling at a downtown hotel goes awry because the police forgot what every journalist knew: the promoters had paid their police protection money, but since the city's regular gambling dens are closed on Catholic feast days, a different venue had to be found for the action. Harry also learns how to "smith out a list" of attendees at a major funeral. When the mourners are not as numerous or distinguished as the deceased's social standing deserves, fake names have to be added to the list. But not any names will do. "They've got to sound Montreal and they've got to sound like they have bank accounts … If the deceased really had money, you want lots of those Scotch names, but go easy on the Irish ones." When Harry suggests adding a "Pierre Leduc" as well, the veteran reporter tells him: "No, on your French names, try for something longer, classier, like 'Bellefeuille,' or 'Préfontaine.' Those Leducs and Carons sound as though they don't have a dime" (24–5).

The novel's references to politics are equally confident in their knowingness. Waldron, a reporter fired by the *Witness* for poking his nose where it didn't belong, jokes about founding a political party advocating the dissolution of the Canadian federation. The provinces would be given to the United States or, in the case of Ontario, back to Britain. With one exception: "Quebec, being the only part of the country with any distinctive character – such as it is – becomes an independent nation. Brother, there'd be no trouble selling that to the Quebec voter!" (67). Harry is impressed, but when he repeats what Waldron told him at an artsy cocktail party, everyone laughs at such "pure Dada" ideas (111). The moment is characteristic of the way the novel expresses its awareness of latent social tensions without any sense of an actual threat to the status quo. For the comic satirist, the absurdity of social arrangements does not portend their immanent collapse; on the contrary, it may be the key to their longevity. Sophisticated Montrealers may be receptive to progressive ideas, but the city they inhabit remains exasperatingly – but also comfortably – resistant to fundamental change. The defensive cohesiveness of its linguistic communities, and the peculiar mixture of contention and collusion between them, gives Montreal a certain impervious solidity that makes it an ideal target for satire, but also a safe one. The Weintraub of *Why Rock the Boat?* was by no means alone in taking such a view, as we have seen in discussing *The Watch That Ends the Night* and will see again in Bessette's *La Bagarre*. What distinguishes Weintraub's novel from the other two is the relish with which that assumption seems to be entertained.

Weintraub's barbs certainly do not challenge his implied readers' deep-seated values. By the standards of an "enlightened" Montrealer in 1961, Harry's reluctance to "smith out" a funeral list hardly makes him much of a rebel. His scorn for his paper's obsequious response to its advertisers is hardly revolutionary and leads to no disruptive action. The young man's eager perusal of medical manuals about "conjugal love" is hardly likely to cause a scandalous reaction; on the contrary, he is comically ignorant of the actual pornography readers assume must be available to those in the know. "Modern" spiritual leaders whose popularity rests on their ability to add a pious gloss to secular activities, like the rabbi who gives inoffensive talks on "Sport in the Old Testament" (173), are another easy target. Far from protesting the exclusion of Jews from Montreal's WASP country clubs, he takes pride in being a member of the "Disraeli Hunt" (171). The reader laughs but is not led to question this social segregation. Like the separation between French and English speakers, it is an arrangement just as much taken for granted as it was fifteen years earlier, in the wartime Montreal portrayed by Gwethalyn Graham. Yet, in comparison with the heroes of the earlier novels we have discussed, Harry's own background is significantly different in that ethnically it is as "unmarked" as it could possibly be. Weintraub could not avoid giving him English as a native language, but he compensates by giving him a fluency in French whose origin is never explained. Harry has no particular religious affiliation (though from this fact the reader understands he isn't Jewish). His economic status is modest, but not too modest to prevent him from being socially presentable. Harry's naivety makes him an outsider, but nothing prevents him from becoming an insider if he smartens up.

Like the novels of the previous decade, therefore, *Why Rock the Boat?* takes Montreal's social arrangements for granted, but, despite the specificity of its local references, it does not historicize that civic consensus, as to some extent at least MacLennan and Callaghan tried to do. Although the story of this 1961 novel is set in the present, nothing seems to distinguish the city it portrays from the one in which Weintraub began his career a decade earlier, and which he himself would later describe in delightfully circumstantial detail in *City Unique* (1996). This non-fiction work, part memoir, part historical chronicle, differs from the novel in its awareness of how and why that era came to an end. *Why Rock the Boat?* omits any reference to harbingers of change, notably the crusade against vice and corruption led by lawyer Jean Drapeau, elected mayor on a reform program in 1954, and by his legendary colleague, police commander "Pax" Plante. It is true that Drapeau was defeated in 1957 and was re-elected as mayor only in 1960, around the time the book was completed. Given the city's history of resistance to change, Weintraub may have felt that the outcome of the anti-corruption campaign was sufficiently in doubt as to make predictions unwise. On the other hand, from the evidence he offers in *City Unique*, public attitudes, and not just about public morals, were clearly shifting by the time *Why Rock the Boat?* was published. Weintraub may perhaps have kept "history" out of the novel so that his satire could appeal to a broad international audience, but the effect is to allow Montreal anglophone readers to have their cake and eat it too. They could applaud Harry's virtuous indignation without worrying whether the underground currents of change might eventually erode the ground on which they stood.

Another key feature of the narrative is its framing of the hero's education as one of social more than moral discovery. There are no revelations about how to negotiate conflicting ethical imperatives. Rather, through his blunders and faux pas, none of lasting consequence, Harry comes to learn "what's what," to borrow the title of the talismanic gossip column in *Duddy Kravitz*: the practical things you need to know to navigate the city. There is, to be sure, a moment of moral trial. In order to save a fellow journalist from being fired, Harry has to admit he was the reporter who invented the scurrilous story about Butcher, the *Witness*'s editor, that one day was slipped into the paper. Of course, if the stingy Butcher had not hired low-cost, non-union French proofreaders who didn't understand the copy they checked, the story would never have made it into print, but Harry can't let another reporter take the blame, even if it means losing his job. It turns out that Harry's immediate superior, a sub-editor who also chafed under Butcher's rule, deliberately let the story go through, and that the other reporter deserved to be fired for incompetence. Harry thus has no real reason to feel guilty. In any case, he suffers no consequences for his actions, since at the moment of crisis Butcher is replaced by another editor determined to make the *Witness* a "real" newspaper. Harry plays no role in this outcome either. By the end of the story, Harry has indeed learned what's what, but his knowledge is not transformative. By relieving the hero of moral responsibility, the author keeps the comedy light but at the cost of trivializing the hero's trials.

In similar fashion, Weintraub's satire minimizes what might be called the collective dimension of his hero's agency. Harry is neither empowered nor burdened by his lineage, in the manner of Paul Tallard or Mathieu Normand. Yet he is not simply a Candide, the orphan or bastard picaresque hero whose freedom from obligation to the past gives him greater social mobility. The vagueness of Harry's origins seems designed simply to forestall any consideration of where he comes from and how that location might affect his point of view. He is simply the "average Joe" of sociological abstraction. Similarly, the future to which Harry aspires involves no redefinition of the political or linguistic character of the community in which he sees himself flourishing. His concern is with the immediate obstacles that obstruct his path, not with the direction of the path itself.

The one, crucial exception involves what Flaubert would call Harry's sentimental education. The young man's eagerness to gain sexual experience modulates into a more thoughtful apprenticeship to love. During a ski weekend for reporters, Harry is seduced by the alluring Mrs Scammell, the neglected wife of yet another editor. This episode does not "rock the boat" of moral order very hard. Far from being the first episode in a libertine career, it is a one-time occasion for the virginal hero to learn "what's what" inasmuch as this is a necessary precondition for moral growth. His brief liaison thus bears some resemblance to Mathieu's affair with Annette and Danielle's night with Jacques in Loranger's *Mathieu*. Harry's night of pleasure generates just enough guilt to prompt him to become more self-aware and transform his erotic pursuit of fellow reporter Julia Martin into a quest for personal intimacy.

Like Callaghan's Peggy, Julia is from Ontario, but her misunderstanding of Montreal has none of the tragic quality found in *The Loved and the Lost*. She believes she speaks fluent French when in fact she barely understands the language. Her delusion is exposed in some comic encounters with local francophones in which the bilingual Harry can ride to her rescue. After treating Harry's awkward advances with amused detachment, the more experienced Julia comes to appreciate his qualities, and once Harry has gained the necessary experience, no rival stands in the way of their union.

Contrary to comic convention, however, the story does not end with the young couple's marriage. Julia leaves for an extended assignment in Brazil, and while there is some suggestion she and Harry may pick up their relationship later, the novel leaves the matter open. Like Mathieu, Harry has not yet fully matured; he has more growing to do. Yet, in striking contrast to Loranger's hero, Harry's social career is clearly mapped out. His professional future is secure but at the same time less pregnant with possibility. While the new editor of the *Witness* will no doubt give him the opportunity to write something meaningful, there is no indication that Harry defines his career, or his role in public life, in significantly new ways.

The novel's conclusion is thus somewhat ambiguous. Harry's sentimental education, which schools him in the mysteries of life and the need to respect their unknowable dimension, contrasts with the pursuit of an easy worldly knowingness. Harry learns that what he doesn't know about

Julia and the prospects for a relationship with her cannot be remedied by greater savvy about what's what. Though not at odds with the satire, the romance plot modifies its perspective. Yet the implications of Harry's sentimental education are limited to the sphere of personal experience. When it comes to his relationship with the city, Harry is never led to wonder about what he doesn't know, still less to worry, so to speak, about what's *not* what. Of course, to dramatize those questions would push the novel beyond the bounds of comic satire. Weintraub doesn't want to spoil our fun. We can be grateful for that while recognizing that the novel's success depends on its limitations.

THE LUCK OF GINGER COFFEY

Brian Moore's Ginger Coffey is just as immature as Weintraub's Harry Barnes, but a man pushing forty with a wife and a teenaged daughter to support has less excuse than a youth just out of school. In the months after his arrival in Montreal from Ireland, Ginger makes only one real friend: a child named Michel, the lonely son of his landlady, Madame Beaulieu. Admitting that "I don't parleyvoo" (87), Ginger would rather escape with Michel into the world of toy trucks than face the challenge of finding a job. Ginger's dream of marketing Irish tweeds and liquor to Montreal stores has come to nothing, yet rather than go home in defeat, he stubbornly insists that success lies just around the corner. The disparity between his unsinkable optimism and the undignified jobs he is forced to take provides much of the novel's satirical comedy. Thanks to a tip from a political cartoonist who has designs on his wife, Ginger gets an interview with the tyrannical editor of the *Tribune*, a newspaper much like Weintraub's *Witness* (and also based on the Montreal *Gazette*). His fantasy of becoming a man-about-town reporter is quickly dashed when the editor makes him a proofreader, a position so poorly paid that to make ends meet Ginger takes a second, equally humiliating, job delivering diapers. While less malicious than the editor, his boss at the *Tiny Ones* service, a veteran of the Canadian army transport corps, is equally obsessed with order and discipline, his military rhetoric comically at odds with the business he runs.

It is surely no coincidence that MacGregor the editor and Stanley Mountain the diaper man (as well as Ginger's cartoonist acquaintance

Gerry Grosvenor) bear the names of real city streets: they symbolize the odd character, at once comical and coercive, of the novel's Montreal. It is a mostly British city, but Moore also offers briefer caricatures of two potential employers of other backgrounds. Georges Paul-Emile Beauchemin is "public relations director of Canada Nickel" (22), a position with more prestige than real power and indicative of the status of French Canadians in the city. H.E. Kahn, whom Ginger takes (no doubt correctly) to be Jewish (26), is an executive for a "professional fund-raising group" (he might be raising capital for one of the hospitals mentioned in *Alexandre Chenevert*). Both men are younger than Ginger, who would like to believe he is turned down because of his age. The real problem is that Ginger is a walking anachronism. He continues to dress in the style he adopted years ago in Ireland to look the part of a "Dublin squire," but his green Alpine hat and suede boots are not only ill suited to the Montreal winter; to the uncomprehending Beauchemin, they give him the air of a spoiled college boy. Ginger, who prides himself on his gift of the gab, is also surprised to discover that his inability to speak even a word of French disqualifies him in Kahn's eyes. Moore's English Montreal may be a blinkered and compartmentalized city, but his hero lives in an even more airtight bubble of ignorance and entitlement. The issue at stake in *The Luck of Ginger Coffey* is thus more urgent than the one in *Why Rock the Boat?* Harry had to learn "what's what" to get ahead; Ginger has to get outside himself if he and his family are to survive at all.

In an interview recorded in the early 1970s, Moore said that *The Luck of Ginger Coffey*, like his other early novels *Judith Hearne* (1955) and *The Feast of Lupercal* (1957), were focused on "the moment in a person's life, the crucial few weeks or months, when one suddenly confronts the reality or unreality of one's illusions."[6] Indeed, Ginger's misfortunes lead him to confront "the mirror man" (160), to see himself as he appears to others.[7] Interestingly, the incident that triggers that self-confrontation is Ginger's one direct encounter with Montreal's semi-colonial identity. Waiting one night at a bus stop after too many drinks, he relieves himself against a wall and is arrested for indecent exposure by the police. The Irish Ginger did not realize the wall he watered was that of the "Royal Family" hotel (221; Weintraub would have appreciated the name), and that he was standing scandalously close to the main entrance. The policemen themselves are French. Like the francophone officials with whom he deals, first in jail and then in court, they speak functional English, but Ginger does not know how to talk to them. His old-boy bombast is even more incongruous here than it was in his job interviews. The radical estrangement he experiences here for the first time is what finally drives him to change his life.

In an ironic twist, Ginger redeems himself through a different kind of fakery: he gives a false name to the judge. His goal is not to avoid punishment but to protect his family from shame. Of course, by calling himself Gerald MacGregor, he is also striking back at the two men who have humiliated him the most. One is the editor of the *Tribune*. The other is Gerry Grosvenor, the freelance cartoonist who befriended Ginger in order to seduce his wife. At the moment of Ginger's arrest, Veronica had been on the verge of giving in to Gerry's advances. Her husband's gallant gesture rekindles her love for him, while Gerry's refusal to help Ginger get out of jail earns him her scorn. The same lie also helps Ginger get a suspended sentence from a sympathetic judge. The novel ends with the hero's resolving to grow up and become a responsible adult at last.

Whether Ginger will keep his promise remains an open question at the end of the book, but this openness becomes more troublesome when we look more closely at what Ginger has in mind when he makes that promise. Looking at the man in the bathroom mirror, Ginger mentally recommits to his marriage and vows to be a better man. Yet his thoughts take a curious turn. Instead of focusing on his obligations to his family, or on the prospect of renewed intimacy with Veronica, that is to say, on responsibilities and relationships, he looks forward to a time when he won't have to struggle or strive at all, to a time "when sex and daydreams, fights and futures – when all that's on the shelf and done with" (243). Despite its disenchanted tone, this is less an acceptance of responsibility than another dream of escape, this time into a world beyond desire.

Nor does Ginger say anything about his relationship to his adopted city other than to predict he will die "in humble circs" (243). It is characteristic of Ginger to avoid picturing that future in any detail, but the absence of any clue about what those circumstances might or might not be, about the context in which his life might play out, suggests that for all the satirical detail about Ginger's Montreal, in the end the city serves only as a backdrop for the story. Unlike the fully realized Belfast of *Judith Hearne*, the Montreal of *Ginger Coffey* merely provides a stage on which the hero's existential crisis can be displayed. In this respect, the novel's instrumental rather than organic use of its Montreal setting is unwittingly akin to that found in some of the abstractly existential francophone novels published earlier in the decade, Charles Hamel's *Solitude de la chair* (Solitude of the flesh, 1951), for example, which also includes satirical elements, or Jean-Marie Poirier's *Le Prix du souvenir* (The cost of memory, 1957). And yet, in the interview cited above, Moore insisted that public issues related to the novel's specific location are crucial to the novel. Readers in the Soviet Union, he says, may have seen in Ginger Coffey "an attack on migration to capitalist countries" that he himself did not intend, but "the book is totally critical of the Canadian system" even if "that criticism is not stated in political terms."[8]

How can one make sense of this claim? Moore's depiction of the *Tribune* and the *Tiny Ones* diaper service hardly matches the ruthless "total critique "of Céline or even the early Evelyn Waugh. Sclerotic as Moore's Montreal may be, the hapless Ginger's dealings with its social "system" hardly show it to be a city more hostile to individual aspiration than any other in which he might have tried his luck. Montreal is certainly no more oppressive than Dublin or Cork, stuffy towns to be sure, but ones where Ginger had failed in large part because of his own faults before he left for Canada. But perhaps it is just the similarities between Ireland and Canada, and not any supposed difference, that is the point. That Moore should have made his hero an Irish immigrant like himself is natural enough, and on the surface Ginger's Irishness simply makes him a more "colourful" character. Perhaps we need to look closer. Is it merely by chance that an Irish writer makes the turning-point of his story an incident in which the hero urinates on the wall of a hotel named for the British monarchy in a city a good many of whose inhabitants still thought of as an outpost of the empire?

Ginger's Irishness is in fact crucial to the novel as a whole. First, it gives the story its distinctive voice, since the third-person narrator for the most part reports Ginger's thoughts from the character's point of view and in his own words. Like McGregor's Scottish accent or the colloquial French mixed into the policemen's English, Ginger's speech is ethnically marked. Yet Ginger's Irishness does more than enhance the comic incongruity of his verbal interactions with the locals. Ginger left Ireland because he was angry at the power the Catholic Church exercised over the nation's public life as well as over personal relationships by its opposition to birth control. Yet here he is in Quebec, which at the time of the story was still a very Catholic province.[9] At home, Ginger had been frustrated by the refusal of his employers to look beyond their comfortable mediocrity and take big entrepreneurial risks. Yet here he is in the hide-bound and slowly declining metropolis of Canada, a city that has not changed much since the war. Montreal, admittedly, was not Ginger's destination of choice. He first planned to go to New York, but the distillery he wanted to represent already had a man there. The irony is that the city he settled for is in important ways another Dublin. Ginger's dream of reinventing himself would seem to be doomed from the start.

A further analogy between Ginger's New and Old World city has to do with the recent war. Ginger's "large military moustache" spoils his interview with a potential French Canadian employer because "Georges Paul-Émile Beauchemin had not served" (23), a pointed reference by the narrator (Ginger is ignorant of the fact) to the reluctance of many Québécois to fight for the British Empire in the Second World War. Yet, although Ginger gained junior officer rank during his own military service, as a soldier in neutral Ireland he saw no action either, a fact he hides from prospective English Montreal employers. He wants to use his military credentials as an advantage while glossing over the reality behind them. Ginger Coffey's greatest stroke of "luck" is that Stanley Mountain, his boss at *Tiny Ones*, is also a veteran who never saw combat. Mountain, too, likes to fudge that fact, and for this reason he is happy to take Ginger at his word.

Yet, if these various implicit and explicit ironies add up to more than a series of satirical barbs, it is hard to see what message they are meant to convey. While Ginger's Irishness serves to expose some of Montreal's social contradictions, it plays little role in the hero's actual dealings with the city. For example, Ginger makes only minimal contact with Montreal's sizeable Irish community. His one half-hearted attempt to win the sympathy of an employment agency clerk named Donnelly only proves the rule. Ginger married above his station (Veronica's family is from Dalkey, a prosperous Dublin suburb), and, as his clothing suggests, he cultivates the image of a "gent." To mix with Montreal's Irish would be to risk exposure as a fraud, for they would be able to "place" him. His one other encounter with an Irish immigrant suggests as much. Delivering diapers to a fancy Sherbrooke Street apartment, he discovers that his customer is an old Dublin acquaintance of his wife's (131). The humiliation he feels at being seen standing on her service stairs in his work outfit is one of the most acute in the book. Just as his other greatest experience of embarrassment occurred at the symbolic intersection of English and French power, here he finds himself trapped by the Irish class structure he had sought to escape. Yet the incident does not prompt Ginger to reflect on his ethnic identity, or the narrator to comment on its implications for Ginger's possible integration into Montreal life.

Looking back on the novel, Moore acknowledged that he had left some loose ends. Financial pressures, he said, had forced him to finish the book in a rush. He also realized that the form he chose, "a first-person novel written in the third person," had its drawbacks, but he did not have the time to address them.[10] Luckily, he thought, these drawbacks were outweighed by the form's advantages. The character's limited perceptions and lack of self-awareness restricted the extent to which the narrative could contextualize his experiences, but writing from a point of view so close to Ginger's own allowed Moore to infuse the story with the hero's distinctive and certainly memorable voice.[11] But can the problems of *Ginger Coffey* be explained away so easily? A hero with a comically limited range of perception can be an effective vehicle for a satire of manners, but on its own this device cannot carry out the broader critical mission Moore claims for his book. It is also does little by itself to put that criticism into a meaningful literary perspective.

In *Why Rock the Boat?*, the romance plot, though conventional, provided a counterweight to the satire, complicating its message while complementing its comic energy. Ginger's bond with his wife might have played a comparable role in *The Luck of Ginger Coffey* if Moore had given us access to Veronica's thoughts. It is never made clear, for example, why a woman of her upbringing would so openly admit her attraction to Gerry (though she is firm in refusing to sleep with him), or, after she has separated from Ginger, so casually leave her daughter Paulie to the care of her estranged husband. Veronica's readiness to return to Ginger after enjoying a brief period of independence, like her decision to marry him in the first place, cannot simply be taken in stride as a necessary means to a comic tale's happy end. The novel is too circumstantial in its realism for that. Like Ginger, Veronica has moved from one particular time and place to another, and like Ginger's her move is fraught with specific social and psychological implications. For example, we infer from the fact that she has only one child after many years of what seems to be a sexually active marriage that Veronica has defied the Catholic prohibition of birth control. She seems to share her husband's wish to escape the repressiveness of Irish life generally. But whereas Callaghan withheld information about Peggy's motivations in *The Loved and the Lost* as part of a deliberate narrative strategy, Moore simply leaves Veronica's character underdetermined. The dynamic of her relationship with her husband does not expand or complement the scope of the satire.

On the other hand, Veronica's gradual integration into Montreal life is given interestingly thicker description. When Veronica separates from Ginger, she has no trouble finding what can be considered a good job for a 1950s woman fresh off the boat and lacking in professional skills. The francophone owner of a fancy Montreal hat shop finds in Veronica, with her Dalkey manners, just the saleswoman she needs to increase sales to English-language customers. Veronica, who gets along well with her boss, easily adapts to her work of linguistic as well as social mediation. When Ginger first left the family home, he took refuge in the YMCA of downtown English Montreal, but when Veronica leaves she ventures farther east, to "an Edwardian gingerbread" boarding house "on the dividing line between the English and French sections of the city" (182). When Ginger tracks her down, he is too focused on his mission to notice the other lodgers, and so we don't know if they in fact include French as well as English speakers (MacLennan had been similarly vague on this point when he spoke of this borderline neighbourhood in *The Watch That Ends the Night*). Still, Veronica's relocation to this neighbourhood suggests that she possesses a capacity to deal with the diversity of Montreal life far greater than Ginger's.[12]

Veronica's trajectory is rich in social, even political, potential, and so it is unfortunate that *The Luck of Ginger Coffey* does no more than sketch it. Perhaps her experience was too much at odds with the novel's supposed critique of the "Canadian system." In any case, when Ginger confronts the "mirror man" and recommits to his wife, he returns to the novel's centre stage. Swept up in the emotion of their reunion, Veronica not only identifies her future completely with his, she even starts to speak about the future in her husband's idiom: "'Oh Ginger," she said, 'I'm starting to sound like you,'" an echo that pleases Ginger enormously (242). With this, the couple's story comes to a rather disappointing end, and so the reader is not surprised to learn that Moore himself later felt dissatisfied. "I don't like the ending anymore," he admitted. Unfortunately, his only elaboration on that comment was more personal than literary: "I don't like the way I came out of that book."[13] This existential phrasing of the problem no doubt refers to events in the author's personal life that affected the conclusion of the novel. He and his first wife, Jacqueline, to whom the novel is dedicated, were in the process of separating. By the time he finished *The Luck of Ginger Coffey*, Moore was no longer living in Montreal, settled, as it turned out for good, in the United States.[14] Knowing this, it is tempting to view Ginger and Veronica's declaration that they have more in common than they realized as a wistful, retrospective one at odds with the most adventurous aspect of the book. When Veronica says, "Home is here, we're far better off here" (201), she may be overestimating her husband's ability to keep his good resolutions, but she is expressing more than just a pious wish. What she says about "home" is warranted by her actual experience of the city.

Unfortunately, Ginger's flash of moral self-knowledge does not make him see Veronica any more clearly than he did before. Here, a comparison with *Why Rock the Boat?* is instructive. Julia's role in that book was also limited to helping the hero grow out of his fantasies, but her relationship with the city was one whose opportunities and limitations were of constant interest to Harry and integral to his process of self-reflection. Moore may have wanted to avoid claiming too distanced a form of satirical authority by deliberately adopting Ginger's limited world view, but he ended up settling too easily for a narrowly individual resolution of the "mirror man" problem. The city the hero cannot see impinges sufficiently on the author's consciousness to edge its way into the story, but, in his haste to bring his story to a neat and tidy close, Moore set aside the disruptive potential that awareness carried with it.

THE APPRENTICESHIP OF DUDDY KRAVITZ

Richler's portrayal of Duddy's girlfriend Yvette Durelle in *The Apprenticeship of Duddy Kravitz* is even more problematic than Moore's characterization of Veronica. Attractive as she is, Yvette is not an object of wonder for Duddy, as Julia was for Harry. Whether Yvette stays or leaves will affect Duddy's future, but he never wonders what she might do, as Ginger does when he thinks about the woman in his life. Ginger shows no more interest in Veronica's thoughts about the world around them than Duddy does in Yvette's, but unlike Richler's hero he does at least worry about what his partner thinks of him. In Richler's defence, however, it can be argued that Duddy's lack of curiosity (for which the narrator does not compensate by offering any insight of his own) is consistent with Duddy's general self-obsession, on whose implications we are invited to reflect.

Duddy likes that Yvette desires him and, unlike most of his family, seems to love him for himself, but his desire for her is instrumental, not personal. Unlike Ginger, who is unwavering in his attachment to the woman who anchors his existence, or Harry, who finds in Julia his romantic ideal, Duddy treats his relationship with Yvette as a sexual and social convenience. As a French Canadian who grew up in the Laurentian countryside near the Jewish resort where she works, she negotiates on Duddy's behalf to get him what he really wants: the lakeside property that will fulfill his dream of becoming a man of substance. "A man without land is nothing" (98), Duddy says, citing his grandfather (44). For Duddy, who has always taken this principle literally, without any of the qualifications or reinterpretations he applies to other admonitions, the converse must be equally true: a man who owns land is by that very fact something. Since the farmers who currently own the fields around the lake would never consider selling to a stranger, Duddy buys their properties using Yvette's name. Of course, he plans to develop a resort on the land, but we are made to feel this is only a secondary goal (and it is worth noting that, when we meet an older Duddy again in *St. Urbain's Horseman*, nothing is said about that resort, which seems never to have been built). Just as it is enough for Duddy that Yvette be there when he needs her, proof that someone accepts him as he is, owning the land is enough to make Duddy feel accepted by the wider world.

Duddy's mother died when he was young, and his other relatives have never given him the kind of unconditional love that tells children they already are something, without them having to prove it. As a result, Duddy acts out his desperate need to compensate for that lack. That Yvette sticks with Duddy even though he often takes her for granted and makes it clear he would never think of marrying a woman who wasn't Jewish is precisely the kind of unconditional support he seeks. What makes Yvette love Duddy, and whether she would want to marry him, are questions the novel never raises because they do not matter to the hero. The one time she is asked what she sees in Duddy, all she says is "plenty" (164). Readers will find the answer unsatisfactory, but from the hero's point of view it says all that needs to be said: someone exists who sees Duddy in terms of the qualities he has rather than those he lacks. Nor does the novel explore why Yvette continues to work with Duddy after she discovers the consequences of a risky action she had warned him not to take.[15] Looking for someone to deliver projection equipment from one summer camp to another for his movie-night business, Duddy hires a man named Virgil Roseboro, knowing he was epileptic. Virgil has a seizure while driving the truck, and the resulting accident leaves him a paraplegic for life. Only when Duddy forges the crippled Virgil's signature on a cheque to make a crucial payment on his land does Yvette finally break with Duddy for good. Since we are not told what she's thinking, Yvette's motivation remains a mystery. Richler would later concede that his depiction of female characters in his early novels was sexist as well as artistically inadequate. Measured by the standards of maturely realistic fiction, this is certainly true. In a satirical context, however, *Duddy Kravitz*'s lack of interest in Yvette's perspective makes more sense, the resulting discomfort being part of the alienation effect the novel seeks to produce.

Indeed, the sword of satirical attack has seldom been so fiercely wielded in Montreal fiction as in *Duddy Kravitz*. Richler depicts the amorality and blinkered vision of his hero with the same jaundiced eye as he exposes the hypocrisy and moral meanness of the world in which he operates. The novel's great achievement is to make us identify with Duddy's revolt even as we recoil from his ruthlessness, and to prevent us from easily resolving our contradictory responses. Realist novels of urban "apprenticeship," from Balzac's *Père Goriot* to Bellow's *Adventures of Augie March*, often evoke conflicting feelings of this kind, but usually try to mediate them by showing the hero acknowledging, if not always seeking to resolve, the tension between his aspirations and the compromises attendant on becoming a mature adult. In *Duddy Kravitz* there is no such acknowledgment. For better and for worse, Duddy refuses to take in the "life-lessons" the grown-ups in his life are so eager to offer. And yet

Duddy is neither a comically hapless naif, like the protagonist of Weintraub and Moore's satires, nor a self-deluded dreamer like the Frédéric of Flaubert's *Éducation sentimentale* (*Sentimental Education*) or the Pip of *Great Expectations*. He is capable of decisive practical action. It is this paradoxical mixture of cleverness and cluelessness that Richler sets out to dramatize, along with the urban context out of which he emerges and whose equally paradoxical characteristics he brings into focus. Duddy's inability to desire or even to "see" Yvette, I would argue, is of a piece with the novel's intention. The ultimate value of the result may be debated, but only once we have discerned the appropriate terms for framing that debate.

A first step in this direction is to examine how the story's Montreal setting and satirical shape relate to what George Woodcock called "a fundamental dichotomy which runs like a rock fault through all of Richler's work." This is "the division between an irrational, half-conscious nihilist drive that so often gains control of his imagination, and a conscious moralism that is intolerant of weakness in behavior and deviousness of thought."[16] The literary framework of social realism cannot easily accommodate such a division, but the latter can find artistically productive representation in satire, a genre predicated on the difficulty (at times, the impossibility) of overcoming that division in a fallen world. In satire, the key aesthetic mediation is not roundness of characterization or thickness of description but rather a cutting sharpness of style. Richler's imagination excels in expressing resentment and conceiving fantasies of revenge, but he also has a keen sense of just how far to go in going too far.

What gives Richler's satire its distinctive flavour, however, is how both sides of the "fundamental dichotomy" of his work are inflected by the peculiar local context to which his work responds. Straitlaced yet lacking in structuring form, Richler's Montreal gives insufficient purchase to extreme forms of either moralistic fulmination or subversive critique. Richler adopts each of these attitudes in turn, but ultimately in the service of a moderately liberal, moderately secular set of values to which his readers, as self-consciously "modern" people, pay lip service but which they act out only in timid and ineffectual ways. It is as a response to this situation that Richler's decision to make Duddy both more visibly immature and richer in initiative than those around him makes the most sense and helps us understand the novel's relation to its historical moment.[17]

One of the most striking and yet least discussed features of *Duddy Kravitz* is that the story stops before the hero comes of age. At the end of the novel, Duddy may be a landowner, but from a legal as well as a moral point of view he is not yet an adult.[18] In this respect, *Duddy Kravitz*'s short chronological arc stands in marked contrast with that of two other ironic tales about young men on the make, stories Richler clearly had in mind as he wrote. Budd Schulberg's *What Makes Sammy Run?* (1941), explicitly cited in *Duddy* (147), traces Sammy Glick's life over many years, from his childhood on New York's Lower East Side to life as a Hollywood mogul. While working on *Duddy Kravitz,* Richler did uncredited work on the film adaptation (1959) of John Braine's novel *Room at the Top* (1957). Braine's hero, Joe Lampton, the prototypical "Angry Young Man" of postwar British fiction, is a former prisoner of war already well into his twenties when his story begins.

Another difference is that, in the American as in the British novel, the passage from the fantasies of youth to the disenchantment of adulthood is marked by the hero's marriage, in both cases to a woman he doesn't love but who helps him achieve social success. In *Duddy Kravitz,* by contrast, the hero entertains no thoughts of marrying at all, for money or for love. There is no romantic disenchantment because there is no romance to disenchant. But neither is Yvette really a means to social advancement, once she has helped Duddy buy his land. She provides the (limited) amount of erotic satisfaction the hero needs (Duddy is not portrayed as sexually voracious, on the contrary), but that is it. Neither the nature of the relationship nor its emotional or practical future is ever a *question* for the hero. It is certainly believable that a young man of Duddy's upbringing would not consider marrying a Gentile woman. But Duddy's lack of guilt suggests that his investment in Yvette is not strong enough to create any internal conflict about the possibility of doing so. More puzzling is that Duddy never seeks to ingratiate himself with the rich men of his own community in order to marry one of their daughters. His hatred for these men is too immediate to allow for long-term thinking, and even his financial dealings with them are restricted to short-term arrangements. The few times he goes on a date with an eligible Jewish girl, he spoils his chances. His off-putting tendency to boast rather than seduce seems to be an unconscious way of avoiding interpersonal engagement. It would be nice to think of Duddy as defiantly rejecting the compromises of conventional adulthood, but in reality he is unable to think strategically, as opposed to tactically, at any point.

For similar reasons, Duddy never dreams either of participating in a more diverse society or of fleeing the constraints of civilization to wander freely in the wilderness, in the manner of American heroes who don't want to grow up. Duddy may be undomesticated, but he stays close to home. He is driven by the need to be recognized by the people closest to him, not by the wider world. His last words in the book are a triumphant "You see!" to his family when the waiter at Lou's Bagel and Lox Bar, who has heard about his land deal, extends him credit (328). Duddy never looks beyond the circle formed by the people who knew him from the beginning. Only within that circle does he seek a person who will see something in him he does not already see in himself, and who thereby might elicit and realize the potential this same family had failed to nurture. The only exception to this pattern is Hugh Calder, a rich WASP man whose wayward daughter Duddy brings back from Toronto, and with whom, until in desperation he asks for a loan, he enjoys a quasi-filial and non-competitive relationship, precisely because he views their worlds as too different for any rivalry to be conceivable.

Duddy has every reason to leave Saint-Urbain Street behind, yet he never moves far from where he was born. His family treats him badly, comparing him unfavourably to his older brother, Lennie, exploiting his yearning to earn their love by demanding all sorts of favours and mocking his ambitions. It is true Duddy is still very young, and that he manages to succeed without having to separate and find recognition elsewhere. His father, grandfather, and brother are all present at the end to "see" his triumph, and so it doesn't matter that no other witness is present. Duddy's father, Max, is so impressed that he starts turning his son's childhood into the stuff of legend, but the telling and retelling of that legend does not spread very far either. The greatest public recognition that Duddy, like the rest of his neighbourhood, can imagine a young Saint-Urbain tycoon receiving is not a profile in Montreal's business press, and still less a photo in the society pages (no doubt less than welcoming to Jews), but a glowing reference in Mel West's "What's What," which, along with the sports section, is the only part of the newspaper his family reads. What counts as "making it" is not storming the citadel of power. To qualify as a Montreal "insider" it is enough to get mentioned in a gossip column.

Duddy becomes a name to conjure with, though conjure what exactly, beyond further local storytelling, is a question no one cares to ask.

The Apprenticeship of Duddy Kravitz not only stops short of taking the hero across the threshold into what might be called the symbolic world of adulthood; it insinuates that this critical moment may never arrive. Duddy's first experience of sex with the surprisingly amenable Yvette is not presented as a significant rite of passage. Obsessed with the land he wants to buy, Duddy is not fully present at his initiation, except in the most basic physical sense, and the experience reveals nothing to him.

Duddy's acquisition of that land is also stripped of any symbolic significance, even though it, too, should mark his entry into the world of adulthood. As I suggested earlier, Duddy's quest for land is fact regressive and fetishistic in character. Although a city boy, Duddy never thinks of buying property in Montreal. Since grandfather Simcha has never really adjusted to city life and likes to grow vegetables in the little yard of his tenement, it seems obvious to Duddy that when Simcha says "a man without land is nothing," he has rural land in mind. He never questions the meaning or the contemporary applicability of the old man's injunction. There are good reasons, of course, for having Duddy focus on the countryside. Rural land is more affordable than urban property, and it is easier to imagine Yvette negotiating with simple French Canadian farmers than Duddy dealing with commercial brokers in Montreal. It is also plausible that the adolescent Duddy thinks of building a family resort rather than an office tower. Yet, if we look closer, Duddy purchases the farmland with questionable ease. Neither hero nor narrator ever wonders why the farmers aren't more suspicious of what lies behind the deal. Duddy's plan to reserve some of the property for a farm for Uncle Mischa is unrealistic in a different way. The vegetables Mischa has grown in his backyard plot have never been edible, a fact Duddy prefers to overlook.

The idea of developing a summer resort is not a "mature" one either. Duddy does not want to urbanize, or suburbanize, the country by building a residential community or a commercial centre. He wants to replicate the camp that employed him as a teenage waiter – a child's fantasy rather than a grown-up's vision. Richler tries to bring the transaction into the adult urban orbit by having Jerry Dingleman, the "Boy Wonder" of Saint-Urbain Street legend and in reality a small-time gangster whose Montreal gambling houses have been shut down by the police, attempt to muscle in on Duddy's project. But, when Dingleman shows up at the lakeside property, Duddy chases him away without fear of reprisal. If the gangster's threat was only a hollow one, then Duddy's defiance is less than heroic. The value of the incident lies only in the story that can be made of it. We are reminded of an earlier moment when Duddy had defied the WASP holiday-makers at a resort that excluded Jews. That incident, too, had no significance beyond the momentary satisfaction it procured. At no point does Duddy think of working to put an end to an exclusionary practice whose continued existence he seems to take for granted.[19] At the end of the book, Duddy doesn't see himself supplanting Hugh Calder either. He doesn't want to change the world, or himself; he just wants to arrange things around him in such a way as to make further change unnecessary.

Richler can hold together the moralistic and anarchistic tendencies of his satire without too much strain, at least in the earlier sections of the book, because he focuses on a protagonist who in plausibly adolescent fashion resents being judged while pronouncing irrevocable judgments on others. As the story progresses, however, the expanding scope of Duddy's urban agency complicates the picture. In an effort to make up for earlier neglect – though also to force his nephew into becoming a responsible adult – Duddy's Uncle Benjy bequeaths him his rather substantial house, on the twofold condition that the nephew live in it and never try to sell it. One can see why Duddy would resent this attempt to control his actions from beyond the grave, and his anger is understandably aggravated by the fact that he inherits the house just at the moment he desperately needs cash to make the final payment on his Laurentian land. However, the incident also makes a broader symbolic point. Here is property located in the middle of the city, property Duddy holds free and clear of debt. If he had the necessary patience, he could use this home as a base of operations until he made enough money to dispose of it. Yet this asset, which would normally serve as a springboard to independence, appears to Duddy only as another constraint. Usually quick to spot an angle he can exploit, Duddy is blinded by an impotent rage all the more painful for being mixed with a gratitude he can't handle.

The novel's urban chapters give two other rites of passage particular twists. These allow Richler's anarchistic and moralistic energies to be combined in plausible fashion while arranging things in such a way that neither Duddy nor the narrative has to seek a mediating position between them. The first of these rites is Duddy's high school graduation. Richler's exuberantly comic depiction of Fletcher's Field High School made its real-life model, Baron Byng, an iconic Montreal locale. Conflict between the rigid (here, the exasperated WASP teachers) and the raucous (their exuberant Jewish students) is a staple of comic satire, setting up literary expectations Richler exploits to good effect. Moral judgment of the school's failure to live up to its mission alternates with anarchic protest against the repression of natural instinct, and the absence of any mediation between the two enhances rather than diminishes the force of the satire. At the same time, the teachers' world view is so radically alien to the population it serves that nothing Duddy experiences in the years leading up to his graduation makes him question any of the attitudes or assumptions with which he started school. In this regard, I think it significant that only at graduation do we learn that Fletcher's Field is a coeducational institution. Until that point, there has been no mention of interaction between boys and girls, or of dances and dates, and the reader may be forgiven for assuming that Duddy was attending an all-male school.[20] As a result, Duddy and his friends seem even younger than they are, since there is no pressure on them to become more civilized. Their scorn for the school's uselessness is not offset by appreciation for the opportunity to meet girls, and the boys' anarchic behaviour is never checked by the desire to win feminine approval.

Richler does include in the school chapters one incident designed to illustrate the dark side of the hero's anarchism and add some psychological depth to his portrait of the hero. The late-night crank calls Duddy makes to the home of a resented teacher, Mr MacPherson, hasten the death of the latter's invalid wife. However, it is only much later in the story that we hear about the consequences of Duddy's action. Richler may have postponed this revelation so as not to undercut the comedy of the novel's early scenes. Another reason for inserting a retrospective mention of the guilt Duddy felt when he heard about Mrs MacPherson's death is to soften our reaction to Duddy's later bad behaviour. The irony is that this play with the story's temporality underscores an even more disquieting fact: whatever guilt Duddy felt at the time of the incident has had no effect on his subsequent behaviour. He never internalized the feeling.

The second rite of passage into adulthood dramatized in the story is the Jewish bar mitzvah. Just as famous as the school scenes (and just as disproportionate in length), is the account of the Cohen boy's bar mitzvah as filmed by Peter John Friar, a director of dubious talent driven out of Hollywood, or so he claims, by the postwar anti-Communist witch hunt. Hired by a Duddy desperate to launch his fledgling Dudley Kane Enterprises with a film commission, Friar delivers an art-house montage, cross-cutting between Jewish ritual practices and African tribal ceremonies, while at key moments interspersing cannily flattering depictions of the officiating rabbi. Like his counterpart in *Why Rock the Boat?*, Rabbi Goldstone preaches an up-to-date, that is, watered-down, spirituality to his bourgeois flock, peppering his sermon with sports analogies. When Duddy's Uncle Benjy complains that modern rabbis have "taken all the mystery out of religion," he seems to speak for the author. "With a severe orthodox rabbi there were things to complain about," he declares, whereas with "this religious drugstore, you might as well spend your life being against the *Reader's Digest*" (146). Benjy, an old socialist, looks back regretfully on the time when a rebellious dissidence that was not anarchic confronted a moralism that hadn't declined into bourgeois convention. But those days are gone.

Benjy's outburst is typical of the plague-on-both-your houses rhetoric commonly found in satire. Curiously, though, Duddy is not addressed by Benjy's words, since he is busy elsewhere. Only the narrator is there to report what Benjy says. Nor is Duddy present when old Mr Cohen, the bar mitzvah boy's grandfather, insists the temple is too fancy to be a real synagogue and must be a church. When Duddy comes up to Cohen a moment later, their conversation is immediately interrupted by other people. What, in any case, could Duddy have said in reply to either man? Nothing in what we are shown of his intellectual or spiritual development has prepared him to engage such issues. The savviness with which Duddy undertakes the filming of young Cohen's bar mitzvah and his comic distress at the result prevents us from noticing that the novel has said nothing about Duddy's own bar mitzvah. On one level, this makes sense. Richler's conception of Duddy's character requires that we never see him as having even once enjoyed his family's full attention. All the same, it is odd that his entry into Jewish manhood (for surely it did occur) is never so much as mentioned, even when Duddy is shown arguing with his ostensibly devout relatives, or when he lists his grievances against them. Even more than in the account of Duddy's sexual initiation, the novel avoids drawing any clear symbolic line between a "before" and an "after" in the development of the hero's consciousness.

It is thus up to Richler's readers to answer Benjy if they can, and perhaps the writer's intention is to make us wonder if we are any better placed than Duddy to do so. Just as the absence of girls in the chapters about Duddy's school days forestalled any potential mediation between nihilism and moralism in Duddy's education, the narrative prevents religion (even a crisis in religious belief) from playing a mediating role either. Duddy literally, not just metaphorically, hears nothing of what Uncle Benjy or Mr Cohen say. Whether Duddy would have taken their complaints to heart is, of course, unlikely, but he is spared the challenge of dealing with them at all.

At the end of the novel, however, Duddy's immaturity does involve a culpable failure to assume adult responsibility. Just before he dies, Uncle Benjy writes Duddy a letter, a kind of testament. He tells him he is "two people … The scheming little bastard I saw so easily and the fine, intelligent boy underneath." One day soon, Benjy warns, Duddy will have to choose between these two people, and he urges him not to let his "brute" instincts win. "Be a gentleman. A *mensh*" (sic, 267). We are not told what Duddy thinks of the letter, only that he folds it up and puts it away (288), but what he does next indicates a deliberate flouting of Benjy's admonition. Hurrying to buy the last part of the land he craves, Duddy throws both morality and prudence to the winds. He tries to blackmail Dingleman into giving him money; he sells off Benjy's antique furniture since he can't sell the house itself; he spoils his relationship with Hugh Calder by asking him for a loan; and, finally, he forges Virgil's signature on a cheque.

There can be no doubt that in these episodes Duddy acts in full awareness of what he is doing. Yet once again the novel emphasizes the context more than the character of Duddy's agency. What really drives Duddy is not a calculus of risk and reward but a daydream about the story his father Max might one day tell his cronies about his son. The morality of his actions is subordinated to the dramatic power of the legend to which they will give rise. This hierarchy of value is paralleled by a preference for one discursive medium over another. Benjy's appeal to universal ethical standards had taken the form of a written text, a document that, like other such documents such as the contracts and deeds that feature in the novel, belongs to the wider world of adult transactions, a world in which Benjy's moral standards carry meaningful weight. Max's story about Duddy, like the tales he used to tell about the "Boy Wonder," is oral, insular, and, as the nickname suggests, located in a world of precocious but perpetual youth. Like Dingleman, the Duddy of legend will always be a neighbourhood kid, a folk hero whose feats are admired rather than critically assessed.

The novel also gives an important role to another form of discourse that stands somewhere between these two. This is the newspaper gossip column "What's What," which I have already mentioned in other contexts. The column has the authority of an institutionally sanctioned written word, yet it is exempted from the requirements of responsible speech – you might want to consult other sources before acting on its tips. In this respect, "What's What" has something of the status of novelistic fiction, though its "knowingness" is perhaps more akin to that of satire than of a multi-dimensional realism. The question that arises now is where to locate Richler's novel on this spectrum of genres. A more concrete way of formulating the question would be to ask whether *Duddy Kravitz* dramatizes immaturity in such a way as to explore its critical potential, or merely highlights its outrageous aspects in order to assert its own moralism. Put another way, one might ask whether Richler does not merely send up but questions, in a self-involving way, the notion of maturity which, as I have suggested, informs the predilection for satirical comedy displayed at this historical moment by Montreal's anglophone writers.

Richler's treatment of Benjy's letter offers the beginnings of an answer. Despite the heartfelt quality of Benjy's text, Richler's novel is not unequivocally on the side of Duddy's uncle. In making his legacy conditional, Benjy undermines his good intentions. Even more problematic is the language Benjy uses to define the decision he wants Duddy to make. "A boy," he writes, "can be two, three, four potential people, but a man is only one. He murders the others" (287). It is certainly true that entry into adulthood necessarily forecloses some career paths, and the foolishness of Max's stories celebrating the protean resilience of men who never cease to be "boy wonders" is obviously in view here. Still, the notion that one has to "murder" diversity within the self is too extreme for us not to be skeptical of the need for so radical a gesture.

Richler's less than wholehearted endorsement of Uncle Benjy's forward-looking perspective is motivated by his appreciation for people whose community accommodates a contradictory mix of traditions and ways of living and which refuses to make the sacrifices Benjy's single-minded ethic demands. As *Duddy Kravitz* shows, such a community can be stifling to those who grow up in it and hostile to those outside. But, when the community involved is a minority group, these objections must be weighed against the desirability of preserving the group's cohesiveness. Unlike Moore or Weintraub, in whose books ethnic particularity is more ironically distanced, Richler speaks explicitly from a "minority" point of view even as the satirical genre he adopts trades on its appeal to the "universal" values of enlightened modernity. While preserving cultural particularity is not incompatible with commitment to universal values, there is inevitably some tension between these concerns. In this respect Richler gives local artistic expression to the situation of the modern Jewish writer familiar to readers of American fiction of the same period. I would go further, though, and argue that the peculiar satirical dynamic of *Duddy Kravitz* does not arise from this tension alone. As in *Why Rock the Boat?* and *The Luck of Ginger Coffey*, it is also generated by an embryonic awareness of the peculiar cultural position of the Montreal English-language novelist, writing in a dominant but minority language in a city whose francophone majority was still held back by its own defensive minority mentality – and therefore considered by outsiders to be culturally immature.

Richler's key move in *Duddy Kravitz* was his decision to abandon the form he had adopted in *Son of a Smaller Hero*: the realistic "social problem" novel in which such cultural contradictions as the narrator could articulate were reflected through the hero's complex internal consciousness. Duddy's stubborn failure to "mature" means that he never internalizes the contradictions he experiences and so cannot articulate them; they are dramatized only through his actions. This limitation can be liberating, however, in a situation where the prospects for authentic articulation are constricted. Richler's strategy offers a necessary corrective to the over-confident manner in which MacLennan invested his heroes with a "representative" function. Over-confident, because the notion that the fundamental tensions of his time and place could be embodied in one person is at once obsolete – modern society is too complicated for that

– and also premature, since from another point of view the situation on the ground is fragmented and compartmentalized rather than multifaceted and complex, and so still lacking symbolic integration. This, I think, was the lesson Richler drew from his own initial attempt at serious realism. Like the shift from narrative omniscience to a more partial perspective, the immaturity and irresponsibility that characterizes Duddy's actions – and the comic excess of their narration – is thus paradoxically a step forward rather than backward. *The Apprenticeship of Duddy Kravitz* speaks authentically to its time by rejecting a "responsible" seriousness too closely identified with a merely superficial modernity and too abstracted from the reality of the historical situation to be artistically convincing.

I have suggested that the distinctive relationship between *Duddy Kravitz* and its Montreal context emerges most clearly when we set Richler's novel alongside the works by anglophone contemporaries and friends contemporary with it. But two further comparisons may help round out the picture. The first is with the novel's film version (1974), which for all its "period" accuracy fails to capture the subtle spirit of the novel. Ironically, the bravura breakout performance by the young Richard Dreyfuss is the problem. Dreyfuss's Duddy, vibrating with kinetic energy, so fills the screen with his presence that he changes our perspective on the character. Simply by his being *there* all the time, the film Duddy acquires a consistency he does not have in the book. Another distorting factor is that the film makes Duddy more sympathetic. This is not an unusual move when a novel is adapted for a mainstream commercial film. Yet it should remind us that, although by the 1970s *Duddy* had become a Canadian classic, the novel never enjoyed the success in the American market for which Richler hoped. At a time when stories of young Jewish men on the make often became best-sellers, and although Richler had good connections with New York book critics, the novel didn't do well.[21] While any explanation for this must remain speculative, I would suggest that in the assimilationist United States of 1959 the "ghetto" life that in Duddy's Montreal was still a living reality had already become a memory, in wish if not quite in fact. In Montreal, too, that life was disappearing, but the city's enduring linguistic divides meant that the symbolic resonance of that segregated mode of urban existence had not faded in the same way. Just as important, while Duddy's ambition and ruthlessness were recognizable variants of traits found in characters such as Saul Bellow's Augie March, his refusal to grow up and the ineffectiveness of the usual rites of passage to encourage or compel him to mature were at odds with the more socially connected lives imagined for their heroes by the American novelists of the day. Yet these features, too, had strong, if perhaps not consciously discernible, symbolic resonance in the Montreal context.

While Richler's *Duddy Kravitz* is productively read in relation to the works of his anglophone contemporaries, it is also worth comparing the novel with French-language novels of the same period, some of whose protagonists have important things in common with Richler's protagonist. Ambivalence about conforming to their society's conception of "maturity" is a defining characteristic of the hero in Gérard Bessette's *La Bagarre* and Pierre Gélinas's *Les Vivants, les morts et les autres.* So is an ironic self-consciousness on the author's part about the artistic plausibility of a protagonist fully embodying the cultural tensions of the late post-war, pre-Quiet Revolution moment. As we shall see in the next chapter, these two francophone novels also use the resources of satire to distance themselves from the constricting effects of the mimetic realism on which they relied to get their projects under way. As their projects take shape, however, they leave satire behind, adumbrating more capacious and nuanced forms of realistic fiction for a community slowly awakening from its dogmatic slumbers.

6

Failing Better

Francophone Novels on the Eve of the Quiet Revolution

Among French-language Montreal novels of the late 1950s, two works stand out for a searching exploration of the conditions and limits of their enterprise that avoids the trap of didacticism. Each in its own way dramatizes the contradictions of the city's social imaginary, whose historical contingency had earlier been highlighted by Callaghan and MacLennan but was only now coming into focus for Montreal's francophone writers, hitherto reluctant to engage it explicitly. Unlike Gabrielle Roy, who in *Alexandre Chenevert* struggled with the demands of a social realism she found increasingly uncomfortable, Gérard Bessette in *La Bagarre* and Pierre Gélinas *Les Vivants, les morts et les autres* found satisfying ways of incorporating artistic self-awareness into a solidly grounded, three-dimensional urban story. If *La Bagarre* and *Les Vivants, les morts et les autres* deploy some time-honoured realist tropes, the confidence and flexibility with which they do so is new.

Each of these novels also addresses some of the literary problems that bedevilled earlier francophone writers. *Alexandre Chenevert* is a more fully realized because concretely circumstantial version of spiritual-distress stories such as Robert Élie's *La Fin des songes* (*Farewell My Dreams* is the title of the 1954 English translation) or André Giroux's *Le Gouffre a toujours soif* (The bottomless pit). Similarly, *La Bagarre* and *Les Vivants, les morts et les autres* rework Giroux's attempt in *Au-delà des visages* (Beyond the faces, 1946) to compensate for the inadequacy of the protagonist's perceptions by incorporating into the narrative a variety of points of view. Giroux's story of a man whose discomfort with his sexual desires leads him to murder his mistress is told by a series of different narrators, each offering a partial view of the murderer's character and expressing in different ways their conviction that his action somehow expressed the essential "purity" of his soul. Giroux intended this multiplication of points of view to illustrate the failure of ready-made, dualistic categories to capture the complexity of human motivations. Unfortunately, his experiment is no more than another exercise in abstraction. It ends by invoking transcendent mysteries less convincingly than does the conclusion of *Alexandre Chenevert*, which was enlivened by the witnessing presence of a variety of concretely embodied characters. Not coincidentally, the urban setting of Giroux's story is even more schematically sketched than Roy's.

The conflicting perspectives dramatized in *La Bagarre* and *Les Vivants, les morts et les autres* are better integrated into the world of the story, and the protagonists' idealist aspirations more fully contextualized. When Bessette has the hero of *La Bagarre* express the desire to "bring Montreal to life, give it a soul of some kind" (31), the soul of which he spoke was something very different from Giroux's ethereal spiritual entity. The life he had in mind is that of the city's "wide range of social classes" and its "two ethnic groups, with different ways of thinking and different languages" (30). This urban soul is thus also very different in conception from the unitary soul of the nation invoked by Lionel Groulx, the language of whose 1922 novel *L'Appel de la Race* (*The Iron Wedge*) is parodied by Bessette's *pure laine* writer-hero.[1] Gélinas is animated by a similar spirit, granting an unexpectedly respectful hearing to a factory owner and a bourgeois lawyer as well as to members of the working class.

In tracing the arc of their protagonist's trajectory, the realist fictions of Bessette and Gélinas also display an ambivalence about the ideal of maturity that in some respects echoes that of the Anglo satirists, though the difference of genre means that ambivalence is thematized from another point of view. Their unease is focused on the psychologically alienating potential of the maturity for which they strive; the Anglo writers had worried about enjoying a maturity based on a presumed exemption from alienation's effects. Bessette's Jules Lebeuf and Gélinas's Maurice Tremblay criticize their people for fatalistically accepting – at times embracing – their lot. But because they believe this fatalism is to be overcome primarily by sheer force of will, the summons to become mature is experienced as yet another inhibiting external compulsion. In different ways, both Jules and Maurice are aware of this bind, but they cannot allow themselves to be anything less than grown-up, even when it would be better to indulge the immature part of themselves they are so determined to outgrow.

This same constricting view of adulthood, ironically, governs the early and influential interpretations of *La Bagarre* that gave it pride of place in the development of Quebec's *texte national.* Writing in the mid-1960s, André Brochu wondered why the heroes of Quebec fiction were much less convincing than the villains. His answer was that even up to his own day "adult" figures are still "snapshots that a photographer would not have the resources to develop."[2] Thus, for Brochu, the value of *La Bagarre* lies precisely in its weakness. The novel diagnoses a cultural problem that remains to be solved, but the literary steps it takes to solve it – or to question the solutions on offer – are dismissed as uninteresting. For Brochu, the urgent political as well as artistic task was to finish processing the negatives Bessette had been unable to develop. Brochu's view was fairly typical of the *parti pris* generation of Quebec nationalist intellectuals, whose teleological conception of psycho-social development, informed by a rigidly heteronormative, narrowly "productive" definition of maturity, has since been subjected to justified critique.[3] Another kind of critical teleology for many years prevented Gélinas's novel from being given the recognition it deserved. Indeed, *Les Vivants, les morts et les autres* never found a place in the national text at all. One reason is its presentation of what seemed already in 1959 to be an anachronistic, old-left perspective, one that gave greater weight to class solidarity than to ethnic identification in its analysis of the French Canadian predicament. At the same time, the novel's disenchanted insider portrayal of local Communist apparatchiks (for some years Gélinas edited the Party journal *Clarté* [Clarity]) embarrassed "progressive" intellectuals of every stripe, reluctant to play into the hands of the anti-Communist right.[4]

While Quebec's cultural and literary historians now take a much more expansive and pluralistic view of the province's development, the continuing importance of the national paradigm means that, although Gélinas's achievement is now recognized and Bessette's finely controlled irony better appreciated, some key aspects of their novels and of their cultural "moment" have remained unexplored. Indeed, I would go further and argue that a new understanding of that moment might begin and not just culminate with a new reading of these works. Such, at least, would be the hypothesis of a literary history centred on the city and on the urban itineraries – discursive well as geographical – traced in and by the authors' works.

A first step toward understanding the novels' urban "moment" is to highlight some common or complementary features in the thematic structure of *La Bagarre* and *Les Vivants, les morts et les autres*, just as we did with *Earth and High Heaven* and *Mathieu* in order to complicate the traditional accounts of the novelistic "moment" of the 1940s based on the contrasting visions of MacLennan and Roy. That this time I will be comparing two works in the same language rather than one in French and one in English reflects my conviction that one key difference between this moment and the earlier one is a greater differentiation in literary articulation of the same problematic within francophone literature, such that one work finds a dialogue partner in a novel contemporary with it in the same language, as well as significant contrasting echoes in work published at the same time in the other.

In *La Bagarre* as in *Les Vivants, les morts et les autres*, the action takes place a few years prior to the time of writing. Both stories begin in the late 1940s, the same period as *Mathieu* and *Alexandre Chenevert*, though significantly the gap between the time of the story and the date of publication has become progressively greater as we move from Loranger to Gélinas (whose story also concludes, interestingly, at a datable time close to the present). Bessette's hero, Jules Lebeuf, is a working-class man who, after spending some years in the United States, has returned to Montreal with the intention of continuing his education and becoming a writer. During the day, he attends university and works on a novel about the city. During the night, he cleans streetcars to make money. What is new about Jules's literary efforts is that they are not depicted as a purely intellectual struggle: his thoughts are constantly connected to his interactions with his fellow workers and the students with whom he drinks. They are also mediated through the idioms of the language in which the narrator has him think. The Maurice Tremblay of Gélinas's book is in some ways Lebeuf's mirror opposite. The son of a Quebec City factory owner who could easily have become a writer like his brother Lucien, he, too, has spent a period "away," in his case working as a union organizer in a remote mining town called Windigo. After his efforts fail, he goes to Montreal, where he thinks he can do better. He, too, wants to become a spokesman for his chosen community, but his preferred vehicle is ideological rather than aesthetic speech, and his college is the Communist Party.

Reading the novels side by side also reveals a curious cross-connection between the concerns named in their titles. Gélinas dramatizes "brawls" (strikes and political demonstrations) far more consequential than the one brief bar fight which in Bessette's story ends in fatigue and fatalism almost as soon as it begins. Conversely, Gélinas's tripartite division of people into the "living," the "dead," and the "others" (or "the rest") applies less neatly to his sprawling cast of variegated characters than it does to Bessette's trio of protagonists. Unwilling to give up yet unable to fully live their life, his Jules, Ken, and Augustin all find themselves in an unsettling, in-between state. Both novels, however, also show how difficult it is for decisive action to occur when the world the characters inhabit is itself lacking in creative energy. Like Bessette's streetcar workers of the late 1940s, Gélinas's union militants of the early 1950s see their dreams crushed by the forces of economic and political authority, the inertia of the people around them, and the Machiavellian tactics of the Party leaders. No wonder they, too, take refuge in a kind of suspended animation.

Both authors reject any simple dualisms in accounting for their characters' decisions – or for their lack of decisiveness. Gélinas shows how embryonic new initiatives can be perverted by the with-us-or-against-us Communist Party, as absolutist in its attitude as the authoritarian church it opposed. Thus, the expression "the others" turns out not to be quite the derogatory epithet it first seems to be. As we shall see in a moment, it refers to people stuck in a situation that is more one of liminality than of alienation: a state of in-betweenness that may offer respite from the pressure of either-or dualities, including that of life and death, or "mature" and "immature." Similarly, *La Bagarre* criticizes its three main characters less for their lack of manly decisiveness than for their failure to shake off paralyzing cultural dualisms. Bessette's depiction of Augustin Sillery's homosexuality, for example, while not completely free of stereotype, is largely sympathetic. Even more notably, Augustin's straight friends are untroubled by his sexuality. The novel does not judge Sillery for acting out his queerness, only for the inauthentic, self-hypnotizing manner in which he does so. Ken Weston is an American veteran who returned from the war with happy memories of his time in France. Eager to put his experience to better use than he was able to do working for his hometown newspaper, he has come to Montreal to write a thesis on French Canada. Struck by the gap between what he has read and what he sees around him, he finds himself stymied in his effort to bridge that gap, and precisely because he defines it in dualistic terms. "'*Statistics vs. life*,' he mused. 'How could the two be reconciled? How could you fuse these two opposite poles [*antinomies*] in the form of a thesis on French Canadians?'" (40, translation modified).[5] Ken seeks an experiential and epistemological mediation between these two "antinomies," but instead of entering more deeply into the life of the city around him, he does no more than shuttle between his boarding-house and the bars where he spends his evenings with Augustin and Jules, fellow students he met when briefly attending classes at a local university. Otherwise, all he does is toy with the idea of visiting the countryside to see how it compares to the image presented by Louis Hémon (author of the rural classic, *Maria Chapdelaine*). The implication seems to be that he would have explored Montreal more enthusiastically if he had been able to read some good novels about the city. The lack of enabling fictions about the city is implicitly to blame for Ken's inability to formulate a thesis about French Canadian life.[6]

Meanwhile, Jules Lebeuf is struggling to write just such a novel. The problem is his assumption that fiction originates in a thesis rather than the other way round. Like Ken, he despairs of arriving at a holistic understanding of his object, one that would combine a "panoramic" view with insightful *aperçus* into Montreal's inner life. Looking over the few pages he has managed to draft, he is overcome by despair. "'A panoramic setting! Such naivety! Then why not a full-fledged census of Montreal's population?'" (101). Indeed, the excerpt we are given to read lacks literary vitality, precisely because of a demographical abstraction that dominates Jules's way of thinking. "To the west, the English; to the East, the Québécois [Canadiens]. Between the two, a trickle of Israelites [*une coulée israélite*]," Lebeuf says to himself (101). Yet, schematic as this mapping may be, what prevents it from serving as a starting-point from which a more three-dimensional panorama of the city's life might be developed? Jules's beginning is not all that different from the opening pages of MacLennan's *Two Solitudes* or Mordecai Richler's *Son of a Smaller Hero*. The answer seems to be that Jules's literary "census" merely confirms what is *already* known; it does not mediate a new or renewed form of knowledge. Unlike MacLennan and Richler, who think of their readers either as foreigners who don't know the city or as locals who, as in all large cities, are necessarily to some extent strangers in their own town, Bessette's Jules imagines an audience with exactly the same degree of familiarity with Montreal as he has himself. Even worse, the Jules who writes and the Jules who reads what he writes are one and the same – a fact that Bessette underscored by composing a novel about a writer who is not like his creator. Whereas Ken can't write his thesis because he sees no way to reconcile the intellectual polarities (40) which make it hard to conceptualize French Canadian life, Jules is stymied by the absence of any gap for his imagination to bridge.

Bessette's depiction of Jules's predicament, as I suggested, does more than reproduce it. The image of the city he attributes to Jules would be just as flat a mirror of "the facts" as Jules fears were it not for a particular word choice that gives the passage a discreetly provocative and colourful twist. It is probably not a coincidence that this word occurs in the final part of the sentence, in which we are reminded that Montreal's French-English dualism is complicated by the presence of a third element. The word *coulée* in *une coulée israélite* is a richly suggestive term. Like the English "trickle" which has been used to translate it, *coulée* can mean a flow of water or liquid metal, a delicate addition to gastronomic dish, or a streak of colour in a painting. But a *coulée* is also a path created by animals as they make their way through the woods, a meaning related to the English adoption of the French word to designate a ravine. These connotations give colour to Jules's thoughts and expand the imaginative potential of the sentence in which the *coulée* is slipped.

Within the story, though, nothing can come of this potential, since Jules is too focused on thinking grown-up ideas to waste time playing with words. This, however, is just what Bessette does. He declines to depict the city in panoramic terms. Rather, he widens the perspective of his text by attending carefully to language, and especially to the speech patterns of his characters. Ken's stilted phrasing, Augustin's virtuoso flights of rhetoric, the passionate eloquence that shines through the tramway workers' fog of rote phrases – these are what give "soul" to the city these people inhabit. Gélinas is more interested in the ideological inflections than in the lexical or grammatical idiosyncrasies of language, but, like *La Bagarre*, *Les Vivants, les morts et les autres* marks a step forward in the development of the Montreal novel by eluding inhibiting expectations about what a "mature" social novel should be like.

LA BAGARRE

The *bagarre* of Bessette's title is not the kind of brawl we expect will break out after reading a few chapters into the book. The tension between workers and management at the Compagnie de Transport Métropolitaine (closely based on the real Montreal Tramways Company) never degenerates into violence. Because of his years of experience in American factories and his high level of education, Jules is called upon to play a mediating role when that tension comes to a head. This task serves as a practical counterpoint to his artistic vocation as a would-be novelist of city life. His success in the former, however, proves to be as dispiriting as his failure in the latter, and it is through the interplay between the two plots that Bessette integrates into his story a thought-provoking perspective on the challenges of his own artistic enterprise.

The long-simmering resentment of the streetcar maintenance workers toward their bosses turns to overt protest when a feisty old sweeper nicknamed Bouboule, just two years away from retirement, is fired and denied a pension for assaulting the foreman Lévesque.[7] Though angry at this injustice and unhappy with their low wages, Bouboule's co-workers, fearful of losing their own jobs, hesitate to take aggressive action. And so they ask Jules, an outsider, to accompany another senior worker named Charlot to convey their complaints to Stevens, a one-time sweeper like themselves who now manages the maintenance crews. Jules's impressive physical stature (the narrator refers to him several times as a "big man [*colosse*]," together with his mastery of English, will, the workers hope, persuade the manager to reconsider. But Stevens turns out to be sufficiently bilingual not to need Jules to interpret for him. Instead, he proposes a deal that puts the would-be mediator in a bind. He will reinstate Bouboule, and even give the workers a little raise, but only if Jules agrees to replace Lévesque as foreman (142). We learn that Stevens has for some time had his eye on Jules as someone who has the skills to become a manager like himself. Jules's first instinct is to refuse. Not only does he dislike being co-opted by the bosses, he knows that taking on new responsibilities will deprive him of the time and psychological freedom to pursue his "real" vocation as a writer. In the end, though, he feels he has to accept the deal.[8]

Jules soon regrets his "noble" sacrifice. Though grateful at first, the other sweepers, even his good friend "Bill" Lafrenière, soon distance themselves from their new overseer; Jules no longer enjoys that feeling of solidarity with the working class that made his drudgery bearable. He gets no pleasure either from the enthusiastic response of Marguerite, the practical-minded waitress with whom he lives in what until now has been just a convenient arrangement. Someone has to be the boss, she says, and so it might as well be Jules (151). What's more, now that he has a secure position, they should think of getting married. Feeling trapped yet reluctant to do anything about it, Jules lapses into listlessness. He abandons work on his novel. He also fails the philology exam required for his university degree. Becoming a teacher in a Quebec school, he believes, would be as soul-destroying as being a shop foreman (227). This is not just a self-justifying excuse. As Bessette himself could attest, the statement is no more than the truth. The author's reputation as an atheist prevented him from getting a job in Quebec. At the time he wrote *La Bagarre*, he was teaching in Pittsburgh. Bessette would make his own dispiriting experience at a Montreal teachers' college the basis for his next novel, *Les Pédagogues* (The pedagogues, 1961), a bitter portrait of the Quebec educational system as he experienced it in the years just after the war.[9]

In recent decades, critics have highlighted the creative role played in Montreal writing by the figure of the *passeur*, a mediating character who helps the protagonist of a story to negotiate the fluid reality of a culturally diverse city and whose representation allows writers to explore their own mediating mission.[10] These figures are defined by their ability to cross ethnic or racial lines, to move back and forth between languages, often also to blur erotic boundaries – in short, to expand the networks of urban communication through acts of "translation" in the broadest sense of the term. In *La Bagarre*, however (and the same, as we shall see, is also true of *Les Vivants, les morts et les autres*), the hero's qualifications as a *passeur* neither facilitate better communication nor enhance his own social mobility. The only advantage Jules gains from his hybrid status as what his young admirer Gisèle amusingly calls an "student-sweeper" (85) is the opportunity to become a foreman, a go-between despised by both sides of the labour divide, thus the very opposite of a *passeur*. Jules's bilingualism is of no more creative use than that of the streetcar conductor who mechanically repeats "*attention aux portes*, mine de door!" (146, translation modifed). The world of Bessette's novel is one of social and linguistic inequality, a place with little room for creative translation.

Jules's friends are equally ineffectual in putting their linguistic talents to productive use. Augustin dazzles other people with his rapier wit and his rhetorical flights of fancy, but he is incapable of sustained dialogue. The anglophone American Ken has made so much linguistic progress during his four months in Montreal that he has started to think directly in French and wonders at the stubborn refusal of Montreal's native anglophones to learn the language (42). Ken earnestly records unfamiliar idioms in his notebook and, ironically, he is the only one of the three main characters to read contemporary French Canadian novels, including Roger Lemelin's 1944 (and therefore recent) novel *Au pied de la pente douce* (*The Town Below*, 160).[11] Yet he is no closer to getting a handle on his dissertation project than he was when he arrived in town. Both men, it is true, are hindered by their personal histories. Augustin's homosexuality forces him to be wary of potential hostility and to conceal his feelings, a tendency reinforced by his straitlaced bourgeois upbringing. Ken wants to recapture in Montreal something of the freedom and sense of discovery he had enjoyed as a GI in wartime France, but he cannot quite escape the constricted world view of his working-class Missouri background. In both cases, however, the real obstacle is the character's failure of erotic nerve. Critics of the novel have paid surprisingly little attention to this deficit of desire, perhaps because the book does not draw explicit attention to it. In the extensive bar-room discussions that form the core of the book, the three men sympathize in a general way with each other's relationship troubles, but there seems to be a silent agreement among them (another form of that tacit consensus that is a recurring theme in works of the period) to avoid asking, let alone answering, uncomfortable questions about each other's erotic agency.

Thus, it is left unclear why Ken cannot extricate himself from a merely embryonic but already burdensome relationship with Thérèse, his landlady's adult daughter. Thérèse has used Ken's request to help him correct his French as a pretext to push him into getting more closely involved with her. Although Ken finds Thérèse an unattractively bitter and jealous woman and realizes she is desperately looking for a husband, he is curiously unable to escape her machinations; it is all he can do to hold her at bay. How is it, we wonder, that an American combat veteran who wants to bridge the gap between "statistics" and "life" never seeks to meet, let alone romance, a woman other than this pinched and pious boarding-house spinster? It may well be true, as Ken says, that "when you're new in a place, you're after all the girls [*toutes les femmes vous tentent*]" (41). And no doubt Thérèse's lack of charm was initially offset by her interest as a supposedly "typical" representative of the French Canadian people. Yet, even after Ken gets around more, he never tries to pick up another woman at the bars he frequents with Jules and Augustin (though some of these may be all-male beer taverns), at the university where he attends classes, or in the street. Indeed, he never seems even to notice other women at all. Admittedly, Ken has only enough money to stay in Montreal for a few months, but he gives up on his thesis, and on the city, even before the academic term has ended. Whatever desire he had to engage the city has exhausted itself without ever finding full expression.

Augustin's erotic behaviour is similarly self-defeating. He seeks out men younger and less sophisticated than himself; yet, though he often persuades them to accept his advances, they soon rebel against his neediness and turn to more conventional forms of sexual outlet with female prostitutes. Augustin's friends are remarkably non-judgmental about his homosexuality, but neither they nor the narrator who reports Augustin's inner monologues ever mentions the possibility of his going to a gay hangout to find a more compatible partner. Augustin wanders in and out of all sorts of places, from downtown clubs to seedy Saint-Laurent cafés and bowling alleys, but this supposed connoisseur of Montreal's red-light district never thinks of entering one of the places Michel Tremblay would later describe in his multi-volume *Chronicles of the Plateau Mont Royal*, most notably in *Des nouvelles d'Édouard* (*News from Edward*, 1984), whose action is set in 1947, the same year as the story of *La Bagarre*.

This omission cannot be explained simply by the literary censorship still prevalent at the time Bessette wrote. In 1956, for example, Eugène Cloutier's *Les Inutiles* (The useless ones, 1956) openly referred to the "effeminate" men who congregate in certain Montreal pool halls. Several years earlier, the heroine of Roger Viau's *Au milieu la montagne* (In the middle, the mountain, 1951) was said to be surprised but not particularly shocked when she realizes why the conventional-seeming male diners at the "Joseph Inn" where she waitresses never try to pick her up. Had it served Bessette's purposes to place Augustin in a setting of homosexual sociability, he surely could have done so.[12]

It is possible, of course, that Augustin is interested only in men who do not identify as gay. He certainly gets a masochistic thrill from the possibility of a violent reaction to his advances, as he does from a glimpse (or is it a hallucination?) of a sinister-looking man lurking in the shadows near his home (32). Bessette's Augustin is somewhat reminiscent of Sartre's Daniel in *L'Âge de raison* (*The Age of Reason*, 1945), a novel in which homosexuality is presented as a form of self-deluding "bad faith." Yet *La Bagarre* differs in significant ways from its Sartrian predecessor. In addition to talking freely about his affairs, Augustin "performs" his sexuality in ironically self-aware ways, delighting, for example, in the queer twist he deliberately gives to the classic "Un Canadien errant" when he sings it in *La Bougrine*, the tourist-trap nightspot where he meets Ken and Jules on a regular basis. Perhaps this is because he knows the tourists have to rely on translators less concerned with linguistic accuracy (or with morality) than with the tips they get for showing their clients a "typical" French Canadian show (16–17). Nonetheless, at the end of the novel, like Ken, Augustin decides to leave Montreal, perhaps for Africa like his hero Rimbaud (228). He had earlier declared his intention to live a life of "Rimbaudian immoderation" in Montreal (11), but that no longer seems to be a possibility. His flight is the manic double of Ken's depressive retreat. In complementary ways, Ken and Augustin mirror Jules's inability to project a "panoramic" of vision Montreal or to infuse it with erotic – or aesthetic – vitality.

Finally, although Jules recoils from Marguerite's self-centred delight in his promotion to foreman, her outlook is hardly different from his own egotistical approach to their relationship. When he invited her to live with him (23), he was looking not for a muse but for a cook and a sexual partner. His physical needs satisfied, he would be free to concentrate on his writing. For Jules, erotic yearning is not a creative spur, merely a distraction from serious work. Ironically, he now finds himself trapped by Marguerite's expectations. Even worse, precisely because his immediate needs are met, he has no excuse for failing to get the book done. Yet the writer's block from which he suffers never drives him to think, let alone desire, outside the box he has built for himself. With one important exception that we will discuss in a moment, he no more thinks of breaking off with Marguerite than of looking at his novel from another angle.

Of course, if the three protagonists of *La Bagarre* were more committed to pursuing their erotic quests, they would not be spending their evenings in the long conversations among themselves in which Bessette revels. Like the characters, Bessette is more interested in talk than in action, but in portraying the characters' predicament the author does more than reproduce it at another level. Like Jules, Bessette may not be able to offer a novelistic "panorama" of Montreal as a dynamic whole, but he can provide the next best thing: he can "animate" the city by attending to the diversity of its speech patterns. Jules's colloquialisms, Augustin's hyper-correctness, and Ken's anglicisms illustrate the range of the city's linguistic registers, along with the expressive inhibitions of Montreal French.[13] Augustin, the most self-conscious of the three men, speaks for the author as well when he sings the praises of "philology," the discipline that traces the transformation of languages and language uses across time and space. In particular, the study of philology offers a potential remedy for French Canada's crippling inferiority complex. "'In demonstrating the relativity of all languages [*toutes langues*] and their constant evolution,' Augustin remarks, 'it makes one feel less singular, less of an outcast'" (59).[14] The ironic insertion of an English word to highlight the linguistic alienation he is talking about is as typical of Augustin's style as his omission of the definite article before *langues*, a flourish he draws from the French classics written in the century of French Canada's founding. Augustin's sentence thus encapsulates the history of his people. We sometimes forget today that, in the academic world of the nineteenth and early twentieth century, philology included cultural history and criticism as well.[15] In "reducing" action to conversation, Bessette's own philological attentiveness actually expands the revelatory potential of his narrative.

It is also significant that Augustin should use his knowledge of philology to explain Jules's writing block. Jules, he suggests, can blame his failure on the "quasi-ineluctable laws of philological and semantic evolution" (60).[16] While the discovery of such "laws" gives historical legitimacy to the varieties of French that have evolved over time and distance, and while it relativizes moral judgments about their richness or poverty, the notion of necessity may also seem to leave little room for individual linguistic responsibility. As the discussion continues, it becomes clear that this is not Bessette's view. He has Ken upbraid Jules for his pessimism, telling him that he has "the chance of belonging to a different milieu which has a slightly different language" from that of the inarticulate common people (60). Jules gives a dispirited reply. "'Different environment, that's true. But the milieu you want to write about, you're immersed in it. And if it's disorganized, indifferent and incoherent, you …'" (60, translation modified). The issue is thus not an inadequately structured language, which philologically makes no sense, but a failure in the structuring power of the discursive context in which that language is deployed. So formless is Jules's milieu that he cannot finish the sentence in which he tries to define his experience of it.[17] This situation can be explicated only by a higher-level philology of which Jules, for whom philology is just a course required to earn a college degree, seems to be unaware.[18] Indeed, for all his self-consciousness about language, Jules fails his philology exam. His real failure, though, is not to have learned what philology is really about. No wonder he finds it impossible to write his book.

By making his novel about speech, about bar-room bull sessions and factory break-room grumbling rather than about physical *bagarres*, Bessette gives his novel the animating form Jules seeks in vain. One might say that Bessette's conversation scenes follow a colourful path through the interstices of the city's linguistic, national, and sexual dualities. These scenes, it is true, do not directly answer the questions Jules asks about the possibility of writing a panoramic Montreal novel. They challenge the questions themselves by doing something different, by suggesting that the formulation of theories should follow rather than precede the dramatization of practices. Some of the novel's early reviewers missed the point, criticizing the author for using a range of language registers incompatible with aesthetic coherence and dignity.[19] That Jules, with his own high idea of art, would have agreed with this judgment just shows how mistaken and self-sabotaging Bessette thought those judgments were. Over the following decade, however, critical opinion shifted to Bessette's side. The story of Jules's failure came to be seen as one of the most successful novels of the decade, precisely because of its artful use of oral idiom.[20]

Bessette does not eliminate action from the novel altogether. There *is* a *bagarre* in *La Bagarre*. It is precipitated by the protagonists' inability to maintain their compromised erotic equilibrium and their tacit agreement not to meddle in each other's lives. Earlier in the story, Jules's co-worker Bill Lafrenière had introduced him to his teenage daughter, Gisèle, and asked him for advice on her future. Gisèle excels at school, especially in mathematics, but in 1940s Quebec there was no free French schooling beyond grade nine. A priest is willing to sponsor Gisèle's admission to a convent boarding school, but Bill is wary of the clergy. He turns to Jules for help, asking him to assess Gisèle's intellectual abilities and advise him on her future. Jules is reluctant to get involved, but when he meets Gisèle, he is smitten by her beauty. She reminds him of a picture of Natasha he had seen in an illustrated edition of Tolstoy's *War and Peace* (88). The literary allusion is significant not only in suggesting that, like the young Natasha, Gisèle embodies the spirit of a nation in need of redemption, but because it is a *literary* allusion: Gisèle is the only person Jules meets whom he instinctively sees in novelistic terms. In her own unself-conscious – and thus all the more effective – way she bridges the gap between life and literature. She thus appears as a potential mediating figure though whom Jules might become in turn the cultural mediator he dreams of being. By helping Gisèle, Jules would contribute to the betterment of his people. "Raising the individual's level, wasn't that raising the whole group's level?" (191). It might even "elevate" him as well.

Gisèle certainly awakens in Jules something more than a charitable concern for her welfare, though he prefers to think of his interest in Gisèle as "fatherly" rather than romantic (181). It is also clear she is attracted to him. Jules limits his initial involvement to arranging for an aptitude test, and then, after the positive results come in, to advising her on her educational future. He encourages Gisèle to attend Sir George Williams College, the only local institution where she could study while also working to help out her family. As he tells her later, "there's no French girls' school for you to go to, so it seems to me that Sir George Williams is the only place" (222).[21] Meanwhile, he has Augustin persuade his stockbroker father to give her an office job so she can earn some money for her family.

Like his mediation on behalf of Bouboule, however, the action Jules takes to help Gisèle backfires on him. Monsieur Sillery's all-too-obvious delight at seeing his son interested in a girl makes Augustin uncomfortable. Augustin takes his resentment out on Jules by bringing Gisèle to *La Bougrine* on what she thinks is a real "date." When Jules arrives on the scene, he is enraged to see Augustin taking advantage of Gisèle's naivety, and his "fatherly" self is offended by her exposure to the vulgar songs of the stage show (176). Adding to the tension is Ken's arrival with Thérèse in tow. The latter is just as deluded as Gisèle in interpreting the invitation as a sexual overture. Ken has asked her only out of pity. Jules reaches his breaking point and punches Augustin in the face. The waiters intervene, and Ken, who is happy to find an excuse to drop Thérèse, rushes to help Jules in what degenerates into a free-for-all. Augustin slips away, and the brawl ends with Jules and Ken being thrown out of the club.

While trivial in comparison with the conflict at the streetcar company, this incident proves to be the turning-point of the story. Ken's mixed feelings of guilt and relief about abandoning Thérèse make him eager to leave town as soon as possible. Augustin quickly puts an end to his fake courtship of Gisèle. When Jules speaks to him later, he has become less "outlandish" (227) than before and so Jules lets go of any lingering animosity, but just as Jules's entreaties do not make Ken change his mind about returning to St Louis, his renewed declarations of friendship do not shake Augustin's resolve to go abroad. He may not really go to Africa like Rimbaud, but like Ken he is determined to leave Montreal.

The effects of the *bagarre* on Jules himself are more complex. He feels an unexpected swell of pride for having "defended" Gisèle, though he is reluctant to admit that his action was triggered by jealousy rather than by paternal concern. Yet, by acting out his "immature" impulse by punching Augustin, he begins to acknowledge his repressed romantic feelings for his protégée. Gisèle's own attraction to Jules, momentarily redirected to the more demonstrative Augustin, is also rekindled by his aggressive action on her behalf. The quality of their relationship starts to change. Jules somewhat tentatively opens up to Gisèle about his creative struggles. Her thoughtful responses delight him: "'She understands me,'" he says to himself (222). The remark echoes Gisèle's earlier intuition that Jules will understand her (91). If Gisèle is Natasha, the novel seems to imply that Jules, whose awkward physique and moral befuddlement are reminiscent of Tolstoy's hero, might become her Pierre.

The idea that a man who is twenty-nine (221) might legitimately consider marriage to a girl of sixteen would not be acceptable today, but in the world of the novel the age difference is not considered problematic.[22] Bill is not at all scandalized by the fact that grown men have been showing interest in his teenage daughter. In fact, he almost tells Jules he would be happy to see Gisèle marry "a guy like you" (201). The only reason he doesn't give Jules more of a nudge is that he thinks Jules isn't ready to settle down. He knows Jules is living with Marguerite, but for him this could only be a temporary arrangement.[23]

Jules's hesitation has nothing to do with age either. True, despite his joy at discovering someone who understands him, he resists the impulse to take Gisèle's hand across a restaurant table. Yet his subsequent decision to change the subject, "Well, all this is getting us nowhere" (222, translation modified), is not an indication of mature self-restraint. His renunciation is an act of hopelessness, not high-minded virtue. His "all this" refers to more than a potential relationship with Gisèle; it includes the dream he has just shared with her of "expressing something," of seeking something beyond the ordinary world of money and bourgeois marriage altogether (223). When a moment later he shifts his focus back to the practical issue of Gisèle's education, Jules likes to think he is being selfless, but when he tells her "you have to make up your own mind" (as the English translation has it)] whether or not to go to Sir George he is seeking primarily to avoid taking any risk. He does not want to repeat the mistake he made in pleading for Bouboule (223). In the end, it does not matter, since Gisèle's parents make the decision for her. Although they still fear that the convent will pressure her to become a nun, they worry even more that attending an English school will end with Gisèle losing her French and marrying a "English bloke." "It's happened," Bill had insisted when Jules had tried earlier to dismiss the possibility as mere speculation (200). Jules concludes that Gisèle "was not the girl for me" (227), but while this may well be true, it is also true that he never dared imagine she might be "for him" in the first place, and that he turned down the mediating role he might have played.

I am not suggesting that things could or should have turned out otherwise. The point is that Jules never imagines himself either as a character in a romance story or as a potential arranger of such a story. Realist novelists, including the Balzac and Tolstoy Jules takes as his models, often show us a character who at the start sees himself or herself as the hero or the heroine of a story and then discovers the disenchanting difference between literature and life. The paradox of realism is that such disenchantment becomes a springboard for the writer's own creative imagination, *Madame Bovary* being the paradigmatic case. Like Flaubert's Emma, Bessette's Gisèle has read a lot of silly romances (84). On the other hand, her mathematical talent is real, and the novel never makes her an object of mockery. Although she is naive, she is also thoughtful, and it is significant that of all the characters in the novel she is the one most willing to ponder the paradox of Jules's being a "student-sweeper." Thus, the disenchanted realism with which *La Bagarre* portrays its imaginatively and erotically impoverished Montreal, and which finds ultimate expression in Jules's giving up – and giving up on – Gisèle, may conform to the European model in some respects, but it deviates from that model in important ways. The real theme of *La Bagarre* is not the danger of the romantic imagination but rather its arrested development. That is to say, if Jules struggles in vain to write a novel, one important reason is that he has never been able to picture himself as the hero in one. Not even for a moment does he imagine himself as the "Pierre" his "Natasha" needs. The desire to be a storybook hero may be a "teenage chimera," as Jules says of his attraction to Gisèle (227), but maturity can be achieved only by living that desire before redirecting it toward a more appropriate goal.

When Jules wonders why he is helping Gisèle, he does not take a closer look at what he really wants. Nor does he use his conversation with Gisèle to learn more about her as a person. Instead, he determines to follow "a reasonable course, an objective approach" (191). Jules's failure to respond authentically to Gisèle is thus of a piece with his failure to write. In both cases, his haste to achieve the equanimity he believes an author needs to depict other people's desires artistically alienates him from his own life. He thinks his problem is gaining the right distance from his world when the more basic issue is his lack of intimate involvement in it. Jules knows he should avoid generalizations and make his book livelier by showing the city "in motion" (102). But he cannot conceive of himself as a self-moving being within the world he wants to depict, a self out of whose experiences, not ideas, a perspective might begin to emerge.

The only way Jules can think of to get his novel moving is to consult a booklet summarizing the "Plots of 100 Best Novels" (102). He believes he can energize his work by clarifying its structure from the outside. The chaotic *bagarre* in which for a brief moment Jules does play the chivalrous hero, and thereby momentarily frees himself to experience the desire he had repressed, is not an incident Jules would think of making the centre of a story. This, however, is exactly what his creator does. Just as Bessette's attention to philological detail in the protagonists' aimless conversations contrasts with Jules's paralyzing obsession with the expressive deficiency of the local language, the author's decision to have the title of his book refer to this "minor" incident highlights the difference between his conception of a revelatory plot and that of his would-be writer hero.

If Jules undermines his project by a false maturity, a premature disenchantment with life and art, the blame, Bessette suggests, is not borne by him alone. As mentioned earlier, Jules's sabotaging of his career prospects in the teaching profession is justified by the dismal future that would await him in that line of work, although the reasons are only hinted at in *La Bagarre* itself. A happy future with Gisèle may not be conceivable either, for a similar though even less explicit reason. While Jules is tempted to see Gisèle as a symbol of the French Canadian people he wants to "elevate," she may in the author's eyes be a less representative figure than Marguerite. The novel may criticize Jules for his often-cavalier treatment of his practical-minded girlfriend and for his scornful dismissal of her neediness, but it never blames him for not trying to raise Marguerite's consciousness or expand her ambitions as he imagines doing with Gisèle. That Marguerite might think of something beyond getting promoted to manager at the restaurant where she works is not a possibility Jules – or the novel – ever considers, not even in order to dismiss it. This surely says something about the limits, not just of what *La Bagarre* thinks is feasible to do in fiction, but of what is imaginable in the world that fiction reflects.[24]

There is, however, an intriguing and, I think, artistically crucial element of compensatory fantasy in the author's portrayal of his protagonist. Bessette later admitted he had enjoyed giving his hero a physical stature more impressive than his own. But Jules is not just tall and strong. He is repeatedly referred to as a *colosse*, a word that suggests a giant, even a monster. It is a designation more suited to a character in a folk or fantasy tale than in a realist novel. Given Bessette's philological self-consciousness, however, his incongruous choice of this word suggests that something more than personal vanity is involved in its use. In *Beautiful Losers*, Leonard Cohen will use his protagonists' adolescent obsession with the "Charles Axis" he-man of American comic-book ads to imply something about the stunted growth of the culture that has shaped them. Bessette is not as clinical as Cohen in his depiction of body images, but Jules's disproportionate size makes him paradoxically less like a larger-than-life adult and more like an awkward adolescent who hasn't fully grown into his body.

Just as fantastical as the hero's size is his relation to the temporal parameters of realist fiction. For reasons that are never specified, Jules was forced to go work in the United States when he was very young.[25] On his return to Montreal at age twenty, Jules took several years to complete the *cours classique*, Quebec's traditional elite course of study for boys. Now that he is in university, he pays his way by cleaning streetcars, but how and with what money he is supposed to have made it this far is never explained. Critics have also observed that it would be physically impossible for Jules to work a full night shift, attend day classes at the university, and still have enough waking hours to write, devote some time to Marguerite, and spend long evenings drinking with his friends.[26] The ease with which Jules somehow maximizes the limited number of hours in a day stands in marked – though in the narrative unremarked – contrast with the sense of temporal confinement he shares with his less fortunate friends.

I would argue, however, that this improbability is not, or not only, the artistic flaw it appears to be. This is because the narrative is generally so convincing and the conversations are so vivid that we hardly notice the problem as we read. Indeed, I would argue that what makes it possible for the reader to overlook these implausibilities is precisely the author's willingness to indulge the kind of "teenage chimera" his hero disdains. By doing so, Bessette infuses his novel with the vitality the hero could not give his own, more scrupulously "objective" and realistic book.

LES VIVANTS, LES MORTS ET LES AUTRES

Pierre Gélinas's sprawling story of social unrest in 1950s Montreal raises the question of maturity more explicitly. "What is maturity?" asks Maurice Tremblay, a young man rebelling against his bourgeois background. His answer mocks the humanist discourse of the day: "tailoring yourself to fit 'other people' … It's what they call … putting yourself on a level with other men, who take comfort in being similar to each other" (209). Maurice is wondering whether to join the Communist Party, and so in a sense his statement is more ironic than he realizes, since the Party would not view its opposition to the capitalist order as a counter-cultural refusal to grow up but rather as a step toward historical maturity, not least in Quebec, whose economic development has lagged behind the rest of the first world and whose labour unions are only belatedly getting off the ground. We are in 1952, the year of historic strikes at Dominion Textile and Dupuis Frères, Montreal's francophone department store. These strikes, following on from the landmark 1949 miners' strike in Asbestos, signalled the belated rise of militant labour organizations bent on breaking the grip of the Anglo capitalists and traditional francophone elites judged to have colluded in blocking social progress in Quebec. Gélinas's novel will depict these episodes in vivid detail. But there are other ironies as well. At the moment he rejects the conformism of maturity, Maurice does not yet realize what the novel has already shown: that, while his union organizing is motivated by sincere concern for the poor, he, too, wants to become like other people, in the sense that he wants to be at one with the working class. Maurice's fateful decision to join the Party, his declared refusal to accept the compromises of maturity, is also ironic on another level. Determined to resist the anti-Communist hysteria of the McCarthy era, he will suppress his growing discomfort with the Party's strong-arm tactics and intolerance of dissent until Khrushchev's 1956 revelation of Stalin's crimes triggers a crisis of faith that forces him to ask again what maturity means for him.

Gélinas's novel tells a familiar tale of political disillusionment, but with a distinctive local twist. *Les Vivants, les morts et les autres* is filled with fascinating insider details about how Communist militants struggled to accommodate French Canadian national feeling while insisting that class issues must trump ethnic concerns. It also shows how the eagerness of American labour leaders to purge suspected Party members from positions of power in Montreal union locals stemmed not just from political pressure at home. The Americans found in anti-communism a convenient pretext to quash the autonomy of Canadian unions. In Quebec literary history, however, Gélinas's novel is best remembered today for its account of a very different historical episode: the 1955 riot by Montreal hockey fans angered by the presence in the Forum of Clarence Campbell, the English Canadian president of the National Hockey League who, under American pressure, had suspended hockey hero Maurice Richard. Yet just as important in the story as this quintessentially Québécois moment is an event that occurs outside the province. Gélinas's account of the equally controversial, if less violent and now largely forgotten, Canadian Peace Congress, held in Toronto in 1952, is as detailed as his treatment of the 1955 Montreal riot; and, as we shall see, it plays an equally important role in the hero's development. In Gélinas's novel, local issues are connected to larger ones in a variety of ways.

The novel's geographical breadth is matched by its ideological range. Readers may be surprised to find a sympathetic portrayal of Maurice's elder brother Victor, a Quebec City factory owner struggling to protect his workers from the effects of Ottawa's free-trade policy. Another character, Édouard Patry, a highly placed federal civil servant representative of the "mandarins" of the era, is just as paternalistic in his ideas of governance as Victor. His fondness for the Greek and Roman classics makes him even more an alien figure than the old-school Quebec City entrepreneur, yet there is no personal hostility and even a large measure of understanding in Gélinas's account of his views, too. Gélinas's mastery of narrative technique may not equal MacLennan's, but *Les Vivants, les morts, et les autres* shows a deeper appreciation for the complexity of historical forces than *The Watch That Ends the Night*.

The context in which Maurice raises the question of maturity is artistic as well as psychological and political. He has just been comparing his situation with that of two childhood friends, each of whom has settled into a comfortable media career. One man writes radio and television scripts; the other edits a tabloid sensation sheet. The other creative people he knows also make one question what maturity is supposed to mean. When Party boss Roger Picard proposes to use Hurteau, a well-known poet, as a front man in their political rallies, Maurice objects. Hurteau holds impeccably left-wing views, but he is a notorious womanizer. Maurice's writer-brother Lucien, on the other hand, is morally irreproachable, but his novels are politically as well as artistically inconsequential. The writer whose "career" (if we can call it that) is described in the greatest detail presents an even more problematic image of artistic life in the novel's Montreal. Roma Dostie, a distant cousin of Maurice who has recently died, was an invalid who couldn't leave home, but his adoring wife would peddle his work to every newspaper and magazine she could find. Thanks to her persistence, and to the editors who took pity on her, she succeeded in getting several dozen of Roma's insipid short stories into print. Roma died a happy man, and at his funeral the widow proudly displayed clippings of the publications as a memorial. This *reductio ad absurdum* of literary achievement would have delighted Weintraub or Richler. No wonder Maurice finds maturity so distasteful.

In its skeptical view of the link between writing and social maturity, *Les Vivants, les morts et les autres* complements the perspective adopted in *La Bagarre*. Bessette's Jules complained of finding no support in the local culture for his literary aspirations. Looking back on his situation with Dostie's case in mind, we realize that Jules never thought of starting his career, as Gélinas's character did – and as so many budding writers still do today – by submitting short stories to local papers or magazines, or by seeking mentorship or patronage. He is determined to start at the top, by producing an ambitiously "panoramic" novel all on his own. He will be Balzac (or at least, Jules Romains) or nothing. Note that, although he is obsessed by literary models he can't appropriate, it doesn't occur to Jules to write about the difficulty of writing, as his creator does with such striking effect. He will write a big book or none at all. Maurice's problem is the opposite of Jules's, and the result is a very different relationship between story and novel. He has the education and the economic means to undertake a literary career, and (perhaps naively) he doesn't worry about inspiration, but in his view to become a writer in the Montreal he knows is to pursue a career unworthy of a real man. When Gélinas's disillusioned hero decides at the end of the story to make what he calls "charity," and not political ideology, his guide (314), he begins to articulate what has already taken form in the book we have just been reading.

One reason for the narrower gap between intention and achievement, between hero and writer, is the modesty of Gélinas's literary ambition. The author is as diffident about transmuting experience into the "higher" realm of art as his hero is bashful about claiming philosophical significance for his actions. The loose construction and sometimes awkward style of *Les Vivants, les morts et les autres* stand in striking contrast with the tight organization and linguistic sophistication of *La Bagarre*.[27] Gélinas's novel is the work of an experienced journalist – for some years, he edited the Communist Party journal *Clarté* – rather than that of a career novelist.[28] Many of the novel's scenes take the form of quasi-independent set pieces, accounts of what Victor Hugo called "things seen" (*choses vues*), stitched together in a plot whose seams are still visible. Thus, it is tempting to view *Les Vivants* as a novel to be mined for its documentary value rather than admired for its narrative shape.

Yet a curious and crucial elision of time in the novel, one the author is at pains to conceal, makes the question of its narrative shaping one of artistic as well as historical interest. The novel's account of the 1952 Dominion Textile strike (the company's name is not used, but there is no mistaking the reality that inspired the fiction) flows into the story of a second dispute whose historical coordinates are more difficult to pin down. A number of clues, including its close juxtaposition in the narrative with the description of the Forum riot, suggest that we have moved forward to 1955. Three years seemed to have gone by without any clear sense of their passing. This and other departures from chronological clarity suggest that *Les Vivants, les morts et les autres* is not concerned with documentary accuracy alone. As we have seen, when *La Bagarre* first appeared, Bessette's book was deemed insufficiently literary because of the colloquial, even vulgar nature of its dialogues. Only later did it come to be seen as a turning point in Montreal literary history, precisely because of its innovative use of language. I would argue in similar fashion that the sometimes condensed, sometimes loosely connected sequence of episodes in Gélinas's narrative deserves greater appreciation for its literary-historical significance even if it reflects the author's awkwardness of craft. For, just as Maurice seeks to make coherent sense of history while respecting the stubborn contingency of local circumstances and the irreducibility of individual aspirations, the novel that tells his story struggles to incorporate the insight that aesthetic truth is compatible, indeed somehow connected, to temporal under-determination. In the "emplotment" of his characters' decisions or actions, Gélinas shows how people are embedded in multiple chains of causes and effects that cannot be reduced to a single controlling scheme of historical development, even if such schemes are useful heuristic points of departure. What the author's passage through Marxism has taught him is that no one is in a position to say what is true "in the last analysis." This is not because life is random or because the human heart is a mystery – Gélinas's disenchantment with communism does not drive him to embrace its ideological contraries – but because the truth lies at the intersection of a variety of sometimes overlapping, sometimes conflicting personal and historical dynamics.

Gélinas's effort to give this conviction narrative form is not entirely successful, but it is worthy of respectful and sympathetic assessment.

A first step toward that end, paradoxically, is to take a fresh look at the author's handling of place. Although most of the story takes place in Montreal, its portrait of the city is framed by images of three other locales. Each of these involves labour conflicts related to those in Montreal, but each also represents a different moment of historical development, despite their being situated in close chronological proximity. The novel begins with a "prologue" set in a fictional northern Quebec logging town called Windigo, a few years after the end of the Second World War. This is where Maurice, a recent graduate of Laval's pioneering social-science program, begins his career as a union organizer.[29] He arrives at a moment when, because of a downturn in demand, the logging company simply has no need for labour, and so his efforts come to naught. After a brief standoff between the police and the disgruntled labourers, the company agrees to pay the men's fare back to Quebec City, and Maurice goes with them. Although a couple of minor characters from this prologue turn up again later in the Montreal chapters, neither they nor Maurice ever refers to their Windigo experience. While valuable as the memorialization of the kind of event official histories would either distort or dismiss as trivial, and as "background" for the hero's later struggles, the prologue's connection to the rest of the plot is thus a tenuous one. Yet this tenuousness has a significance of its own. Instead of projecting the countryside as a place of moral refuge from the city, as traditionalist Quebec authors often did, or, like Gabrielle Roy, using a country episode to drive home the point that there is no escaping the anguish of urban life, Gélinas highlights the absence of any way for the self to bring the two locales into meaningful relation. On the one hand, conditions in Windigo are dictated by the same overall historical dialectic that governs the capitalist system as a whole. On the other, this dialectic manifests itself in the still quasi-feudal world of Windigo very differently from the way it appears in the more advanced capitalist economy of Montreal. No wonder the young Maurice finds himself at a loss. He knows there is a connection between the two forms, just as there is between the two landscapes of his home province, but as yet he can neither define it intellectually nor appropriate it existentially for himself.

On his return from Windigo, Maurice stops off in Quebec City, a town that belongs to a curious, historically idiosyncratic moment somewhere in between the old and the new. Quebec City has its long-established factories, but it is also a kind of backwater, insulated by its linguistic and political walls from the winds of capitalist modernization, or at least it was until recently. The clothing factory owned by Maurice's father has no labour problem. During the First World War, the old Monsieur Tremblay had taken advantage of a sudden spike in demand (and of federal contracts lavishly distributed to win French Canadian support for the war) to build a thriving business. He also looked after his employees in the time-honoured, paternalistic manner characteristic of that old city. Maurice's older brother Victor is now following in his father's footsteps, and all would be well were it not for Ottawa's decision to lower tariffs on foreign goods as part of a general loosening of trade restrictions in the years after the war. Though in line with international trends, the new policy threatens to flood the local market with cheaper American imports. The big decision Victor has to make has therefore nothing to do with wage demands. It is whether or not to stop supporting the governing Liberals, to whom, like many French Canadians, the family had long been loyal, and embrace the culturally alien Conservative Party in the hope that it will oppose free trade. Victor's determination to defend his legacy will lead him later in the story to consider the even more shocking step of changing tactics entirely and merging with a US firm. In the meantime, he hires productivity consultants to keep him going. In a further twist on conventional notions of modernization, these consultants show Victor how he might profit by making his employees feel wanted and paying the same wage for fewer hours of work: a new version of the old-school paternalism of Victor's father.

There is clearly an element of wish-fulfillment in the novel's Quebec City chapters, yet at the same time their dreamlike quality reflects an important – and enduring – aspect of a social imaginary that continues to inform the novel despite its Marxist allegiances. That internationalism is compatible with Quebec's quasi-autarchy is a belief still shared by many in the province's elites. Gélinas's reluctance to subject Victor's utopianism to dialectical critique reflects a complex of class and cultural forces that ultimately defies easy ideological categorization. On the other hand, the Quebec City episodes are only way stations in the narrative of the hero's journey to Montreal. This is because the provincial capital cannot accommodate the more open-ended and problematic action of a novelistic hero of the kind Gélinas wants Maurice to be. In terms of political orientation, Victor may have a "new geography" in his mind, and his firm may look different after being made over in the image of an international corporation (244), yet the walls of his factory, like those of his city, remain comfortably the same. Indeed, Victor is at ease only within the confines of old Quebec; he is put off by the casual mingling of French and English businessmen in Montreal (76). Maurice needs a wider stage to develop his potential. It is interesting that he doesn't even consider doing any labour organizing in his native city. Perhaps he tacitly recognizes the futility of the idea. Only in Montreal, a city Victor doesn't like and rarely visits, will Maurice finally be able to flourish.

A first key point about the novel's Montreal is that Victor has no counterpart in that city. There is no equivalent of Hugh MacLennan's Huntly McQueen or Sir Rupert Irons or of Michel Garneau, the francophone entrepreneur figure in Ringuet's *Le Poids du jour* (The burden of the day, 1951). Although Gélinas includes characters from many walks of life, the only businessman we see in this novel about Montreal industrial disputes is the comic and peripheral figure of an adman marketing laxatives (85). Since the companies Gélinas describes are only thinly fictionalized, he may have been reluctant to portray bosses whose lives, unlike those of the workers, he did not know.[30] A more important consideration is that the actions of such large corporations are dictated by impersonal economic forces, not by personal decisions, as they still are in a place like Quebec City. But there could be another reason for the absence of such figures. Any plausible portrayal of the men who run Montreal's big businesses would prompt a comparison with Gélinas's depiction of Victor, and give the impression that the latter is merely an anachronism. But Gélinas's Victor is not meant to be a throwback like MacLennan's Athanase Tallard, but a living link between the past and a future not yet completely determined. He thus needs to be kept apart, in reserve, as it were. Meanwhile, a more immediate link between past and future will be forged in Montreal, as in *Two Solitudes*, by the family's *déclassé* son, Victor's brother Maurice.

With the exception just mentioned, the range of Montreal characters is admirably wide, and each is vividly individualized. Like the Gabrielle

Roy of *Bonheur d'occasion* or *Alexandre Chenevert*, Gélinas respects the integrity of each person's point of view, but his narrator is more willing than Roy's to point out the limitations of their perception and scrutinize the logic of their reasoning, through the same indirect discourse that reports their thoughts. A good example is the debilitating effect of the traditionalist French Canadian notions of what family life is supposed to be like. "It was Montreal," the narrator tells us, "that had undermined for good all the family structures familiar to Rachel," who looks back longingly to the days when "the mother ruled over a peaceful household in a land where no one raised a fuss" (45) and who still likes to see herself as the matriarch of the Lussier family. Rachel's distress is genuine, but she forfeits our sympathy when she uses that self-image to legitimize her refusal to accept other people's reality. After her son dies in the Korean War, she drives her daughter-in-law Yolande out of the house when she refuses to settle for permanent widowhood and begins to date again. Rachel also cannot comprehend why her otherwise well-behaved daughter Réjeanne should get involved in union work at her textile plant instead of focusing on marriage. At the end of the novel, Rachel is reduced to recreating a parodic version of the traditional family. She rules over a boarding-house that accepts only mature single men as tenants, one of whom, she is not at all distressed to discover, likes to fondle the bed linens that belonged to his deceased mother (293).

The breakdown of family unity and authority among the Lussiers pales in comparison, however, with the disintegration of Montreal's Communist Party when in 1956 word gets out about the "secret speech" Khrushchev gave in Moscow, acknowledging Stalin's crimes. For its members, the Party was a new kind of voluntary or chosen family, one that crossed linguistic lines and that prided itself on transcending ethnic particularity. In this sense, it embodied something of the urban promise of liberation from inherited identities. The Party's values would thus seem to be the opposite of Rachel's. And yet, as the novel makes clear, Communist ideals have been perverted into a more insidious, because ostensibly more progressive, justification of the same intolerant authoritarianism. In the end, some Party members succeed in confronting inconvenient truths while others do everything possible to suppress them to protect their position or, in some cases, their psyche from collapse. Gélinas's account of the bitter arguments between militants calling for renewed solidarity with the

Party leadership and those whose zeal has cooled echoes in unexpected and thought-provoking ways the era's more familiar French Canadian debates about continued fidelity to the nation's sacred "mission" in a materialistic North America. The novel exposes the habits of mind that in both cases insulate authority from necessary critique.

The analogy between Party cell and urban community then leads us to ask how Montrealers would respond to an event in their own city as shocking in its revelations as Khrushchev's speech. As we shall see, for Gélinas the Forum riot is just such an event. It exposed as nothing had done before the brittleness of the city's social consensus, and it did so for people of all backgrounds and degrees of political consciousness. In contrast with *Alexandre Chenevert*, however, the juxtaposition of local and international events is not ironic or deflationary. On the contrary, it is through this juxtaposition that the true historical significance of the local may be perceived, and the connections between the personal and the political in the local context may be illuminated.

In carrying out this project, Gélinas faced the same difficulty Bessette confronted (or cleverly eluded) in *La Bagarre*: the absence in the francophone Montreal they knew of the kind of erotic energy they could tap to give dynamic fictional form to the interaction of private and public life in the city. The great realist novels dramatize this interaction by representing how the dynamic of personal desire reveals unforeseen possibilities or unacknowledged blockages in the public world. Bessette had likened his Jules and Gisèle to the heroes of *War and Peace*, but only to acknowledge the incongruity of the idea that his novel could emulate Tolstoy's and to underscore the need to find other ways of linking individual and collective destinies, to develop novelistic strategies more suited to the task of giving shape to Montreal's once brittle and inchoate imaginary. Although it is only fanciful speculation, I wonder if in similar fashion Gélinas had *Doctor Zhivago* in mind as he wrote Maurice's story. The decision to give Pasternak the Nobel Prize in 1958 was opposed by the Soviet Union, and was surely a topic of controversy among Montreal Communists. Zhivago's spiritual reflections might be said to find some echo in Maurice's musings. Yet if Gélinas had Pasternak in mind, either as inspiration or irritation, he would have realized that his characters could not plausibly be endowed with either the intensity of desire or the depth of disenchantment experienced by the Russian writer's characters.

In order to mediate between individual and collective experience, Gélinas had to begin with a frank acknowledgment of an erotic deficit in the culture he sought to energize. This he does in a variety of illuminating and imaginatively productive ways.

Gélinas gives a number of instances in which discoveries about sex fail to sharpen a character's perception of the world or their experience of desire. The teenage Réjeanne Lussier hears a lot about her female co-workers' sex lives, yet although she is lively and sensitive she seems unaffected by what she learns. She is not even curious to know more. After her trade union ends its strike in defeat, she accepts a marriage proposal from Jean-Guy, a childhood friend of conventional political views whom she does not love. Her personal decision is consistent with her political disenchantment, but we cannot help wondering why she never saw any romantic potential in her relationship with fellow militant Georges Duchesne. This more vital man piqued her interest, but she never pursued him, just as he never really pursued her. That she does not even imagine an alternative future for herself may or may not be a deliberate authorial decision, but the novel's silence makes an important point about its world.

Another aborted erotic sub-plot involves Réjeanne's country cousin Gérard. In a chapter reminiscent of similar passages in Gabrielle Roy's *Bonheur d'occasion* and Eugène Cloutier's *Les Inutiles* (The useless ones), we follow Gérard as he walks down Sainte-Catherine Street through the red-light district, assailed on every side by what Roy's Alphonse called the "temptations" on display. Like his predecessors, Gélinas includes movies among these temptations, but by having Gérard put Hollywood romances on the same level as night clubs and brothels, the author highlights the incongruity of an equivalence asserted by French Canadian traditionalists, for whom Americanization, commercialization, and immorality were all of a piece. Gérard discovers what city moviegoers already knew, that there was nothing pornographic in the films being shown, but he still can't help equating the suggestive enticement of the cinemas with that of the strip joints on the same street (145–7). Yet, whereas in *Bonheur d'occasion* Alphonse is tormented by desire and tragically aware of his degraded state, Gérard is saved by his imaginative imperviousness. Following some men into a club, he comes into a room where two women are having sex in front of a crowd. Not only does the show fail to arouse Gérard, he fails to comprehend what he has just seen. "Gérard hadn't really understood, and what he had managed to grasp had not awakened his desire, but instead had left him in perplexity" (147), a state of mind he never seeks to shake off.

The supposedly mutually reinforcing effect of social curiosity and sexual excitement could hardly be put into question more explicitly than it is here. The novel gives no explanation for Gérard's cluelessness, the implication being that there is nothing peculiar about it. Nor is Gérard presented as a man immunized against the corruptions of the city by any kind of moral purity. Gélinas could have used the incident to reassure the anxious reader of his day that sexual knowledge does not necessarily lead to sexual promiscuity. But, as in the case of Réjeanne, virtue is not the issue. The character's imperviousness to the temptations of desire is neither good nor bad; it is simply a fact.[31]

Of course, Gérard and Réjeanne are only secondary characters designed to illustrate the mentality of their milieu, not to dramatize its capacity to change. Yet Maurice and his distant cousin Claude, the novel's second and contrasting Montreal protagonist, suffer from an erotic deficiency just as severe as Réjeanne's or Gérard's. What makes *Les Vivants, les morts et les autres* much more than a documentary work is the author's struggle to forge a dramatically convincing connection between the evolution of the two men's political thinking and their development into self-aware desiring subjects in a world as deficient in erotic energy as the individuals in it.

Claude Jobin is a young Montreal lawyer being groomed for leadership by his uncle Alcide Patry, a prominent local judge, and tutored by his cousin Édouard Patry, deputy minister of external affairs in the federal government – the latter thus a francophone equivalent of Arthur Lazenby in *The Watch That Ends the Night*. Édouard explains to Claude that democracy works only when it is guided by enlightened but prudent elites. Politicians should not do what they want, only "what it would be a mistake not to do" (79), an elegantly Tocquevillian gloss on the more pedestrian pragmatism of Mackenzie King (74). Claude finds Édouard's cosmopolitan point of view attractive because it seems to transcend ethnic or other local prejudices, and he is flattered when the older man vouches for him in Montreal's fashionable salons. What he does not realize is that co-opting amenable young outsiders like Claude is one of the ways the Liberal Party keeps its grip on power, in the same way that the Communists recruit people like Maurice to increase their Party's appeal to French Canadians. In neither case are the young men encouraged to offer ideas of their own. Just as Maurice is ridiculed for objecting to the womanizing poet, Claude is scolded for his willingness to represent some arrested strikers at their bail hearing. If he wants to get ahead, he has to be less scrupulous (248).

Édouard also plays a key role in Claude's *éducation sentimentale* by introducing him to the socialite Margot Sauvé. When Margot seduces him, Claude immediately thinks of their affair as a great romance, although it is clear that for Margot it is just sex. In his own way, Claude is just as clueless as Gérard. He cannot understand why Margot never worries about keeping their affair a secret, failing to grasp that liaisons of this kind, affairs of no consequence, are tolerated in her milieu. Thus, Claude's sexual initiation does nothing to remedy his social naivety. Nor does he apply to his personal life the cynical insights of his political education. Just as important, though, is the fact that Édouard does nothing to enlighten his protégé on this point. His mediating role stops short of providing the understanding the protagonist most needs to gain. In this respect, Claude's erotic deficiency is more than a reflection of diffuse cultural circumstances, like Gérard's or Réjeanne's. Claude's ignorance can be blamed on the very man charged with initiating the young man into the ways of the world. Here the novel's cultural critique is expressed through the actions and inactions of a character in the story, rather than from a mere absence in the narrative.

The arc of Maurice's education is similar to Claude's, though its ideological inflection is very different. Soon after his arrival in Montreal, Maurice is noticed by Roger Picard, a local Communist leader. Picard's apparently open-ended but in fact carefully leading conversations with Maurice gradually convince the young man that working with the Party is the best way to advance the workers' cause. Like Édouard, Roger speaks of historical necessity, this time with the Party as its authoritative interpreter. Picard flatters Maurice by inviting him to help represent French Canada at the Peace Congress about to be held in Toronto, stressing that he can speak as what Callaghan's Jim McAlpine calls an "independent man."

Neither French- nor English-language critics have paid much attention to this episode, closely based on a real event that occurred in 1952, even though it is just as central to the novel as the story of the 1955 Forum riot. Since it is set in English Canada, the episode has held little interest for Quebec literary historians, while the critical portrayal of Communists and their naive fellow travellers was not appreciated by the few scholars in English Canada who noticed the book at all.[32] Yet the Toronto scene is crucial both to the documentary and to the artistic ambitions of the novel. With a wealth of insider detail, Gélinas shows the Party quietly controlling the Congress's resolutions committee and packing the schedule with speakers who supposedly represent a variety of progressive viewpoints but who can be counted on not to raise awkward questions about the Soviet Union or North Korea. At the big closing rally in Maple Leaf Gardens, unofficial "security" teams mobilized by the Party beat up anyone (especially fiercely anti-Communist refugees from Eastern Europe) who might dare to heckle James Endicott, the Protestant minister whose speech accusing the United States of war crimes in Korea was the climax of the Congress.[33]

Maurice is charged by Picard to get himself delegated to attend the Congress as an "observer" for his union, on the grounds that war is bad for the working class. At this stage, he is largely ignorant of international politics and just as clueless about Toronto. He doesn't realize that the monolingual public of that city will not understand a word of the text over which he obsesses. No wonder Roger doesn't worry about what Maurice might say. All that matters is that he speaks in French. English Canadians will think the peace movement enjoys broad support in Quebec, and French Canadians, it is hoped, will be grateful that their "national sensitivities" have been accommodated (125). Just like Jules's attempt to mediate the labour dispute in *La Bagarre*, therefore, Maurice's intervention across the language divide is an exercise in futility and bad faith. Gélinas's hero fails to see this, however. The uncomprehending but enthusiastic applause he receives gives him a new confidence in himself. Moreover, for what seems to be the first time in his life, he feels the pull of sexual attraction.

Until this point, the "mystic Jansenism" (10) that inspired Maurice's political activism prevented him from taking much interest in women. Nothing comes of his brief acquaintance with Olga, an attractive young Macedonian woman working for the Congress, for Maurice is still as erotically artless as he is politically nave (129).[34] Yet, in contrast with

Gérard or Réjeanne, Maurice, like Claude, needs to have his desire stimulated so it can then be channelled to proper political ends. On their return to Montreal, Roger introduces Maurice to an amenable female fellow-traveller who captures Maurice's attention just as Margot does Claude's.

It is surely no coincidence that Gélinas gives Maurice's new girlfriend the name Margaret, an English variant of Margot. But making her an anglophone is an even more intriguing decision. Of course, ethnicity is not supposed to matter to a Communist, but one wonders whether her origin is supposed to make her sexual availability more plausible, for, unlike Margot, Margaret Webster is unmarried, the better to accentuate the contrast between the two protagonists' sentimental education. Whatever the case, like Margot's socialite connections, Margaret's English Montreal circle introduces the protagonist to a different social world. Like Margot, too, Margaret's moral code is more flexible, more sophisticated, than that of her new partner. Her vaguely defined position in an advertising agency is reminiscent of Peggy's initial situation in *The Loved and the Lost*. Like Callaghan's character, Margaret lives in bohemian near-poverty near McGill, though on the eastern rather than the western side of the university, in the liminal space between English and French described by Moore and MacLennan. Margaret happily accepts Maurice's gifts of groceries and other supplements to her meagre resources, and she seems to welcome his attentiveness, yet their relationship seems never to get past the friendship stage. In a different way than Claude with Margot, Maurice doesn't become central to Margaret's life.

Margaret is no prude; on the contrary, she is surrounded by other men with whom, the novel hints, she has casual and perhaps mercenary sex (as in *The Loved and the Lost*, the reader is not given access to the character's thoughts). But, whereas Callaghan's Jim was tormented by jealous suspicion, Maurice seems to accept his situation with a tranquility only occasionally troubled by moments of perplexity that, like Claude's doubts about Margot, for a long time have no effect on his behaviour.

At this point, the novel becomes deliberately fuzzy about the parallels between the characters' development and the sequence of external events. We know that both men's affairs begin in the wake of the 1952 Dupuis Frères and Dominion Textile strikes, but these seem hardly to have concluded when the 1955 Forum riot erupts. The narrative elides the passage of the three intervening years by avoiding any reference to datable events in that time period. The implication seems to be that, while the protagonists' erotic potential had been energized by disruptive historical moments, its momentum cannot be sustained without further external stimulation. Having "readjusted" their lives to fit what others expect from them and settled for compromise in the fulfillment of their desires, the two young men have arrived at a "maturity" just as inauthentic as the one Maurice had rejected at the beginning of the book.

Only with the Forum riot will this maturity be thrown into question, which is a way of saying how fundamental that event is to Gélinas's story. Not only is the riot a turning-point in both the history of the city and the lives of the individual protagonists; it provides the means by which the novel can articulate an understanding of the interrelationship of public and private histories. With the benefit of hindsight, we have come to see the riot as the result of long-growing cultural and political tensions. For the protagonists of the novel, however, the significance of the event lies in its being unforeseen. Although Maurice and Claude have been trained by authoritative mentors to discern (according to opposing philosophies, of course) the underlying logic of historical cause and effect, the riot comes to them as a complete surprise. The disruption is such that they are forced for the first time to find meaning for themselves.

The task the story sets for its protagonists is one that the narrative also sets for itself. Gélinas introduces his account of the riot with the only significant instance of meta-commentary in the novel. "Some petty dramas," he tells us, referring ironically to the love lives of Maurice and Claude, "have less to do with events, which provide the setting or even just the pretext for them, than with the nature of the protagonists. But afterwards it is the broader 'societal' event, so to speak, that implants the moment of the private drama in our memory" (245). What's interesting about this modest-sounding statement is how far-reaching its implications prove to be. As if worried about sounding sententious, or of presenting as a new insight what for sophisticated readers is merely a banality of the human condition, the author ironizes his characters' private experiences by labelling them "petty drama," while downplaying the significance of the external events they confront by deeming them "societal" only "in a manner of speaking." This sounds disappointingly timid, but the statement may also be read as a rueful wariness of overarching explanatory systems. Any attempt to apply such a system to real life risks being belied by the elusive complexity of the very reality the system initially helped us to perceive. What Gélinas says here is not new; it repeats what many self-conscious modern novelists have also said. What gives his statement its distinctive edge is his awareness that the most urgent danger is of an opposite kind. As the narrative's blurring of chronological clarity suggests, the dynamic of the public-private dialectic may founder on the amorphous or flattened reality of a particular historical situation before it even gets off the ground. The Montreal Maurice and Claude experience in the in-between years of the book does not frustrate them because its complex differentiation cannot be captured by the terms they use, whether intellectual or emotional; rather, the city they inhabit prevents those terms from gaining any traction at all.

All this changes when the Forum riot erupts.[35] As André Laurendeau recognized, in the famous editorial he wrote in *Le Devoir* a few days after the event and which he titled "On a tué mon frère Richard" ("They Killed My Brother Richard"), the riot was no mere outburst of vandalism by disgruntled hockey fans. It was a revolt against political and linguistic oppression, a sign that the days when French Canadians would passively accept their inferior status were coming to an end.[36] Published four years later, *Les Vivants, les morts et les autres* confirms and amplifies Laurendeau's analysis. For Gélinas, however, a writer whose judgment is clearly based on first-hand experience of what happened in the streets after the crowd spilled out of the Forum, the rioters were as angry at the complacency of Montreal's francophone elite as they were enraged by Clarence Campbell and the anglophone-dominated National Hockey League. One would expect Gélinas, as an orthodox Marxist, to make class rather than nation the dominant factor, but what he actually does is to present the rioters, who included fans of all backgrounds, not just French Canadians, as rebelling against repression or inhibition in general, including, as we shall see in a moment, the erotic paralysis afflicting Maurice and Claude.

Gélinas's enthusiastic description of the riot thus stands in pointed contrast with his disenchanted account of how the Toronto Peace Congress rallies were only sham expressions of a "spontaneous" popular will. On the formal level, the novel emphasizes the difference between the two events by presenting the two stages of the Forum riot from the complementary viewpoints of two characters in the story, instead of supplementing what one character saw with observations from the anonymous narrator. The latter takes us backstage at Maple Leaf Gardens, but the events unfolding inside the Forum are reported only as they are heard by Claude, who, along with the Patry family, listens to them on the radio. They try to make sense of an event they do not control or even see. Ironically, it is just at this moment that Claude's eyes are opened to the reality of his personal situation. Édouard lets it slip that Margot has more than one lover (249). The humiliated Claude finds himself identifying with the resentment of the hockey fans that explodes as they leave the Forum. As the Patrys call for the police to quell the riot in the streets, Claude discovers a nationalist fervour unexpectedly welling up in his soul. The public-private parallel is a bit too neat, but the reader's attention is soon drawn to other, more intriguing aspects of the episode. Particularly interesting is the narrator's insistence on the epistemological opacity of the event. Claude's emotional insight is contrasted with futile attempts of the Patrys to understand what is going on. Hearing the crowd is beginning to spin out of control, Édouard accuses the city's mayor (the unnamed Jean Drapeau, elected to that position in 1954) and French Canadian nationalists generally of identifying too closely and too sentimentally with their people. True political leaders, according to Édouard, must cultivate a clear-eyed detachment (253). Yet Édouard's clarity is shown to be delusory; he has no sense of what is actually happening on the ground. Ironically, it is Claude's intuition of the riot as "a burst of national indignation" (253) that comes closer to the truth. The "petty drama" of his personal life opens a path to political insight. The dialectic of public and private experience of which Gélinas spoke so tentatively at last finds a grip in local reality, just at the moment when Claude rejects the "maturity" modelled for him by his uncle.[37]

Gélinas goes on to describe the "street" phase of the riot more directly through the eyes of Maurice, who is not listening to the radio but immersed in the crowd. After hearing about the protest, he and Margaret instinctively gravitate toward the Forum and are quickly caught up in the mass of people sweeping down Sainte-Catherine Street. Until this point, Gélinas tells us, the western downtown area around the Forum had been considered alien territory by many francophone Montrealers. Even those living in the southwest of the city would normally take a detour in order to approach the Forum from the east along a section of Sainte-Catherine Street that Gélinas compares to the "Danzig corridor" (261). Fears that the rioters would turn in the other direction and threaten anglophone Westmount can be quickly dismissed: it is psychologically impossible for francophone fans to do anything but return the way they had come. What is new is that at least they take possession of what was then a thoroughly English section of the street. Maurice, too, experiences a new freedom as well as a new erotic excitement as he leads Margaret back toward the francophone east. For once, Maurice is not worried about the working class getting a bad name. He is no longer the mature and disciplined union leader. That night, he makes love to Margaret for the first time.

In every way, therefore, the Maurice who emerges from the Forum riot is a different man from the militant who returned from Maple Leaf Gardens. His triumphal march down the western part of Sainte-Catherine can also be read as a deliberate contrast with Gérard's uneasy walk down the eastern end of the same street earlier in the novel, an erotic journey that ended in bafflement rather than bliss. Gélinas had used that earlier episode to undercut French Canadian moralizing about the corrupting effect of urban life on family order. Here, he goes further: he embraces the contingency and unpredictable novelty of human experience, culminating in erotic communion between two free individuals.

Gélinas's sensitivity to the seductive appeal of ideological systems makes him wary of turning this insight into the basis of an alternative philosophical system. His two principal male characters renew their quest for an authentic political future, but their search takes on a more moderate and open-ended quality. Claude distances himself from his Liberal patrons, but he does not become a rabid nationalist. He joins a group of young intellectuals who, along with some "progressive members of the clergy," seek to form a "Social-Christian Party" as an alternative to both the traditional right and, it is implied, the compromised establishment Liberals (300). Though unsuccessful as a candidate in the provincial election of 1956, Claude wins enough votes to encourage him to persevere, even though the landslide victory of Duplessis's Union Nationale (not named as such) means that, for now, "nothing had changed in the Province" (308).

Maurice's career prospects are not so rosy. The sexual and social euphoria he experienced after the Forum riot makes him question the way he lives, but his life and his beliefs remain compartmentalized. Like Claude, he stands for election in 1956, emphasizing the authenticity of his personal commitment to people's welfare more than the specifics of the platform. His decision to distance himself from ideological debates, however, works against him. He barely notices the publication of Khrushchev's speech and fails entirely to foresee its devastating impact not only on public opinion but on the Party itself.[38] Nor does his new intimacy with Margaret give him any greater insight into the dynamic of their relationship. It is as if the mental fog which the Forum riot had momentarily dissipated has enveloped him once again. Under pressure from Roger Picard to get married so as not to offend the voters, Maurice proposes to Margaret. He also suggests that they do the responsible thing by moving to the southwest Montreal riding he wants to represent. To his astonishment, Margaret says no. Her friends would never visit her in that faraway neighbourhood, and besides, she has no intention of giving up the bohemian lifestyle she enjoys, just as Margot never thought of leaving her husband for Claude. Furious at first, Maurice finds himself experiencing an unexpected sense of relief. Realistically speaking, wouldn't a French Canadian woman be a more appropriate partner for the public man he soon will be (284–6)? But this is only another fantasy. Maurice garners only a few dozen votes in the election, far fewer than Claude. He realizes at last how disconnected he is from political as well as emotional reality, from the world and from himself.

Maurice is not alone in his distress. His "petty drama" has a more tragic analogue in the story of one of his erstwhile comrades, Ben Ruben, a Party cadre who has a solid voter base among the immigrant Jews of the Main. In earlier scenes, Ben was shown to be the consummate Machiavellian, a man with no qualms about doing what had to be done for the sake of the cause, drumming up fraudulent votes and drumming his rivals out of the Party as revisionist heretics. After Khrushchev's speech, he can no longer deny what he had dismissed when it was reported only in the bourgeois press: far from enjoying freedom from anti-Semitic prejudice in the Soviet Union, Russian Jews had suffered horribly under Stalin's rule. The shock does not simply disillusion Ben; it undoes him altogether.[39] Here is another example of that *effondrement*, or psychic collapse, whose threat had haunted *Bonheur d'occasion* and lies beneath the surface of *Mathieu* and *La Bagarre* as well.

Maurice is luckier in being able to pull himself back together, but at the end of the book he has taken only a first step toward a more genuinely integrated existence. "Above and beyond all systems, he had come to discover men, his brothers: the conquerors and the defeated, the living, the dead, and the others" (314). When he adds that he needs to learn "charity," this religiously freighted word makes him sound a bit like Claude, just as his humanist generalities recall those of Loranger's *Mathieu*. These similarities in moral language, however, conceal a significant evolution in outlook. Unlike Claude, who almost overnight embraces a new vocation, Maurice remains wary of any hasty new commitment. Indeed, he seems to number himself among "the others," that is, among those who are condemned, at least for the moment, to live in a liminal space between life and death. Maurice seems finally to realize that, in his eagerness to reject the flawed "maturity" of his writer friends, he ended up pursuing a more subtly deceptive version of the same specious ideal. He must not make that mistake again.

Another key difference between Claude and his cousin is that Maurice does not feel obliged to repudiate his past entirely. He may have been deluded in becoming a Communist, but at least he was disinterested, and however equivocal his relationship with Margaret, it was not based entirely on a lie. Looking around his apartment, Maurice notices for the first time how messy it is, but he comforts himself with the thought that the disorder was caused not by his preoccupation with foolish dreams but rather by his excessive commitment to "adult" responsibility (313). Instead of rushing to clean up the mess, he will dwell in it as he discerns a way forward.

There is, it is true, something a bit clerical about both Claude's and Maurice's revitalized sense of mission, in that it includes no erotic dimension. In this respect, Gélinas's protagonists resemble the Jules Lebeuf of Bessette's *Les Pédagogues* ("The Pedagogues"), which, though published two years later (in 1961), was probably written around the same time as *Les Vivants, les morts et les autres*. The new Jules, a union leader himself, seems immune to the enticements, and free from the entanglements, of the sexual desire that caused him such problems in *La Bagarre*. One wonders what Maurice and Claude would have become in a sequel to their story. Regrettably, Gélinas did not write one. What we do know is that Quebec politics took a rather different path from what the characters or their creator could have anticipated at the time.[40] The groundwork for the Quiet Revolution of the early 1960s was indeed laid in large part by an alliance of practical-minded union activists and progressive clergy, but soon the course of that revolution would take a turn few members of these groups could have foreseen in 1959, not least because of the tidal wave of sexual liberation that hit the province in the later 1960s. As Gélinas's novel had already taught us, however, the interconnection of such developments appears only in retrospect. The merit of *Les Vivants, les morts et les autres* lies in its effort to incorporate into its narrative a hard-won understanding that the dialectic of public event and personal drama cannot be defined in advance but must be kept open to the unexpected.

PART THREE

Solutions and Dissolutions

By the mid-1960s, the Montreal familiar to the novelists of the preceding chapters, as well as the kind of future they could imagine for the city, were rapidly being relegated to the past. With the clearance of old neighbourhoods in the name of progress, the erection of new high-rise buildings, and construction of the Metro subway system, Montreal's cityscape was being radically transformed. A brash new generation of francophone writers had burst upon the literary scene, supported by new publishers and subsidized by governments eager to accelerate the province's modernization. The spirit of the 1960s is often thought of as anti-authoritarian, and many writers in those years did take more confidently assertive stances than they had done before. The qualms about the legitimacy or the adequacy of the writer's *prise de parole* we have found in the French-language novels of the 1940s and 1950s were resolved, I believe, only with the realization that embracing the unauthoritative nature of their speech was a complementary and crucial step toward literary liberation. Working through instead of willing their inhibitions away, they turned the language of abjection against itself.

Some writers, including Jacques Renaud, whose novella *Le Cassé* (*Broke City*, 1964) remains the most eloquent example of the style, did so by writing in *joual*, the sociolect of Montreal's francophone working class. Characteristic of this speech were an excessive use of English loanwords to express what ignorance or mental subjugation prevented them from naming in their own language, and phonetic deviations from the norms both of international and of educated Quebec French, most seriously by syntactic malformations that were seen by many as blocking the proper articulation of thought.[1] Earlier novelists of lower-class life, notably the Gabrielle Roy of *Bonheur d'occasion*, had incorporated some features of *joual* in their dialogues, but, except in some deliberately dialectal first-person stories, none had considered making it the language of narration, that is, the language in which the characters' lives were told. By having the literary superego express itself in the language of the id, so to speak, *joual* writing undid the former's inhibiting power. It is significant, though, that *joual* was less prominent in fiction than in poetry, its expressiveness being more suited to subjective lyricism than to analytical subtlety.

Despite its limitations, *joual* nonetheless had a salutary effect on novelists, encouraging them to take greater stylistic liberties with the standard language. Jacques Godbout's comic *Salut Galarneau!* (*Hail Galarneau!*, 1967) was enlivened by an easy colloquial tone that gave artistic conviction to its story of the hero's reconciliation with life. Réjean Ducharme's *L'Avalée des avalés* (*The Swallower Swallowed*, 1966) analyzed the manic pursuit of impossible ideals in an equally hyperbolic but carefully controlled style. Hubert Aquin's *Prochain épisode* (*Next Episode*, 1965) memorialized his speakers' defeats in laments that oscillated between the labile and the lapidary. Another common feature of these three novels, however, is that while some events in the story take place in or around Montreal, the city itself hardly features in the narrative. Montreal, that is to say, is not the world within which the characters move, or even a significant context of meaning. One reason for this, of course, is that for most francophone authors in this period, the agonistic space of a resurgent Quebec nation constitutes the milieu in and against which the actions of the characters and their creators gain cultural definition.

Meanwhile, the literary authority that English writers had been able to claim in speaking of the city, an authority grounded in mastery of the language of global urban modernity, was being challenged because the new Quebec nationalism also deployed the discourse of modernization, sharpened by the rhetoric of global anti-colonialism. Satirical distance and ironic self-deprecation were no longer adequate strategies of response. Hugh MacLennan upped the discursive ante, turning to the vocabulary of myth and collective psychology to shore up his critique of Quebec nationalism in *The Return of the Sphinx* (1968). Yet in doing so he misread the signs of the times; the judgments that language encouraged him to make were more specious than shrewd. The most talented English writers of the generation after MacLennan's, Mordecai Richler and Mavis Gallant, did not pursue in Montreal the careers they began there. By the turn of the decade, both of them were living in Europe and were setting their fiction in locations abroad. Richler would return to Montreal in 1972, but his next Montreal novel, *Joshua Then and Now*, would not appear until 1980, and it too used foreign settings for crucial episodes in its plot. Similarly, it was not until the mid-1970s, with her "Linnet Muir" stories, that Gallant returned in imagination to the Montreal setting of some of her early stories. Published in the *New Yorker* and other magazines, those stories had been largely ignored at the time, and it was only when they were collected, along with the Linnet Muir sequence, in the volume *Home Truths* (1981), that Gallant gained the local recognition she deserved. While other novelists remained in the city, their careers did not develop as smoothly or as continuously as might have been expected. Constance Beresford-Howe, for example, a contemporary of Gallant's, published several well-received novels between 1946 and 1955 but fell silent until 1973, when she re-emerged with her most enduring work, *The Book of Eve*. The vitality of anglophone Montreal's literary culture was sapped by another form of displacement: the long-resisted realization that the once-ridiculed Toronto the Good, to which Beresford-Howe among others had eventually relocated, had become the epicentre of English Canadian culture and Toronto's media the arbiter of writers' reputations. It would take two decades and two political referenda before a new generation of anglophone writers, adapting to their minority status, would find a way to thrive in closer interaction with, and not just in reaction to, the city's francophone majority.[2]

The story of these developments, however, is a matter for another volume. In the final chapter of this book, I focus on two works poised on the cusp of the changes I have just sketched. Jacques Ferron's *La Nuit* (1965) dramatizes an underground journey from abjection to agency, though the scope of that agency, like that of the *pays* he had imagined in the two volumes of *Contes* (*Tales from an Uncertain Country*, 1962–64) published before *La Nuit*, would still be *incertain* at the end of the book.[3] Leonard Cohen's *Beautiful Losers* (1966) is equally inconclusive, both in its engagement with the new Quebec nationalism and in its questioning of the literary authority it asserts. If Ferron relishes the resentments from which he seeks to be rid, Cohen remains enthralled by the mastery he deconstructs. Each of these works thus occupies a pivotal position in the literary history of its language community. I want to suggest, however, that we read these works as complementary stories of the equivocal city in which they are set, for the central personal and cultural conflict they dramatize takes provocatively similar and mutually illuminating forms.

7

Twilight of the Idols, Dawn of a New Day

Jacques Ferron's *La Nuit* (The Night) and Leonard Cohen's *Beautiful Losers*

An impressionable man of weakly defined identity, occupying a liminal position on the fringes of urban life, struggling with an admired and resented mentor figure, "master" of the city he surveys: this is the situation Ferron and Cohen dramatize in the novels that became turning-points in their career. We have already encountered other versions of this tension: for example, in the relationship between George and Jerome in *The Watch That Ends the Night*, and in the responses of Maurice and Claude to their mentors in *Les Vivants, les morts et les autres*. Never before, however, had the conflict culminated in violence. In those books, the authority figures were discredited or displaced; in *La Nuit* and *Beautiful Losers* they have to die.

No doubt the difference may be attributed in part to the greater cultural and political turbulence of the 1960s. But there is a key difference between Ferron and Cohen's plots and the apparently similar stories of, say, Hubert Aquin. The mentor-doubles about whom the protagonists of Aquin's first novels, *Prochain épisode* (*Next Episode*, 1965) and *Trou de mémoire* (*Blackout*, 1968), feel so paralyzingly ambivalent are all foreigners. Whether they are European, African, or English Canadian matters less in the end than that they hail from a world that is not the hero's own. The mentor figures of *La Nuit* and *Beautiful Losers* are certainly "other" in terms of language and ethnic identity, yet they are also neighbours. The two adversaries grew up in what for all its estranging factors was nonetheless recognizable in important ways as the same place. For a Montreal writer to make a character from the other language community so central a figure in the protagonist's quest was in the 1960s a revolutionary gesture; even today, it is still far from common. Of course, this character is ultimately eliminated, but he is not brought into the story simply to be sacrificed as part of some emancipatory rite of passage. Comparing the French novel with the English one will show how they subject the notion of liberating violence to ironic examination and subvert the symbolic dualisms – of life and death, of freedom and obligation – associated with it.

A second feature common to both books is the distinctive role played by the city of Montreal in the plot. Both Ferron and Cohen view the city as an essentially agonistic space but also one in which unexpected moments of communion occur. Like Gélinas before them, they make a political demonstration a key moment in the story.[1] In *La Nuit*, a Communist-led protest against the formation of NATO (based on a real event of 1949) triggers the plot. In *Beautiful Losers*, a Quebec nationalist rally set against the background of early 1960s FLQ bombings and later an undated, apocalyptic, and anarchic takeover of the streets serve as turning-points in the story.

In contrast with Gélinas, however, the point is not so much to raise the underdog protagonist's political consciousness as to shock him into a new awareness of the complex interconnection of the city's two linguistic communities. Each scene also has a ritualistic element, in that the character, at first merely a spectator standing at the edge of the crowd, is swept up in the unfolding event and then violently expelled from the scene. In *La Nuit*, François Ménard is arrested as a Communist agitator by Frank Archibald Campbell, éminence grise of the city's Anglo power structure, convicted, and shamed into leaving the city for the suburbs. The unnamed first-person narrator of *Beautiful Losers*, generally referred to by critics as "*I*," narrowly escapes being assaulted by a crowd whipped into nationalist frenzy by a francophone radical identified only as "F." (122). Yet *I* is saved from harm by none other than F. himself, a man who has mentored as well as tormented him ever since the years they spent in the same Montreal orphanage.[2] Similarly, François's arrest by Frank is a form of protective custody, and when François leaves his soul behind at the courthouse, Frank picks it up and holds onto it for him. In each book, the relationship between the two main characters is thus as intimate, even complicit, as it is hostile. Today we might call these men "frenemies," recalling that in 1963 Solange Chaput-Rolland and Gwethalyn Graham had already conveyed the same idea by publishing the two versions of their epistolary exchange under the titles *Chers ennemis* and *Dear Enemies*.[3]

Another feature of urban geography common to the two books is an "underground" downtown locale associated with the more shadowy aspects of the mentor-figure's power, which includes the ability to stage erotic encounters across ethnic and racial lines. In Callaghan's *The Loved and the Lost* such transgressive encounters were mostly a matter of fantasy for the white patrons who frequented the black nightclub on Saint-Antoine but who only flirted with racial taboos. In Ferron and Cohen's novels these fantasies can be acted out. In *La Nuit*, Frank holds court at the seedy Alcazar nightclub. Inverting the symbolic pattern of the *La Bougrine* bar of Bessette's *La Bagarre*, where waitresses dressed up as old-time French Canadians for the benefit of tourists, Ferron's Alcazar offers French Canadian bar-girls arrayed in exotic foreign costumes, the better to entice local customers to escape for a moment into other worlds. The club's name evokes the sophisticated hybrid culture of Moorish Spain rather than provincial rusticity. In *Beautiful Losers*, F. haunts the System Theatre, a cheap movie house where people come to grope each other in the dark, but where, as its sign suggests, insight into the hidden logic of reality may be found.[4] These places give the Montreal of these novels a phantasmagorical quality, a dimension highlighted by Ferron's calling the city a "Castle" and by Cohen's references to it as a site of "magic." I use the term "phantasmagorical" because, while the narratives include elements that can be called "mythical" or "allegorical," the symbolic connections, I will argue, are suggestively disorienting rather than systematically directive.

Behind these parallels of form and theme lies an important commonality in the authors' creative situation. Unlike many novelists of the 1960s, Ferron and Cohen were far from hostile to the past that shaped them. Both writers came from families well established in their community; they were secure in their identity and unashamed of where they came from. Their attitude to the religion in which they were raised, while somewhat detached, was neither emotionally hostile nor intellectually adversarial. Though mindful of their abuse, *La Nuit* and *Beautiful Losers*, in contrast to many other works of the period, treat religious beliefs and symbols in a playful and often affectionate manner. Ferron and Cohen are less intent on exposing religion's inhibiting influence than on exploiting the expressive resources of its language, for their own ends to be sure.

Similarly, both writers took a measured, if critical, view of their literary inheritance. The past was a history of real but hitherto unfulfilled opportunities they now had the chance to realize. Each writer had a predecessor who had failed but in whose failure they found instruction. For Ferron, it was Saint-Denys Garneau, whom he accused of fleeing from the challenges of worldly existence into a simulacrum of transcendent spirituality, but whose example provided an energizing source of oppositional imagination.[5] Cohen's attitude toward A.M. Klein was more compassionate. In his 1964 lecture "Loneliness and History," Cohen described the older poet as torn between a "priestly" calling to express, indeed embody, his community's aspirations and his "prophetic" mission to criticize the failings and compromises of that community from a disinterested position on its margins.[6]

The real obstacle to innovation, as Ferron and Cohen saw it, was not the lack of literary insights on which to build, but the failure of their predecessors to produce work of sufficient power to make negating it an enabling existential challenge. Ferron would never forget the impact of reading Paul Valéry, and Cohen defined himself in relation to poets such as Federico Garcia Lorca throughout his career; but, though they would have relished the opportunity, neither was compelled to wrestle, at least for very long, with a local writer. After the success of his first collections of poetry, Cohen pushed the aesthetic envelope with *Flowers for Hitler* (1964), but the provocations of this riposte to Klein's *Hitleriad* (1944) might have resonated more deeply if Klein's painfully earnest satire had forced Cohen to think harder about the emancipatory value of his amoral lyricism. While Cohen held Klein in great affection and sympathized with his plight, he did not have to struggle against those feelings in order to become himself. In a somewhat different way, Garneau did not find in his work a mode of expression robust enough to offset the spiritual contortions Ferron disliked so much in his life. As a result, the fantastical portrait of Garneau that might have expanded the imaginative scope of *Le Ciel de Québec* (*The Penniless Redeemer*, 1969) turned what should have been Ferron's magnum opus into a petty settling of accounts.[7]

These contrasting but I think complementary literary genealogies help us appreciate the significance of *La Nuit* and *Beautiful Losers* for Montreal's literary history. In the absence of an admired and envied mentor in the writer's "local" tradition as that is conventionally defined, that is, by linguistic lineage, they open a way forward by revising that definition. Ferron and Cohen dramatize their struggle for full literary expression by staging a confrontation with a representative from the "other" culture, a man who serves as the mediator, at once respected and resented, of their protagonist's emancipation. *La Nuit* dramatizes its francophone hero's sly victory over Frank Archibald Campbell (modelled on the distinguished poet and public intellectual F.R. Scott), who is presented as a man caught between his allegiance to the established order and his sympathy for French Canadian aspirations. François heals his own divided consciousness by turning Frank's split mind against itself. *Beautiful Losers* celebrates the seductive vision of sexual, political, and spiritual liberation offered by a charismatic francophone figure who for *I* embodies the revolutionary energy of an insurgent Quebec nation. Yet F. comes to harbour doubts about the authority he exerts over his disciples, allowing the privileged but paralyzed *I* to appropriate the subversive power of the loser and displace the master. In each case, the confrontation between the two protagonists does more than allegorize historical rivalries. In telling the story of the hero's admiration, resentment, and overcoming of the mentor figure, both Ferron and Cohen extend the imaginative reach of the "minor" cultural and literary tradition from which their books emerge. They do so by staging a confrontation with an authority figure who turns out to represent a community just as de-centred and fragile as their own. One might go so far as to say that in these novels both the francophone and the anglophone protagonists belong to "minority" groups in the sense that term was used in Callaghan's *The Loved and the Lost*, that is, as a marker of communal precariousness rather than numerical proportion.

This point is linked to a second one. The breadth of learning and agility of imagination that gives the representative of the "other" community his enviable power, a power paradoxically enhanced by his ability to identify with his victim, also, and by the same token, makes him vulnerable to psychic collapse. The conflict between the characters serves also as a means to explore the emerging writer's ambivalent relation to the intimidating yet fragile otherness of culture itself.

Each story opens with the protagonist addressing the reader from a liminal position on the margins of Montreal, François Ménard from a South Shore suburb, *I* from a treehouse somewhere outside the city. For anthropologists, liminality designates an "in-between" situation, a transitional place or moment in a religious ritual or rite of passage. Stripped of their former identity or status in the community, the participants undergo a period of testing or trial before they can return to the community and take on new roles in it. The collective order also benefits from the ritual, redeeming and reintegrating the potentially disruptive energies of the new generation. Such rites of passage lose their efficacy, however, if the fundamental consensus of minds and mores that underpins them becomes too fragile to handle the dislocations the ritual enacts. Momentary liminality may freeze into permanent marginality, into a pervasive alienation that can be healed only by a creative reconstruction of the collective symbolic order itself.

The situation addressed here is thus more complex than the problem dramatized in *Earth and High Heaven* or *Mathieu*. At issue in those novels was the incorporation of an outsider into a community whose basic cohesiveness was not in question but which needed revitalization, just as the outsider, whose suitability was also clear, also just needed a boost in order to realize his potential. In *The Loved and the Lost* or *Alexandre Chenevert*, on the other hand, the governing social imaginary was presented as being too fragile to survive a challenge which therefore should not be risked. The liminal protagonist we meet in the first pages of *La Nuit* and *Beautiful Losers* is in different ways both an insider and an outsider, and for precisely that reason seems condemned to remain in limbo indefinitely.

Ferron's François Ménard is a middle-aged man leading a routine existence in a modest tract house in a South Shore suburb that is never named but is clearly Ville Jacques-Cartier. Later incorporated into Longueuil, this district, where Ferron lived and practised medicine, was still well into the mid-1960s a zone of unregulated development and minimal public infrastructure, with modern subdivisions springing up amid the detritus of a depressed rural past.[8] François settled in this neighbourhood after being humiliated by Frank to the point of having to leave Montreal for what threatens to become permanent exile. François now manages the branch of a bank and lives in a neat suburban house with his wife, Marguerite.

Cohen's *I* writes the first part of his story from a place that is only vaguely located, but he too has fled Montreal, in his case because F.'s death has left him helpless to deal with his spiritual abjection. Having taken refuge in a treehouse, he lives alone except for visits from the young boys he seduces to distract him from his solitude and self-loathing.

Like François's exile, though, *I*'s banishment has little to do with social disqualification. *I* is a recognized anthropologist; his regressive behaviour in the treehouse could thus be interpreted as a perverse form of fieldwork, just as François's financial activities are a distorted form of moral accountability. Both men remain in a state of suspended animation because they haven't been able to shake off the paralyzing influence of their mentors. Frank and F. continue to hold their envious admirers in thrall, even at a distance, through a mixture of affectionate concern for their victim's welfare and ruthless exploitation of his vulnerability. We have seen a similar combination of attitudes in the Catherine and Jerome of *The Watch That Ends the Night*, or the Roger Picard and Édouard Patry of *Les Vivants, les morts et les autres*. The crucial difference is that in *La Nuit* and *Beautiful Losers* the mentor's prestige derives in large part from his authority within a language community other than that of the protagonist, an authority as much spiritual, for lack of a better word, as it is political.

The Frank Archibald Campbell of *La Nuit* is a prominent figure in Montreal's anglophone establishment. A cultured man of liberal outlook, he is also a police agent, monitoring the movements of francophones who threaten the status quo. Frank's Quebec roots are as deep as those of François. Both men grew up in the same small Quebec town, and though their families, separated by language and religion, were not actually acquainted, they are spectrally linked by the ghosts who scare François and who live in the decaying Anglican church whose last vicar was Frank's father. The satisfaction with which François witnessed the gradual decline of his town's English community has made him all the more resentful of the continuing English domination of the city. Yet François seems to be incapable of turning his bitterness into action. Ashamed of the cowardice that made him deny his Communist sympathies in order to avoid being sentenced to jail after the anti-NATO demonstration, François let his soul fall onto the courthouse floor. The ever-vigilant Frank retrieved it and has held on to it ever since, keeping it safe for future use.

Cohen's F. and *I* also share a common background. Although F. seems to be several years older than his friend, they grew up together in a Montreal orphanage. In contrast to *La Nuit*, *Beautiful Losers* says nothing about its main characters' families of origin. This raises an interesting question. For many years, readers have largely taken for granted that *I* is an anglophone Montrealer, and most likely a Jew like Cohen himself. As Frank Davey has pointed out, however, Québec orphanages were historically segregated by both language and religion.[9] He infers from this that we cannot take *I*'s anglophone identity for granted. He may well be just as much a francophone as F.[10] The fact that *I* reads American comic books and is fascinated by the "New Jew" of postwar Zionism is inconclusive since F. shares these interests. Davey's argument has the merit of warning us against too closely identifying *I* with his creator. When *I* is targeted as an English Jew at the nationalist demonstration, he neither confirms nor denies that identity. Similarly, when F. speaks of having "worked among the Jews" and pointedly adds, speaking to *I*, "(You own the factory)" (152), once again *I* neither confirms nor denies the accusation. The most we can conclude from all this, however, is that *I* does not *define* himself as a Jewish anglophone, not that he isn't one. Certainly, he claims no other identity. When he talks about French Canadians, or about Native peoples, he never says "we." The only time he uses the collective "we" is in reference to Canada. This self-identification, interestingly, seems intended to confirm rather than contradict *I*'s refusal to let his identity be pinned down. He tells F., "You've turned Canada into a vast analyst's couch from which we dream and redream nightmares of identity" (133). The Canadian "we" is thus an inclusive one because, at least until now, it has remained underdetermined. Now, however, everyone, whether French, English, or Native, and including *I*, is subject to these "nightmares of identity." The obvious implication is that Cohen's *I* represents what used to be called an "unhyphenated" Canadian, a subject who, in refusing to name himself or let himself be defined by a single language or ethnicity, insists on his transcendence of particularity.

This Canadian *I*, however, is identified with a specific geographical location within that country. The jacket copy Cohen wrote for *Beautiful Losers* identifies the book's protagonist as "a contemporary Montrealer."[11] In the absence of further specification, the 1966 English-speaking reader of a 1966 English-language book would, I think, immediately think of him as anglophone. (So, most probably, would any francophone reader, since it would be rare for a French-language novel of this period to refer to its hero in terms of his urban rather than ethnic or national identity.) But attentive readers of Cohen's first novel, *The Favorite Game* (1963), would want to give this phrase an additional gloss. The central figure of that book, Lawrence Breavman, declares that each man in the city speaks with "his father's tongue," so much so that "just as there are no Canadians, there are no Montrealers. Ask a man who he is and he names a race … in Montreal there is no present tense, there is only the past claiming victories" (125). The implication is that, as a contemporary Montrealer, *I* is a character who does not yet exist.

Cohen's claim about Montrealers thus echoes what MacLennan had written about Canadians in *Two Solitudes* two decades earlier. Yet, despite the similar use of the word "race," the differences between the two statements are as significant as the similarities. In *The Favorite Game* there are three "races," not two, and not only are they stuck in the past, their personalities are fundamentally distorted. Breavman reproaches his friend Krantz for leaving Montreal at a moment when the city is "on the very threshold of greatness, like Athens, like New Orleans." Krantz responds: "The Frogs are vicious … the Jews are vicious, the English are absurd."[12] Breavman's final retort, "That's why we're great, Krantz. The cross-fertilization" (113), transforms MacLennan's idealistic marriage of virtues into a perverse threesome of vices. This ironic view of the city's intercultural transactions finds an echo in François's characterization of Montreal near the beginning of *La Nuit* as a "marché de dupes" (37). The implication is that a "Montreal" identity can be constructed only out of recalcitrant negativities. To live in the "present tense" requires a radical break from the past. Thus, Cohen's point is that whatever his original identity, *I* is now simply the one who says "I," the grammatical marker for the person speaking at this moment and identifying himself in his speaking. In this respect, *Beautiful Losers* is a story of the Montrealer *The Favorite Game* said did not exist, and who now is only beginning to exist thanks to this novel. Whether such a "contemporary Montrealer" identity can plausibly be appropriated by other "I"s outside the text is another question.

Like Ferron's Frank, Cohen's F. is also a connoisseur and collector of souls. Popular among French Canadians for having opposed conscription in the Second World War, F. is now an influential member of the federal

Parliament and a wealthy businessman. At the same time, he presents himself as a rebel underdog, a guerrilla fighter for Quebec independence.[13] His rhetoric is the seductive and slippery speech of one who wraps himself in the righteousness of victimhood even as he plots the seizure of power. *I*'s freedom from the burden of collective memory does not prevent him from being seduced by F.'s charisma, for F. offers a more extreme form of liberation: liberation from the self. *I* is eager to empty his ego, as F. urges him to do, but when he sees how F. turns the rhetoric of disempowerment into a tool of domination he finds himself clinging all the more tightly to the defences he wants to shed. What F. calls *I*'s "constipation" (in his case a literal as well as a psychological affliction) may seem to be poles apart from François's abjection, but the effect is much the same. F.'s therapeutic guardianship of *I*'s psyche is as paralyzing as Frank's safekeeping of François's soul. Like Frank, F. will eventually be made to pay for his mastery with his life.

In both novels, the relationship between the male protagonists is mediated by enigmatic female figures. I say "figures" because these women straddle the boundary between the earthbound world of novelistic fiction and the cosmic one of myth. The name Ferron gives François's wife, Marguerite, reinforces the impression we get from the beginning of *La Nuit* that François's struggle with Frank echoes Faust's quarrel with Mephistopheles.[14] Later in the story, a black prostitute named Barbara becomes for François an avatar of his mother, but also of the eternal feminine celebrated in the second part of Goethe's drama. In *Beautiful Losers*, the mythic references are more explicit. *I*'s dead wife, Edith, a woman of indigenous origin, reappears speaking Greek and identifying herself as the goddess Isis (183). In Apuleius' Latin novel *Metamorphoses* (also known as *The Golden Ass*), Isis shows the foolish hero Lucius, imprisoned in the body of an ass as punishment for playing with magic, not just how to become a man again but how to attain a new and higher humanity. This is also the transformation for which *I* now yearns, having failed to follow Edith's lead when she was alive.

These allusions refer to a supra-historical level of meaning, but in doing so they also reveal the political stakes of the quest undertaken in each book. Ferron's version of the Faust legend, which has François reclaiming his soul by regaining confidence in the consistency and cohesion of his alienated self, clearly resonates with the francophone Montreal imaginary of his time. Cohen's Isis allegory, in which *I* must abandon his power fantasies and engage more modestly with the world around him, anticipates the changes the city's Anglo *têtes carrées* will have to accept. In each case, however, transformations of political agency must for the male protagonist go hand in hand with the renegotiation of other, less easily categorizable forms of agency dramatized in their encounters with the novels' female figure.

The stories' upbeat endings suggest that Ferron and Cohen were convinced that their art successfully synthesized these two forms of metamorphosis, and that in doing so they were inaugurating a new era in which old political and cultural dualities would soon be overcome. This mood of literary optimism was short-lived. The October Crisis of 1970 soured the tone of Ferron's fiction, and even before then Cohen had abandoned narrative fiction altogether. In each case, personal circumstances in the author's lives were also a factor,[15] yet, from a literary-historical point of view, the two novels can be said to mark an endpoint as well as well as a beginning. In the years that followed the publication of *La Nuit* and *Beautiful Losers*, the prospects for articulating a cross-cultural vision of the city comparable to what Ferron or Cohen attempted were less than favourable. Of course, historical factors, including the increasing and divisive pressure of Quebec nationalism on both French- and English-speaking Montrealers, played a key role in hindering such developments. But aesthetic considerations should not be discounted. Despite the enduring and trans-historical availability of the literary myths to which they appeal, in both Ferron and Cohen we find lingering doubts the imaginative capaciousness of their art.

LA NUIT

Although it is labelled a *roman* and not a *conte* or *récit*, the novella-length *La Nuit* would seem to belong to the genre of myth or fable, like the short tale "Le Pont" ("The Bridge") out of which it emerged.[16] In contrast with novelistic heroes, who change over the time of their experience, characters in a mythical tale can emerge from their ordeals much as they were before, like Jonah, ejected undigested from the belly of the whale. Similarly, the soul François regains is unaffected by its long years of captivity. The mythical world of *Faust* is much more complex than that of folktale, but in Goethe's work, too, the hero can sell and recover his soul without loss or remainder, since this spirit is a purely metaphysical entity, unaffected by time. When François regains his soul from Frank, his personality, too, is reinvigorated but not refashioned. Yet his quest is social and historical as well as mythical. Ferron's distinctive achievement in *La Nuit* is to have found a delicate balance between novel and fable.

Ferron gives his version of the Faust myth a decidedly local twist. François does not sell his soul to the devil in exchange for superhuman knowledge. Indeed, he cannot be said to sell it at all. While the judge gives him a suspended sentence in return for denying his Communist sympathies, that transaction did not require him to give up his soul. Indeed, from the Communist viewpoint, such lies were justifiable responses to government persecution. Self-loathing is the real reason François abandons his soul on the floor of the Palais de Justice. Leaving the courtroom with his head down, François almost welcomes an abjection that is political in a more fundamental sense. As he makes his way through the crowd "comme un immigrant de la gare Windsor," he excuses himself in English: "I kept saying, 'Sorry Sir' to my new fellow citizens, all of them English" (73).[17] Like these immigrants, François experiences his foreignness in a city dominated by the English. As he walks away under Frank's watchful eye, François shrivels even further: "I would have been happy to change my name, be naked and rebaptized in the throng by the first person to come along, the lowest and most wretched of passersby" (73). François's despair is deepened by the feeling that his betrayal has validated Frank's patronizing judgment of him. Yet Frank's gesture of putting François's soul in his pocket is in its way an act of compassion. François will not actually need to be "rebaptized," since Frank will keep his soul safe and intact.

Thus, while this episode dramatizes in miniature the dispossession of vulnerable French Canadians by a more self-confident anglophone power, its political meaning cannot be "read off" from the text in simple allegorical fashion. At the time of the demonstration, François has just been released from the "Royal Edwardian Hospital" in Sainte-Agathe after being treated there for tuberculosis. According to Ferron, the causes of this disease were not just biological. Ferron's experience as a doctor in a remote Gaspé town just after the war had convinced him that poverty and psychological deprivation were not just environments in which tuberculosis was liable to spread but actual causes of the disease.[18] This helps us understand why the most important factor in François's physical recovery should be the political education he receives from Smédo, a fellow patient who teaches him about communism. Given the later depiction of the immigrant mentality as one of obsequious obedience and English assimilation, it may seem odd that François's ideological mentor should be a leftist of Hungarian origin. As we shall see, however, Smédo is one of several immigrant figures who play important mediating roles in François's liberation. One reason seems to be their ability to speak French, although how they avoided the English assimilation of the Windsor Station newcomers is never explained. The key point, however, is that *La Nuit* sets up the geopolitical duality of native and foreigner, insider and outsider, only to deconstruct it.

Smédo's teaching also prepares the way for an epiphany that expands François's mental horizons even farther. In a moment of mystic perception reminiscent of Hans Castorp's sanatorium visions in Mann's *Magic Mountain*, François realizes that behind the hills he sees from his hospital window lies not just an ordinary Laurentian village but another dimension of reality. He records his discovery in capital letters. "LIFE IS A FAITH. SAINTE-AGATHE EXISTS. REALITY HIDES BEHIND REALITY" (45). Yet, just as the hero's tuberculosis was more than a biological phenomenon, his mystical vision is not just a metaphysical one. This becomes clear in the demonstration episode that follows. Knocked out of commission by one of Frank's cops, who stand guard over him as he lies prostrate in a storefront entryway, François has another quasi-mystical experience. Once again, political enlightenment is linked to another form of awakening consciousness.[19] Next to him in the "sanctuary" to which he is confined is another detainee, a young man François describes as "handsome as the squire to a Knight of Malta" (52).[20] This queer historical reference casts a curious light on François's attraction to Marguerite when he meets her a few months later, for the fact that her smile reminds him of the "not very Marxist" smile the young man gave him is what draws François to his future wife (52).

The fluidity of sexual, political, and spiritual boundaries here suggests another, deeper explanation for the difference between the François who abandons his soul and the Faust who sells his. If François's gesture is not transactional, it is because François is not yet in a position to engage in productive symbolic exchange. He has not yet become a subject capable of defining, appropriating, and negotiating his desires. His interactions with the world are stuck at a more primitive, less articulate level. Although his visions have awakened him to realities beyond the prison of the present, he cannot yet believe that to desire and pursue that goal is to exercise meaningful agency whether or not it results in final success.

Thus, we are not surprised that after his trial François never confronts Frank or seeks out Smédo's Montreal counterparts. Instead, he abandons the city, the site of negotiated desires, and buries himself in a South Shore suburb whose chaotic settlement mirrors his psychic landscape. This reading of the text as a fable of pre-political, or more generally, pre-symbolic existence would also explain how the soul François eventually recovers is still pristine: it didn't have enough of a defined shape for that shape to be distorted. This same amorphousness, on the other hand, could be what dissuades Frank from seeking to reshape that soul according to some alien pattern: that pattern, too, would not "take." If this interpretation is correct, then it also leads us back to politics. For François's recovery of his soul would then be more than a moment of mythic closure; it would offer a pointed lesson about the unexpected power of the weak, in their very weakness, to elude the grasp of the strong.

Frank's handling of François's soul also calls for closer examination. He does not exploit his possession. On the contrary, he phones François every so often to check on him. Frank treats François's soul with what we might call fiduciary care; he is like a trustee waiting for François to return and claim his property. For a long time, nothing happens. François deflects Frank's phone calls by telling him he's reached the wrong number, as indeed he had: François is not yet able to enter into conversational exchange. Only after François is promoted to bank manager, that is, when he has shown himself able to safeguard other people's assets, does he respond differently when Frank calls again.[21] Even now, François does not demand the return of his soul. He goes only so far as to speculate that Frank, captive in his own way to his ethnic identity, is impelled by the financial probity of the Scots to offer belated compensation for François's loss (61–2). Yet, as often happens in the history of decolonization, it is precisely when naked exploitation gives way to a still unequal but at least formally structured exchange, one that offers a modicum of mutual recognition, that François finds himself emboldened to escalate his demands and envisage a violent reckoning with his oppressor.

So it is that François refuses payment and goes for payback. The drama begins rather curiously with Frank asking for "Frank" and François responding that "Frank" is ill, then a little later that "Frank" is dead. The identity of this "Frank" is only gradually clarified. At first, it seems that Frank, by speaking English and using an English version of François, is reminding the latter of his dominance. By telling his caller that *this* "Frank" is dead, François would then be declaring the death of his former, abject self. And if this "Frank" is dead, this means that the other, Scottish Frank has shamefully failed in his fiduciary obligation to keep his ward alive, a failure implicitly acknowledged by Frank's contrite attitude. This in turn allows François to shift the dead "Frank" identity from himself to his adversary, first as a joke and then with increasing seriousness. His lament becomes a prophecy whose full import he will himself only grasp in a moment: that he is going to actually kill Frank. A further ambiguity arises when Frank asks François to bring what he calls "my corpse" to the Montreal morgue (24). Is he asking for François's corpse or anticipating his own demise at François's hand? Such a reversal of fortune would be ironically appropriate, since, if François regains his soul by killing Frank, he will have proved his enemy had honoured his commitment to keep that soul alive. But there is a further irony. Since Frank is the one who in a sense gave François the time and space he didn't know he needed to become a self capable of desiring agency, François remains in Frank's debt for his emancipation. This is not as disastrous as it seems. If the self were not always in relation and thus inevitably in some sense dependent on the other, its freedom would be an empty one. Subjectivity emerges from engagement, and far from being incompatible with acknowledgment of the other, its agency is often enhanced by gratitude.[22] This paradox becomes a problem only if you mistakenly believe that dependence by definition diminishes the self, that autonomy is an absolute. Such a belief may understandably arise, however, in someone whose long experience of mistreatment or misrecognition has made any further acknowledgment of dependence intolerable. This seems to be the case for François, and so his path to liberation will not be straightforward.

To put an end to Frank's "containing" of his soul, François brings Frank a container of his own: a jar of Marguerite's home-made quince jam laced with poison. Frank is delighted by the gift, for in this jar of preserves he finds preserved his forgotten memory of the quince jam he used to eat as a child, back in the little town where he and François grew up. With this Proustian present, François shows himself to be a trustee of Frank's past. By poisoning the jam, François uses that past against his mentor, so that Frank is undone from within.

The jam has a second symbolic meaning, however, one whose significance is missed if we focus only on the political allegory. Jars of quince jam symbolize in the present the prudent economy of François's life with Marguerite. Marguerite makes the jam once a year in season, and then the Ménards carefully limit their consumption so they won't run out before the next year begins. In other words, they discipline their desires so the resources available to satisfy them won't be depleted. At the end of the novel, Marguerite's decision to open a new jar of jam for François on an ordinary day that wouldn't normally justify such extravagance signals the couple's liberation from this constricting economy of desire (132). Following François's use of the jam as a weapon against Frank, Marguerite's gesture celebrates her husband's victory over his oppressor. But it also suggests that François's psycho-social struggle has other dimensions we must not neglect.

The novel makes this clear when the confrontation between the two male antagonists is about to reach its climax. François goes to downtown Montreal to bring Frank "his" corpse, but before Frank eats the jam he introduces François to Barbara, a black prostitute trolling for clients at the Alcazar club where the two men meet. The introduction of this new female character is crucial to the novel's complication of political dualities and to its reconfiguration of François's relationship to Montreal. The city he had fled after his trial was one in which such ethnic or racial differences as existed were of no consequence compared to François's conviction that the immigrants it welcomed would all become English (73). We have already seen how the character of Smédo began to expand François's mental horizon. On his way across the river into Montreal, François makes the acquaintance of a second character who belongs to neither of the city's original two solitudes. Like Smédo, taxi driver Alfredo Carone addresses François in French, and Carone's easy familiarity with the city impresses François even more than Smédo's mastery of Marxist theory. Carone has not assimilated into the English population; moreover, he is unfazed by the notion that Montreal might be a "fool's game" (37). The importance of this character was first noted by Simon Harel in an important book about the changing image of *l'étranger* (the foreigner or stranger) in Quebec literature, and about the role this figure plays in challenging entrenched notions of Quebec identity.[23] Although, like his quasi-namesake, the mythological Charon, Carone ferries his passenger across the river to Montreal's "nighttown," his jocular conversation offers François a new perspective on the hitherto hellish city and prepares him to envisage a more productive interaction with it.

Carone's role is nonetheless a limited one. When, like Aeneas and Dante before him, François returns from the underworld, Carone does no more than chauffeur him back home. François will not share his newfound wisdom with a man who for all his savvy would not understand it. The real mediator figure of *La Nuit* is Barbara, even though the journey on which François embarks with her is confined to a brothel bedroom and takes place without the exchange of a single word.[24] Legally speaking, of course, Barbara is not an immigrant, since she comes from Nova Scotia, but as a black woman who arrived in Montreal by way of Buffalo she is more of a foreigner than the white Italian Carone, and certainly more genuinely "other" than the French Canadian hostesses at the Alcazar, dressed in their cheesy foreign costumes (86). Nor is Barbara an ordinary prostitute. She does not carry herself like a victim but projects an air of self-possession; indeed, she breathes a kind of mystic calm. With Frank's blessing, a gesture that transfers the responsibilities of trusteeship to her, Barbara takes François (in Carone's taxi) to her room in a run-down Stanley Street mansion.[25] When he emerges a short time later, François is a different man: "I must have got back my soul" (102).

By the time they get back to the Alcazar, Frank is dead from eating the poisoned jam. It may be that François recovers his soul at the moment Frank dies, but the novel makes it clear that making love with Barbara is the turning-point in the hero's story. This shift of emphasis gives another surprising twist to the political allegory.[26] Just as curious is that, in a novel so strongly focused on language as an identity marker, the encounter with Barbara takes places without her uttering a single word in English or French.[27] François trades sardonic quips with Frank about politics and literature; he and Carone speculate on philosophical and theological questions; but François and Barbara communicate only through bodily contact. This does not necessarily make their encounter any less rich in political significance, but the overlay of personal and political relationships is more like a palimpsest than a one-to-one mapping. In order to understand the political meaning of François's night with Barbara, we need to look more closely at his relationship with his wife before returning to Frank.

If we look back at the beginning of the story, we see that communication between François and Marguerite has also been non-verbal, at least much of the time, but not in a good way. François sometimes wonders whether his wife is happy, only to conclude: "I couldn't say. It's possible that happiness was not something she sought, or that she even thought about" (10). The idea of asking her directly does not cross his mind. Instead, François seeks reassurance from her body, though not through sexual union. During the daytime, she shows signs of age that make him uncomfortable: "Seeing her didn't make me feel any younger." At night, however, "her skin was as soft as it was when we first set up house" (10). François snuggles up against her so he can sleep "under her protection," more like a child than a husband. On those occasions when Marguerite "humbly" approaches him with a silent request for sex, François rather uneasily reports that "I felt obliged to behave in outlandish ways [*extravagances*] that may well have made her regret her impulse" (10). The word *extravagances* suggests that for François sex is a kind of manic play-acting that frustrates rather than fosters mutuality.

Whether François is correct about Marguerite's regret we don't know, but his discomfort with his sexuality is clear. François likes it best when Marguerite "holds" him, preserving the integrity of his physical self, not when she makes the demands of a lover pushing him out of his comfort zone into "extravagant" behaviour. Although he entertains the idea that what Marguerite most wants from marriage is security, François is the one who prefers security to risk. He senses that Marguerite knows it, and judges him for it: "The next day, her expression was still the same, a mixture of pity and envy" (10). The reason for the pity is obvious enough, but the reference to envy is curious.[28] Perhaps what she envies is François's greater ability to deny or stifle his desire, or his capacity to remain a child and avoid growing up.

François's relationship with Marguerite in the first part of the novel is thus strangely analogous to his relationship with Frank. In each case, a key dimension of François's desiring agency is "contained" – held, safeguarded, neutralized – to both reassuring and disquieting effect by a person about whom the hero feels ambivalent. Only at the very end of the story, as a result of François's awakening to new life – which is to say, after he has sex with Barbara – does Marguerite adopt a more positive attitude. The last words she says in the book, "Go on," are a call to action, issued as she urges François out the door and into the public world of work (133). She accompanies this injunction with a "joyous" wave of her hand that also expresses her sense of renewed life. Significantly, this "daytime" gesture recalls the gesture of blessing with which Barbara blessed François's nighttime departure from her room (101).

François's recovery of his political soul is thus inseparable from his recovery – or perhaps discovery – of real sexual agency. Both processes, however, involve a transformation of the relationship between self and world at a more fundamental level. The first step in that transformation was François's sanatorium vision of a "reality behind reality." The second occurs in Barbara's room, and it, too, has something mystical about it, something that goes beyond sexual consummation just as the earlier experience went beyond physical healing. When François returns to the taxi Alfredo Carone has waiting for him on Stanley Street, he says that what he experienced in Barbara's room was "a first stage of ecstasy" (104). Carone sardonically asks if he has seen the holy Virgin. François answers: "Virgin, I'm not sure about that, but I'm inclined to believe she was even though she wasn't an untouched maiden" (105). Turning Carone's anti-clerical humour back on him, François's witty reply shows that he no longer splits women into demandingly sexual and de-realized spiritual beings. But the "I'm not sure" also implies there is more to the story. François tells Carone the truth, but he does not tell him everything.

Ferron's works are not prudish in their treatment of sex, but they are more allusive than crudely explicit. In *La Nuit*, this is because in François's encounter with Barbara, the "ecstasy" he experiences involves more than a symbolic passage into erotic adulthood. In their conversation at the Alcazar club, the confrontation between François and Frank had been complicated by reminiscences of their childhood in the same small town. Frank says this makes them "compatriots," but François agrees only to the extent that they are both haunted by the ghostly "Tarlanes" (hybrid figures having the head of a horse and the body of a man) of the old Anglican church, now fallen into ruin (89). When François notices Barbara sitting next to him, the attractive yet frightening sexuality of her black body initially stirs up that same childhood fear of the monstrous combination of the human and the animal: "Barbara, you are my childhood fear, yes, remember, my fear when the Tarlane rose up between the two poplars from the ruins of the meeting-house" (95).[29]

But this fear gives way to another, deeper anxiety, when Barbara's colour reminds François of a figure closer to home. "No, Barbara, it isn't possible! Your black skin isn't the uniform worn by the Ursuline Nuns of the convent in Trois-Rivières" (99). François's mother had worn this uniform when she had been held "captive" there, as François puts it, between the ages of five and eighteen (92). A young woman imprisoned by an oppressive institution: this is Barbara's situation, too, since the Stanley Street bawdy house where she lives is guarded by a couple of thuggish doormen. The identification of the urban immigrant Barbara with a *pure laine* provincial Quebec woman is made even more disconcerting by the implication that François's relationship with his mother included a curiously twisted form of incestuous fantasy. "Are you my kid mother?" (100), François asks, gazing wonderingly at Barbara. The expression "kid mother" (*mère cadette*) is one Ferron seems to have invented (by analogy with *soeur cadette*, "younger sister," and *fille cadette*, "younger daughter") to convey something of the disorientation he felt as a middle-aged man when he thought of his mother as a woman younger than himself. Like the real Ferron at the time he wrote *La Nuit*, the François of the story is at this point older than his mother was when she died.[30] The expression would then perhaps symbolize François's false adulthood, one based on the mother's infantilization rather than on the son's coming to maturity. But, when François tells Barbara/mother "we're going to travel down the long cascade of waterfalls" in the river that flows into the St Lawrence at Louiseville, "and starting out from the end of the world, find ourselves, you'll see, back below Saint Léon" (100), the adult son reverts to the incestuous child. François turns the geography of his childhood landscape into a symbolic landscape in which origin and end, kinship differentiation and erotic fusion, are happily "contained." Yet, insofar as François's encounter with Barbara allows him to bring this regressive yearning to the surface, acknowledge it without flinching, and symbolically act it out, the middle-aged child succeeds in finally separating from his parent. "Then you looked at me with the smile of a mother whose grown-up boy is saying goodbye," François says in concluding his account of his ecstasy. "It was over" (100). Barbara in turn dismisses François with a smile,[31] which he understands as telling him: "Go on, now, you're no longer a child" (100), a phrase that anticipates Marguerite's later injunction. If Alfredo Carone was the *passeur* who helped François cross the bridge into Montreal, Barbara is the mediator who ferries François back across the river of memory into the streets of a city he feared was only a fool's game [*marché de dupes*] but now has become the site of the crucial symbolic transaction through which he recovers the agency he had lost, or rather never really possessed.

More is involved in this transaction than the resolution of a childhood Oedipal fantasy. Barbara channels the spirit of François's mother, but she also morphs into his wife. "And would you also at the same time be a Marguerite at last come into her own, her face radiant with sweat? I cried out: 'Marguerite!'" (100). The text pivots from mother to wife with a suspicious abruptness, as if the hero (or his creator) were anxious to return to a more "normal" kind of fantasy, but the move is psychologically consistent with what has just taken place. In Barbara, François had found someone who could "contain" his desires without "capturing" them, just as she herself was not a prisoner of any identity projected onto her. She is thus able to mediate François's emancipation from regressive melancholic attachment to his mother into mature appreciation of his wife, whose face he now sees for the first time. For this to happen, François needed to be accepted as a desiring subject in the most basic sense. That is, he needed reassurance he is entitled to demand that the world satisfy his desires, even if his desires incorporate questionable impulses and in turn question the existing order of things.[32] This reassurance is Barbara's gift to François, the positive counterpart to François's poisoned gift to Frank. (The reassurance might also be considered an unwitting gift from Frank, since the tryst he apparently arranged to keep François under control has the opposite effect. But this is a possibility the novel does not entertain.) Significantly, the contrast between the two gifts is also a linguistic one. François's offering emerges from an equivocal power play with words, while Barbara's is transmitted in a silence untroubled by interpretive anxiety. Indeed, only by transforming the situation at a pre-linguistic level can Barbara's gift enable François to begin negotiating the process of separation and differentiation that structures the symbolic world of linguistic and other intersubjective transactions.

Not the least important of these negotiations is that of the conflictual difference between English and French. In her silent communication with François, Barbara relativizes the importance of that difference, just as her behaviour denies racial and economic inequities their ultimacy. In this respect, Barbara goes beyond Smédo, the immigrant Marxist whose outsider perspective had enabled François to gain his first critical perspective on the world around him. Thanks to the "beginnings of ecstasy" he enjoyed with Barbara, François realizes that not every urban encounter is a confidence trick. Back in Carone's taxi after leaving Barbara's house, François decides that "the night is not a marketplace for suckers." On the contrary, he declares, "the night is the meditation of the day, and the world becoming sacred once more" (105). We are reminded here of François's sanatorium epiphany. That vision, along with the worldly insights he gained from talking to Smédo, had helped François overcome the disease undermining his body from within and opened his eyes to the reality beyond the realm of the immediately visible. Nothing he learned in the sanatorium, however, had prepared him to deal with the psychological breakdown that resulted from his courtroom betrayal of faith. Now, thanks to Barbara, François has been freed of the guilt that had burdened him and empowered to complete his political as well as his personal emancipation.

When François returns to the club, he finds Frank dead. Lying next to the body is an object François eagerly picks up, mirroring the earlier moment in which Frank had retrieved something he had left behind. This object is not François's soul – which, as we saw, he had already recovered (102) – but a notebook titled "GOTHA OF THE QUEBEC" (118). The allusion seems to be to the *Almanach de Gotha*, for many generations the social register of Europe's noble families. Frequently mentioned in Proust's *A la recherche du temps perdu*, the *Gotha* was written in French, the cosmopolitan world language in the days before English took over that role.[33] Frank had apparently been using this book in his police capacity to record information on prominent French Canadians. The more important purpose of the notebook, however, was to record what Frank really thinks about the *Canadiens*, by which, François says, are meant the *Québecquois* (sic, 128).[34] François cites a long paragraph in which Frank claims that the only way to "save" the Canadiens is to seek their ruin (129). Just as federal poet-bureaucrats like Duncan Campbell Scott eulogized Indigenous ways of life they believed had no future, and whose destruction they therefore sought to hasten (130), Frank believes the Canadiens, like Canada's Native peoples (and like the aristocrats of the

Almanach de Gotha) have held on to an "atavistic" identity unsuited to the modern world. For their own protection, therefore, they must be kept as wards by a paternalistic English state.

Yet the notebook also records Frank's intuition that the docility of the Canadiens may be a ruse, and that "this patient and unsubdued people" is only waiting for its hour of independence to come (130). This may explain why Frank seems to have welcomed his death. Indeed, his final words express regret for having spent all his life on what he calls the "WRONG SIDE OF THE WALL" (130), an expression whose phrasing and capital letters underscore the connection with François's crucial sanatorium insight. Frank thought of himself as erecting a protective fence around the Canadiens; he now realizes that in doing so he built a prison for himself. To borrow François's language from the earlier episode, Frank cut himself off from the "reality beyond the reality" familiar to him.

The novel ends, however, on a less triumphalist note than the reversal of power relations between François and Frank would lead us to expect. For, by putting the notebook in his pocket, François assumes guardianship of it. Although in one sense he has killed Frank, in another he has made himself the preserving "container" for Frank's subjectivity. François's gesture may be said to exemplify the strategic Canadien patience Frank had described. This is not to minimize the importance of the changes François has undergone. On the contrary. When after returning home he slips back into bed with Marguerite, she senses there is something different about him. Her affection for her husband is renewed and, just as important, so is her respect. No longer obliged to deprive herself in order to fill the void in him, Marguerite greets the dawning day with a happy boldness that is matched by François's equally serene mood. They are now authentically connected because they each have their own separate self. "It was much more normal this way, with each of us having our own soul" (132). The MacLennan of *Two Solitudes* would have agreed. François does experience one last pang of self-doubt. Although Marguerite was joking when she called him a "shabby man" as he left the house (133), her words make him wonder if he is not really just as pathetic as he was before. Perhaps his night in the city had been "fool's bargain" after all (134). But the notebook he feels in his pocket confirms that what happened to him was not just a dream (133). He is also heartened by the sight of a traffic sign "corrected" by the young FLQ man he had met as he made his way home from the place where Carone had dropped him off (134).[35] Most important, François realizes he doesn't have to be single-minded or absolute about anything. He can be "alderman and Buddhist, bank manager and communist" as and when the situation requires (122).

The author of *La Nuit* similarly takes the long view in relation to his art. Just as François does not feel obliged to become a single-minded militant, Ferron feels no compulsion to make his work a political instrument. To do so would be to go on defining oneself in terms of the envied and resented other. The more creative alternative is to incorporate the other into one's own self-definition. Just as François pocketed Frank's notebook rather than destroy it, so Ferron accommodates the anglophone other within a more differentiated, more structurally complex, internal space. In his final words, Frank had spoken about climbing over the wall of separation, not of demolishing it. Earlier, François's sanatorium vision had been one of a reality "behind" ordinary reality, the distance between them remaining even as it was bridged by an intuitive imagining. To discern this second reality was to take a decisive step toward becoming a fully individuated self, genuinely separate from the day-to-day world and just for that reason better able to enter into an authentic relationship with it. Because it is non-fusional, this relationship is also less liable to the danger of *effondrement* or psychic collapse. I would suggest that in *La Nuit* Ferron views his art as working along similar lines: mediating separateness-in-relation both for its protagonist and for the author who wrote it. The positive response the novel received suggests that *La Nuit* succeeded in playing this mediating role – dramatizing a necessary struggle yet relativizing its ultimacy – also for its readers (though at the time they were a happy few). Even F.R. Scott apparently took no offence at being symbolically murdered by an author whose talent he appreciated.[36]

The nature of Ferron's literary achievement becomes clear if we set *La Nuit* alongside another, more famous, 1965 francophone novel about a melancholy hero's violent confrontation with his double. One reason the nameless narrator-protagonist of Hubert Aquin's *Prochain épisode* fails to overcome his sense of alienation is that he cannot bring himself to trust in fiction's capacity to "hold" his contradictions while he works them through. Though he projects himself as the hero of a story-within-the-story in the manner of a sophisticated, multilayered modernist fiction,

Aquin is unable to keep self and other, friend and enemy, indeed writer and character, separate from each other long enough to create room for a productive imaginative negotiation between them.[37] In Aquin, every transaction thus turns out to be a *marché de dupes*, a game of smoke and mirrors, and every action only serves to mark time.

I would argue that the aesthetic contrast between *Prochain épisode* and *La Nuit* is related to the difference of setting, that is, to the kind the space in which each story unfolds. Where Ferron has his hero travel to Montreal from the nearby South Shore, Aquin sends his character away from the city to faraway Switzerland. In the early 1960s, Ferron, like a number of other Quebec writers concerned about the future of the French language, looked to Switzerland as a model for a reformed Canadian Confederation, one composed of loosely linked unilingual cantons. In the course of his journey to that country, however, Aquin's hero never traverses any of its linguistic frontiers or travels across any of its rivers and lakes. Instead, he rushes back and forth along the north shore of Lake Geneva from one French-speaking canton to another. Nor does he negotiate any cultural otherness within francophone space. The variety of real-life and fictional figures he meets – French, Swiss, Belgian, Senegalese authors and secret agents – only aggravates the protagonist's feelings of inadequacy. The narrator-hero cannot "contain" them in a narrative that soon spins out of control. Unable to loosen the hold of the cultural superego represented by Balzac and Simenon, the "I" of *Prochain épisode* is defeated even before he returns to Montreal and is captured by the RCMP. Ferron, by contrast, eludes any confrontation with French writers, preferring to exercise his capacity for literary play by incorporating English-language writings into his text in deliberately distorted form.[38] Ferron's François succeeds in recovering his soul and in reintegrating the split-off parts of his sexual and social self at least in part because the mixed linguistic context of Montreal proved better able to accommodate his struggle for liberation than the compartmentalized Switzerland of Aquin's fantasy.

Unfortunately, *La Nuit* has never attained the iconic status enjoyed by the more flamboyant *Prochain épisode*. Ferron's novel might in time have exerted greater influence had the delicate psychological and political equilibrium it modelled not been upset by the October Crisis of 1970. Suspected by the police of sympathy for the FLQ, Ferron ended up serving as a mediator between the government and the FLQ cell responsible for the death of the politician Pierre Laporte, and whose peaceful surrender he helped secure. The strain of this experience seems to have been exacerbated (the story is still not entirely clear) by recurrence of the psychological problems he had suffered in the late 1960s and which would mark the final decade of his life. Whatever the case, Ferron decided to replace *La Nuit* with what he told his publisher Gérald Godin was a "corrected version" of the story, to which he gave the title *Les Confitures de coings* (*Quince Jam*).[39] This later version, which appeared in 1972, is the one reprinted since that time and the only one translated into English.[40] Yet *Les Confitures de coings* does more than sharpen the political edge of *La Nuit*; it sacrifices the artistic tension of the earlier work to polemical tendentiousness.

As its title suggests, *Les Confitures de coings* narrows the focus of the story from the nighttown space in which François undertakes his political, erotic, and spiritual journey to the material cause of Frank's death.[41] Ferron could not forgive the real F.R. Scott for supporting the invocation of the War Measures Act by Prime Minister Pierre Trudeau, Scott's disciple, to quash an apprehended FLQ "insurrection." In Ferron's view, the champion of civil rights and sympathetic translator of French Canadian poetry had betrayed his principles – or perhaps finally shown his true colours. Among other significant changes, Ferron removed the capital letters from Frank's expression of regret for having spent his life on "the wrong side of the wall" (183),[42] thereby erasing the typographical parallel between Frank's epiphany and François's sanatorium vision of reality. The most important change, however, is a shift in the book's overall shape and literary mode. No longer convinced that the novel could stand on its own, Ferron added a six-part supplement titled "Appendix to Quince Jam, or, The Sacking of Frank Archibald Campbell" (209–62).

In this text, Ferron almost completely blurs the distinction between fiction and reality that *La Nuit* had played with but still maintained. The author now regrets that the quince-jam poisoning was only an imaginary murder. He launches a withering ad hominem attack against Scott, who though still called "Campbell" is now clearly identified with his real-life model. The attack is political, to be sure, but at the same time it is an assault on fictional writing as an activity with its own distinct integrity. Ferron rejects the separateness-in-relation of life and art just as he repudiates the relation-in-separateness of the novel's two principal figures. Nor is this all. In a manner oddly reminiscent of Aquin, militancy turns into melancholy as the author is compelled to acknowledge that the psychological emancipation dramatized in the novel has not been existentially effective. Merging his voice with that of the hero who supposedly had left his mother behind when Barbara set him free, Ferron is intent on being rid of her once and for all just as he wants to "fire" his political nemesis. Recalling the day of his mother's funeral, Ferron writes: "My mother is on her way in her carriage from the house to the church along Main Street in Louiseville. Let her go!" (256).

This summons to depart has been read as marking a decisive turn in the author's creative development: the son has finally succeeded in ending his crippling identification with his mother.[43] Psychological deliverance is thought to parallel, and perhaps in some way follow from, the writer's resolution of his politically and poetically ambivalent relationship with Scott. Taken together, the two gestures would then signal Ferron's definitive triumph over his inhibitions and his entry into full, autonomous adulthood. This interpretation ignores the fact that the original *La Nuit* had *already* enacted the writer's process of emancipation and had done so with a finely controlled irony very different from the unstable mixture of bitterness and sarcasm characteristic of the "Appendix." In its determination to spell things out more explicitly, the Appendix retreats from the original novel's confidence that fiction provides a sufficiently sturdy container in which inchoate feelings can be clarified and worked out in a manner no less "real" for being symbolic. In retrospect, Ferron seems to have become convinced that the distance between the author and his fictional projection is not a space of creative potentiality, but instead an open wound that needs immediate suture. From this point of view, the "Let her go!" of the passage just cited (like its more vehement equivalents in the passages about Frank) is a desperate injunction that has little in common with Marguerite's invigorating "Go on!" (*La Nuit*, 133) or Barbara's blessing of François's departure. It bespeaks a self eager to abjure what it despairs of integrating.

It was precisely because the original novel had created a separate space ("la nuit") in which Ferron's fictional representative could engage with Frank as the admired *and* abhorred embodiment of masculine mastery, and with his "mère cadette" as both the desired *and* depleted figure of feminine vulnerability, that François could recover a sense of genuine agency. Even if fiction could not effect it, it could at least model that recovery so that readers, including the author, could appropriate it over time. In the wake of the October Crisis, however, such a conception of fiction, with its trust in an imaginatively open future, no longer corresponded to what Ferron thought were the urgent demands of the moment. Curiously, though, after *Les Confitures de coings*, Ferron mined more personal veins of memory and madness more than he engaged in political polemic, though, of course, the personal was always political too.[44] In any case, Ferron would never again publish a full-length fiction set in the diverse urban world of Montreal.[45]

BEAUTIFUL LOSERS

Beautiful Losers is at once thematically denser and more loosely constructed than *La Nuit*, so it is difficult to say in a few words what the book is "about," but one of Cohen's recurring concerns is the problem central to Ferron's work. When trapped between admiration and resentment of another's power, how can you disentangle the esteem from the envy, the desire to appropriate from the urge to destroy, when you claim power for yourself? In Ferron's novel, the solution depended on François becoming a good "container" of his rival's spirit, reversing but also emulating Frank's earlier trusteeship of François's soul. The paradox was that François could recover that soul only indirectly through the positive mediation of Barbara, who first gave him an experience of being "contained" without being captured or consumed. In this sense, one could say, the reassuring but static compartmentalization that earlier anglophone writers such as Callaghan and MacLennan had seen as crucial to the coexistence of Montreal's various communities is put to emancipatory use in Ferron's quietly revolutionary work.

Cohen's response to the problem is somewhat different. One would expect as much, since the challenge in his novel is for the privileged but guiltily paralyzed anglophone *I* to loosen his defences and let himself be revitalized by the energy of the newly insurgent francophone community represented by F. That energy, however, is wilder and more polymorphous than the decorous desires dramatized by Ferron. The initial answer the novel gives to the question of internalizing the other while preserving one's integrity is to view the act of what Cohen calls "receiving," not as passive acceptance, but rather as another and higher form of self-assertion. In this way, the self's agency is affirmed, not abandoned. Cohen's appeal to the religious notion of sainthood is intended to make clear that abnegation is not the same as abjection. On the other hand, the story the novel tells about the Mohawk saint Tekakwitha, as well as other incidents involving Edith, the native woman *I* and F. both claim to have loved, makes one wonder whether a will-driven reception of the other is not a contradiction in terms, a ruse by which a narcissistic ego shields itself from any real change while proclaiming its noble intentions. To avert this danger requires another kind of paradoxical move. As with François's ability to contain, an authentic will to receive cannot be self-generated. It is itself a gift that comes from outside the self, a gift that enables you to receive it. Though its theology is far from orthodox, *Beautiful Losers* follows a long tradition of biblical thought, Jewish and Christian, in identifying the giver of this gift with a personalized divinity. To receive this gift, in turn, is to discover a greater sense of agency, to become a self no longer obsessed by the need to dominate, as F. is always at risk of becoming, and no longer imprisoned, like the passive-aggressive *I*, by the defences of the ego. But this insight about receiving is itself not easy to accept, and Cohen is clearly aware that the will to receive can degenerate into another instance of the Nietzschean will to power. That he displays this awareness in *Beautiful Losers* has seemed sufficient reason for many critics to praise the novel for its honesty. However, the extent to which the novel actually integrates this awareness into the narrative is more difficult to measure.[46] Reading *Beautiful Losers* alongside *La Nuit* may help us arrive at an answer.

Like *La Nuit*, *Beautiful Losers* begins with one character whose spiritual bankruptcy has put him, as it were, in receivership and with another character serving as his guardian. However, F. and *I* are more complexly entangled than Frank and François. Not only are they linked by an affectionate rivalry going back to their orphanage days; they have been sexually intimate, both directly and indirectly though Edith, who was *I*'s wife and F.'s lover. This greater degree of fusion also affects the novel's vision of their future. The end of *La Nuit* saw François looking forward to a new era, but, as the stop-sign "corrections" and François's "commencement d'extase" suggest, an era that does not mark a complete break with the old. Cohen's characters anticipate an "apocalypse," the sudden manifestation of a radically transcendent reality that will not merely adjust existing power relations but reconfigure them in entirely new ways. This higher reality the novel calls "Magic." To be sure, this Magic takes nameable historical forms: "Magic Canada, Magic French Québec, and Magic America" (161). However, these are not mutually exclusive, or even entirely distinct, entities. Rather, they are aspects or extensions of a Magic Montreal, which is never named as such because the city in question is not a bounded territory but rather the space in which the "contemporary Montrealer" named in the "paratext" of the novel's dust jacket will live and move and have his being.[47]

Unfortunately, the more F. and *I* work at becoming receptive, the more they fail to let their magical vision transform their lives. The characters' impotent awareness of their plight is what gives the first two parts of the book, *I*'s "History of Them All" and F.'s "Long Letter," their sometimes melancholy but more often hysterical lyricism. *I* especially cannot overcome his resistance to F.'s exhortations because after Edith's suicide that resistance is all he has left to shore up his self; he fears collapse more than alienation. To "let go" of a self he had never fully owned would be a gesture not of spiritual abnegation but of dispiriting abjection. F. may like to see himself as *I*'s mentor and protector, but he has none of the cool detachment that allowed Ferron's Frank to hold François's soul in trust. On the contrary, he depends too much on his ward's continuing to be dependent on him. Instead of embodying the magic he preaches, F. provokes continued resistance in *I* to the magic the latter professes to want.

Viewed through a political lens, the relationship between F. and *I* could be said to dramatize the attempt of a francophone nationalist less autonomous than he thinks and an anglophone sympathizer more reluctant than he realizes to abandon their brittle sense of privilege. Cohen shows, for example, how F. uses the language of victimhood to claim an authority *I* cannot critique without sounding insensitive. Yet, just as Frank's compassion was the source of his undoing, F.'s claim to exclusive occupation of the moral high ground deconstructs itself, but not in a way conducive to greater receptivity of otherness. F. can never "own" his power, and thus contend authentically with a rival power, since to do so he would have to give up his victim persona. As a result, F.'s politics remain essentially rhetorical and theatrical in nature. His only concrete political action is to blow up the statue of Queen Victoria at McGill

University.[48] This explosion does nothing to overthrow the social order; its only purpose is to give F. an opportunity to boast that he caused it. F. puts the thumb wound he got from setting off the bomb to personal advantage, using the stub that was left to pleasure women better than his full thumb could do. F.'s delight in the sexual power of infirmity is, however, ironized by the fact that he exercises that power only in the confines of the mental hospital to which he is confined (184). F.'s cavalier disregard for practical influence is also illustrated when he buys a factory, not to participate in the marketplace exchange of goods, but only so he can talk to its "Jewish ghosts" and "play with the machines" (42).

F.'s one sustained project is his mentorship of *I*. In the "Long Letter" he arranges for his disciple to discover after his death – like Frank's "Gotha of the Quebec," a testament of failure – F. reveals that out of "professional pride" he didn't want *I*'s "exodus to be too easy" (162). He had to make *I* suffer in order to free him from the bondage of his ego and open him to ecstatic experience. F. concedes, however, that his strategy has probably backfired: "What is more sinister is the possibility that I may have contrived to immunize you against the ravages of ecstasy by regular inoculations of homeopathic doses of it." *I*'s defensive retreat to the suburban treehouse where he reads F.'s letter confirms this diagnosis. F.'s failure is almost the mirror opposite of Frank's in *La Nuit*. Frank thought that the sexual gratification François would get from Barbara would help keep him under control. Frank did not expect François to use that ecstasy to achieve his own "exodus" from psychological captivity. Cohen's F. did not foresee how his therapeutic technique would prevent *I* from being healed.

Just as F.'s aspiration to liberated mastery is undercut by his perverse attachment to victimhood, *I*'s desire to drop his defences conceals a stubborn imperviousness to critique. In *La Nuit*, François stuck with the security of being "contained" by Marguerite and Frank, even at the price of being separated from his soul. *I* resists change because of what F. calls his "constipation." *I* fears that, if he lets go of the social and sexual privileges he had enjoyed without qualm until Edith's suicide, there will be no self left to receive the new identity he is promised. His anxiety, which is so great that it manifests itself in perverse attachment to his own physical excrement, is aggravated by his awareness that F. actually needs *I* to resist him. The shortest and surest way to secure evidence of one's agency, after all, is to provoke angry opposition; it is a lot harder to be sure your actions have had a positive effect. *I*'s counter-move, though not acknowledged as such, is to display a passive-aggressive submission that affords F. no satisfaction because it denies him the kind of victory that would make him proud. Yet this strategy also has the effect of keeping F. involved in *I*'s life. Hidden in all this is perhaps the fear that, if *I* stopped resisting, F. would lose interest and leave.

The relationship between *I* and F. is so twisted that one wonders how the two men could ever free themselves from the hostile dependency that binds them. The first two parts of the novel, *I*'s grandiose yet fragmentary "History of Them All," followed by the frenzied "Long Letter from F.," suggests that an imaginative pathway can be mapped only by an imagination unconstrained by conventional notions of temporal development and emotional logic. Any reconstruction of "what happens" in *Beautiful Losers*, at least insofar as the sequence of events is concerned, can only be tentative and will inevitably omit details other readers may find significant. Cohen does, however, give us one explicit starting-point for interpretation and assessment. In his "posthumous" letter to *I*, F. writes: "I believed I had conceived the greatest dream of my generation: I wanted to be a magician. That was my idea of glory. Here is my plea based on my whole experience: do not be a magician, be magic" (164). Having failed to gain this insight in his own life until it was too late, F. enjoins his disciple, and by extension the reader, to learn this lesson by reading his text, before their own lives have run their course.

"Glory," F. realizes, is not something to be appropriated by the self; it is a reality disclosed to the self, dissolving its defences. In this respect, Cohen's "glory" recalls the "reality behind reality" glimpsed in the sanatorium by the François of *La Nuit*. In *Beautiful Losers*, however, the vision of glory does not lift the self out of dejection; rather it strips the hospitalized F. of his last Promethean pretensions. Cohen calls this disclosure "*apocalypsis*" (98). The word means "revelation," but in the biblical book of that title, as in the literary tradition of "apocalyptic" on which it draws, including the Hebrew Book of Daniel, the point is not just to reveal a higher spiritual truth; it is to expose the vanity of earthly imperialisms that seek to create a new magic country by a conjuring act of political will.[49]

The clarity of this insight, however, is at odds with the desperate, indeed often hysterical tone of Cohen's narrative. Although the first two parts of the novels are told in the first person, *I*'s "History" and F.'s "Long Letter" are composed at some distance from the events they relate. Yet, if this gap is sufficient to permit the formulation of retrospective insights like the one just cited, what has been learned about the past does not affect how that past is told. Similarly, the future projected in the narrative remains the unrealized future of that past rather than the future as it is at least partially realized through the recollection of that past.[50] One explanation for this is that the central insight the characters gained from their experience is one they remain determined to deny. "We did not train ourselves to Receive," F. says in a revealing parenthesis of his letter to *I*, "because there wasn't Anything to Receive and we could not endure with this Belief" (178–9). This would explain why the instruction to "be magic," though properly self-disciplining in encouraging us to abandon whatever wands or weapons we have been using as would-be magicians, still enjoins us to perform heroic acts of will in order to fill the gap left by the absence of the divine. The contradiction inherent in seeking to transcend wilfulness by self-assertion is not overcome; it re-emerges at a higher metaphysical level. The narrative mimics the temporal confusions and stylistic excess of apocalyptic writing in order to conceal the hollowness of its revelations.

Yet this is only a partial explanation. We have not yet taken account of the mediating role played by a series of "third" parties whom *I* and F. call upon to free them from their interlocking neuroses. Even if there is no higher revelation to be had from a transcendent divine agent (though it is important that, while F. doubts there is "Anything to Receive," he does not address the issue of whether there is Anyone to offer it), these figures, some human, some larger than life, may provide F. and *I* emotional and imaginative resources for the personal, and perhaps also for political, liberation of the "contemporary Montrealer" whose story *Beautiful Losers* is intended to be.

The first of these mediating figures is *I*'s wife, Edith. Like Alfredo Carone and Barbara in *La Nuit*, Edith is neither French nor British. She is a Native woman, a member of a particularly unfortunate tribe the novel refers to only as the A_____s, a people reduced to what seems to be permanent abjection by centuries of mistreatment by both the French and the English who have settled in what is now Canada.[51] By a curious coincidence, Edith is said to have grown up near Trois-Rivières, that is, in the region nostalgically evoked in *La Nuit*. Ferron's novel, however, while noting the complexity of its French and English history, made no mention of local Native or Métis populations, or of French Canadian attitudes toward the land's Indigenous inhabitants.[52] When in other passages *La Nuit* evoked the extermination of Native cultures, it blamed that catastrophe solely on the power of an anglophone-dominated federal government. The implication was that French Canadians and Native peoples were on the same side rather than in conflict with each other.[53] *I*, an anthropological expert on the A____s, wants to give them, and especially Edith, the place they deserve in his "History of Them All," and also, presumably, in a future Magic Montreal. Yet, as the novel opens, Edith is dead, having committed suicide by crawling into the bottom of the elevator shaft in the apartment building where she lived with *I*, and waiting there until she was crushed. The symbolism is clear: the high-rises of modern Montreal are built on a foundation of violence, and whether those above speak French or English makes little difference to the Indigenous people buried below.

I and F. are united in lamenting the woman they have lost, and for a moment it seems as if mourning Edith might provide a catalyst for change. Yet *I*'s guilt for failing to properly reciprocate Edith's love or understand the depth of her distress is outweighed by memories of his frustration when she resisted his sexual demands. F. seems to have appreciated Edith more. As a French Canadian, he knows what it means to belong to a community robbed of its history (121). But he, too, recalls most vividly the moments when he exploited Edith for his own purposes. On a hallucinatory trip to a country the novel calls "Argentine,"[54] he watched as Edith was assaulted by a self-propelling "Danish Vibrator" before joining with a sinister Hitler-like double in orgiastic three-way sex. This sadistic ritual is supposedly justified by the mystical apocalypse it triggers. When asked "who are you?," the abject victim of sexual and historical domination suddenly replies in Greek that she is the goddess Isis (183), a feminine divinity transcending time and change. Yet this metamorphosis does not reverse the power relation between Edith and F., or make the latter a more receptive man. On the contrary, the Native woman's divinization gives him the reassurance he needs that his aggression is neither as destructive nor as futile as he fears. The relief is only momentary, however, being soon spoiled by Edith's suicide. Like *I*, F.

cannot really mourn Edith because any gratitude he felt for having known her is overwhelmed by defensive self-obsession. There is a striking and instructive contrast here between Cohen's Edith and Ferron's Marguerite and Barbara.

How far the novel goes in acknowledging the problematic role it assigns to Edith is unclear, at least in comparison with the story's second mediating figure, a polar opposite of the first: a man not a woman, a victor instead of a victim, a type rather than an individual. This is the "New Jew" figure that emerged after the Second World War as the embodiment of Jewish determination never to leave themselves vulnerable again. No longer rootless but at home in the world (and especially in the state of Israel), at ease in a muscular (and heavily masculinized) body, the New Jew is a model not only for more timid Jews in the North American diaspora (including *I*, if we identify him as such) but for all those who want to stop being victims. F., the would-be founder of an independent Quebec, is one of them. The New Jew may be Jewish, F. declares, "but always he is American, and sometimes he is Québécois" (161). Indeed, it is under the aegis of the New Jew that F. prophesies the advent of "Magic Canada, Magic French Québec, and Magic America."

The New Jew is "always" American because America – that is, the United States – is the source of another form of emancipatory energy associated with Jews: pop culture. During their years in the orphanage, F. and *I* pored over American comic books, and they still listen to American pop songs. As Cohen was surely aware, and as Mordecai Richler would later remind us, Superman, the most famous of the comic superheroes, was created by a Canadian Jewish writer, Joe Shuster, who even introduced biblical motifs into his character's origin story.[55] Superman quickly became a symbol of American power, but Cohen extends the scope of the New Jew to make him the mediator of a more globalized magical empowerment, "confirming tradition through amnesia, tempting the whole world with rebirth" (161). The New Jew "dissolves history and ritual by accepting unconditionally the complete history." Like American pop culture, the energy of the New Jew can be appreciated and appropriated by anyone, whatever their native language. Rooted in tradition, yet needing no translation to be understood, the New Jew models the possibility of overcoming all boundaries and divisions. He would seem to make it possible for F. and *I* to become "queer, militant, invisible" members of a "new tribe bound by gossip and rumors of divine evidence" (161), that is, by forms of communication that need no authentication, of evidence that needs no proof.

Yet, as F. admits in the same passage, the dream of becoming "New Jews, the two of us," turned out to be a nightmare. When they read their comic books, the young F. and *I* were less interested in the superhero stories at the front than in the ads they found at the back. These ads told more down-to-earth stories about skinny weaklings, tired of being mocked and having their girlfriends seduced away by bullies at the beach, and about the body-building programs that transform them into he-men who turn the tables on their oppressors. By changing the name of ad's sponsor from the "Charles Atlas" of the real-life comics to "Charles Axis," that is, from an idealistic allusion to the Greek god holding up the sky into a disturbing reference to the Second World War alliance of Germany, Italy, and Japan (116), Cohen implies that the characters' fascination with the "New Jew" was really another form of Fascist temptation, a would-be triumph of the will. Indeed, it is shortly after his paean to the New Jew that F. enjoins *I* not to become a magician but to be magic (164).[56]

It is thus understandable that Edith and the New Jew make only cameo appearances in part three of the novel, whose subtitle, "Beautiful Losers," is also the title of the novel as a whole. A woman in moccasins gives *I*, now an "old man" after incorporating F.'s spirit, a lift into downtown Montreal, but this avatar of Edith just drops him off at the System Theatre, leaving him to undergo his final metamorphosis alone. We get a glimpse of a New Jew "laboring on the lever of the broken Strength Test" at the Main Shooting and Game Alley just long enough to illustrate his irrelevance. When he exclaims, "Hey, Somebody's making it!" (242), he points to what is happening, but like the biblical Moses, he cannot share in the triumph. The final section of the novel moves beyond the contradictions dramatized in the first two parts by postulating a new ideal, that of "beautiful losing," in which the polarities of energy and enervation, audacity and abjection, wilfulness and welcome, are held together in creative balance.

The novel's third and most prominent mediating figure, Catherine (or Kateri) Tekakwitha,[57] a seventeenth-century Mohawk convert to Christianity, appears in all three parts of the book, beginning with its first sentence. Like Edith, Tekakwitha was subjected to mistreatment and manipulation by men, and not just by the French. Like the New Jew, she is a figure of resilience and renewal. Taking ascetic control of her own body, she turned alienation into autonomous agency and transformed the disfiguring disease that caused her death into a display of strength and beauty. According to *I*, Tekakwitha is a saint, that is, "someone who has achieved a remote human possibility" (95). In her case, the possibility is that of containing within herself all the contrary impulses that make up "the energy of love." What makes her worthy of veneration, and indeed of emulation, is that her quest seems at first sight to be unsullied by wilful self-consciousness. She seems to have overcome the opposition between activity and passivity, between resistance and receptivity, between victimization and domination. She thus would seem to herald from the past a new and freer future for the protagonists. *Beautiful Losers* in fact had opened with the question, "Catherine Tekakwitha, who are you?" (3, the same question posed to the transfigured Edith/Isis, 183). Both *I*'s "History" and F.'s "Long Letter" include extended passages retelling parts of her story. The fact that, as the third-person narrator of the novel's third part explicitly states, "this book ends" with a plea for Tekakwitha's beatification by the Catholic Church suggests that here at last a genuine spiritual mediator has been found.

Yet the space Tekakwitha occupies on the penultimate page of the novel is said to have been "rented out to the Jesuits" (242). They, not the narrator of the "Beautiful Losers" section, are the ones demanding her "official beatification" by the church. The narrator's role is limited to reproducing a passage from a biography of Tekakwitha written by Édouard Lecompte in 1927 that ended with this pious request. Most of Cohen's information about the "Lily of the Mohawks" is taken from this book,[58] though his familiarity with the text did not prevent him from introducing a number of mistakes in citing the French original or from offering a noticeably stilted English translation of it.[59]

Lecompte's wish had partially been fulfilled at the time Cohen wrote. The pope had declared Tekakwitha "venerable" in 1943. The implication is that, however outrageously the novel portrays her, Tekakwitha will remain unsullied by the protagonists' perverse devotion. Ironically, by the time she was canonized in 2012, Catholic fervour in Quebec had declined so sharply that the gesture had little religious resonance compared to the literary fame she had gained by being featured in Cohen's novel. Lecompte's prediction that North Americans would draw new "strength" from the "lily" of the Mohawks, a prediction Cohen cites (242–3), has come true in a way the Jesuit historian could not have anticipated. Yet the fact that the plea for Tekakwitha's beatification appears in a "rented" space, that is, in commercial rather than aesthetic relation to the main narrative, should give us pause. Is this only a way of ironizing a piety more naive than the novel's? Or does it signal a deeper unease?

It might be helpful to begin by contrasting Tekakwitha's mediating role with that of Barbara, for she too was haloed with a religious aura. Ferron's character embodied the possibility of being "virgin ... and yet not a maiden" (105). She could be a nurturing Madonna to François even though, indeed because, she was fully sexual. Cohen's Tekakwitaha is dedicated to virginity – as F. puts it, she "sailed her cunt away" (192) – but precisely because she is eternally inviolable she can safely be made an object of sexual fantasy. What makes Tekakwitha even more appealing to F. and *I* is that she figures a mystic receptivity to the divine, yet one whose ascetic self-fashioning makes her immune to disappointment. Tekakwitha would still be a saint even if the God she believes in doesn't exist (179). The intuition that Tekakwitha's receptivity operates independently of actual divine action leads F. to suspect her of being "a little saintly faker" (12). Yet it also makes her the ideal object on whom *I* should carry out F.'s injunction to "fuck a saint" (12) so as to learn from her how to transcend the dualities of ego and other.

Curiously, though, while they like to dwell on Tekakwitha's eroticized body and speak wistfully about the traditional Mohawk "fuck cure" for diseases of the body and spirit (130), neither *I* nor F. fantasizes actually having their way with the saint. This may be a sign of an unconscious resistance to an unwelcome truth. Because if training in receptiveness is what you seek, shouldn't you want the saint to fuck you? The novel never considers *this* scenario. In fact, *Beautiful Losers* never dramatizes any receptive experience of sex. By this I don't mean the adoption of "passive" as opposed to "active" postures, but the emotional taking in of the other's desire as a part of one's own. Whether hetero- or homosexual, sexual activity in *Beautiful Losers* consists almost exclusively of extracting from another person (or from oneself) tangible evidence of one's erotic power. In this sense, the critics who have called the novel pornographic were justified in doing so. Just as hardcore-porn filmmakers insist on "money shots" of visible ejaculation to prove the actor isn't faking it, the protagonists of *Beautiful Losers* are obsessed with external evidence of climax, whether in the form of semen or of vaginal discharges. The Tekakwitha of their fantasy is no different, for she is not satisfied until her self-mortifications make her bleed. What gratifies *I* and F. is empirical proof of their agency, not the inwardness of ecstasy. Similarly, the subject from whom a response is extracted (again, it could be another person or another side of the self) does not experience this extraction as abnegation, as an inner emptying of the ego, but rather as evacuation, whose result, again, is a product one can point to as evidence of agency. Here, we are no longer in the realm of genitality but in that of a regressive and controlling anality: the "constipated" *I*, alone in his treehouse after F.'s death, delights in the shit he manages to produce and which he refuses to clean up. His ego is perversely reinforced by the other people's reactions of disgust, the only response he can be sure of eliciting in his derelict state. The same pattern might be said to obtain in the novel's mode of communication with the reader. Cohen's sex scenes are designed primarily to extract a gasp of shock or awe more than to invite the reader into imaginative participation. Or perhaps they are designed to provide readers with an opportunity to show their openness of mind.

The language and practice of religion are beset with similar contradictions. F. is impatient with *I*'s manic chatter: "Are you disarmed and empty, an instrument of grace? Can you stop talking?" (153), but F. never stops talking either. He praises self-effacing, non-verbal communication at bombastic length. In his first novel, *The Favorite Game*, Cohen had his hero acknowledge the contradiction. "I'm not a good lover or I'd be with you now," Breavman writes to his lover Shell near the end of that book. "I'd be beside you, not using this longing for a proof of feeling" (234). *Beautiful Losers*, at least in its first two parts, is too enamoured of its religious rhetoric to see its narcissism. There is, to be sure, one sustained moment of prayer in the novel, included as chapter 17 of *I*'s "History" (53–5), and it offers an eloquent and seemingly authentic expression of need. Yet it is so overstuffed with words that God would have a hard time getting a word in edgeways. Of course, the strategy has its upside: if God is dead or absent, the person who voices this prayer will have not have heard the silence.

In the following chapter, the idea that "Prayer is translation" (56) seems to provide a more promising basis for a devotional practice characterized by chastened attention and respectful reception. But what F. has in mind has little to do with contemporary translation theory. "A man translates himself into a child asking for all there is in a language he has barely mastered" (56). Beneath its apparent modesty, the statement envisages the translation process as taking place entirely within the self, at the self's initiative. The other language is only an instrument to be mastered, an object out there to be appropriated for one's own ends, not an initiative calling for, or enabling, an answering response. Moreover, to ask for "all there is" is to want to possess everything, that is to say, it is to want to be God, not God's servant. The only other vision of translation in the novel is the one implied by the reproduction of pages from a Greek-English phrasebook at the end of *I*'s "History" (142). Here, it is true, we have examples of depersonalized, ego-free translation, and to that extent the passage ironizes F.'s Promethean prayers. Poetically, however, these lists are inert. Worse, the phrases translated are all about buying and selling, not about giving and receiving.

These commercial transactions bring us back to the page "rented out" to the Jesuits at the end of the novel. I understand this statement to be Cohen's attempt to distance himself from the rhetorical and religious excess in the novel. Along the same lines, the translation flaws in the passage taken from Lecompte, whether or not they were deliberate, can be read as a means of prodding Montreal readers, who should be better at moving between French and English than between English and Greek, to devote closer attention to the challenges of communicating across the local language divide. Still, the idea of "renting" out space sounds like an admission of imaginative vacancy. There seems to be no other way to mediate the novel's intimations of a "reality behind reality," and no way to resolve the political tensions between the French and English (and Jewish) communities, at least until the arrival of the messianic figure whose advent is announced in the last paragraph of the novel, the "end" that follows "the end of this book" and that points to a future beyond what fiction can imagine.

Yet the third part of *Beautiful Losers*, disjointed and disconcertingly abbreviated as Cohen later admitted it to be,[60] tempers this fatalistic conclusion by offering a few clues to a more creative kind of "beautiful losing" through which a new civic community could be created here and now. The first clue is the suggestion that the hostile dependency that binds *I* to F. and vice versa might be resolved without appealing to any external agency. Instead of waiting to receive new identities through the intervention of a third party, the protagonists can themselves create the "third" magic figure by merging their current selves. This would be another way to resolve the paradox of wilful selflessness. Most critics have understood the unnamed character who in the last part of the novel arrives in Montreal along with the spring of a new year to be a combination of F. and *I*. It has become customary to call him "IF," an acronym that nicely captures the figure's purely hypothetical quality.[61] Whether *I* has assimilated the spirit of F., or whether F. has taken over *I*'s body and given new life to a derelict "old man" (230) – or, to borrow the metaphor I used in discussing *La Nuit*, who "contains" whom – is unclear. Both interpretations may be equally true or equally inadequate. In some way that can't be formulated, they seem to have been received into each other.

In any case, IF's existence is evanescent. His mission is limited to a single action, one that reveals the city to itself. The old man dropped off at the System Theatre by the Edith-Isis avatar appears to be a decrepit version of *I*, and he attracts the same reaction of scorn and disgust that *I* did at the nationalist rally earlier in the book. But when a crowd gathers around him in the streets adjoining the "Main (as St. Lawrence is called)" (237), he appears to channel F., being identified by various people as a "Terrorist Leader," a "Patriot," a "pervert," and the would-be "President of our country" (239). Unlike that nationalist rally, however, the new gathering that coalesces around this figure is not unified by the idealization of a leader or by the "othering" of a scapegoat. What defines the crowd is not a call to take sides, or, more precisely, the sides they take are not mutually exclusive. "For the first time in their lives, twenty men experienced the delicious certainty that they were at the very center of action, no matter which side" (240). The fact that the word "action" is preceded neither by a definite or indefinite article I take to mean that what Cohen has in view is a paradoxical fusion of certainty and indeterminacy that cannot be captured using ordinary grammar. "Action" is not a conflict producing winners and losers, but rather an ongoing contention whose energy serves to enliven an overarching sense of connection. The political rally on top of the mountain was an event about Quebec, with francophones demanding that their history be given back to them

(121). In itself, that demand was legitimate, as were Native complaints – unmentioned at the rally, it should be noted, but echoed elsewhere in the narrative – about the history of which they had been robbed by both settler nations. The new, more inclusive event occurring here, by contrast, belongs to another history in the making, that of the city. "They could all sense it as they closed in on the Main: something was happening in Montréal history!" (240). The urban crowd is not defined by language, class, or ethnicity. It includes businessmen as well as bohemians, while the "androgynous hashish smokers" among them point to a fluidity of sexual and psychological identities as well. This civic community does not replace national solidarities, but it subordinates them to enactments of diversity that are moments in a process, not steps toward a unifying goal. Again, no explanation is given as to how the fusion of *I* and F. makes this community possible. All we can say is that "action" of the kind modelled here, action without stable or permanent mediators, itself mediates the emergence of the magical city. It follows from this that IF, having served his purpose, must disappear so that people can interact directly among themselves. In a pop-culture apotheosis, he disappears into a light beam projecting a movie image of Ray Charles across the sky.

There's a hint of authorial self-congratulation as the novel celebrates IF's "remarkable performance" (241), but it is worth noting that this final part of the book (until the final, messianic paragraph) is told by an anonymous third-person narrator who is only a vicarious witness to the drama. In this respect, the "Beautiful Losers" section recalls the novels of witnessing we looked at in chapter 4. In fact, you could say that the witness-figures in *The Loved and the Lost*, *The Watch That Ends the Night*, and *Alexandre Chenevert* were looking to "lose beautifully" too. Cohen's novel, however, goes further in that he offers what might be called a poetics as well as a pathetics of losing. He does so by means of a metaphor startlingly different in its delicate handling from the insistent imagery of the first two parts of the book. The narrator compares the dynamic of IF's presence in the city to that of "an hourglass, strongest where it is smallest. And that point where he was most absent, that's when the gaps started, because the future streams through that point, going both ways. That is the beautiful waist of the hourglass!" (241). The sand in the hourglass "goes both ways" because to keep the clock going you have to flip the hourglass over as soon as the sand in the top "flask," as Cohen calls it, has finished emptying into the bottom one. Here is an image of reciprocal receiving over time. Each flask is only on top until it is emptied and the other is called upon to take its place.

Important as it is, however, this reciprocity is not what interests Cohen most about his poetic hourglass. "For a lovely briefness," he says, "all the sand is compressed in the stem between the two flasks" (241). Even if it were possible to achieve it without bursting the glass vessel, such compression is imaginatively problematic. What distinguishes it from the "constipation" the novel attacks, or the overstuffed writing of the prayer chapter in the first part of the book? The notion of compression makes better literary sense if we link it to the novel's other significant use of the word "stem." This occurs in a passage about the System Theatre, the place where F., *I*, and sometimes Edith used to play their mind games, and to which the "old man" of the "Beautiful Losers" section first gravitates when he returns to Montreal. "Outside on Ste. Catherine Street," the narrator notes, "the theater marquee displays the only neon failure in miles of light; dropping two letters which will never be repaired, it signals itself as stem Theatre, stem Theatre, stem Theatre" (221). The symbolic importance of this passage has often been noted. Out of the breakdown of the "System" of mastery emerges the serendipitous magic of the "stem," the fragile conduit through which flowers draw life from the earth. We are reminded of Cohen's *Flowers for Hitler* (1964), the provocative collection that preceded *Beautiful Losers* and in which he explored the antinomies of poetry and power. We also think of the song "Sisters of Mercy," written around the same time as *Beautiful Losers*, and which famously speaks of a "love that is graceful and green as a stem."[62] In this image, compressed fullness is achieved by the linguistic sparseness of lyric.

Beautiful Losers, I think, would be a more satisfying work of art if Cohen's novelistic practice had been more consistent with the poetic vision briefly glimpsed at its end. Although the novel takes the form of a series of fragments – even *I*'s "History of Them All" consists only of a series of brief episodes – it often stuffs those fragments to the point that, although they are short, they are no longer "brief" in the desired sense. Perhaps most unfortunately, at the end of the novel the third-person ironic-witness narrator who directed our attention to the "stem" and the hourglass disappears, as does his vision of a non-teleological urban community. Instead, the narration reverts to the first person, with a speaker who may or may not be a more self-assertive version of the third-person narrator taking on the mantle of the biblical Moses by prophesying that the divinity "will uncover His face" (243) to him. If, like Moses, this speaker will not enter the Promised Land himself, he does not intend to vanish like IF. His final words, "Welcome to you, darling and friend, who miss me forever in your trip to the end" (243), are not a prediction contingent on later verification or a prophecy whose meaning is yet to be discerned. It is a presumptuous declaration of established fact, a fact not subject to time and change but enduring "forever" until time itself comes to an end. It is a statement profoundly at odds with the "lovely briefness" of the hourglass and the brokenness of the stem.

The manic conclusion of *Beautiful Losers*, it seems to me, betrays a lack of trust in art's capacity to create on its own terms the conditions for its reception. In this respect, the novel's final paragraph is not unlike the fevered Appendix that Ferron attached to the revised version of *La Nuit*. It is thus not surprising that Cohen would subsequently abandon novelistic fiction. His decision not to write another Montreal story, it is true, was in large part dictated by practical considerations rather than by the political and psychological factors that led Ferron not to write another urban novel like *La Nuit*. *Beautiful Losers* enjoyed a satisfying *succès de scandale*, but sales were disappointing.[63] It brought in too little money for Cohen to make fiction writing a career. Yet there is something politically appropriate about Cohen's change of direction. The project of writing a story centred on the figure of a "contemporary Montrealer" whose identity was as multi-dimensional and receptive to otherness as Cohen would like it to be was, in the mid-1960s, politically naive, or at least premature. Even before the October Crisis that so traumatized Ferron and embittered so many of his contemporaries, the chances of *Beautiful Losers* being "received" across the city's linguistic lines as a creatively anarchic vision of fluid urban identities were no greater than those of *La Nuit* being taken seriously as an ironic but irenic program for upsetting Montreal's hierarchies of power. Cohen's boast a decade later that he was both Canadian and French Canadian,[64] however sincere, would still at that time sound more wilful than culturally warranted. Only when the militancy of the post-October Crisis era gave way to a new, "post-national" interest in urban diversity, and once French and English writers began to read each other's work as mattering to them, would it become possible to read

Ferron and Cohen alongside as well as against each other as part of a more comprehensive literary conversation about the city.

Of course, Cohen's voice did not gradually fade away into silence, as Ferron's would do and as Klein's had already done. On the contrary, Cohen would go on to win worldwide fame through his music, while at home he would be adulated by both francophone and anglophone fans. More to the point, while *Beautiful Losers* falls short of the vision it glimpses, many of the songs Cohen wrote after he abandoned novelistic fiction dramatize elements of that vision to admirable effect. The spiritual logorrhea of *Beautiful Losers*' prayer chapter is replaced by "broken Halleluiahs,"[65] while the fantasy of a self-image magnified on the sky by a movie-projector beam gives way to a chastened acknowledgment of the "cracks in everything" that let outside light in.[66] His best songs have the "lovely briefness" Cohen's novel praised but his prose could not perfect. On stage, Cohen projected his stage persona as the "leader of a government in exile" with a more relaxed irony and a greater imaginative credibility than he could give his fictional protagonists. Perhaps most important, in setting the poems to music, he created spaces between the words, making room, as the novel did not, for listeners to inhabit the world of which they speak. As a result, by the time of Cohen's death in 2016, the claim made by the final "I" of *Beautiful Losers* to be "missed forever" no longer sounded as outlandish as it did fifty year earlier, when the novel first appeared.[67]

Conclusion

In this book, I hope to have shown how novelists writing about the Montreal of the postwar decades were challenged – in some ways stimulated, in others stymied – by the peculiar character and self-conception of the city they saw. This Montreal was a place governed by what Hugh MacLennan in *The Watch That Ends the Night* thought of as a set of implicitly accepted rules. According to these rules, the languages, memories, and modes of living of its constituent communities were granted various degrees of legitimacy as long as their lives were kept compartmentalized. Of course, every community is shaped by what contemporary thinkers, notably Montreal philosopher Charles Taylor, have called a social imaginary: a complex of images through which that community's sense of what holds it together is represented, not always explicitly, and a complex of practices that enact the community's self-understanding, often in unthinking ways. According to MacLennan, what made Montreal's social imaginary distinctive was, first, that it actually consisted of two social imaginaries co-existing side by side. In the period we are considering, neither of these imaginaries – let us call them "francophone" and "anglophone," to oversimplify a complicated history of political, religious, or cultural self-identifications in each language – could conclusively out-narrate what MacLennan called the "legend" of the other, but neither was content with being seen as a less than comprehensive interpretation of the whole. From their various social and historical starting-points, the other novelists studied in this book encounter a similar narrative impasse. Some of them are more explicit than others in diagnosing the problem, but all seek in some way to meet the obstacle it presented to any effort to give Montreal life intellectually coherent and imaginatively compelling fictional form.

The problem was aggravated by a second feature of this Montreal of the mind. This was the city's reluctance to engage, and not just acknowledge, the conflicting visions of its constituent imaginaries. By engagement, I mean a willingness to concede that the imaginary from within which one spoke could not be hermeneutically authoritative. But willingness by itself is not a sufficient precondition for action. Also required was a leap of faith that one would end up with something more than just another contestable view. The authors I discuss thus were faced with a daunting prospect. In their Montreal, differences of language and outlook between Montreal's francophone and anglophone communities, as well the internal differentiation of those communities along class, religious, or ethnic lines, became themes of critical reflection only so that those who engaged in such reflection could avert the conflict that would be triggered by going too far along this road – that is, to the point of exposing the intractability of competing claims. Boundary lines could be crossed, but their continued existence was taken for granted. The spaces defined by those boundaries may have afforded only limited room to flourish, yet they accommodated what on the evidence of the works I examine seemed to be a need surprisingly common among Montrealers of various backgrounds: the need to shore up their identities against an always imminent threat of collapse.

As we saw in discussing *La Nuit* and *Beautiful Losers*, by the mid-1960s writers began to be more optimistic about the city's capacity for change as well as about literature's transformative potential. Yet it is remarkable how long it took to gain this confidence, and how persistent the undercurrent of doubt remained. Neither the pressure of a second world war nor the prosperity of the years that followed was enough to impel a reconfiguration of the old imaginaries. This would happen only over the course of the following decades, as the explosive forces of state modernization and sexual-liberation movements combined to re-energize Quebec's francophone nationalist imaginary and then, by virtue of their success, ironically weakened its hold. Quebec's greater acceptance of the internal diversity created by new waves of immigrants integrating into the francophone community, coupled with the rise of revisionary, decentred conceptions of Canada, in which not just immigrant but

Indigenous populations and regional affiliations became more salient, created a set of conditions for Montreal anglophones to embrace their own minority status. As optimism grew about the capacity of so-called "national texts" to accommodate a plurality of historical and identity narratives, Montreal novelists in both languages gradually found themselves in a better position to transform their predecessors' stories of compartmentalized diversity into narratives of open-ended interrelationship and to instantiate in their work new and more inclusive literary visions.

Opportunity is no guarantee of success, of course. Projects often fall apart in performance, and I have tried to be candid about where that happens in the novels I analyze. Yet the terms in which those projects are conceived may also fail to capture everything the performances enact and in the process bring to light: contradictions as yet unacknowledged, unanticipated possibilities, questions latent in answers proposed. I have argued that attending to what the novels do as distinct from what they say they are doing shows them working toward just these kinds of insights. I contend that the task of literary history is to recover these insights, since they illuminate aspects of the past we can recover from no other source and by no other method than by closely tracking the inner process through which the work is made – and unmade.

Thus, I showed in chapter 1 how Hugh MacLennan's conception of a marriage symbolizing the union of two national "races" in *Two Solitudes* was complicated by an ambivalent appreciation for the sexual and social promiscuity of modern life. The novel's not-quite-avowed fascination with promiscuity, I suggested, was both a reflection of and a response to an experience of historical and metaphysical solitude deeper than ordinary social isolation. The weakness of the novel's national allegory, most egregiously manifest in the author's decision to make the French Canadian partner the bilingual son of an anglophone mother, can be traced in part to the author's literary dilemma. How could he include within his programmatically realist "Canadian" novel a more experimental work about the mixing and levelling forces of an impersonal modernity without undermining his nation-building project? The ambiguity of his novel is that it seeks to found a national realist tradition so that the cosmopolitan consciousness of modernity has something local with and against which to develop, but at the same time to provide a positive response to modernity's negations before they have done their work. From this perspective, *Two Solitudes* may be called a novel of the late colonial predicament.

Similarly, we saw in chapter 3 how Gabrielle Roy wanted to infuse *Bonheur d'occasion* with the positive and in that sense "unliterary" feeling of tenderness exemplified by Rose-Anna; and how she was determined that, in writing a novel exposing the misery of the poor, she would not, under the guise of selfless sympathy, give in to the "temptations" of a self-assertive and socially disruptive desire. In faithfully following the lives of the characters, however, the novel shows how this tenderness can be a trap, and how it can legitimize a defensive narrowing of perception. Conversely, the novel shows how Florentine finds in hostile feeling a heightened understanding and how Emmanuel recognizes in the "temptation" to fight an invitation to a fuller and more integrated life. These are inconvenient truths with which the self-protective author herself grappled in writing the book she hoped would bring her acclaim without notoriety, the negative face of fame, and this in a city whose francophone writers were more likely to become notorious for challenging the social status quo than to win recognition for the merits of their art.

In Gwethalyn Graham's *Earth and High Heaven* and Françoise Loranger's *Mathieu*, discussed in chapter 2, the exploratory dynamic of the fiction takes different paths. Instead of working through the conflicting connotations of a particular idea like promiscuity or temptation, these novels highlight the unstable kinship structures that provide an enabling context for the heroine's agency while also limiting its scope. Thanks to the status and indulgent attitude of their family, Graham's Erica and Loranger's Danielle enjoy a considerable degree of freedom. They also find some institutional outlet for their talents. They are frustrated, however, in their efforts to help the "outsider" male protagonists (and potential life partners) achieve the same combination of personal autonomy and social integration. In contrast with *Two Solitudes* and *Bonheur d'occasion*, these novels do not end with a marriage symbolizing the overcoming or the repression of the social contradictions dramatized in the story. This lack of resolution at the level of the plot, I suggested, reflects the authors' uncertainty about whether their art might play a positive mediating role in the community to which they belong. The same uncertainty finds expression in another symbolic moment found in each book: a panoramic vision of the city as a space open to imaginative occupation. A closer look, however, reveals that in Graham what is open is also empty, while in Loranger the openness cannot actually be seen. Whether the urban space glimpsed in these moments can be lived in, and more important, whether it can be lived *into* more fully and concretely over time, is a question these novelists leave hanging, perhaps because they fear that, for writers and especially for themselves as women, the answer is still no.

In each of the novels examined in the first part of this study, a key underlying concern is the difficulty in making any sort of claim for the work it does. While the compromises and submerged contradictions found in these fictions can be attributed to a large degree to the conflicting ideological forces in which the writers, as francophone or anglophone Montrealers conditioned by their context, find themselves caught, these problems also stem from the absence of a solid local literary support structure on which emerging authors can lean or against which they can creatively define their vision. In such a situation, to think too much about the cultural warrant for one's project is to risk never carrying it to completion. In the culturally defensive and morally censorious world of 1940s Montreal, it is therefore unrealistic to expect that the intuitions of novelistic practice will be explicitly reflected in the writers' self-presentation. The writers of the period are already too inhibited as it is, and so their most probing intuitions have to find their way through the cracks.

The 1950s novels I analyze in the second part of this study mark a new stage in the development of Montreal fiction in that they integrate into the world of the fiction a greater self-consciousness about the devices used to depict it. The writers I study also seek to gain in other ways a more nuanced perspective on the novelistic enterprise itself, on what it can and cannot reveal or hope to discover. This is especially true of the works examined in chapter 4, all of them composed by writers who had already published successful books but who were wondering how to follow up on them in writing about a Montreal that had changed less than expected in the years after the war. Morley Callaghan had suffered a decade of writer's block after publishing several novels, moral fables really, set in a Toronto deprived of its name and portrayed as an abstract epitome of the North American city. The experience of doing practical writing for the radio during the war helped him overcome his creative paralysis, and he became so fascinated by Montreal's peculiar and stubbornly resistant social consensus that he was inspired to make the city the concretely specified setting of a new urban novel. *The Loved and the Lost* is not only a novel about Montreal; its subject is also what one can and cannot know about individual people and places, and what writers can and cannot say about the limits of their knowledge. Callaghan dramatizes the problem by adopting what I call the device of the double witness: one protagonist serves as witness to the actions of a second protagonist, actions that themselves consist largely of testifying, through the experience of suffering, to the moral reality of the Montreal in which both protagonists live.

This device takes different but not entirely dissimilar forms in *The Watch That Ends the Night* and *Alexandre Chenevert,* the second Montreal novels published by MacLennan and Roy. Instead of presenting us with a resourceful hero or heroine emblematic of the author's hopes, these books revolve around a chronically ill character and conclude with that character's death. As in *The Loved and the Lost,* the narrative is primarily one of witness, since the death cannot be prevented, though, in MacLennan and even more starkly in Roy, the witness role is assigned to the personalized narrator of the story rather than to a character within it. Both novels express a more thoroughly disenchanted vision of the city and its future than did *Two Solitudes* and *Bonheur d'occasion.* Those novels put their hope in history, while the new narratives place their trust in a more transcendent power. The deliberate vagueness with which that trust is articulated suggests that what is being professed is not so much religious belief as faith in the literary imagination and its capacity to persist, as witness if not as transformative agency, even in the absence of adequate social support. Without questioning the earnestness, or the practical benefits of this faith, one may feel it to be artistically wishful. Transcendent forces are not so easily harnessed to energize novelistic forms.

The effort to dramatize in the work the literary perspective that shaped it takes sharply divergent directions in the novels examined in the other chapters of Part Two. The three anglophone writers studied in chapter 5 use the generic resources of comic satire to highlight the absurdities of a Montreal they see as stiff and stuck in the past. Unlike the novels of witness, these satirical novels begin from a standpoint external to the story world, indeed explicitly distanced from it, the interesting tensions of such novels lying precisely in the split between the "insider" knowledge they display and the "outsider" perspective they adopt –the outside not of religious transcendence but of social self-assurance. In *Why Rock the Boat?, The Luck of Ginger Coffey,* and *The Apprenticeship of Duddy Kravitz,* William Weintraub, Brian Moore, and Mordecai Richler also relied on the reader's acceptance of the standards presupposed in satirical fiction of the mid-century anglophone world. These standards appeal to a set of universal, "common sense" values in fact shaped by a specific ethos, the secular liberal modernity the authors see themselves as representing. From this standpoint, the authors lampoon the rigidity of those who cling to the anachronistic or eccentric values of their particular milieu. They also mock, to even more bitingly comical effect, those who think of themselves as embracing modern values but whose lack of genuine self-awareness makes them as ridiculous as their more obviously anachronistic neighbours.

The satirical confidence of these writers, I argued, reflected their privileged imaginative position in a Montreal that at the turn from the 1950s to the 1960s anglophones could still comfortably call their own, indeed even more so as at that time the city's gradual modernization seemed to bind it ever closer to a mid-twentieth-century world in which English was the hegemonic language. In the narrative working out of that satire, however, this privilege proved to be more defensively brittle, the cosmopolitanism more superficial and circumscribed, than they seemed at first. Could the satirical gaze these writers cast on the city's would-be with-it people not be turned back on the satirists themselves? The possibility of doing so is not explicitly countenanced in the texts, but the force of the question informs the ways certain episodes are enacted and certain descriptions of the city are shaped. This is particularly true of *Duddy Kravitz*, a novel which, unlike Richler's first Montreal novel, *Son of a Smaller Hero*, is defiantly partial, in every sense of that word.

If these anglophone satires can be thought of as externalizing the witness perspective by moving it from the structure of the plot to the framing of the narrative while also making the attitude of that witness more worldly, the two francophone novels on which I focus in chapter 6 move, aesthetically speaking, in the opposite direction. The actions of the central character are not conceived merely as testimony to resistant urban realities, although they do serve that purpose, and the literary dynamic of the work is not structured around the fate of another character whose principal function is to provide the hero, and through the hero the reader, with a perspective on that reality. In Gérard Bessette's *La Bagarre*, Jules Lebeuf fails to write his great Montreal novel, and in Pierre Gélinas's *Les Vivants, les morts et les autres* Maurice Tremblay is frustrated in his efforts to inspire Montreal's working class to revolutionize the social order, but each of these characters wants to act, not to watch. Their failure, it is true, dramatically illustrates the obstacles to genuinely transformative action in a socially and psychologically hidebound city. But Jules's artistic striving and Maurice's political struggle also provide an opportunity for the author to develop a perspective on their world otherwise than by following another character's life story. The necessary mediation is provided instead by an intellectual interpretive toolkit for making sense of that world.

In *La Bagarre*, this toolkit is philology. For Bessette, if not for the teachers of the university course in which Jules and his friend Augustin are enrolled, philology is to be understood in its broadest sense as the historical and encyclopedic study of languages and the evolution of linguistic expression. From a philological point of view, for example, the peculiarities of Quebec French are not deformations but merely variations legitimately derived from earlier patterns of pronunciation and syntax. The study of philology thus helps to overcome feelings of cultural inferiority. Philological attentiveness is also what enables Bessette to make his dialogues so lively in style and so suggestive of each character's social position. From this point of view, Jules's dismissal of philology as useless is of a piece with his failure to realize his literary ambitions. On the other hand, his dismissal is to some extent justified, for, as he discovers when he tries to mediate a labour dispute at the streetcar company, linguistic skills alone cannot resolve social or cultural problems. Philology is thus not to be idealized as the key to imaginative transformation. On the other hand, as Bessette shows by putting it to literary work in his novel, philological deftness does open some doors. *La Bagarre* is not the epic *oeuvre* its hero aimed to write, but it is a book that gives us a better, because more rounded, view of the issues at stake.

In *Les Vivants, les morts et les autres*, Marxist theories of historical development and political change play a role much like philology in *La Bagarre*. That is to say, they are shown to be of genuine but relative usefulness. Even when he loses his illusions about the Communist Party, Gélinas's hero Maurice never repudiates his past. Flawed as it was in its justification of dubious tactics, the ideological education he received during his years as a militant provided him, and the author he represents, with tools for understanding the world that continue to be valuable even as belief in the universal and exclusive applicability of those tools has to be given up. Maurice's experience also gives him a healthy reluctance to embrace any other ideology in the same wholehearted way. In constructing works predicated on the relative value of the intellectual schemes to which they appeal, these two authors succeed in modulating the oscillation between over-confidence and despair, between flights of idealism and dejected descents, to which, despite their best efforts, earlier writers often fell victim. In these novels, acknowledging and embracing the relative goodness of philology or historical dialectics as a heuristic framework of inquiry and interpretation is also a key step toward gaining, and being able to portray, a more rounded view of the world.

The explosion of literary production in the 1960s makes it risky to view any small selection of works as representative of a rapidly evolving situation, and even more hazardous to identify a clear turning-point with which this essay in Montreal literary history might appropriately conclude. In the final part of this book, I argued nonetheless for the pivotal significance of an imaginative mid-1960s moment whose contours may be traced through a comparative study of Jacques Ferron's *La Nuit* and Leonard Cohen's *Beautiful Losers*. Each work occupies a somewhat paradoxical historical position. Ferron's work seemed to inaugurate a new mode of francophone fiction, at once militantly ironic and modestly irenic, but the synthesis it modelled was undermined by subsequent events and it found few imitators. Cohen's triumphantly apocalyptic vision was also soon belied by events that made anglophone writers much less sanguine about their prospects in the new, more nationalistic Quebec. Like *La Nuit*, *Beautiful Losers* had no immediate literary progeny, though at the end of my discussion of each book I have added a note about another work of its period that might profitably be read in relation with it.[1] Both these novels stage an encounter between a francophone and anglophone protagonist and dramatize a complex story of rivalry and kinship between them. I argue that in them we may find as yet untapped resources for gaining an alternative perspective on the moment in which they were written and for constructing a different literary history narrating the work of that moment in relation the earlier moments explored in this book, and perhaps in relation to those that came after.

The coincidence in 1960s Quebec of revolutions in political and sexual self-expression generated dreams of a fusional merger of individual and collective liberation, and this fusional aspiration informed literary creation as well. The lyrical *poésie du pays* (poetry of the land) is the best-known illustration of a dynamic that is also present in a novel such as Hubert Aquin's *Prochain épisode* or, in negative, nihilistic form, Jacques Renaud's *Le Cassé*. In this context, one can understand how the realist fictional aesthetic of Bessette and Gélinas, based on the appreciation of the relative, conditional value of explanatory theories and expressive ideals, should give way to the ideal of *vécrire*, a word coined by the hero of Jacques Godbout's *Salut Galarneau!* to capture his wish to live and write at one and the same time. Yet Aquin's work shows how the ambition to embody the ideal of *vécrire* in telling the story of its attainment (something the ironic Godbout did not attempt himself in his own modest fiction) risked collapsing the narrative scaffolding on which the writer relied before he could get to the point where he could dispense with its support. It says something about the hidden undercurrents of 1960s optimism that Aquin's work achieved immediate iconic status precisely because of the vividness with which he conveyed the pathos of that collapse. There is pathos in Ferron's *La Nuit*, too, but the novel's distinctive achievement is to have balanced the fusional ideal of wholeness with a nuanced appreciation of difference (psychological, linguistic, even political) as something good to preserve even as the energies and perspectives generated by differentiation are incorporated into an expanded sense of self. The notion that the "container" should incorporate but not assimilate the "contained" is one with important implications for a more hospitable conception of literature as well. Retrieving that conception and exploring its possibilities and limits as they were explored in a work like *La Nuit* may help us move beyond the mixture of nostalgia and embarrassment with which we look back on the fusional *vécrire* ideal, and against which so much later writing has felt obliged to define itself.

Whether the same revisionary case can be made for Leonard Cohen's *Beautiful Losers* is a matter for debate, though I think that having that debate is also important for developing more nuanced forms of literary-historical understanding. *Beautiful Losers* picks up Ferron's exploration of how the other can be incorporated, or, to use Cohen's favourite term, "received" in ways that affirm rather than abase the self. As in Ferron, the issue is at once psychological, cosmic (although maybe we should put "cosmic" in scare quotes), and concretely political. And, as in Ferron, too, the issue is dramatized through the relationship between a cross-cultural pair of Montreal "frenemies," although the confrontation is complicated in Cohen's case by the haunting presence of Indigenous ghosts. What is hard to say, however, is whether the acts of "beautiful losing" the third part of the book projects as resolving the problem open up a genuine way forward, or only express in more cunning form the aspiration to mastery the earlier sections of the novel profess to abjure. The problem, as I see it, is that while the chastened modesty of key poetic images such as the hourglass "stem" support the first interpretation by offering a vision of fragile reciprocity over a series of "brief moments," the novel's apocalyptic rhetoric betrays an overweening and stubbornly insistent desire to "be" the magic it talks about. In this respect, the Cohen of *Beautiful Losers* could be said to have fallen victim to the same temptation to fuse literature and life that vitiated the work of someone like Aquin. Yet to stop there would be to downplay the ruthless irony with which *Beautiful Losers* exposes the will to power that drives the writing of histories, irrespective of whether they are deemed good or bad, rebellious or redemptive. Not just histories of the winners but histories of the losers too (and to which of these categories does the history of the [now] canonized Saint Catherine Tekakwitha belong, anyway?). Even any comprehensive "History of Them All," as the subtitle of the novel's first part has it, is subject to suspicion. Retrieving the critical side of Cohen's vision, uncomfortable as it is, may be even more relevant today than it was fifty years ago. There was an aesthetic logic, I concluded, in Cohen's abandoning novelistic narrative for the brief lyricisms of song. Historical logic, too, in that the ambitions of the novel were at variance with the need at the time to deconstruct the pretensions of anglophone writers to speak authoritatively about a majority francophone city. The situation is different now. Identity politics have hardly disappeared, but writers cannot claim, at least for very long, any authority beyond what they earn through their work.

Cohen's skepticism about historical narratives, or perhaps better, the skeptical perspective gained through a close reading of his novel, surely extends to the writing of a literary history like this one. As Montaigne insisted and illustrated in his *Essays*, however, skepticism proves its value when it stimulates further inquiry, not when it shuts it down. In this book on Montreal fiction in the postwar decades, I have tried to follow that example and offer, as Montaigne did, sense-making connections between events, experiences, and the books written about them. My analysis of Cohen's novel is, I believe, more appropriately skeptical than most of Cohen's critics. I have explored the significance – the literary value but also the cultural import – of what I argue are serious contradictions between what he says about history and what is enacted in the narrative he writes. But I hope that this exploration will also lead to a new appreciation of how *Beautiful Losers* makes sense in and of its literary and social context. The contours of that context I do not take as given. Rather, I argue that they emerge when this novel is read alongside other works in both French and English which, seen in relation, help us define the "moment" each of them marks. Literary history, in other words, is much like Bessette's philology and Gélinas's dialectical ideology, and indeed I am tempted to define it as a combination of the two. Despite its taking narrative form, literary history should be heuristic, not holistic. Its linking up of a succession of "moments" is an imaginative construct, a provisional story about what was being made over time in the writing of literary works and is being remade as those works are reread in the here and now. For me, that "here and now" is that of a trans-linguistic Montreal as diversely national in allegiance as it is ethnically diverse in composition. It is a city in which imaginary walls still exist but where, to use the words of Ferron's *La Nuit*, there is no "mauvais côté du mur" (130). Of course, this ideal of inclusiveness is very imperfectly honoured in economic and political practice, and it is an ideal still to be fully realized in literary activity as well. Works in one language are being published in another more quickly and in greater number than ever before, and cross-linguistic dialogues among writers at festivals and other civic venues have multiplied. However, criticism not centred on translation or current trends has yet to catch up. My hope is that readers of this book, and perhaps especially those skeptical of its general thesis, will be stimulated to take a new look at the past of their "here and now" too.

Notes

INTRODUCTION

1 Mills, *The Empire Within*, 10. A well-received French translation of his book appeared a year later under the title *Contester l'empire. Pensée postcoloniale et militantisme politique à Montréal 1963–1972*.

2 The key work here is Simon's landmark *Translating Montreal* and its more recent complement, *Cities in Translation*.

3 See Harel, *Le Voleur de parcours, Les passages obligés,* and *Braconnages identitaires.*

4 See also Moisan and Hildebrand, *Ces étrangers du dedans.*

5 These are the titles of two of Nepveu's important books, *L'Écologie du réel* and *Lectures des lieux.*

6 A full bibliography of publications associated with the "Montréal imaginaire" project is available at http://oreilletendue.com/2013/10/26/ecrire-montreal/. For a brief review of the 1992 *Montréal imaginaire* essay collection, see *Québec Studies* 18 (1994): 181–2. The "traffic" image comes from Simon's early book, *Le Trafic des langues.*

7 Nepveu, *Lectures des lieux*, 200–1. Nepveu's use of the term "mosaic" picks up an image more favourably invoked by earlier, mostly English Canadian thinkers, to characterize the relationship between Canada's various communities. The use of this image had been subjected to critique from a sociological perspective by John Porter in his 1965 classic *The Vertical Mosaic*, a work, ironically, never translated into French.

8 "Une diversité sans mise en relation n'est qu'une juxtaposition inerte, et … une pluralité qui ne fait pas bouger de manière significative les termes en présence est une mosaïque" (Nepveu, *Lectures des lieux*, 200–1).

9 For samples of their many publications, see Germain and Rose, *Montreal: The Quest for a Metropolis*; Germain and Radice, "Cosmopolitanism by Default"; Radice, *Feeling Comfortable*.
10 Le Bel, *Montréal et sa métropolisation*.
11 Godard's "Geography of Separatism" was one of the inaugural essays of this type of approach.
12 See Moyes, "Writing the Montreal Mountain." Similar concerns appear in Moyes's work on Gail Scott. For Beneventi, see "Lost in the City."
13 See notably Davies, *The Isles*, and Tombs, *The English and Their History*.
14 See Morgan, *Mindscapes of Montreal*. Morgan has also begun to develop an interactive digital map of the city linking particular locations to recordings of writers reading passages of their work set in those places. https://www.google.com/maps/d/viewer?mid=1-18wFHR5vG6O-Pjloh1vqwUgnuk&ll=45.52892971436903%2C-73.58391831190181&z=13 (accessed 9 January 2018).
15 Žižek, "What Donald Rumsfeld Doesn't Know."
16 See Popovic, *La Contradiction du poème*, and Biron, *L'Absence du maître*. My review of the former appeared in *Spirale* 125 (1993): 8. More recent work inspired by Biron, and combining archival investigation with sophisticated historiographical reflection, has been collected in Cellard and Lapointe, *Transmission et héritages*.
17 For an overview of Marcotte's writings on the city, see Cambron, "Gilles Marcotte, Montréaliste."
18 Coleman, *The Limits of Sympathy*.
19 Marcotte, *Écrire à Montréal*, 167.
20 In the French original, *mise en intrigue*. See Ricoeur, *Temps et récit*.
21 Roy, "Retour à Saint-Henri," 167.
22 Cameron, *Hugh MacLennan*, 171.
23 Bessette, *Mes romans et moi*, 82.
24 Siemerling, "A Political Constituency," 162.
25 On this question, see Willmott, *Unreal Country*, and Marcotte, "Jacques Ferron, côté village." For a discussion of the tension between modernism and provincialism in the instructively different case of Irish literature, see Kiberd, *Inventing Ireland*.
26 See the essays collected in Jauss, *Toward an Aesthetic of Reception*.
27 For extended discussion of this expression, see Taylor, *Modern Social Imaginaries* and *A Secular Age*.
28 Perkins, *Is Literary History Possible?*; Blodgett, *Five-Part Invention*.

29 For a recent discussion, see the essays in part one of Sugars, ed., *The Oxford Handbook of Canadian Literature*, though the whole volume addresses the issue in one way or another. There is also a brief review of the issue in the introduction to Howells and Kröller, *The Cambridge History of Canadian Literature*. An important earlier example of this shift with particular relevance for Montreal writing is Greenstein, *Third Solitudes*.

30 Notable examples of these include Moisan, *L'Âge de la littérature canadienne*; Sutherland, *Second Image* and *The New Hero*; Jones, *Butterfly on Rock*; and Stratford's more chastened *All the Polarities*. The groundwork for these essays was laid by Frye, "Conclusion," and Falardeau, *Notre société et son roman*.

31 The massive *Dictionnaire des oeuvres littéraires du Québec*, for example, which presents itself as a comprehensive encyclopedia, includes only works written in French. For details on this and other pedagogical works, see Chapman, *What Is Québécois Literature?*

32 See Cambron, *Une société, un récit*.

33 See, for example, Green, *Women and Narrative Identity*.

34 See the early studies collected in Groupe de recherche Montréal imaginaire, *Montréal: l'invention juive*, and its English counterpart, Robinson et al., eds., *An Everyday Miracle*. More recent work includes Anctil et al., eds., *New Readings of Yiddish Montreal*, and Simon, *Cities in Translation*, chapter 5. Mention should also be made of Massey's memoir, *Identity and Community*.

35 The terms are those used by Garand, *Accès d'origine*, 314n.6. For Garand, it remains a valid distinction, the *peuple québécois* consisting of those citizens who, whatever their origin, participate in the construction of a francophone culture and identify with "the cultural group formerly called French Canadian" (314).

36 See, for example, Chamberland, "Fondation du territoire" ("Founding the Territory"), as well as any number of the "poèmes du pays" of that decade.

37 Nepveu and Marcotte, *Montréal imaginaire*, 9.

38 See the sets of essays collected in the following: Moyes, ed., "Écrire en anglais"; Moyes and Lane-Mercier, eds., "Textes, territoires, traduction"; Moyes, ed., "Fitful Colloquy"; and Leclerc and Simon, eds., "Littérature anglo-québécoise."

39 See Leith, *Writing in the Time of Nationalism*.

40 This is perhaps even more true of English Canadian literary histories than of Quebec ones. Even when they adopt a narrative form, as in New, *A History of Canadian Literature*, the approach takes an encyclopedic turn in which cross-linguistic analysis plays only a minor role.

41 Garand, *Accès d'origine*, 394–7. In this context, "answerability" I think best translates Garand's *responsabilité*.
42 Weinstock, "Four Kinds of (Post)nation-building," 51–68.
43 Garand, *Accès d'origine*, 435.
44 Roy, *Fragiles lumières*, 163.
45 These include Roger Viau, *Au milieu la montagne* (In the middle, the Mountain, 1951); Charles Hamel, *Solitude de la chair* (Solitude of the flesh, 1951); Eugène Cloutier, *Les Inutiles* (The useless ones, 1956); and Jacques Renaud *Le Cassé* (*Broke City*, 1964). See also Jean Basile's "Mongols" trilogy (1964–70): *La Jument des Mongols* (The mare of the Mongols), *Le Grand Khan* (The Great Khan), and *Les Voyages d'Irkoutsk* (Irkutsk trips).
46 In this respect, the argument made here develops what I said about Roy's creative process in *The Limits of Sympathy*.
47 MacLennan was irritated that American reviewers likened his novel to Graham's. Reacting somewhat resentfully, for the charge is clearly unjust, he declared her novel to be "not really Canadian" (Cameron, *Hugh MacLennan*, 184). Whatever the case, *Two Solitudes* was almost finished when *Earth and High Heaven* appeared. There is nothing in *Mathieu* to suggest any awareness of Roy's work.
48 Though it is worth remembering that the idea for *Alexandre Chenevert* first came to Roy in Paris, and that, well before the novel was published, she had left Montreal for good.
49 Renaud's *Le Cassé* was first translated by Gérald Robitaille in 1964 under the title *Flat Broke and Beat*, and again in 1984 by David Homel as *Broke City*. The two versions are compared in Lane-Mercier, "Untranslatability."
50 See Leith, "Quebec Fiction."
51 To my knowledge, the original *La Nuit* has never been translated into English.

PART ONE

1 On these early works, see Marcotte, "Mystères de Montréal, 114–15, and *Écrire à Montréal*, 42–3.
2 See, Popovic, "Le Mauvais flâneur," 92. English-language writing of the inter-war period remains to be fully explored. J.G. Sime's 1921 novel *Our Little Life: A Novel of Today*, for example, can be seen as articulating a critical sense of the city, but this rather obscure novel does not seem to have been known to MacLennan.
3 On the English poetry of this period, see Trehearne, *The Montreal Forties*.

4 In the absence of publicly available biographical details about her life, I cannot say the same about Loranger, but it is interesting that a secondary female character in *Mathieu* has been to Paris.

5 The epigraph reads: "Love consists in this, that two solitudes protect, and touch, and greet each other," a phrasing MacLennan took from a book review that cited Rilke only in an incidental way (Cameron, *Hugh MacLennan*, 177). The quotation comes from Rilke's *Letters to a Young Poet*, published posthumously in 1929 and since then translated many times and in various ways into English. A current translation reads: "love consists in two solitudes protecting, defining and welcoming each other" (Rilke, *Letters*, 36). In the context of that book, Rilke is heralding the arrival of a new and independent kind of woman, represented by some female Scandinavian writers, as a potential partner for the creative man, though he is also thinking about poetic creativity more generally.

6 There may be an echo here of Somerset Maugham's 1925 novel *The Painted Veil*, and more distantly, of Schopenhauer.

7 Of all MacLennan's critics, Linda Leith is the only one who to my knowledge has seen the importance of his enigmatic reference to "the ultimate solitude" (Leith, *Introducing* Two Solitudes, 71–3). While her interpretation of this solitude as a reference to death seems to me incomplete, her analysis of *Two Solitudes*, here as elsewhere, has been an important stimulus to my own thinking about the novel.

8 See Blanchot, *L'Espace littéraire*, which includes a discussion of Rilke.

9 Heidegger and Sartre might well be invoked, but of the writers discussed here only Loranger mentions Sartre, in the context of a planned performance of the latter's *Les Mouches* (*The Flies*). In the novel, the play is banned because of its alleged immorality, but it is interesting to note that Sartre's *Huis clos* was performed in Montreal with great success in 1947 (Whittaker, *Setting the Stage*).

CHAPTER ONE

1 It is important to remember how important a role was played in the development of European realism by historical novels, as well as by fictions set in the present but depicting historically "backward" regions or provinces. Walter Scott's work in both genres was widely imitated throughout Europe.

2 The word has no colour connotations here. It is used more in the sense that Walter Scott in *Ivanhoe* spoke of the need to reconcile the Saxon and Norman "races" in England.

3 The most acute demonstration of how this genealogy skews the novel's national politics is found in Leith, *Introducing* Two Solitudes, 53–65.

4 See *Statutes of the Province of Quebec*, 1968, chapter 82. The unavailability of civil marriage would be an issue of considerable though, as far as I know, critically unexplored importance for a writer I will discuss later in this book, Jacques Ferron. The fact that, as a divorced man, Ferron could marry his second wife in a Protestant but not in a Catholic ceremony (Murphy, *Le Canada anglais*, 63) may lie behind the many ambivalent references in Ferron's works to the so-called "mitaine" (Ferron-speak for "meeting-house," that is, Protestant church) of Louiseville as a haunting symbol of the English presence there.

5 The real-life heart condition that afflicted MacLennan's wife, Dorothy Duncan, made it unadvisable for her to bear a child, yet it did not prevent her from writing books of her own or from helping her husband develop his creative potential. Whether or not MacLennan consciously exploited the ambiguity of the heart image – and it is hard to imagine it did not inform his choice in some way – it is there in the text.

6 MacLennan has since been faulted for ignoring the country's Indigenous populations, whose acknowledgment would also have complicated the novel's dualistic vision (Leith, *Introducing* Two Solitudes, 67).

7 There is surely an echo here of "A Man Should Rejoice," the modernist novel MacLennan himself wrote in the 1930s, and which he never published (Cameron, *Hugh MacLennan*, 95–6).

8 The connection with Grant is made in Nick Mount, "On Hugh MacLennan's Watch," *The Walrus*, July/August 2009, http://thewalrus.ca/on-hughs-watch/ (accessed 31 January 2018).

9 Hoy, *Hugh MacLennan*, 193. In what respect this "Celtic" background differs from that of the Ontario Scotchman Huntly McQueen is not made clear, but the implication is that the Nova Scotian Celt has an earthy quality that contrasts with McQueen's puritanical fussiness.

10 We are told the studio is on "rue Labelle." There is a street with that name near the present-day site of the Université du Québec à Montréal.

11 MacLulich's *Hugh MacLennan* is an important exception, though MacLulich reads the scene rather conventionally as one of human warmth and vitality.

12 Leith, *Introducing* Two Solitudes, 77–8.

13 There have been a few French-language Protestants in Montreal, but their numbers have been negligible and their history largely ignored.

14 I cannot help thinking about Gabrielle Roy in this context. Coming to Montreal as an outsider, she really became the kind of journalist the fictional Paul did not,

but she never gave that career to one of her fictional protagonists. She also might have depicted Jean Lévesque's rise from poor orphan of uncertain parentage to social success, but, as is well known, she found the prospect unappealing.

15 While MacLennan recognized Waugh's talent, he thought him morally corrupt (Cameron, *Hugh MacLennan*, 199, 220–1). He seems to have missed the metaphysical anxiety in Waugh's early work.

16 None of the critical works on MacLennan that I have seen comment on this fact. Peepre-Bordessa's *Hugh MacLennan's National Trilogy*, for example, has a section of a chapter explicitly devoted to "cityscapes" in the novel that does not mention Kathleen's childhood street. The issue is complicated in that current Montreal maps do not include a "Rue de l'Assomption." (The city's "Boulevard de l'Assomption" does not match the novel's description, and in any case it received its name only in 1951.) One can imagine MacLennan not wanting to locate his fictional brothel on a real street. MacLulich's *Hugh MacLennan* remarks on the sympathetic treatment of Kathleen's fling with the army officer, but without reference to her personal background.

CHAPTER TWO

1 Graham herself had a relationship with a Montreal Jewish man, whom her father refused to meet (Meadowcroft, *Gwethalyn Graham*, 96).

2 Housman, *Collected Poems*, 74.

3 It may be that what Graham could not imagine was a career for Marc that did not involve deeper engagement with his Jewish identity. In a different way, how Mathieu could move from internal liberation to engagement with religious and other institutions may have been a question Loranger could not address.

4 The shunning is all on the part of the WASP establishment into which Betty Rosenberg, like Erica, was born. Nothing is said about the Jewish community, which for Graham is irrelevant since the only social integration that interests her is into the dominant caste. I return to this point below.

5 This confidence may implicitly be predicated on the novel's acceptance by an American publisher. While *Earth and High Heaven* was also published in the United States, the stakes were different. The theme of anti-Semitism was more instrumental than Canadian issues in drawing attention to the work, just as the theme of Graham's first novel, *Swiss Sonata* (1938), the rise of fascism in Europe as seen through the lives of girls in a Swiss finishing school, resonated more broadly for its British and American audience than McLennan's Canadian concerns in *Barometer Rising* (1941).

6 If, as is likely, Bruno's career is based on that of the actor-director Pierre Dagenais, Loranger may have wanted to distinguish the character from his real-life counterpart. Dagenais had close links with the English Montreal theatre scene, and one of the productions of his Théâtre de l'Équipe was directed by the anglophone Herbert Whittaker. See Godin, "L'Équipe"; Forsyth, "Drama in French"; and Whittaker, *Setting the Stage*. Still, the decision not to include any reference to English Montreal is symbolically significant.

7 Nicole says that she saw Louis Jouvet's production of Giraudoux's play *Ondine*. The play's 1939 opening run in Paris was cut short by the outbreak of war. News of Jouvet's revival of the play in May 1949 may have reached Loranger as she was finishing *Mathieu* (according to its date of printing, the book appeared in October of that year), but, although the story's chronology is vague, Nicole cannot plausibly be supposed to have seen the postwar production.

8 Personal experience no doubt played an important part in this. Graham's struggles with relationships as well as with her writing have been well documented (Meadowcroft, *Gwethalyn Graham*). A biography of Loranger is yet to be written, although it is clear she was personally familiar with the travails of radio and stage actors. From a literary point of view, perhaps the most interesting point is that neither writer published another novel after the one discussed here. Demoralized by a disastrous marriage and poor health, Graham was able to complete just one more book, *Dear Enemies*, a work of social commentary based on an exchange of letters with Solange Chaput-Rolland. Loranger shifted her focus to writing radio drama and then plays for the stage. What is common to both cases is a turn away from narrative fiction.

9 As we shall see, Étienne's paternalistic approach anticipates that of Victor Tremblay in Pierre Gélinas's *Les Vivants, les morts et les autres*, a novel with a much more explicit political agenda.

10 This detail reminds us of Canada's involvement in colonial Caribbean trade.

11 This episode is based on a real incident of 1946 involving Pierre Dagenais and his Théâtre de l'Équipe, whose work Françoise Loranger described in notes for one of their programs. Dagenais had managed to put on *Huis clos* (*No Exit*) at the Gésu theatre (owned by the Jesuits) before Sartre's name had become well known in Montreal circles. The Jesuits tried to ban the play, not just because of Sartre's atheism but because the actress Muriel Guilbault (the muse of poet Claude Gauvreau) appeared on stage in a provocatively transparent costume. But the play's run ended before the matter was resolved. A special performance in the Windsor hotel was arranged a little later for Sartre himself, who visited

Montreal after the play closed. Plagued by debts, Dagenais's troupe folded in 1948. For these and other details, see Godin, "L'Équipe."

12 That Loranger had any knowledge of these journals is unlikely (they were not published until 1954), but she may have known something of the *Relève* group to which Garneau belonged.

13 One can imagine how his story might be rewritten by the Ann-Marie MacDonald of *Fall on Your Knees*, for example, or, had he been bold enough to overcome his inhibitions, by the Ernest Buckler of *The Mountain and the Valley*, whose (non-Jewish) hero is also named David.

14 Housman, *Collected Poems*, 74.

15 Roy, "Retour," 174.

16 One thinks of Saint-Denys Garneau and of the heroes of such novels as Anne Hébert's *L'Enfant chargé de songes* (*The Burden of Dreams*) and Michel Tremblay's *Des nouvelles d'Édouard* (*News from Edward*), written much later but set in the immediate postwar years. It is interesting to note that Rochat's real-life model, Émile Maupas (1874–1948), was in fact French. Significantly, Loranger's Rochat is less "cultured" than the real Maupas, who was a painter as well as a fitness buff. See Marie-Christine Blais, "Mathieu de Françoise Loranger: femme d'aujourd'hui," http://www.lapresse.ca/arts/livres/201407/04/01-4781087-mathieu-de-francoise-loranger-femme-daujourdhui.php (accessed 29 October 2017).

17 All of this will be repeated in parodic form in *Beautiful Losers*, whose protagonist "*I*" is fascinated by the "Charles Axis" ads at the back of his comic books, and who has fallen under the spell of F., a perverse avatar of Loranger's Rochat.

18 Pascal, *Provinciales*, 1300.

19 Le Moyne, *Convergences*, 46–66.

20 "Je marche à côté d'une joie / D'une joie qui n'est pas à moi / D'une joie à moi que je ne puis pas prendre." Garneau, *Poésies*, 101. The translation is that of F.R. Scott, in *Collected Poems*, 312.

21 For an insightful analysis of this dissociation, see Biron, *De Saint-Denys Garneau*, 167ff.

22 Honoré de Balzac, *Père Goriot*, trans. A.J. Krailsheimer (Oxford: Oxford University Press 1991), 263.

CHAPTER THREE

1 See Coleman, *The Limits of Sympathy*. I was glad to find my earlier reading of *Bonheur d'occasion* endorsed in Alain Roy, *Gabrielle Roy*, 259n.31. His book has

in turn helped stimulate my more recent thinking about the novel. Though my interpretation later in this chapter of Gabrielle Roy's use of the "unliterary" term *tendresse* differs significantly from Alain Roy's, it owes much to his path-breaking and, it seems to me, insufficiently appreciated analysis.

2 In "The Artist at Work," one of the short stories in his collection *Exile and the Kingdom*, Albert Camus makes a famous play on the one letter that distinguishes *solitaire* from *solidaire*.

3 Ricard, *Gabrielle Roy*, 258–62.

4 See Roy, *Heureux les nomades*, 25–92.

5 The French text has "out for the big things," in English (307).

6 Thanks to Benoît Melançon for information on this point. See also Douglas and Greenhous, *Out of the Shadows*, 53.

7 Alphonse's "us" might well be understood as a marker of ethnic commonality rather than economic status.

8 Maclennan, *Watch*, 119. It is interesting that Alphonse says nothing about food, thus keeping desire separate from appetite.

9 Compare the moment in *Ulysses* when Stephen, like Alphonse, borrows money to visit a prostitute. In Joyce, the incident prompts an extended imaginative exploration of credit and debt (*Ulysses*, 241–2). On the local level, one might compare this scene with MacLennan's depiction of the neighbourhood brothel in *Two Solitudes*.

10 The translation omits the word "bears," which precedes "animals" in the French text (61).

11 Emmanuel's use of the feminine form "naines" probably reflects the tendency of popular Quebec speech to feminize certain words that are masculine in international French. Yet today it is hard not to read this quirk of grammatical gender in symbolic terms.

12 The question was given considerable thought. See Ricard, *Gabrielle Roy*, 282–4.

13 With the exception of Alain Roy (*Gabrielle Roy*, 242–3), critics of the novel have not wanted to raise the issue either. To be clear: I am not saying Rose-Anna could or should have acted differently, or even that Roy should have included the scenes and explanations she omits, only that the story is shaped by decisions that invite discussion of their artistic implications.

14 The word *revanche* Roy uses here for the re-establishing of balance is the one used by losers at cards or chess who request the favour of getting their own back in another game. The same word will also be used to describe Florentine's feeling of triumph at being loved by Emmanuel even though she does not love him (401).

15 Roy, *Fragiles lumières*, 163.

16 Roy, *Le Pays de* Bonheur d'occasion, 93.

17 In this respect, Rose-Anna is a bit like her creator, who talked about having to turn away from the reality of the people who inspired her characters in order to make them figures in her fiction. See Roy, *Le Pays de* Bonheur d'occasion, 87–100, and the discussion in Coleman, *Limits of Sympathy*, 50–4.

18 Paul Socken, *Concordance de* Bonheur d'occasion, provides indispensable help for such word studies.

19 The Russian literary critic Mikhail Bakhtin called this phenomenon "finalization." See Gary Saul Morson and Caryl Emerson, *Mikhail Bakhtin*, especially 216–17.

20 This phrase, omitted by the translator from the sentence in the English text that begins "Oh, a pleasant prison …" (288), appears in the French original as "une prison de tendresse" (302).

21 The darker possibility of a tenderness that collapses rather than avoids differentiation (incest, for example, or pedophilia) is not one Roy ever entertains, with the one very limited exception of the attraction between the schoolteacher and Médéric in her final work of adult fiction, *Ces enfants de ma vie* (*Children of My Heart*).

22 Simon Harel has often used the psychoanalyst D.W. Winnicott's seminal 1974 paper on "Fear of Breakdown" in his work on migrant literature in Quebec to help analyze the difficult passage from the home culture left behind into an insufficiently structuring *culture d'accueil.* Harel's critical framework is somewhat different from mine, but his references to *effondrement* alerted me to the significance of Roy's use of the term in speaking of the experience of native-born characters.

PART TWO

1 Ricard, *Gabrielle Roy*, 347.

2 MacLennan freely acknowledged that in writing *The Watch That Ends the Night* he was dealing with the final illness and death of his first wife, Dorothy Duncan. While Roy made no public statements, we now know that *Alexandre Chenevert* reflects her struggle with what would prove to be chronic health problems (Ricard, *Gabrielle Roy*, 342). In the same period, both writers were feeling the pressure of the public's expectation that they would once again produce a culturally "representative" work.

3 See Coleman, *The Limits of Sympathy.*

4 I am thinking for example of "The Temptations of Marie-Blanche" (*The Other Paris,* 1956), and of some of the stories that first appeared in book form only years later, in the first section of *Home Truths* (1981).

5 For a more extended critique of Viau, see Leahy, "Race, Gender, and Class," 38–41.

6 Belleau, *Romancier fictif,* 75–9.

7 At the end of the decade, John Buell's *The Pyx* (1959) will also combine the spiritual and the forensic in a fable of redemption, although his novel's elegant spareness of style is at odds with its lurid conception of spiritual forces.

8 *The Loved and the Lost* is listed in Sirois's 1968 survey *Montréal dans le roman canadien,* but to my knowledge it has hardly ever been cited since. Callaghan's novel does not, for example, feature in Chassay's otherwise comprehensive *Bibliographie* of 1991.

9 *The Loved and the Lost* was preceded by the young adult novel *Luke Baldwin's Vow* (1948).

CHAPTER FOUR

1 MacLennan had certainly read Callaghan's book with close attention (Verduyn, *Dear Marian*); whether Roy knew it I do not know.

2 Cameron, *Conversations,* vol. 2: 25.

3 It is interesting that, with the exception of her late autobiography, most of Roy's later works are assembled from separate stories or vignettes rather than continuous novelistic narratives.

4 For this reason, I think it justified to refer to the narrator as "she."

5 Callaghan, *A Literary Life,* 144.

6 No one has so far identified a literary source for the title of *The Loved and the Lost.* In my view, the title has a soap-opera sound. Callaghan did a lot of radio (and later television) work in the later decades of his career. He would return to the biblical world for the title he gave his second and more overtly religious Montreal novel, *The Many Colored Coat* (1960).

7 See Desmond Pacey, *Creative Writing,* 214.

8 Verduyn, *Dear Marian,* 45. As Verduyn notes, MacLennan tended to use capital letters instead of underlining in his letters when he wanted to stress a point.

9 Conron, *Morley Callaghan,* 78.

10 See Gregor and Nicholas, *The Moral and the Story.* I am also intrigued by the fact that Montreal critic Philip Stratford, whose essay *All the Polarities* helped

pioneer comparative studies of Canadian fiction in English and French, had earlier written a comparison of Catholic novels in those languages. See Stratford, *Faith and Fiction*.

11 See Taylor, *Modern Social Imaginaries*.

12 I find it interesting that neither of the two foreign critics who gave sustained attention to *The Loved and the Lost* decades ago echoed the moral objections raised by their Canadian counterparts. They focused instead on what they felt was a vivid representation of Montreal's urban life. William Walsh, an English pioneer in the field of what used to be called "Commonwealth Literature," spoke of "the quietly insinuated but effectively established presence of Montreal" in the novel, and went on to add, "In no other novel of Morley Callaghan is the city context so significantly part of the story and – at least to a British reader – so attractive" (Walsh, *Manifold Voice*, 203). The American critic Edmund Wilson's high opinion of Callaghan is well known, and he, too, attributed much of the merit of *The Loved and the Lost* to the "charm" of its setting. "Montreal, with its snow-dazzled mountain, its passionate winter sports, its hearty and busy bars, its jealously guarded French culture and its pealing of bells from French churches, side by side with the solid Presbyterianism of its Anglo-Scottish people, is a world I find it pleasant to explore" (Conron, ed., *Morley Callaghan*, 107). For these critics, what the novel does or does not know about Peggy, or any other character, is not an issue at all.

13 See Leahy, "Race, Gender, and Class."

14 Place of publication, it is true, also matters. "Now That April's Here," often taken as a portrayal of John Glassco's relationship with Graeme Taylor, like Callaghan's lesbian story, "No Man's Meat," appeared in Paris, where anglophone writers could publish daring material in avant-garde magazines without fear of censorship.

15 Cited in Conron, *Morley Callaghan*, 124.

16 McDonald, "The Civilized Eye," 90.

17 The bar is based on a famous watering hole of the day known by the nickname Slitkin's and Slotkin's. See Callaghan, *A Literary Life*, 181–8; and Weintraub, *City Unique*, 133, 138.

18 Note the ironic use of the word "possession." The passage may profitably be compared with the description of a similar party involving anglophone and francophone media people of the early television era in Hugh Hood's *White Figure, White Ground* (1964).

19 The building at 8232 avenue de Gaspé in Villeray now bears a plaque commemorating this fact.

20 In 2017 a white pine tree was added to the centre of the cross to represent Indigenous peoples.

21 In this respect, the novel may be said to anticipate discussions about the advantages and disadvantages of not defining Quebec's place in Canada in a clear and final way.

22 The "would be" of Callaghan's text suggests that Jim (who is seated close to the ice) doesn't actually see any black spectators and that he doesn't take the trouble to check his claim. Whether the expression "Canadian" faces is shorthand for English, Scottish, and Irish, or includes all other ethnicities except Jewish and French, is unclear.

23 The original edition of the novel has "innocent" here (Callaghan, *The Loved and the Lost* [1951], 165). While it is possible that Callaghan changed his text, other variants in the same passage, especially the surely inadvertent change of "the stout French Canadian" standing next to Jim into "the stout French Canadiens," make editorial negligence a more likely explanation for the change. The 2010 edition says nothing about the text on which it is based.

24 See Proulx, *Ce qu'il reste de moi*, 401.

25 See Woodcock, "Lost Eurydice."

26 See MacLennan, "City of Two Souls," 66.

27 As we shall see, the same is true in *Alexandre Chenevert*, the most significant francophone novel of the mid-1950s.

28 One wonders how much this emphasis reflects MacLennan's need to write a book that would appeal to readers in the United States. By the mid-1950s, the wartime strategic interest in Canada that created an audience for *Two Solitudes* south of the border had long waned.

29 This passage is one in which the original text of 1954 was modified for the 1979 and later editions of the novel. Fontaine was said to think in English because he liked to think of himself as bilingual, *en bilingue qu'il était*, as Roy put it (1954 edition, 95 [cf. Socken, *Myth*, 96]). Roy probably deleted this part of the sentence because it implied that bilingualism was a form of alienation, a claim that would be made in the nationalist 1960s but one that Roy did not endorse. The English translation, based on the original text, adds another spin by making Fontaine think "bilingually, as he had every right to do" (62).

30 The English version omits the French "HÔPITAL." In the French text, the words on the sign appear in different order the second time around: "HÔPITAL/SILENCE/HOSPITAL ZONE (223). The translation again omits the French word (199). For detailed comparisons of the two versions, see

Chapman, *Between Languages and Cultures*, and Kelly, "Lost in Translation." For other examples of bilingual linguistic play in older Montreal signage, see Shell, "The Forked Tongue."

31 See Kwaterko, "La Problématique interculturelle."

32 Roy's procedure here stands in marked contrast with her journalistic method in the articles about the Montreal she wrote in the early 1940s. These seek to give her readers a feel for the diversity of urban life, notably through an extended description of the shops on Saint-Laurent. The articles have been justly praised for an openness of outlook exceptional for the period, but, while they can be read as anticipating the multicultural civic consciousness so prized today, it should be noted that they neither record any actual nor imagine any potential conversation between the writer and the people she describes (Roy, *Heureux les nomades*, 27–92).

33 Shek, "L'Espace," 88.

34 From the documents we have, the novel's genesis lay in a memory flash that happened to Roy in 1948, during a visit to Geneva (a city, of course, that had not suffered during the war). An image came back to her from the year before of people waiting in line at a Paris government office (Ricard, *Gabrielle Roy*, 339). However, the process through which Alexandre became the hero of a story set in the postwar Montreal that had already served as the setting of a story about a lowly bookkeeper, "Feuilles mortes," written and published shortly before Roy's departure for Europe (Ricard, *Gabrielle Roy*, 289), remains a matter of speculation.

35 Significantly, Roy's later "artist" novel, *La Montagne secrète* (*The Hidden Mountain*, 1961), also features a male protagonist.

36 We are reminded that the only hospital mentioned in *The Watch That Ends the Night* has a distinctively British and Protestant character.

37 We know that Camus became one of Roy's favourite authors (Ricard, *Gabrielle Roy*, 340, 389), so we can assume she had read *La Peste* before writing *Alexandre Chenevert*.

38 Shek, "Thoughts," 183.

39 As Isabelle Daunais has observed, in confining her metaphysical questioning to the depiction of Alexandre's last days, Roy blunts the social implications of that questioning (Daunais, *Le Roman sans aventure*, 110–15). Daunais argues that such gestures of avoidance are characteristic of the Quebec novel, and stem from Quebec's failure to achieve full self-consciousness as a nation willing, to borrow a phrase from *Two Solitudes* that Daunais does not cite, to be "alone

with history." As my reference to MacLennan suggests, I think Daunais's francophone-centred political interpretation is open to question.

40 Marcotte, *Écrire à Montréal*, 129.

41 Here is another possible echo of Camus's *La Peste*. In that book, a character named Joseph Grand, like Alexandre a humble clerk, endlessly rewrites the first sentence of a novel, despairing of finding the perfect expression of his idea.

42 Ricard, *Gabrielle Roy*, 343.

CHAPTER FIVE

1 I find it significant that neither Moore nor Weintraub mentions television even though news media play a prominent role in their novels. Whether the action of their stories takes place before or after the arrival of television in Montreal in 1952 makes no difference.

2 Especially in the works of Edward O. Phillips, the detective novel, like other genre fiction, would re-emerge in the 1980s as an expression of a self-consciously "modest" minority anglophone literature (Leith, "Quebec Fiction"). In recent years, Peter Kirby and John Farrow have made the genre a vehicle for a more wide-ranging engagement with the post-nationalist city.

3 For reasons detailed in the next chapter, a somewhat analogous rebellion on the francophone side against a standard of "maturity" felt to be oppressive initially took the form of questioning realist norms from the inside. The literary appropriation of "immaturity" would come a little later, with the *joual* writers.

4 The novel implies the French press is just as bad as the English but focuses only on the latter.

5 In the novel, all the city's best hotels are named after members of the British royal family. One need not have much local knowledge to appreciate the joke, but it is useful to remember the controversy over the 1954 decision by Canadian National Railway president Donald Gordon to name the company's new Montreal hotel the *Queen Elizabeth*. The following year, a petition signed by 250,000 people, including Jean Drapeau, demanded a French name, "Le Château Maisonneuve."

6 Cameron, *Conversations*, vol. 2, 66.

7 "The Mirror Man" was the novel's original title (Sampson, *Brian Moore*, 127).

8 Cameron, Conversations, vol. 2, 74.

9 Whether the year in view is 1956, the year in which the novel is set, or 1948, when Moore arrived in Montreal, makes little difference.

10 Cameron, *Conversations*, vol. 2, 83.
11 Sampson, *Brian Moore*, 132.
12 The teenage Paulie displays a similar adaptability; she is her mother's daughter more than her father's.
13 Cameron, *Conversations*, vol. 2, 83.
14 Sampson, *Brian Moore*, 133–5.
15 Davidson, *Mordecai Richler*, 98.
16 Woodcock, *Introducing* Duddy Kravitz, 22.
17 The older Duddy, who makes a cameo appearance in *St. Urbain's Horseman* (1971), is given to the same juvenile scheming; but, when Richler explains his self-destructive behaviour by having him exclaim, "Who in the hell could love Duddy Kravitz?" (211), he turns him into a very different, more pathetic but less unsettling character, more in line with the more sentimental outlook of that novel.
18 Thus, it may not be for ethnic reasons alone that Yvette's name is on the deed. She is older than Duddy.
19 In this respect, *Duddy Kravitz*'s outlook is hardly different from that presented in *Earth and High Heaven* fifteen years earlier.
20 In the real Baron Byng, classes were segregated by sex, but the school itself was co-educational. Why the widely reproduced photograph of Richler's graduating class includes only boys I have not been able to determine, and it is interesting that no biographer or critic has thought it necessary to explain this fact.
21 Foran, *Mordecai Richler*, 249–51.

CHAPTER SIX

1 See Bessette, *Mes romans et moi*, 63.
2 See Brochu, *L'Instance critique*, 106.
3 See Schwartzwald, "Fédérastophobie."
4 Beaudoin's 1991 *Roman québécois* was the first history of the genre to recognize the merits of Gélinas's novel. Compare Shek's 1977 *Social Realism*, whose uncharacteristically harsh treatment can be explained only on ideological grounds.
5 In the English translation, some of what the characters say to themselves is put in italics, which may mislead the reader into thinking the phrases have been singled out, either by the author or by me, for special emphasis. To avoid this problem, I follow the practice of the French original, which uses quotation marks for internal speech.

6 Interestingly, there is no mention of *Bonheur d'occasion*, a novel whose importance Bessette had recognized early on. Ken doesn't read any novels about Montreal.

7 Although the internal evidence is somewhat vague about the exact date, the story takes place in the late 1940s (Bouboule started working in 1913, and the incident occurs either thirty-three or thirty-four years after that). At that time, the real Montreal Tramways Company (MTC) was a private enterprise. It had seen a major strike in 1943. The MTC's thirty-year contract with the city would expire in 1948, and it has been argued that the company did not bother to modernize its facilities in the postwar years, which include the months in which Bessette worked there to pay for his studies. The MTC would be replaced by a city-owned corporation in 1950, committed to replacing all streetcars with buses within a decade.

8 Though Bessette makes it clear that the raise Stevens "generously" offers will be paid for by attrition and layoffs of other workers, Jules does not give this fact, which a "panoramic" view of the labour situation would have to include, any attention; he is focused solely on the people he knows personally.

9 Ironically, the job he found was at a Catholic institution, Duquesne University.

10 See Harel, *Le Voleur de parcours*, and Simon, *Translating Montreal*.

11 Lemelin's story takes place in Quebec City, not Montreal. If Ken makes no mention of Montreal novels such as *Bonheur d'occasion*, Jules and Augustin cite no Quebec writers at all, only authors from France. See Robidoux, *La Création de Gérard Bessette*, 135.

12 The character of Augustin was based on a real person of the author's acquaintance, but what information that source provided Bessette doesn't say (*Mes Romans et moi*, 60).

13 In what became the classic interpretation of *La Bagarre*, Gilles Marcotte noted the significant fact that Bessette's hero wants to give a soul to Montreal and not, as one would have expected from a novel of the 1950s, to French Canada or Quebec (*Le Roman à l'imparfait*, 214). This decision seems to be clearly linked to the author's interest in the city's diversity of speech patterns. He even includes an episode in which Augustin converses with a French-born sailor that has no relevance for the plot but that allows the author to have Augustin notice his non-local pronunciation (69–70).

14 The French original uses the English word "outcast" here.

15 See Turner, *Philology*.

16 Philology includes the study of historical semantics and so normally should not be listed separately. Augustin may be using the word to refer to phonetics and phonology.

17 The final word, "you," accurately translates the pronoun *tu*, but in the unfinished sentence as its stands *tu* can also be read as a past participle meaning "silenced."

18 André Belleau makes the point from a slightly different point of view in *Le Romancier fictif*, 123n.22.

19 See *Dictionnaire des Oeuvres littéraires du Québec*, vol. 3, s.v. *La Bagarre*.

20 Marcotte's 1976 *Le Roman à l'imparfait* played a decisive role in this regard.

21 What Jules means is there is no French-language institution that offers girls the opportunity to pursue higher education through evening classes.

22 At the time of the story, the age of consent in Canada was fourteen. It was raised to sixteen in 2008.

23 Augustin is twenty-five (18) and so younger than Jules, but still significantly older than Gisèle. Yet his parents are happy to think of her as a potential wife for him.

24 When Jules reappears in *Les Pédagogues*, he is in many respects a changed man. After being fired from the transportation company for making trouble – "There had been some brawls [*bagarres*]" is all Jules is willing to say (195) – he went to work for the textile workers' union and eventually became president of one of its locals. Interestingly, this is the union portrayed by Gélinas in *Les Vivants, les morts et les autres*, published in the interval between Bessette's two works. Even more interesting, though, is that Jules has not married Marguerite. He heads a union local whose membership is largely female, but the key to his success, it seems, is his detachment from desire.

25 Almost nothing is said about Jules's family background. Bessette later admitted that this omission reflected his own fantasy of being an orphan (*Mes romans et moi*, 62).

26 Robidoux, *La Création de Gérard Bessette*, 137.

27 The proofreading is also inadequate. The text of the original edition systematically omits the accents that in French distinguish imperfect and pluperfect subjunctive from otherwise similar indicative verb forms.

28 Gélinas spent much of his later life working in obscurity for the publication services of the Université du Québec à Montréal (Lucie Robert, personal communication). His 1962 novel *L'Or des Indes* (The gold of the Indies) and the

two novels he published late in life have not attracted much attention and are hard to find. For further information on Gélinas, see Jacques Pelletier, "Une représentation totalisante de la réalité sociale contemporaine: Saisons de Pierre Gélinas," in Petr Kyloušek, Max Roy, and Józef Kwaterko, eds., *Imaginaire du roman québécois contemporain*, 16–30 (Montreal: Figura 2006), http://oic.uqam.ca/en/articles/une-representation-totalisante-de-la-realite-sociale-contemporaine-saisons-de-pierre (accessed 27 January 2018).

29 Founded by Georges-Henri Lévesque in 1936, Laval's social-science faculty was known for its progressive outlook.

30 Though the ground-level story of the 1952 labour dispute at Dupuis Frères, like that of the Dominion Textile strike, is dramatized in fascinating detail, discussion of this aspect of the novel unfortunately lies beyond the scope of this study.

31 The novel's readers, however, are presumed to understand what Gérard does not and to imagine scenarios Réjeanne never pictures, and are therefore assumed not to resemble them in these respects. Is this also just a fact without moral implications? The novel doesn't raise this question.

32 See the uncharacteristically harsh judgment in Shek, *Social Realism*. Even the most astute ideological analysis of fictional accounts of the Forum riot (Melançon, *Les Yeux de Maurice Richard*) does not pick up the implied parallel with the Toronto episode.

33 For an account of the speech and its repercussions, see Endicott, *James E. Endicott*, 295–6.

34 Olga's Macedonian origins make Maurice think of Alexander the Great; he seems to know nothing about the complex postwar politics of the southern Balkans that may have prompted her to take an anti-American stand.

35 On 13 March 1955 National Hockey League President Clarence Campbell had suspended Montreal's star player Maurice Richard for the entire playoffs after Richard slapped a referee during a fight provoked by a Boston opponent. The decision was widely seen by Montreal fans not only as unfair given the clear bias of the referee, but as a sign of a prejudice against French Canadians generally on the part of a hockey establishment dominated by English speakers. Undeterred by the demonstrations outside and against police advice, Campbell calmly took his seat in the Forum on 17 March, when the Canadiens were playing the Detroit Red Wings. He was booed by hostile fans, and, after a small homemade bomb exploded on the ice (who threw it is not known), he left the arena. Montreal fans spilled

out into the city, some of them venting their rage on storefronts along Sainte-Catherine Street.

36 For a discussion, see Melançon, *Les Yeux de Maurice Richard*, 160–5. Melançon also analyzes the representation of the riot in Cloutier's *Les Inutiles* and in a number of other subsequent books and films. More recently, John Farrow has dramatized the riot, largely from the (supposed) point of view of the young Pierre Elliot Trudeau, in his historical saga, *River City* (2011). In *Les Vivants, les morts et les autres*, Maurice pays a visit to *Le Devoir* in the hope of persuading its editor to support the Canadian Peace Congress. He is rebuffed by "Omer Martineau," who has not forgiven the Communist Party for abandoning the anti-conscription cause the moment the Germans invaded the Soviet Union (104). In this episode, Maurice's criticism of Martineau's "sophistries" is presented as naive. What Gélinas thought of the real Laurendeau is a question the novel does not help us answer.

37 Édouard, it is worth adding, seems to have no sexual life at all, another feature he shares with Lazenby, his counterpart in *The Watch That Ends the Night*. In both cases, this ostensible transcendence of desire undercuts the existential validity of their teaching.

38 Maurice's obliviousness to the publication of Khrushchev's secret speech in the *Montreal Star* (286, 289) suggests he has forgotten his eye-opening discovery, during his trip to Toronto, that despite its anti-communism the English Canadian mainstream press recognizes the existence of opposing positions on the Korean War, a fact unmentioned in the four newspapers he has been reading in Montreal (122).

39 For a discussion of Canadian Jewish Communists' reaction to the revelations about Stalin and about the reality of the "Jewish republic" of Birobidzhan, see Srebrnik, *Jerusalem on the Amur*.

40 *Les Vivants, les morts et les autres* bears a printing date of 15 November 1959, two months after Duplessis's death on 7 September, but it is unlikely that any awareness of that event could have made it into the novel.

PART THREE

1 In discussions of *joual* over the years, it has often been hard to disentangle the application of scientific criteria from that of cultural judgment, and I make no attempt to do so here. I merely summarize a view commonly expressed in the period.

2 See Leith, *Writing in the Time of Nationalism*.

3 The book would later be revised and retitled *Les Confitures de coings* (1971). This is the only version translated into English (under the title *Quince Jam*). My reasons for preferring the earlier text are detailed below.

CHAPTER SEVEN

1 Compare Aquin's *Trou de mémoire* (*Blackout*), in which the big separatist rally is held indoors, in a hotel meeting room, and from which outsiders are excluded in advance.

2 What "F." stands for is unclear. Since the character's identity is less important than his role, and his roles are various, the initial could just as well stand for "Fuck" as for "French," in the same way that "the A—s," the elided name of the Native people to which Edith belongs, can be read in different ways.

3 See Chaput-Rolland and Graham, *Chers ennemis*; Graham and Chaput-Rolland, *Dear Enemies*. Both editions of this pioneering work are "original" in that each author wrote in her own first language and translated the other's letters. In an additional experiment, each wrote one of their letters in the other's language.

4 Though the System Theatre is gone, the building that housed it still stands just northeast of Phillips Square.

5 Ferron's most extended engagement with Garneau was in his *Le Ciel de Québec* (*The Penniless Redeemer*, 1969).

6 Siemerling, "Leonard Cohen: Loneliness and History," 149.

7 Mordecai Richler's *Solomon Gursky Was Here* (1989) offers an instructive contrast to both these works. His fictionalized portrait of Klein still has some of the pettiness of Ferron's depiction of Garneau, but it also includes a creatively ambivalent reappropriation of some characteristic Kleinian tropes. See Leahy, "A.M. Klein."

8 The unevenness (and inequities) of the area's postwar development are vividly portrayed in the autobiographical sections of Pierre Vallières's manifesto *Nègres blancs d'Amérique* (1968), and later in Michael Delisle's novel *Dée* (2002).

9 Davey, "*Beautiful Losers*," 15–16.

10 Although, according to his biographers, Cohen's models for F. were not themselves French Canadian. They include Irving Layton and the Scottish writer and heroin addict Alexander Trocchi. Sylvie Simmons's portrait of George Lialios, Cohen's neighbour on the Greek island of Hydra, makes me wonder

whether he is not another source. Lialios was an intellectual of complicated political loyalties, and, like Trocchi, he was nine years older than Cohen (the age difference between F. and *I* seems to be roughly similar). Simmons calls him "a significant figure in Leonard's life on the island" (*I'm Your Man*, 85).

11 Nadel, *Various Positions*, 137.

12 Note that Cohen aligns the Jews more with the French than with the English.

13 The story's chronology as well as the age of the characters at any given moment are left deliberately vague, so it is better to think of F.'s activities as a set of historical postures than as stages in a career.

14 We might wonder, retrospectively, about Gélinas's decision to give versions of the same name to Maurice and Claude's lovers in *Les Vivants, les morts et les autres*.

15 Though the details are only slowly coming to light, it is clear that Ferron suffered episodes of severe psychological strain at various times in his life. Cohen's decision to focus on songwriting rather than fiction was in part a practical one, prompted by his need to earn a living in New York.

16 Ferron, *Contes*, 48–50.

17 Ferron often adverted to the use of "sorry" by English-speakers pretending to apologize for not speaking French, and would later give the name "Soçaurez" to one of his characters (Bednarski, *Autour de Ferron*, 136).

18 Olscamp, *Le Fils du notaire*, 360.

19 It should be noted that Ferron's fictionalization of the anti-NATO demonstration omits the fact that very few of the participants were French Canadians. Ferron may have blurred the facts in reaction to the tendency of the francophone press to stigmatize Communists as foreigners (Olscamp, *Le Fils du notaire*, 378–81).

20 The novel does not develop the homosexual overtones of this allusion to the Knights of Malta, a religious and military order whose original mission was to defend Christendom against the Turks but which in later centuries had a reputation for sexual licence. Together with François's encounter at the end of the book with a second young man, the FLQ militant whose action he blesses, the episode hints that for Ferron political dissidence might not be unrelated to the troubling of gender identities. Ferron's most explicit though still enigmatic comments on homosexuality are found in his later correspondence with John Grube, a gay Toronto intellectual who shared Ferron's conspiratorial interpretation of the October Crisis (See *Une amitié bien particulière* [A most peculiar friendship]).

21 François was not completely inactive before this. At some point; he joined a "respectable" socialist party, one he claims never seriously sought power (12). In the 1958 federal election, Ferron was the Longueil candidate of the Parti socialiste démocratique, the Quebec partner of the Canadian Co-operation Commonwealth Federation (CCF).

22 For a detailed discussion of this dynamic in another literary context, see Coleman, *Anger, Gratitude*.

23 See Harel, *Le Voleur de parcours*.

24 It is perhaps for these reasons that Harel does no more than mention Barbara in passing. She does not fit his language-based paradigm.

25 It is tempting to imagine this house as adjoining the building on the same street in which Lawrence Breavman, the hero of Cohen's *The Favorite Game* (1963), rents an apartment when he moves downtown.

26 When he reviewed the novel in 1965, Gilles Marcotte was puzzled by this shift. "If Ménard recovers his soul, is it because Frank is dead, or because he has slept – *horresco referens* – with a hooker?" (Ferron, *Les Confitures de coings*, 1977 ed., 261–2). The question deserves a serious answer.

27 It may be that François has learned something of Barbara's background from preliminary conversation at the club, but the text does not say so.

28 The French *envie* can also mean desire, but not in this context, I think.

29 Ferron refers to all non-Catholic churches as "mitaines," from the English "meeting-house." Though Ferron was not a believer, he liked to think of Catholicism as Quebec's national religion, and so from his point of view there could only be one institution called "church."

30 Ferron, who was forty-four when he wrote *La Nuit*, would do the same when he wrote about his own mother, the former Adrienne Caron, who died in 1931 at the age of thirty-two, in the 1972 appendix to the revised version of the novel. This text, in which, among other things, we discover a second reason why Ferron called his fictional taxi driver Carone, is discussed below. In *Quince Jam*, Ray Ellenwood translates the expression as "child-mother" (164), misleadingly, I think.

31 The French "tu me dis *avec* le sourire de la femme" can mean "with" or "through."

32 For a detailed discussion of the literary importance of this dynamic in the emergence of the realist novel, see Coleman, *Reparative Realism*.

33 The curiously awkward English of "The Gotha of the Quebec" may be a swipe at F.R. Scott's competence as a translator of French-language writing, notably the poetry of Saint-Denys Garneau and Anne Hébert.

34 Ferron liked to spell the word this way, perhaps to emphasize his people's deep historical roots.

35 Though there is perhaps a hint of irony in that the correction probably involved just changing "STOP" to "ARRÊT."

36 Djwa, *Politics of the Imagination*, 419.

37 See Lapierre, *L'Imaginaire captif*.

38 See Murphy, *Le Canada anglais*.

39 See Ferron's letter of 27 July 1971 to Gérald Godin, reprinted in *Les Confitures de coings*, 1977 ed., 8.

40 In 1979, however, Ferron did allow *La Nuit* to be reprinted by a French publisher in an edition for students, for reasons I have not seen explained in the critical literature (Ferron, *La Nuit*, 1979).

41 In 1968 Ferron had already used a number of elements from *La Nuit* in *La Charrette*, a novel that pulled the story closer to the genre of the fantastic folktale and gave greater prominence to the semi-rural South Shore setting. A comparison of these two works, as well as a detailed analysis of the textual differences between *La Nuit* and *Les Confitures de coings*, falls outside the scope of this study. For a fascinating analysis of shifts in the use of translation in the revision of *La Nuit*, see Bednarski, *Autour de Ferron*, 197–216.

42 All quotations from *Quince Jam* are taken from the translation by Ray Ellenwood.

43 Garand, *Accès d'origine*, 69.

44 Although Ferron's psychological state in the years leading up to his death in 1985 is still shrouded in mystery, it is clear from his last works, as well as from the writings of various dates published posthumously, that he suffered periods of severe mental strain.

45 It is tempting to think of Scott Symons's *Place d'Armes* (1967), a novel its title page calls a "Combat Journal," as offering us the notebook of a man of elite WASP background who, unlike Ferron's Frank, jumps wholeheartedly from the "bad" to the "good" side of the wall, but who also, like François, seeks to recover a soul hitherto incapable of full erotic agency. François's deep knowledge of, and appreciation for, the literature and characteristic tropes of the other language are strangely mirrored by Symons's learned narrator. The novel's narrative is a hot mess, but one striking feature deserves, I think, more attention that it has received, and might serve as the starting-point for a reconsidering its place in Montreal literary history. *Place d'Armes* is the first novel I know of that not just describes real buildings in detail, using their real names, but whose "insite," to use Symons's term for site-specific insight, extends to the

layered historical roles and meanings of identifiable elements of the city's built environment. It is curious to look back on the earlier novels examined in this study and realize how rare this is.

46 For a somewhat different formulation of the issue, see Dennis Lee, *Savage Fields*. Lee's conclusion, at the end of a subtle and somewhat idiosyncratic argument inspired by Heidegger and George Grant, was a qualified negative.

47 I use the masculine pronoun here, first because its immediate referent is *I*, but also because the crowd that gathers in the streets in the last part of the story, though sexually inclusive, is primarily gendered male.

48 It may be relevant to point out that in 1964 there was a real attempt, presumably by the FLQ, to destroy this statue, but the dynamite was discovered before it could be detonated. In other words, the attempt failed, as Montreal readers of the time would have known. A statue of Queen Victoria in Quebec City had, however, been successfully blown up in 1963.

49 See Collins, *The Apocalyptic Imagination*.

50 According to Cohen's own account, much of the novel was written under the influence of drugs and the effects of excessive fasting and exposure to the sun (Simmons, *I'm Your Man*, 130–4). While this may explain a lot, it does Cohen's literary project no justice to make it the product of personal circumstances.

51 The typographical effacement of the name serves a variety of possible purposes: to draw a veil over the tribe's abasement; to symbolize their historical erasure; to suggest that the name might be that of many tribes; to suggest, in the manner of the comic books and pulp fictions referenced in the novel's scatological narrative, that the censored word is "Assholes."

52 Cohen got much of the information on which he based his depiction of the A—s from the Abenaki filmmaker Alanis Obomsawin, whose tribe has a long history in the area. The episode of the teenage Edith's rape by a trio of white boys seems to have been based on a real incident, though whether Obomsawin herself was the victim remains unclear. See Lewis, *Alanis Obomsawin*.

53 To be fair, Ferron does address the complex history of French-Native relations, and of Métis genealogies, in some of his later works. According to recently published correspondence, in 1965, just after writing *La Nuit*, Ferron began to investigate these issues. His 1969 novel *Le Ciel de Québec* (*The Penniless Redeemer*), for example, includes a sympathetic portrait of "Les Chiquettes," a beleaguered Métis village based on a real community in his native county of Maskinongé (Ferron, *Le Ciel de Québec*, 488–9). The tone of Ferron's account, however, is more comic than tragic or elegiac. This important topic deserves more space than I can give it here.

54 The spelling is French, but it may also be a way of recalling the older use of "the Argentine" in British English. Perhaps the name is meant to underscore the fantastic character of the scene.
55 See Richler, "The Great Comic Book Heroes."
56 It is notable that no mention is made of a "Magic Israel."
57 The novel uses both "Catherine" and "Kateri" at various points. The latter name supposedly approximates the "original" Mohawk version of her Christian name, but the saint's most recent biographer argues that this supposition reflects a questionable nineteenth-century "fin de siècle primitivism." It is more likely that Tekakwitha had no "first" name at all before she was given a Christian one. See Greer, *Mohawk Saint*, xi.
58 See Monkman, "Beautiful Losers."
59 Some French words (e.g., "enterprise") appear in English or quasi-English form, and the italicized English phrase "*whatever the intentions*" is awkwardly constructed. See Siemerling, *Discoveries of the Other*, 56–7.
60 Siemerling, "A Political Constituency," 162.
61 See Barbour, "Down with History," 140; Scobie, *Leonard Cohen*, 97. While an argument can be made that the figures remain distinct (Wilkins, "Nightmares of Identity"), whatever distinction remains makes no difference.
62 On the novel's connection with the song, see Scobie, *Leonard Cohen*, 101.
63 Simmons, *I'm Your Man*, 139–40.
64 Cohen, *Death of a Ladies' Man*, 150.
65 Cohen, "Halleluiah," *Various Positions*, 1984.
66 Cohen, "Anthem," *The Future*, 1992.
67 The maieutic and erotic complexities of F. and *I*'s relationship are echoed with interesting variations in the novels of Jean Basile's "Mongols" trilogy (1964–70), though it might be more accurate to say, since the first volume of that trilogy, *La Jument des Mongols* (The mare of the Mongols), appeared two years before *Beautiful Losers*, that Cohen's work echoes Basile's. That novel is narrated by Jérémie, one of three disciples (the others are Jonathan and Judith, who in turn narrate the subsequent volumes) of the charismatic painter Victor, whose mysterious disappearance has left them bereft. They seek to reconstruct their lives by inventing a series of sexual games involving various partners they meet in various Montreal locales. As their identical initials suggest, and as the fact that all their lovers' names begin with A (for *Autre*?) confirms, the three friends are really three dimensions of one consciousness that over the course of the trilogy begin, but never quite finish, fusing into one. The characters are all francophones (though Judith is Jewish, not Catholic), but curiously the emblem of

their connection is a sculpture located on the McGill University campus: the grouping familiarly known as *The Three Bares*, Gertrude Vanderbilt Whitney's variation, using male figures, on the theme of the three graces. Although Basile is sometimes cited for his praise of "The Main" as the emblematic Montreal site, his characters spend much of their time in bohemian-bourgeois apartments located near McGill and frequent the restaurants and bars of the western (and significantly anglophone) part of Montreal's downtown as much as they do more francophone spaces like the Parc Lafontaine. Moreover, unlike the writers examined in this study, English or French, Basile uses the real names of his 1960s bohemian hangouts (Pam Pam, New Penelope, Swiss Hut, as well as the Sam Ash of the Main, and, yes, the System Theatre). In this respect, there is an interesting connection to the point I made above about Scott Symons. The tension between this geographical specificity and the narcissistic inwardness of the narrators' monologues is again striking, as is the split between the generally apolitical attitude of the characters and the pointedness of the remarks that every so often punctuate the narrative. Most notably, the vision of a Quebec "séparé de ces cochons d'Anglais" is scorned in favour of a "Montréal futur" characterized by all sorts of promiscuity (*Voyages*, 57–8). How Basile's trilogy works through the tensions between these perspectives is a topic for another study, but one in which Cohen's novel could play an illuminating heuristic role.

CONCLUSION

1 See chapter 7, nn.45, 67.

Bibliography

Where I have used more than one edition of a novel, the one usually cited is indicated with an asterisk.

Anctil, Pierre, Norman Ravvin, and Sherry Simon, eds. *New Readings of Yiddish Montreal.* Ottawa: University of Ottawa Press 2007.

Archambault, Gilles. "*Mathieu.*" *Le Devoir*, 23 January 1993, C22.

Balzac, Honoré de. *Le Père Goriot.* In *La Comédie humaine*, ed. Pierre-Georges Castex. 12 vols. Vol. 3, 3–290. Paris: Gallimard 1976–81.

Barbour, Douglas. "Down with History: Some Notes towards an Understanding of *Beautiful Losers.*" In Michael Gnarowski, ed., *Leonard Cohen: The Artist and His Critics.* Toronto: McGraw-Hill Ryerson 1976. 136–49.

Basile, Jean. *Le Grand Khan.* N.p.: Les Éditions Estérel 1967.

– *La Jument des Mongols.* Montreal: Les Éditions du jour 1964.

– *Les Voyages d'Irkoutsk.* Montreal: HMH 1970.

Beaudoin, Réjean. *Le Roman québécois.* Montreal: Boréal 1991.

Bednarski, Betty. *Autour de Ferron: Littérature, traduction, altérité.* Rev. ed. [Quebec]: Presses de l'Université Laval 2012.

Belleau, André. *Le romancier fictif: essai sur la représentation de l'écrivain dans le roman québécois.* Sillery: Presses de l'Université du Québec 1980.

Beneventi, Domenic. "Lost in the City: The Montreal Novels of Régine Robin and Robert Majzels." In Justin Edwards and Douglas Iverson, eds., *Downtown Canada.* Toronto: University of Toronto Press 2005. 104–21.

Benson, Eugene, and Leonard W. Conolly, eds. *The Oxford Companion to Canadian Theatre.* Toronto: Oxford University Press 1989.

Bessette, Gérard. *La Bagarre.* Montreal: Cercle du livre de France 1958.

– *The Brawl*. Translated by Marc Lebel and Ronald Sutherland. Montreal: Harvest House 1976.

– *Mes romans et moi*. Préface de Jacques Allard. Montreal: Hurtubise HMH 1979.

– *Les Pédagogues*. Montreal: Cercle du livre de France 1961.

Binnie, Jon, et al., eds. *Cosmopolitan Urbanism*. London: Routledge 2006.

Biron, Michel. *L'Absence du maître: Saint-Denys Garneau, Ferron, Ducharme*. Montreal: Presses de l'Université de Montréal 2000.

Biron, Michel, François Dumont, and Élisabeth Nardout-Lafarge, with Martine-Emmanuelle Lapointe, eds. *Histoire de la littérature québécoise*. Montreal: Boréal 2007.

Blanchot, Maurice. *L'Espace littéraire*. Paris: Gallimard 1955.

Blodgett, E.D. *Configurations: Essays on the Canadian Literatures*. Downsview: ECW 1982.

– *Five-Part Invention: A History of Literary History in Canada*. Toronto: University of Toronto Press 2003.

Boutros, Alexandra, and Will Straw, eds. *Circulation and the City: Essays on Urban Culture*. Montreal and Kingston: McGill-Queen's University Press 2010.

Brochu, André. "Un héros semi-sartrien: *Mathieu*, de Françoise Loranger." *Voix et images* 20 (1994–95): 178–88.

– *L'Instance critique 1961–1973*. Montreal: Leméac 1974.

Callaghan, Morley. *A Literary Life: Reflections and Reminiscences 1928–1990*. Toronto: Exile Editions 2008.

– *The Loved and the Lost*. New York: Macmillan 1951.

– *The Loved and the Lost*. Introduction by David Staines. Toronto: Exile Editions 2010.*

– *Such Is My Beloved*. Toronto: New Canadian Library 1957 [1934].

Cambron, Micheline. "Gilles Marcotte, Montréaliste." *Études françaises* 53, no. 1 (2017): 59–73.

– *Une société, un récit. Discours culturel au Québec 1967–1976*. Montreal: Nota Bene 1989.

Cameron, Donald. *Conversations with Canadian Novelists*. 2 vols. Toronto: Macmillan 1973.

Cameron, Elspeth. *Hugh MacLennan: A Writer's Life*. Toronto: University of Toronto Press 1981.

Cantin, Pierre. *Jacques Ferron, polygraphe*. Montreal: Bellarmin 1984.

Cellard, Karine, and Martine-Emmanuelle Lapointe, eds. *Transmission et héritages de la littérature québécoise*. Montreal: Presses de l'Université de Montréal 2012.

Chamberland, Paul. "Fondation du territoire." *parti pris* 4, nos. 9–12 (1967): 11–42.

Chapman, Rosemary. *Between Languages and Cultures: Colonial and Postcolonial Readings of Gabrielle Roy*. Montreal and Kingston: McGill-Queen's University Press 2009.

– *Siting the Quebec Novel: The Representation of Space in Francophone Writing in Quebec*. Oxford: Peter Lang 2000.

– *What Is Québécois Literature? Reflections on the Literary History of Francophone Writing in Canada*. Liverpool: Liverpool University Press 2013.

Chaput-Rolland, Solange, and Gwethalyn Graham. *Chers ennemis*. Montreal: Éditions du Jour 1963.

Chassay, Jean-François, with Annick Andrès and Louise Frappier. *Bibliographie descriptive du roman montréalais*. Université de Montréal: Département d'études françaises 1991.

Cloutier, Eugène. *Les Inutiles*. Montreal: Fides 1981 [1956].

Cohen, Leonard. "Anthem." In *The Future*. New York: Columbia Records 1992.

– *Beautiful Losers*. New York: Vintage 1993 [1966].

– *Death of a Ladies' Man*. Toronto: McClelland and Stewart 1978.

– *The Favorite Game*. New York: Viking 1963.

– "Hallelujah." In *Various Positions*. New York: Columbia Records 1984.

– "Sisters of Mercy." In *Songs of Leonard Cohen*. New York: Columbia Records 1967.

Coleman, Patrick. *Anger, Gratitude, and the Enlightenment Writer*. Oxford: Oxford University Press 2011.

– "A Context for Conversation: Jeffrey Moore's *The Memory Artists* as Anglo-Quebec Literature." *Journal of Canadian Studies* 46, no. 3 (2012): 204–24.

– "Detours to Diversity: Recent French Fiction from Montreal." *Matrix*, 35 (1991): 24–7.

– "The Geography of Identity in Françoise Loranger and Gwethalyn Graham." *Québec Studies* 21–2 (1996): 161–76.

– "The Imaginative Poverty of Gabrielle Roy." In Paul Socken, ed., *Gabrielle Roy aujourd'hui/ today*. Saint-Boniface, MB: Éditions des Plaines 2003. 51–8.

– "Inside, Outside: New English Fiction from Montreal." *Matrix* 41 (1994): 14–23.

– *The Limits of Sympathy: Gabrielle Roy's* The Tin Flute. Toronto: ECW Press 1993.

– *Reparative Realism: Mourning and Modernity in the French Novel 1730–1830*. Geneva: Droz 1998.

– "Le Sens de l'époque: les années quarante dans la littérature montréalaise." In Benoît Melançon and Pierre Popovic, eds., *Montréal 1642–1992: le grand passage*. Montreal: XYZ 1994. 129–42.
– "Slow Down and Read: Landscape and Cityscape." *Topia* 19 (spring 2008): 167–74.
– "Writing beyond Redemption: Hubert Aquin and Mordecai Richler in Postwar Paris." In Paula Gilbert and Miléna Santoro, eds., *Transatlantic Passages: Literary and Cultural Relations between Quebec and Francophone Europe*. Montreal and Kingston: McGill-Queen's University Press 2010. 67–79.
Collins, John J. *The Apocalyptic Imagination: An Introduction to Jewish Apocalyptic Literature*. 3rd ed. Grand Rapids, MI: Eerdmans 2016.
Conron, Brandon. *Morley Callaghan*. New York: Twayne 1966.
– ed. *Morley Callaghan*. Toronto: McGraw-Hill Ryerson 1975.
Daunais, Isabelle. *Le Roman sans aventure*. Montreal: Boréal 2015.
Davey, Frank. "*Beautiful Losers*: Leonard Cohen's Postcolonial Novel." In Stephen Scobie, ed., *Intricate Preparations: Writing Leonard Cohen*. Toronto: ECW Press 2000. 12–23.
Davidson, Arnold E. *Mordecai Richler*. New York: Ungar 1983.
Davies, Norman. *The Isles: A History*. Oxford: Oxford University Press 1999.
Dictionnaire des oeuvres littéraires du Québec. 7 vols. Montreal: Fides 1978–2003.
Djwa, Sandra. *The Politics of the Imagination: A Life of F.R. Scott*. Toronto: McClelland and Stewart 1987.
Douglas, W.A.B., and Brereton Greenhous. *Out of the Shadows: Canada in the Second World War*. New York: Oxford University Press 1977.
Élie, Robert. *La Fin des songes* [1950]. In *Œuvres*. Quebec: Hurtubise HMH 1970.
Endicott, Stephen Lyon. *James E. Endicott: Rebel out of China*. Toronto: University of Toronto Press 1980.
Falardeau, Jean-Charles. *Notre société et son roman*. Montreal: Éditions HMH 1967.
Ferron, Jacques. *Une amitié bien particulière: Lettres de Jacques Ferron à John Grube, suivi de "octobre en question" de Georges Langlois*. Montreal: Boréal 1990.
– *La Charrette*. Montreal: Bibliothèque québécoise 1994 [1968].
– *Le Ciel de Québec*, ed. Pierre Cantin et Luc Gauvreau. Montreal: Bibliothèque québécoise 2009 [1969].

– *Les Confitures de coings*. Montreal: L'Hexagone, collection Typo 1990.
– *Les Confitures de coings et autres textes, suivi de Le Journal des Confitures de coings*. Montreal: parti pris 1977.*
– *La Nuit*. Montreal: parti pris 1971.*
– *La Nuit*, présentée par Diane Potvin. N.p.: Fernand Nathan 1979.
– *Quince Jam*. Translated by Ray Ellenwood. Toronto: Exile Editions 1977.
Forsyth, Louise. "Drama in French 1900 to 1948." In Eugene Benson and William Toye, eds., *The Oxford Companion to Canadian Literature*. 2nd ed. Toronto: Oxford University Press 1997. 313–17.
Fournier, Michael, and Ken Norris, eds. *Take This Waltz: A Celebration of Leonard Cohen*. Montreal: Guernica 1994.
Frédéric, Madeleine, ed. *Montréal, megapole litttéraire: Actes du Séminaire de Bruxelles (sept.-déc. 1991)*. Brussels: Université libre de Bruxelles 1992.
Fredette, Nathalie. *Montréal en prose 1892–1992*. Montreal: Hexagone 1992.
Frye, Northrop. "Conclusion to a Literary History of Canada." In *The Bush Garden: Essays on the Canadian Imagination*. Toronto: Anansi 1971. 213–51.
Garand, Dominique. *Accès d'origine, ou pourquoi je lis encore Groulx, Basile, Ferron …* Montreal: Hurtubise HMH 2004.
Garneau, Hector de Saint-Denys. *Poésies complètes*. Montreal: Fides 1949.
Gélinas, Pierre. *Les Vivants, les morts et les autres*. Montreal: Cercle du live de France 1959.
Germain, Annick, and Martha Radice. "Cosmopolitanism by Default: Public Sociability in Montreal." In Jon Binnie et al., *Cosmopolitan Urbanism*. London: Routledge 2006. 112–29.
Giroux, André. *Le Gouffre a toujours soif*. Montreal: Fides 1953.
Gnarowski, Michael, ed. *Leonard Cohen: The Artist and His Critics*. Toronto: McGraw-Hill Ryerson 1976.
Godard, Barbara. "The Geography of Separatism." *Revue de l'Université laurentienne/Laurentian University Review* 9, no. 1 (1976–7): 33–50.
Godin, Jean-Cléo. "L'Équipe (1942–1948) de Pierre Dagenais." *L'Annuaire théâtral: revue québécoise d'études théâtrales* 23 (1998): 74–89.
Graham, Gwethalyn. *Earth and High Heaven*. Philadelphia: J.B. Lippincott 1944.
Graham, Gwethalyn, and Solange Chaput-Rolland. *Dear Enemies*. Toronto: Macmillan 1963.
Green, Mary Jane. *Women and Narrative Identity: Rewriting the Quebec National Text*. Montreal and Kingston: McGill-Queen's University Press 2001.

Greenstein, Michael. *Third Solitudes: Tradition and Continuity in Jewish-Canadian Literature*. Montreal and Kingston: McGill-Queen's University Press 1988.

Greer, Allan. *Mohawk Saint: Catherine Tekakwitha and the Jesuits*. New York: Oxford University Press 2005.

Gregor, Ian, and Brian Nicholas. *The Moral and the Story*. London: Faber and Faber 1962.

Groupe de recherche Montréal imaginaire. *Lire Montréal: Actes du colloque tenu le 21 octobre 1988*. Montreal: Université de Montréal, Département d'études françaises, 1989.

– *Montréal, l'invention juive. Actes du colloque tenu le 2 mars 1990*. Montreal: Université de Montréal, Département d'études françaises, 1991.

Hamel, Charles. *Solitude de la chair*. Montreal: Cercle du livre de France 1951.

Harel, Simon. *Braconnages identitaires. Un Québec palimpseste*, Montreal: VLB 2006.

– "La parole orpheline de l'écrivain migrant." In Pierre Nepveu et Gilles Marcotte, eds., *Montréal imaginaire: ville et littérature*. Montreal: Fides 1992. 373–418.

– *Les passages obligés de l'écriture migrante*, Montreal: XYZ (Théorie et littérature) 2005.

– *Le Voleur de parcours: identité et cosmopolitisme dans la littérature québécoise contemporaine*. Montreal: XYZ 1989.

Hébert, François. *Montreal*. Paris: Champ Vallon 1989.

Heidenreich, Rosmarin. "Narratological Structures and Ideology: The Case of Hugh MacLennan." In Frank M. Tierney, ed., *Hugh MacLennan*. Ottawa: University of Ottawa Press 1994. 125–33.

Hobsbawm, Eric, and Terence Ranger, eds. *The Invention of Tradition*. Cambridge: Cambridge University Press 1992.

Housman, A.E. *Collected Poems and Selected Prose*, ed. Christopher Ricks. London: Penguin 1988.

Howells, Coral Ann, and Eva-Marie Kröller, eds. *The Cambridge History of Canadian Literature*. Cambridge: Cambridge University Press 2009.

Hoy, Helen. "Hugh MacLennan." In Robert Lecker, Jack David, and Ellen Quigley, eds., *Canadian Writers and Their Works*. Toronto: ECW Press 1990. 147–212.

Jauss, Hans Robert. *Toward an Aesthetic of Reception*. Translated by Timothy Bahti. Minneapolis: University of Minnesota Press 1982.

Jones, D.G. *Butterfly on Rock*. Toronto: University of Toronto Press 1971.

Joyce, James. *Ulysses: Annotated Student Edition*. Harmondsworth, UK: Penguin 1992.

Keith, W.J. *Life Struggle: Hugh MacLennan's* The Watch That Ends the Night. Toronto: ECW Press 1993.

Kelly, Dorothy. "Lost in Translation: The English Versions of Gabrielle Roy's Early Novels." *Studies in Canadian Literature* 30, no. 2 (2005): 96–114.

Kiberd, Declan. *Inventing Ireland: The Literature of the Modern Nation*. Cambridge, MA: Harvard University Press 1995.

Klein, A.M. *The Second Scroll*, ed. Elizabeth A. Popham and Zailig Pollock. Toronto: University of Toronto Press 2000 [1951].

Kwaterko, Jósef. "La Problématique interculturelle dans *Alexandre Chenevert* de Gabrielle Roy." *University of Toronto Quarterly* 63, no. 4 (1994): 566–74.

Lane, Anthony. "Warring Fictions." *New Yorker*, 26 June 1995, 60–73.

Lane-Mercier, Gillian. "Untranslatability, Non-Translation, Retranslation, Creativity: A Case Study." In Ian Kemble, ed., *The Changing Face of Translation*, Proceedings of the 9th Annual Portsmouth Translation Conference, University of Portsmouth, 2010. 28–39.

Lapierre, René. *L'Imaginaire captif: Hubert Aquin*. Montreal: Quinze 1981.

LaRue, Monique, and Jean-François Chassay. *Promenades littéraires dans Montréal*. Montreal: Québec-Amérique 1989.

Leahy, David. "A.M. Klein: Mordecai Richler's Version." In Norman Ravvin and Sherry Simon, eds., *Failure's Opposite: Listening to A.M. Klein*. Montreal and Kingston: McGill-Queen's University Press 2011. 191–202.

– "Race, Gender, and Class Enigmas in *The Loved and the Lost* and *Au milieu la montagne*." *Textual Studies in Canada* 5 (1994): 32–45.

Le Bel, Pierre-Mathieu. *Montréal et sa métropolisation: une géographie romanesque*. Montreal: Triptyque 2012.

Leclerc, Catherine, and Sherry Simon, eds. "La Littérature anglo-québécoise." *Voix et images* 30, no. 3 (2005): 15–132.

Lee, Dennis. *Savage Fields: An Essay in Literature and Cosmology*. Toronto: Anansi 1977.

Lehan, Richard. *The City in Literature: An Intellectual and Cultural History*. Berkeley: University of California Press 1998.

Leith, Linda. *Introducing Hugh MacLennan's* Two Solitudes. Toronto: ECW Press 1990.

– "Quebec Fiction in English during the 1980s: A Case Study in Marginality." *Québec Studies* 9 (1989–90): 95–110.

– *Writing in the Time of Nationalism: From Two Solitudes to Blue Metropolis.* Winnipeg: Signature Editions 2010.

Lemieux, Denise, et al., eds. *Traité de la culture.* Québec: Presses de l'Université Laval 2002

Le Moyne, Jean. *Convergences.* Montreal: HMH 1961.

Lewis, Randolph. *Alanis Obomsawin: The Vision of a Native Filmmaker.* Lincoln: University of Nebraska Press 2006.

Linteau, Paul-André. *Histoire de Montréal depuis la Confédération.* Montreal: Boréal 1992.

Loranger, Françoise. *Mathieu.* Montreal: Cercle du livre de France 1949.

MacLennan, Hugh. "City of Two Souls." In *Thirty and Three.* Toronto: Macmillan 1954. 64–8.

– *Two Solitudes.* New York: Duell, Sloan, and Pearce 1945.

– *The Watch that Ends the Night.* New York: Scribners 1959.

MacLulich, T.D. *Hugh MacLennan.* Boston: Twayne 1983.

Major, André. *Le Cabochon.* Montreal: parti pris 1964.

Marcotte, Gilles. *Écrire à Montréal.* Montreal: Boréal 1997.

– "Jacques Ferron, côté village." In *Littérature et circonstances.* Montreal: L'Hexagone 1989. 243–58.

– *Une littérature qui se fait.* Montreal: HMH 1968.

– *La Littérature à l'imparfait.* Montreal: La Presse 1976.

– "Mystères de Montréal." In Pierre Nepveu et Gilles Marcotte, eds., *Montréal imaginaire: ville et littérature.* Montreal: Fides 1992. 97–148.

Massey, Irving. *Identity and Community: Reflections on English, Yiddish and French Literature in Canada.* Detroit: Wayne State University Press 1994.

McDonald, Larry. "The Civilized Eye and Its Discontents." In David Staines, ed., *The Callaghan Symposium.* Ottawa: University of Ottawa Press 1981. 77–94.

Meadowcroft, Barbara. *Gwethalyn Graham (1913–1965): A Liberated Woman in a Conventional Age.* Toronto: Women's Press 2008.

Melançon, Benoît, and Pierre Popovic, eds. *Montréal 1642–1992: le grand passage.* Montreal: XYZ 1994.

Mills, Sean. *The Empire Within: Postcolonial Thought and Political Activism in Sixties Montreal.* Montreal and Kingston: McGill-Queen's University Press 2010.

Moisan, Clément. *L'Âge de la littérature canadienne*. Montreal: Éditions HMH 1969.

Monkman, Leslie. "Beautiful Losers: Mohawk Myth and Jesuit Legend." *Journal of Canadian Fiction* 3, no. 3 (1974): 57–9.

Montrose, David. *The Body on Mount Royal*. Montreal: Véhicule 2012 [1953].

Moore, Brian. *The Luck of Ginger Coffey*. Boston: Little, Brown, and Company 1960.

Morgan, Ceri. *Mindscapes of Montreal: Québec's Urban Novel, 1960–2005*. Cardiff: University of Wales Press 2012.

Morson, Gary Saul, and Caryl Emerson. *Mikhail Bakhtin: Creation of a Prosaics*. Stanford, CA: Stanford University Press 1990.

Moyes, Lianne. "La Littérature anglophone du Québec." In Denise Lemieux, ed., *Traité de la culture*. Quebec: Les Éditions de la IRCQ 2002. 423–38.

– "Writing the Montreal Mountain: Below the Threshold at Which Visibility Begins." *Canadian Literature* 192 (2007): 45–66.

Moyes, Lianne, ed. "Écrire en anglais au Québec: un devenir minoritaire?" *Québec Studies* 26 (1998/1999): 3–37.

– "Fitful Colloquy." Special issue on Anglo-Québécois Literature, *Journal of Canadian Studies* 46, no. 3 (2012): 5–286.

Moyes, Lianne, and Gillian Lane-Mercier, eds. "Textes, territoires, traduction: (dé)localisations/dislocations de la littérature anglo-québécoise." *Québec Studies* 44 (2007/2008): 1–101.

Murphy, Susan Margaret. *Le Canada anglais de Jacques Ferron: formes, fonctions, représentations*. Quebec: Presses de l'Université Laval 2011.

Nadel, Ira. *Various Positions: A Life of Leonard Cohen*. New York: Pantheon 1996.

Nepveu, Pierre. *L'Écologie du réel*. Montreal: Boréal 1988.

– *Lectures des lieux*. Montreal: Boréal 2004.

Nepveu, Pierre, and Gilles Marcotte, eds. *Montréal imaginaire: ville et littérature*. Montreal: Fides 1992.

New, William H. *A History of Canadian Literature*. 2nd ed. Montreal: McGill-Queen's University Press 2003.

Olscamp, Marcel. *Le Fils du notaire: Jacques Ferron 1921–1949. Genèse intellectuelle d'un écrivain*. Montreal: Fides 1997.

Orange, John. *Orpheus in Winter: Morley Callaghan's* The Loved and the Lost. Toronto: ECW Press 1993.

Pacey, Desmond. *Creative Writing in Canada*. 2nd ed. Toronto: Ryerson 1961.

Pascal, Blaise. *Les Provinciales, Pensées, et opuscules diverses*. Paris: Le Livre de poche 2004.

Peepre-Bordessa, Mari. *Hugh MacLennan's National Trilogy: Mapping a Canadian Identity (1940–1950)*. Helsinki: Suomalainen Tiedeakatemia 1990.

Perkins, David. *Is Literary History Possible?* Baltimore, MD: Johns Hopkins University Press 1992.

Popovic, Pierre. *La Contradiction du poème: Poésie et discours social au Québec de 1948 à 1953*. Candiac: Les Éditions Balzac 1992.

– "Le Mauvais flâneur, la gourgandine et le dilettante." In Pierre Nepveu et Gilles Marcotte, eds., *Montréal imaginaire; ville et littérature*. Montreal: Fides 1992. 211–78.

– *De la ville à sa littérature: Préliminaires et bibliographie*. Montreal: Université de Montréal Département d'études françaises 1988.

Porter, John. *The Vertical Mosaic: An Analysis of Social Class and Power in Canada*. Toronto: University of Toronto Press 1965.

Proulx, Monique. *Ce qu'il reste de moi*. Montreal: Boréal 2015.

Radice, Martha. *Feeling Comfortable?: The Urban Experience of Anglo-Montrealers*. Quebec: Presses de l'Université Laval 2000.

Rae, Ian. "Converting Failure in Klein, Cohen, and Michaels." In Norman Ravvin and Sherry Simon, eds., *Failure's Opposite: Listening to A.M. Klein*. Montreal and Kingston: McGill-Queen's University Press 2011. 203–20.

Ravvin, Norman, and Sherry Simon, eds., *Failure's Opposite: Listening to A.M. Klein*. Montreal and Kingston: McGill-Queen's University Press 2011.

Reid, Gregory S. "Is There an Anglo-Québécois Literature?" *Essays on Canadian Writing* 84 (2009): 58–86.

Renaud, Jacques. *Le Cassé*. Montreal: parti pris 1964.

Ricard, François. *Gabrielle Roy: une vie*. Rev. ed. Montreal: Boréal Compact 2000.

Richler, Mordecai. *The Apprenticeship of Duddy Kravitz*. Toronto: Penguin 2005 [1959].

– "The Great Comic Book Heroes." In Mordecai Richler, *Notes on an Endangered Species and Others*. New York: Knopf 1974. 109–21.

– *Son of a Smaller Hero*. Toronto: New Canadian Library 1989 [1955].

Ricoeur, Paul. *Temps et récit*. Vol. 1. Paris: Seuil 1983.

Rilke, Rainer Marie. *Letters to a Young Poet*. Harmondsworth, UK: Penguin 2011.

Robidoux, Réjean. *La Création de Gérard Bessette*. Montreal: Québec/Amérique 1987.

Robinson, Ira, Pierre Anctil, and Mervin Butovsky, eds. *An Everyday Miracle: Yiddish Culture in Montreal.* Montreal: Véhicule Press 1990.

Roy, Alain. *Gabrielle Roy: l'idylle et le désir fantôme.* Montreal: Boréal 2004.

Roy, Gabrielle. *Alexandre Chenevert.* Montreal: Beauchemin 1954.

– *Alexandre Chenevert.* Montreal: Stanké 1979.

– *Alexandre Chenevert.* Montreal: Boréal 2013.*

– *Bonheur d'occasion.* 2 vols. Montreal: Société des éditions Pascal 1945.

– *Bonheur d'occasion.* Rev. ed. Montreal: Boréal 1993.*

– *The Cashier.* Translated by Harry Binsse. New York: Harcourt, Brace 1955.

– *Heureux les nomades et autres reportages.* Montreal: Boréal 2007.

– *Le Pays de Bonheur d'occasion; et autres récits épars et inédits.* Montreal: Boréal 2000.

– "Retour à Saint-Henri." In *Fragiles lumières de la terre.* Montreal: Quinze 1978. 159–75.

– *The Tin Flute.* Translated by Alan Brown. 1980. Rpt. Toronto: McClelland and Stewart, New Canadian Library, 1989.

Sampson, Denis. *Brian Moore: The Chameleon Novelist.* Dublin: Marino Books 1998.

Sanderson, Douglas. *Blondes Are My Trouble.* Montreal: Véhicule 2015 [1950].

– *Hot Freeze.* Montreal: Véhicule 2015 [1954].

Schor, Naomi. *George Sand and Idealism.* New York: Columbia University Press 1993.

Schwartzwald, Robert. "La Fédérastophobie, ou les lectures agitées d'une révolution tranquille. *Sociologie et sociétés* 39, no. 1 (1997): 129–43.

Scobie, Stephen. *Leonard Cohen.* Vancouver: Douglas and McIntyre 1978.

Scobie, Stephen, ed. *Intricate Preparations: Writing Leonard Cohen.* Toronto: ECW Press 2000.

Scott, F.R. *The Collected Poems of F.R. Scott.* Toronto: McClelland and Stewart 1981.

Shek, Ben-Z. "L'Espace et la description symbolique dans les romans 'montréalais' de Gabrielle Roy." *Liberté* 13, no. 1 (1971): 78–96.

– *French-Canadian and Québécois Novels.* Toronto: Oxford 1991.

– *Social Realism in the French-Canadian Novel.* Montreal: Harvest House 1977.

– "Thoughts on a Rare Privilege: A 15-Year Friendship with Gabrielle Roy." In Paul Socken, ed., *Gabrielle Roy aujourd'hui/ today.* Saint-Boniface, MB: Éditions des Plaines 2003. 181–6.

Shell, Marc. "The Forked Tongue, or the Road Not Taken in Québec." In *Children of the Earth: Literature, Politics, and Nationhood*. New York: Oxford University Press 1993. 41–57.

Siemerling, Winfried. *Discoveries of the Other: Alterity in the Work of Leonard Cohen, Hubert Aquin, Michael Ondaatje, and Nicole Brossard*. Toronto: University of Toronto Press 1994.

– "Interior Landscapes and the Poetic Realm: Contingent Meditations on a Speech and a Song by Leonard Cohen." *Canadian Poetry* 33 (2003): 88–107.

– "Leonard Cohen. 'Loneliness and History: A Speech before the Jewish Public Library." In Michael Fournier and Ken Norris, eds., *Take This Waltz: A Celebration of Leonard Cohen*. Montreal: Guernica 1994. 143–53.

– "A Political Constituency That Really Exists in the World: An Interview with Leonard Cohen." In Michael Fournier and Ken Norris, eds., *Take This Waltz: A Celebration of Leonard Cohen*. Montreal: Guernica 1994. 154–69.

Simmons, Sylvie. *I'm Your Man: The Life of Leonard Cohen*. New York: Ecco 2012.

Simon, Sherry. *Cities in Translation: Intersections of Language and Memory*. New York: Routledge 2012.

– *Le Trafic des langues: traduction et culture dans la littérature québécoise*. Montreal: Boréal 1994.

– *Translating Montreal: Episodes in the Life of a Divided City*. Montreal and Kingston: McGill-Queen's University Press 2006.

Simon, Sherry, and David Homel. *Mapping Literature: The Art and Politics of Translation*. Montreal: Véhicule 1988.

Simon, Sherry, Pierre L'Héraut, Robert Schwartzwald, and Alexis Nouss. *Fictions de l'identitaire au Québec*. Montreal: XYZ 1991.

Sirois, Antoine, et al. *Bibliography of Studies in Comparative Canadian Literature/Bibliographie d'études de littérature canadienne comparée 1930–1987*. Sherbrooke: Université de Sherbrooke, Département des lettres et communications, 1989.

– *Montréal dans le roman canadien*. Montreal: Didier 1968.

Socken, Paul. *Concordance de* Bonheur d'occasion *de Gabrielle Roy*. Waterloo, ON: University of Waterloo Press 1982.

– ed. *Gabrielle Roy aujourd'hui/today*. Saint-Boniface, MB: Éditions des Plaines 2003.

– *Myth and Morality in* Alexandre Chenevert *by Gabrielle Roy*. Frankfurt: Peter Lang 1987.

Srebrnik, Henry Felix. *Jerusalem on the Amur: Birobidzhan and the Canadian Jewish Communist Movement, 1924–1951*. Montreal and Kingston: McGill-Queen's University Press 2008.

Staines, David, ed. *The Callaghan Symposium*. Ottawa: University of Ottawa Press 1981.

Steele, James. "History Repeating Itself as Fiction: Oxyrhynchus and the Novels of Hugh MacLennan." In Frank M. Tierney, ed., *Hugh MacLennan*. Ottawa: University of Ottawa Press 1994. 109–23.

Stratford, Philip. *All the Polarities: Comparative Studies in Contemporary Canadian Novels in French and English*. Toronto: ECW Press 1986.

– *Faith and Fiction: Creative Process in Greene and Mauriac*. Notre Dame, IN: University of Notre Dame Press 1964.

Sugars, Cynthia, ed. *The Oxford Handbook of Canadian Literature*. Oxford: Oxford University Press 2016.

Sutherland, Ronald. *The New Hero: Essays in Quebec/Canadian Literature*. Toronto: Macmillan 1977.

– *Second Image: Comparative Studies in Quebec/Canadian Literature*. Toronto: New Press 1971.

Symons, Scott. *Place d'Armes*. Toronto: McClelland and Stewart 1967.

Taylor, Charles. *Modern Social Imaginaries*. Durham, NC: Duke University Press 2004.

Tierney, Frank M., ed. *Hugh MacLennan*. Ottawa: University of Ottawa Press 1994.

Tombs, Robert. *The English and Their History*. New York: Knopf 2014.

Verduyn, Christl, ed. *Dear Marian, Dear Hugh: The MacLennan-Engel Correspondence*. Ottawa: University of Ottawa Press 1995.

Viau, Robert. *Au milieu la montagne*. Montreal: Beauchemin 1951.

Walsh, William. *A Manifold Voice: Studies in Commonwealth Literature*. London: Chatto and Windus 1970.

Weinstock, Daniel. "Four Kinds of (Post)nation-building." In Michel Seymour, ed., *The Fate of the Nation-State*. Montreal and Kingston: McGill-Queen's University Press 2004. 51–68.

Weintraub, William. *City Unique: Montreal Days and Nights in the 1940s and 1950s*. Toronto: McClelland and Stewart 1996.

– *Why Rock the Boat?* Boston: Little, Brown 1961.

Westley, Margaret. *Remembrance of Grandeur: The Anglo-Protestant Elite of Montreal 1900–1950*. Montreal: Libre Expression 1990.

Whittaker, Herbert. *Setting the Stage: Montreal Theatre 1920–1949*. Montreal and Kingston: McGill-Queen's University Press 1999.

Wilkins, Peter. "'Nightmares of Identity': Nationalism and Loss in *Beautiful Losers*." In Stephen Scobie, ed., *Intricate Preparations: Writing Leonard Cohen*. Toronto: ECW Press 2000. 24–50.

Willmott, Glenn. *Unreal Country: Modernity in the Canadian Novel in English*. Montreal and Kingston: McGill-Queen's University Press 2002.

Wilson, Edmund. *O Canada: An American's Notes on Canadian Culture*. New York: Farrar, Straus and Giroux 1965.

Winnicott, D.W. "Fear of Breakdown." *International Review of Psycho-Analysis* 1 (1974): 103–7.

Woodcock, George. *Introducing Mordecai Richler's* The Apprenticeship of Duddy Kravitz. Toronto: ECW Press 1990.

– "Lost Eurydice: The Novels of Callaghan." In *Odysseus Ever Returning: Essays on Canadian Writers and Writings*. Toronto: McClelland and Stewart 1970. 24–39.

Žižek, Slavoj. "What Donald Rumsfeld Doesn't Know That He Knows about Abu Graib." http://www.lacan.com/zizekrumsfeld.htm (accessed 5 June 2017).

Index